PATRICK
ROY

WINNING. NOTHING ELSE.

A Biography by Michel Roy

Translated by Charles Phillips

TRIUMPH
BOOKS

TRIUMPHBOOKS**.COM**

To Jana

Jonathan

and Frédérick

This book is available in quantity at special discounts for your group or organization. For further information, contact:

Triumph Books LLC
814 North Franklin Street
Chicago, Illinois 60610
(312) 337-0747
www.triumphbooks.com

Printed in U.S.A.

ISBN: 978-1-62937-165-8

Cover design by Andy Hansen

Interior text design and typesetting by Natalia Burobina, Tegan Wallace, Pat Loi

TABLE OF CONTENTS

ACKNOWLEDGMENTS

I wish to express my deep gratitude to all those who have helped me bring this work to fruition, all those who have made this book possible by providing information, sharing stories and offering advice and encouragement.

François Allaire, Donald Beauchamp, Lise Beaulne, Craig Billington, André Blanchet, Mélanie Bouchard, Nicole Bouchard, Pat Burns, Claude Carrier, Robert "Bob" Chevalier, Tim De Frisco, Jacques Demers, Fred Dixon, Sylvain Doyon, Robert Fiset, Patsy Fisher, Julien Gagnon, Pierre Gervais, Andrea Gordon, Luc Grenier, Pierre Jolin, Pierre Lacroix, Georges Larivière, Stephan Lebeau, Gaétan Lefebvre, Michel Lefebvre, Patrick Lefebvre, Jean-Louis Létourneau, Christine Marchand, Jean Martineau, Barbara Miller-Roy, Pierre Mourey, Jacques Naud, Jean Perron, Normand Pruneau, Bertrand Raymond, Alexandra Roy, Gaétan Roy, Stéphane Roy, Daniel Sauvé, Robert "Bob" Sauvé, Serge Savard, Huguette Scallon, Serge St-Michel, Jacques Tanguay, Réjean Tremblay, Yolande Tremblay, Danièle Viger, Damen Zier, and all the dedicated members of the Éditions Libre Expression team.

I would particularly like to thank, in the chronological order in which they contributed their support: Daniel Payette, for introducing me to Éditions Libre Expression; André Bastien, my editor, for his trust and good counsel; Paul Ohl who, out of a friendship of some 40 years, agreed to guide me through this desert crossing and, without ever leading me by the hand, indicated the path that would help me avoid the sand dunes and find the oasis; Monique Lallier, my first reader, for offering wise comments from a woman unfamiliar with the culture of hockey; Romy Snauwaert, editing consultant; as well as proofreaders Denis Poulet and Yvan Dupuis, for their skillful and meticulous work.

Finally, I reserve a very special word of thanks to my son, Patrick, for being the hero of this fabulous story and authorizing me to recount it.

INTRODUCTION

This story is not about hockey.

First and foremost, it is the human story of someone whose determination knows no bounds. Someone who is willing to go beyond his own limits to be the best in the world at what he loves to do. Someone who is willing to exceed his own limits to win.

Culture, education, business or politics could have been the stage. But Patrick Roy was a goaltender—the best in the world at some point in time. And so, hockey is the stage.

Throughout his goaltending career, from the first day he stepped onto the ice until his jersey number 33 was retired, he was driven by a relentless passion to win. And win he did.

There is a belief in hockey that the real season starts with the playoffs. And when the chips are down, Patrick Roy is second to none. Nobody is even close to his record of 151 wins in post-season play. Martin Brodeur is second on the list with 113. The closest active goaltender is 30-year-old Marc-André Fleury, of the Pittsburgh Penguins, who has 52 wins. These numbers emphasize the magnitude of Patrick's playoff record.

In addition, Patrick Roy is the only player in the history of hockey to have won the Conn Smythe trophy three times. Even greats like Bobby Orr, Mario Lemieux and Wayne Gretzky did not win it more than twice. Since 1965, this trophy is awarded every year to the player judged most valuable to his team during the National Hockey League's Stanley Cup playoffs, based on a vote by the members of the Professional Hockey Writers Association.

In 2003, after his illustrious career as a goaltender was over, Patrick suffered from anxiety. The extreme pressure he had carried on his shoulders throughout the previous 18 years was getting to him. He felt there was a huge void in his life.

He wanted to remain connected to hockey in some form or another. As part owner of the Québec Remparts of the Québec Major Junior Hockey League, he served as vice president of hockey operations and general manager of the team. But it was not long before he realized he missed being close to the action, close to the ice, close to the familiar sweaty smell of the dressing room. He missed making the difference between winning and losing.

The passion inside had not gone away.

Age no longer allowed him to be competitive as a player; coaching was the closest he could get to competing on the ice. However, he had too much respect for a trade that has developed into a complex art form over the past few years to jump right in without any preparation. And he had witnessed too many former players burn themselves thinking that coaching would come easy because they had been successful as players.

To get a feel for what it was like and to sharpen his reflexes, he coached a bantam team on which his son Frédérick was playing. Two years later, confident that he was ready for junior major hockey, he took over the Remparts after the team got off to a bad start in 2005–2006. At the end of the season, he led his team to the greatest honor—capturing the Memorial Cup, emblematic of junior hockey supremacy in Canada. His anxiety problems vanished.

Though hockey had made him a multimillionaire, for the next eight years he traveled thousands of miles by bus with a bunch of teenagers, ate chicken on his lap and slept in second-class hotels. But in the process, with the same determination and dedication that he is known for, he perfected his trade, not hesitating to consult with the best in the business, and studied all aspects of his new challenge.

Along the way, he discovered the immense satisfaction of transmitting his expertise and experience to these young kids, making them not only better hockey players but also better people, on and off the ice. He made sure that the educational program of the Remparts was one of the best in minor hockey. At the same time, average attendance at the old Québec Colisée jumped to over ten thousand spectators per game. A huge success story for a junior team.

It was not long before his progress as a coach attracted the attention of NHL teams looking for new leaders. But Patrick's children were still at home and it was crucial for him to spend as much time as he could with them after a career that had taken him away too often. He also valued coaching his two sons, who both played for the Remparts.

But in 2013, when his old teammate Joe Sakic contacted him, the situation was quite different. The children were older and had occupations that took them away from home. The house was empty. Patrick was ready.

Sakic had just been appointed executive vice president of hockey operations with the Colorado Avalanche. Having finished 29th in the NHL standings the year before, his team needed an electric shock treatment. Joe really wanted to turn things around quickly and there was no doubt in his mind that the only person who could help him revitalize the failing franchise was Patrick. They met in Florida and struck a deal.

On May 23, 2013, Patrick Roy was appointed head coach and vice president of hockey operations. In an interview with the *Denver Post*, he not only discussed his adjustment from junior hockey to the NHL but described his basic coaching philosophy:

When you're coaching younger players at the junior level, you're with players who want to be NHL players one day. You have to explain to them what is the NHL journey, what they have to do every day, how hard they have to work on and off the ice. The NHL level is different. I think they need more of a partner, someone they can count on and communicate with. I just give them options. They're in the NHL already. They don't need the same message. Obviously, I'm the coach and I have to draw the line, but it's their team. I said to the guys, "If you want to skip curfews, you're not cheating on me, you're cheating on the guy beside you. If you don't want to work hard, you're not cheating on me, you're cheating on yourself." Obviously, if they're not working hard enough, it's my job to come in and say, "Hey, guys, let's pick it up." But I think our relations with the players have to be based on two words: trust and respect.

And the partnership philosophy really worked. The Avalanche matched the franchise record in 2013–2014 with 52 wins. Their 112 points were the second-highest total in team history and they rose from 29th in the standings to third. Those results earned Patrick the Jack Adams Trophy as NHL coach of the year.

Of course, Patrick was honored and proud that the quality of his work was recognized. But in his heart, personal awards will never replace team accomplishments. The only thing that matters to him now is leading the Colorado Avalanche to the Stanley Cup.

Will he succeed? I certainly would never bet against him, because the only thing that makes a fiery competitor like Patrick Roy happy is winning. Nothing else.

Michel Roy
January 27, 2015

FULL MARKS 1

Guy Carbonneau pounced on the puck at centre ice. Paul Baxter gave him a two-hander across the ankle. But Carbonneau cut in on the Calgary goal, where Jamie Macoun tripped him and he slid into the back of the net, ramming into goalie Mike Vernon on the way. Carbo clambered onto his skates. No penalty: after all, this was the Stanley Cup final with no more than two minutes to go in a do-or-die game for the Calgary Flames, trailing 3–1 in the series.

At the same time, in Yvan Cournoyer's Brasserie No. 12, the Pocket Rocket's place, and in bars and pubs all across Canada, tens of thousands of Canadiens fans slammed their fists on the table or leaped to their feet in rage. They threw their arms in the air, a pint of beer in hand, knocking over chairs and dousing their neighbours with suds. No one noticed; no one cared. The game was what mattered. In Montreal and Calgary, of course, but also from tiny fishing villages in the Maritimes and the Gaspé, to the other side of the Rockies, on the banks of the Pacific, to the remotest regions of the Far North, millions of Canadians had their eyes riveted on the TV. For the first time in 19 years, since 1967, when Canada, hockey's birthplace, commemorated its centennial, two Canadian teams were squaring off in the Stanley Cup final.

The Flames called a timeout. Their fans quaffed some brew to settle their nerves. But Patrick Roy, surprisingly calm considering what was at stake, moseyed over to his bench and sipped a little water. Then he tugged his mask over his sweat-drenched face. The Habs hunkered down to protect their slim 4–2 lead. With nothing to lose, the Flames launched an all-out attack.

With 1:16 minutes remaining, it was the Canadiens' turn to take a timeout to regroup and break the Flames' momentum. While patrons in their local sports bars could watch Patrick twitching his head on six screens at a time, Richard Garneau broke into the colour commentary of analysts Gilles and Mario Tremblay. "There's the Conn Smythe Trophy winner right there! It's normal. Several players deserve the honor, but with a goals against average of about 1.80, it's hard not to pick him. He's had a fantastic playoffs."

Play resumed in the Canadiens' end, and Calgary fans were on their feet, cheering and applauding. Joel Otto unleashed a wicked drive; Patrick made the save. Calgary wouldn't let up. Dan Quinn fired at point-blank range; Patrick rose to the challenge. But Quinn snatched the rebound behind the net and fed Joe Mullen, camped in the slot. Mullen scored, cutting Montreal's lead to a single goal.

Only 46 seconds remained—46 long seconds. Meanwhile, under the Saddledome stands, the champagne was already on ice. Technicians were gearing up for post-game interviews in the dressing rooms.

Could the Flames draw even, snatch the victory, win the sixth game in Montreal and return to Calgary for the final and decisive match with all bets off? Would the Canadiens, the most decorated team in sports history, drop the torch passed them by the battered arms of Richard, Béliveau, Lafleur?

The very idea could haunt Canadiens fans, the brain trust, and even a few players. Nothing tempts fate more than a nervous team playing back on its heels. But Patrick had no time for negativity. He had the same fire in his eyes that we had seen in the Rocket years ago. He focused on the game, not the outcome.

Play resumed. Mike McPhee nearly ended the suspense when he intercepted a pass at center ice and broke into the clear. But his nerves got the better of him. Instead of skating right in on goal and making a play—he had all the time in the world—he took a long shot that was child's play for Vernon. A glorious chance gone begging.

The Flames launched a final assault, a desperately furious siege. Paul Reinhart scooped up the puck from his goalie, raced to center ice and dumped the puck in beside the Montreal goal. Patrick intercepted the puck and cleared it to the corner. The Flames stormed around the Habs' net. Al MacInnis beat the Montrealers to the puck and fired a bullet. Patrick made the save but couldn't control the rebound and the puck bounced off to his right onto Macoun's stick. Macoun ripped the tying goal into the back of the net. Behind him, John Tonelli raised his arms in celebration. But the goal judge hadn't flashed the red light. Incredulous, Macoun strode forward, searched the net. He couldn't find the puck! Patrick had dived, made a miraculous save and smothered the puck. From the Canadiens' bench, Bobby Smith chanted, "Roo-wah! Roo-wah!"

Less than 14 seconds from the end of regulation time, Carbonneau won the face-off in the Canadiens' zone. Chelios picked up the puck and, with three Flames hounding him and seven seconds remaining, he slipped it to Rick Green, who cleared the zone. Mario Tremblay, forgetting he was behind a mike, whooped with glee.

Against all expectations, the Canadiens had won their 23rd Stanley Cup, with eight rookies in the lineup.

It was nearly eleven p.m. in Calgary; almost 1:00 a.m. in Cap-Rouge. I clicked off the TV.

The doorbell rang. Two reporters, one Francophone and an Anglophone, had been waiting in their cars for the match to end so they could come and interview me. Earlier in the afternoon, one of them had suggested they spend the evening with us while a cameraman recorded our reactions during the game for a TV sportscast. I refused. I hate that kind of voyeurism. I wanted the family to savor every moment in peace.

The public hungers for every detail about a superstar's life: the car he drives, his favorite meals, the color of his cat. The media happily put his proud parents on display. People may want to get a look at their idol's folks, but apart from the usual platitudes, they are not interested in what the parents say or think. People would no more expect to hear something insightful from them than from the car or the cat. To most fans, the parents are of little more interest than the objects that are part of the Star's daily life. But if Mom or Dad should happen to shed a tear, it's fodder for the six o'clock news.

I greeted the journalists.

On the Saddledome ice, the Canadiens were jumping for joy, hugging, throwing their arms around each other, releasing the tension accumulated from the nearly two-month playoff grind. Victory is an analgesic. Victory washes away fatigue, pain, even the musty smell of sweat-drenched equipment.

The rink was a ballroom: Claude Lemieux waltzed with Bob Gainey, Larry Robinson with Rick Green. Doug Soetaert gave Patrick a hug—to think that at the beginning of the season the two of them had vied for the backup spot behind Steve Penney! But Penney wasn't there. The club hadn't found room for him on the chartered flight carrying the team staff, although a slew of friends of the upper

4

brass and the wives of quite a few players were on board. No room for Sergio Mommeso or Tom Kurvers either; they had to stay in Montreal, too. An administrative blunder.

Gradually, men like Chris Nilan, Stéphane Richer, Petr Svoboda and Kjell Dahlin, who weren't in the lineup, and the trainers, coaches and assorted friends joined the players on the ice. Photographers formed a cordon around them to capture the emotion.

Stunned Calgary fans kept chanting, "Go Flames go! Go Flames go!" backed by the organist, playing the final chords of the season.

The losers had lined up at center ice for the traditional post-series handshake. The Canadiens finally noticed them and the two teams exchanged congratulations, words of encouragement and pats on the back. The hostilities were over. Team jerseys had divided the players into enemy camps. Now different-colored jerseys meant nothing. Opposing players were united in sharing a common passion. They were brothers in arms.

Calgary fans saluted the Flames for the grit they had displayed in the playoffs. To reach the final, they had upset the heavily favored "Gretzky gang" in the "Battle of Alberta." Still, the crowd gave the new champs a round of applause.

Larry Robinson peeled away from the group and skated over to congratulate Calgary's brass. Meanwhile, one after another, the Flames, heads bowed and faces drawn, filed into the corridor leading to their dressing room for the last time of the year.

At center ice, National Hockey League (NHL) president John Ziegler awarded the Stanley Cup to Habs captain Bob Gainey. The Canadiens' skipper had made sure that veteran defenseman Larry Robinson was there to share the moment in case this was "Big Bird's" last cup.

The other players crowded around them to touch the trophy and raise it up. Slowly, the team did a victory lap to the cheers of the crowd, passing the trophy from one to another: from Patrick to Carbo, from Mats Naslund to Bobby Smith, from Chris Chelios to Ryan Walter, from Mike McPhee to Gaston Gingras, from John Kordic to Mike Lalor, from Claude Lemieux to Serge Boisvert, from Brian Skrudland to David Maley, and so on. Finally the cup came back to Bob Gainey, who hoisted it over his head. Flashguns popped. Then he passed the cup to rookie coach Jean Perron and GM Serge Savard, who posed for the photographers.

On English TV, Dave Hodge said, "I want to go back to something Dick Irvin said when the playoffs started. He said that the one big problem area with Montreal, the big weakness, was goaltending. We said that, he said that, and everybody who watched the Canadiens in the second half of the season said that, and I don't know if there has ever been a more dramatic reversal by one individual player in this sport than by Patrick Roy."

Champagne flowed in the victors' dressing room. As revelers shook magnums of champagne and sprayed each other, John Ziegler officially presented Patrick with the Conn Smythe trophy, emblematic of the playoff MVP. The 20-year-old was the youngest player in NHL history to receive the honor, younger than Bobby Orr, who was 22 when he put his hands on the trophy for the first time in 1970.

Patrick praised his teammates. "To me, winning the Stanley Cup is what's important. You could drop the names of my teammates in a hat and pick one, and it would be a good choice . . . my teammates won the trophy for me."

Some might call it false modesty, but Patrick never played for the money or for individual honors. Only one thing mattered to him: WINNING. Nothing else.

A crew had set up a platform in the middle of the room for the TV interviews. But as the hosts were getting showered with champagne, they retreated to some quieter place.

In the makeshift studio, Lionel Duval interviewed players, coaches and management. "Tonight," said Perron, "Patrick was fantastic again. I'm glad he's won the Conn Smythe. Patrick typifies the young players on our team. I'm really happy a rookie has won the trophy."

Then Ronald Corey, a picture of sartorial elegance, stepped up to the mike. Brandishing a bottle of champagne, Claude Lemieux burst into the interview and drenched his boss. The president managed an indulgent smile. Lemieux had spent the entire regular season with Sherbrooke in the American Hockey League before being recalled. He had almost packed it in a few months earlier. Lemieux had scored all four winning goals in the playoffs, including two in overtime—no one could forget the Habs' last-ditch victory against Hartford in the seventh and deciding quarterfinal game.

—⁂—

Some events make people abandon their values, their inhibitions, even their reason. Along St. Catherine Street in Montreal, revelers of a different sort smashed shop windows, looted stores, overturned or torched cars, hijacked a city bus, and laid waste to everything in their path. Thousands of hardcore Canadiens' fans had flooded the area surrounding the Forum, inadvertently shielding the rioters from the 125 cops dispatched to restore order.

—⁂—

In the dressing room the champagne supplies dwindled and the celebrations ebbed. One by one, the players repaired to the showers, letting the water soothe their aching muscles and rinse away what felt like the sweat of an entire season, mixed with champagne. It was their first moment alone since the match came to its dramatic end, and they began to have a sense of what they had accomplished. The extraverts among them vented their emotions. Others were more reserved. Patrick sat pale and motionless on a red stool. He had focused on one series at a time, one game at a time, one period at a time. He had just won the final period. As the pressure let up, fatigue set in.

There was a bus waiting to drive the team to the Calgary airport. The plane was scheduled to arrive at Dorval around 6:00 a.m., and thousands of joyous fans were already on their way to greet the champions.

In the other dressing room, Lanny McDonald was crying.

—⁂—

Back in Cup-Rouge, when the interviews were over, we packed our bags and headed down Highway 40, for the two-and-a-half-hour drive to Montreal. It was cold and dark, with no moon or stars. The late spring night felt like early autumn. There was no breeze, the pavement was dry and deserted, visibility was good and . . . life was beautiful. To our left there was the St. Lawrence River. We couldn't see it, but we could feel its presence because of the lights twinkling along the other bank and the black chasm that separated us from them. On the radio, Félix Leclerc sang *Le Sentier près du ruisseau*. Beside me on the passenger seat, my wife Barbara was silent. She couldn't wait to give her son a hug. In the back seat, Patrick's sister Alexandra was nodding off with her head on Sophie's shoulder. Sophie was a friend Patrick had met just a few days before. His brother Stéphane had stayed back in Granby, working on a summer job while he was waiting to finish his junior hockey career with the Bisons.

Another few miles went by. My mind started drifting to the past. I murmured,

"It's just like fall!"

THE BEGINNING

It was an October day. The kind of October day when everything seems to die. Trees, flowers, grass, frigid lakes and rivers. A dull, windy day set against a slate background. Days surrender to nights. Gray turns into black. Everything seems to die but hockey. Hockey comes alive again, defying death and bridging the abyss of winter until the warm season returns. Our hopes and illusions come alive, too. Training camps open for kids, the season opens for the pros. Children fidget, parents fret, cars warm up and coaches prepare.

People often wonder how a champion's career gets started. In fact, there are as many beginnings in a champion's career as there are moments when it could end. Looking back over the years, I would point to that "October day when everything seems to die" as the day when Patrick's career began.

October 1974. The tryout camp for the Québec-Centre-Haute-Ville (QCHV) mosquito AA division had been in full swing for two weeks. We read about it in the sports section of a local daily. Patrick, just about to turn nine, had his heart set on hockey. He wanted to be a goalie. He'd spent the summer attending hockey school to prepare for the camp. He was ready. But he hesitated. He was afraid. Afraid of what? I have no idea. Afraid he wouldn't make the team? Maybe. Most likely, he was afraid of the unknown.

He couldn't bring himself to talk about it.

"Look, Patrick, if you want to play hockey, you have to go to Québec-Centre, even if you're a couple of weeks late," I said. "You've practiced all summer, you've played against top opposition, against kids who played mosquito AA last year, and you did fine. There's no reason to be afraid. The worst that can happen is you won't make the team. We'll see. But at least, give it a try."

I didn't want to encourage bad habits but I helped him get his bag ready . . . actually, I packed his bag. Then we left for the arena.

The half-hour drive passed in silence. On that "October day when everything seems to die," Patrick hesitated between letting the athlete in him die like the rest or live.

—⚅—

In those days, the first thing that hit you when entering an arena was the reek of vinegar, fries and cigarette smoke. We were quickly shown along the long, narrow, dark hallway to the players' dressing room. The scene we encountered was played over and over in thousands of arenas. Under a yellowish light, there were open equipment bags strewn all over the floor, hockey sticks piled on top of one another, kids sitting around the room on benches, in a sort of religious silence, busy pulling on socks, lacing up skates, and adjusting knee pads. Two adults were there to help. I went over to one of them and asked:

"Are you Mr. Lafond?"

"No, I'm McNicoll. Mr. Lafond's over there."

Simple things like a father taking his son to the rink and helping him lace up his skates, or a mother straightening his sweater, can help launch a career. You don't realize the influence these gestures may have. How the little things you do may affect the trajectory of a career. You may never know.

Patrick and I stepped through the clutter, and I held out my hand to a man who was lacing up a player's skates.

"Hello. Mr. Lafond, I'm Michel Roy. This is my son Patrick. He's a goalie and he'd like to try out for your team."

The man looked up and shook my hand. Forty-something, ramrod stiff, he didn't beat around the bush.

"Goalie, eh! Well . . . we've already got our 'first year'. . ."

"Can you give him a tryout?"

"Yeah; sure . . . we can give him a tryout."

"A fair . . . tryout?"

"Yes, yes . . . of course!"

And, putting a reassuring hand on Patrick's shoulder, he said, "Sit over there and start putting on your gear. We'll give you a hand."

I patted Patrick on the head, made sure he didn't need me any more, and left the dressing room.

—◠◠—

I didn't know it at the time, but I'd just gotten my first lesson as the dad of a goalie when Mr. Lafond mentioned that he already had his "first year" keeper.

There is room for only two goalies on a team. It's a matter of course. But as every kid stays two years in each category, it is a widespread, entirely understandable practice among hockey coaches to choose one first-year goalie and to pair him with a second-year boy. This allows the coach to play an "experienced" netminder in most of the games, and to get the "first-year" guy ready for the next season.

So it was now or never for Patrick. If he didn't earn a spot in his first season, how could he hope to do it the next year?

Somewhat nervous, I sat down in the arena with a cup of coffee.

One by one the players jumped onto the ice. In their hockey gear they looked about as wide as they were tall. Seeing little Patrick in his green Mickey Mouse sweater made my heart swell with pride. My wife had bought it for herself the day before, but we thought that the Disney icon would inspire Patrick. His face and head were entirely covered by a goalie helmet with fluorescent dragons on the sides, courtesy of my friend, graphic designer Pierre Mourey.

The moppets and two coaches started skating slowly around the rink to warm up. Then Mr. Lafond blew the whistle and led the kids in some stretching exercises.

Next the boys did acceleration drills between the blue lines and the red line. After that, they practiced puck carrying around cones before doing two-on-ones and three-on-twos. The coaches blew the whistle to stop one exercise and begin another. Each time, they offered a few words of explanation.

Not far from me in the stands, a few fathers were locked in a heated argument. They were no doubt settling the fate of the Nordiques, the Canadiens, and while they were at it, the rest of the NHL teams and hockey in general. As some of them were wearing the team's red and white jacket, I figured their sons were second-year boys.

Mr. Lafond skated to one end of the rink to work with the forwards and Martin, the "experienced" goalie. At the other end, Mr. McNicoll looked after the defensemen as well as Éric and Patrick, the lads competing for the "first year" goalie spot. This went on for quite a while and I was starting to get discouraged, when Mr. Lafond changed places with his assistants. He paired up the defensemen and instructed them to pass the puck to each other, alternating between their forehand and their backhand. That way, he could let them practice on their own while he focused on the "first-year" netminders. I had the feeling something important was about to happen, and my heart started pounding.

I moved away from the "hot-stove" analysts, now engaged in a spirited and no doubt profound assessment of the team's strengths and weaknesses for the coming season and in an "objective" evaluation of the rookies. I went over to stand directly behind the goal so I could take in every detail.

Mr. Lafond tested Éric first. Of the ten shots I counted, he stopped six. Then it was Patrick's turn. He stopped every one except the last. Mr. Lafond had put quite a bit more zip into the shot to test him. That was all.

The whistle blew, ending the practice, and the players shuffled off to their dressing room. The Zamboni began resurfacing the ice. For a few moments my eyes were riveted on the reflections of the projectors on the thin layer of water left on the ice. Then I headed to the snack bar to wait for Patrick.

—⚭—

One after another the players came out. Some kids, their hair still damp, were leaning on their elbows, rolling quarters along the counter while they waited to be served. I buried my nose in the newspaper. I had to wait quite a while amidst the comings and goings of parents and players. Kids body-checked the entrance door, or bumped into the door-frame with their bags and sticks. I tried in vain to concentrate, as I kept reading the same damn paragraph over and over.

Finally Patrick emerged with his bag on his back and his stick in his hand, grinning from ear to ear, eyes sparkling.

"That's good, Patrick, you did a great job. Did they say anything to you?"

"No, nothing. But it went OK."

—⚭—

A few days later, we were getting ready for supper when we heard a fan fulminating on the radio.

Times have changed. They're no better, no worse. But they've changed. Things aren't the same. Nowadays, kids play hockey indoors. There's a Zamboni to resurface the ice, just like with the pros. The rink is 200 feet by 85 feet. It's got red and blue lines and circles. There's a rulebook, refs, linesmen and goal judges to enforce the rules. The games last a fixed amount of time. The opposing clubs wear different-colored jerseys so you can tell them apart. A team can ice only six players at a time, including the goalie. At the end of the game, the results are recorded down to the slightest detail—goals, assists, body checks, etc. Hockey's run like a business. It is a business. A stifling business.

In my day, we played outdoors. Nobody cared about the size of the rink. No lines or circles, no rules or referees, no linesmen and no goal judges. The game lasted as long as it lasted, as long as there were kids to play. We didn't care how many players there were or what jersey they wore. We didn't need a record book. Anyway, nobody cared about the score. It was a game. Get rid of the lines and the circles!

We should expose the hypocrisy of phony fans who go to the pro games and are taking up corporate seats, creating the illusion that ticket prices are determined by the market. No god-fearing middle class dad can afford to take his children to an NHL game. But by buying the sponsor's products he is unwittingly paying for a seat he will never occupy. And even if he could afford it, would it be worth the investment? The industrialization of sports has perverted sports. The same applies to baseball. There was a time when going to a game meant enjoying an evening outdoors, in a park, with the scent of freshly mowed grass, with the sky for a roof. Now, they play in closed air-conditioned stadiums on rubber grass. There's nothing left to do but watch the game. Given all that, baseball is a boring game. Hardly surprising that fans are losing interest in pro sports! And it's not surprising there are fewer and fewer youngsters in the arenas!

Let the kids play, he said angrily. *Give hockey back its meaning, its real value, the game . . ."*

The phone rang, cutting into the diatribe.

"Hello!"

"Mr. Roy?"

"Yes, it's me."

On the radio the angry fan was still talking. I motioned to Barbara to lower the volume.

"My name's Maranda. I'm the mosquito AA manager for Québec-Centre. Coach Lafond was impressed with your son's performance. So we'd be real happy to have him on the team. Only . . ."

"Oh! That's good news . . ."

". . . But, I must tell you it's pretty demanding. There's at least one game, sometimes two, on weeknights and two practices early Saturday and Sunday mornings. And three or four tournaments we'll enter this season."

"Well, look, we pretty much expected that; there shouldn't be any problem. Give me your number so I can get in touch with you and I'll call you back to confirm."

He continued. "We'd really like Patrick to be on the team. With the nucleus of players we have, you know, we can go far this year. Oh yes! I forgot; you can pay the first $30 by a check made out to the Cap-Diamant Minor Hockey Corporation."

This was Patrick's first victory in hockey.

—ᴍ—

15

I tossed and turned that night. Ideas kept spinning around in my head. I thought about the radio caller's remark: "Let the kids play . . ."

That's easy to say! But nowadays children are so used to organized activities they find it hard to play on their own. They've been conditioned. They need organized teams and somebody to drop the puck; otherwise all else will break loose. When all is said and done, minor hockey seemed a good way to go.

Barbara and I weren't parents with planned activities, like skiing, for their weekends. For such families, getting involved in minor hockey may pose some problems. They have some tough decisions to make. Do parents have the right to impose an activity on a child because his/her siblings want to do it? Of course, parents can decide, but they have to use common sense. In the end, we all want the best for our family and its members. It's the eternal issue of the collective good versus the individual good. In our case, the issue didn't come up. Stéphane played hockey, too, and Alexandra was only a month old.

Then there was the question of elite versus participatory sports. There are arguments for both sides of the issue. Children are different. Some like to see how they match up against others in sports. Some don't enjoy the pressure and prefer sports for recreation, at their own pace, in a relaxed atmosphere. It depends on the individual. We'd soon see how much Patrick loved testing himself against other kids . . . and winning.

Still no sleep, so I thought about my childhood and summer vacations with my mother at Notre-Dame-du-Portage on the Lower St. Lawrence. There were about a dozen children, aged six to twelve. We organized ourselves. We called ourselves Bouboule's gang. Like the Canadiens, who once had two captains—an Anglophone and a Francophone—we had two leaders, the oldest kids in the gang: Simone and Paul. No sexism in our gang. We were politically correct.

When June arrived, we hitchhiked to the Saint-Patrice Golf Club to work as caddies. We scooped up stray balls and resold them for a little cash. We all wanted to caddy for Canadian Prime Minister Louis Saint-Laurent, who had a summer residence in Saint-Patrice-de-Rivière-du-Loup. It took us only a few weeks to make enough cash to get started on our summer project: building a camp in the woods.

With the money we made, we hitched a ride to Rivière-du-Loup and bought tools, nails, cement—we could hardly do without a fireplace—wire, and so forth. Then a few of us asked Henri, the farmer, for permission to chop down some trees and build our camp on his land. In return, we'd lend a hand with haymaking in August.

One of the kids was a blond-haired, English-speaking boy named Dennis, who was a whiz at electronics. He was a little fellow in glasses and a thick, navy blue woolen sweater. He was the kind of guy that spent his whole summer reading *Popular Mechanics* with a soldering iron in his hand. We had assigned Dennis the incredibly tedious task—perhaps there was a hint of bigotry—of hunting down nails we'd dropped in the thick bed of pine needles on the campsite. The next morning, Dennis showed up at the bottom of the hill where we met before going into the woods, near Henri's cottage. He was carrying a mysterious brown bag. As soon as we arrived at the worksite, he reached into the bag and fished out a sort of magnetic horseshoe attached to a wire. Then he started walking up and down, moving the horseshoe just above the ground, and looking like Professor Calculus divining for water with his pendulum. In ten minutes, he had picked up all the nails.

We were having the time of our lives. We were developing our imaginations and learning a slew of things: respect, working together—in short, teamwork—by ourselves and without supervision. We didn't compete. There were no rules. Another way to spend a childhood.

As I drove along on that late spring night in 1986, heading for Dorval, suddenly, a blinding light jolted me out of my reverie. The flashing light of a police squad car had awakened me. As I had come up to Donnacona, lost in memories of long ago, I had been driving over the speed limit for a few miles with a cop on my tail. Running out of patience, he had pulled me over.

"Papers, please!"

"Here."

He had no idea but at two o'clock a.m. in the morning, he had just caught the happiest dad in the world. I was also a vice-president of the Québec Automobile Insurance Board, and a Highway Safety Code administrator. But mum was the word about those two posts. It wouldn't have helped to mention them.

The cop who stopped me was conscientious and professional. He handed me back my papers and issued me a traffic ticket. I drove off. Life was still beautiful. A few miles down the road, I was drawn back to the past again.

ROOTS 3

Magnificent old maple trees lined both sides of the street, meeting in the middle to form a roof. The mid-summer morning sun made its way through the leaves and dried the pavement that the city water cart had just washed, and licked the red brick façades of the houses. We wouldn't have wanted to be anywhere else on Earth. In 1974, we lived on rue de Montmorency (now rue Barrin), in Québec City's Saint-Sacrement district. The neighborhood was neither rich nor poor. It had an aging population and was a microcosm of middle-class society.

It was a wonderful year for me. In September, Alexandra was born. She was the first girl in the Roy family in at least three generations. Then I received my master's degree in public administration. Finally, I bought my first house, an impressive cottage, in circumstances that I will explain because they are somewhat related to Patrick's genetic heritage.

The Quiet Revolution in Québec began in 1960 with the election of the Liberal Party led by Jean Lesage. Bona Arsenault was elected in Matapédia that year. Lesage was impressed with his skills as a political organizer and invited him to join his team. The two men had known each other since their days as Liberal members of Parliament in Ottawa. Arsenault held a few portfolios during the period that marked the awakening of Québec from 1960 until the Liberal defeat in 1966. A cabinet minister's duties can be demanding, but he still found time to publish an important work titled *Histoire et Généalogie des Acadiens* in 1965. A second edition of the work appeared in six volumes after his political career ended when the Parti Québécois came to power in 1976. In recognition of his Acadian origins and his significant work on the history of the people, the University of Moncton awarded him an honorary doctorate. The street leading to the Musée acadien du Québec in Bonaventure was also renamed after him.

Bona Arsenault was a friend of the family—a longtime friend. When I was very young, I often heard a sonorous voice on the phone asking for Lisette. Lisette was my mother; the voice was his. In my early twenties, I had a long conversation with him in his Parliamentary office. He liked to relax over a drink after work. Like Jean Lesage, he was partial to Beefeater. Like Jean Lesage, he smoked Embassys. As I recall, it was a fine summer evening. Lisette, as was her wont every year, was spending the week on the coast of Maine. Bona was lonely; he felt like confiding in someone. And he made a startling revelation.

"Did your mom ever tell you that you're my son? My biological son."

"Your son . . ."

"Yes, I'm your father. Your biological father."

It was a very emotional moment for me, but when I thought about it, the signs had been there to see. I just hadn't picked up on them. It was as if something new was beginning in my life, yet something that had been there all along.

"What about the other guy, does he know?"

The other guy was Armand (Serge) Roy, whose last name I bore. An only son, he was a brilliant journalist and author. He and Bona had gotten to know each other when Bona ran *L'Événement*, a Québec City daily. Serge was his pen name, the one he preferred to go by. In addition to being a journalist with *L'Événement*, he had penned three novels, *Têtes Fortes, Grisaille* and a two-volume work, *Impasse*. This handsome man-about-town led a very active social life, had traveled extensively in Europe and the United States, and he loved the ladies. As was the practice in some segments of society at the time, he frequented prostitutes. Lisette Fortier, a naïve and pure young woman from a good family, had been absolutely unaware of these activities. But when she found out he had given her a venereal disease on their honeymoon in France, she didn't take kindly to the news. When they got back, she declared her marriage unconsummated and over—in legal terms, null and void. As the customs of the day did not permit divorce, they reached an agreement: they would stay married but live separately under the same roof, in other words, in an open relationship.

When Lisette confided in Bona, he fell in love with her. Lisette, Bona and Serge had an understanding and kept the relationship quiet. The love affair resulted in my birth in the summer of 1942 and the birth of my brother Jacques, nine years later. What a trio! The secret was closely guarded until Bona's death in 1993. When Patrick rented a plane to attend his grandfather's funeral in Bonaventure, the media's curiosity was piqued. One of the journalists who looked into the story was Réjean Tremblay. Despite serious reservations on my part (my mother was still alive), he revealed the whole saga in an article in *La Presse*.

Whenever I think of Serge, I see him chewing on his cigar, banging away on his typewriter, making it sound like a machinegun. He was a virtuoso. He could have beaten secretaries on their electric typewriters! He could carry on a conversation with you while he hammered away on his old Remington. He could be nice enough,

21

but he was difficult to live with. Sometimes you didn't know which Serge you were dealing with. He was one of a kind, a bit of a braggart. He was a character, who loved to tease you, push your buttons, even shock you. I often felt uncomfortable around him.

I'll never forget the incident on Corpus Christi. Every year, sixty days after Easter, people would take part in a procession to celebrate Corpus Christi in the evening. On the radio, Father Lelièvre gave a vivid description of the event, punctuated with *Hail Marys* and *Pater Nosters*, as thousands of the faithful prayed in unison. People would walk through the streets of the parishes along the route announced by the newspapers, holding a cardboard cone with a lighted candle in it for a lantern. It was a warm June evening in 1950, proclaimed Holy Year by the Vatican. As the procession turned onto Marguerite-Bourgeoys, our street in Sillery, they were met with a sight that made their jaws drop: the multicolored Christmas lights that Serge had installed on the big pine tree in front of our home! The laughter was contagious, distracting the pious souls from their religious fervor.

In the mid-1950s, Serge set up a film company, Serge Roy Productions, in Montréal. The studio was located on Boulevard Henri-Bourassa in Montréal-North, and the editing room in Montréal's downtown core, on Guy Street between St. Catherine and René-Lévesque, known as Dorchester at the time. I loved the place. I hung out with artists like Olivier Guimond and Guy l'Écuyer. That's where I learned film editing, my first trade. Television was in its infancy and many programs were filmed in 16 mm. In 1961, I edited some 40 films for Radio-Canada: episodes of *Premier Plan, Express Vingt Ans, Les Uns Les Autres, Opinion*, and more. By the following year I was burned out. I left Serge Roy Productions and returned to Québec City to play music with Les Mégatones. Serge couldn't find it in his heart to forgive me, and our relationship began to deteriorate. A few years later, he founded the *Journal de Québec* for Pierre Péladeau, and became the daily's first editor.

Sometimes reality is stranger than fiction. In 1970, Serge died. The next year, Bona's wife, Blandine, passed away. Then in January 1973, Bona and Lisette finally got married at the Bonaventure Church in the Gaspé. Gérard D. Lévesque, a cabinet minister in Robert Bourassa's Liberal government and Deputy Premier of Québec, acted as a witness for Bona. As my mother's father was deceased, I stood as a witness for her and gave her hand in marriage to . . . my father. Things had fallen into their rightful place.

There was no question of Lisette living in the house where Bona had raised his eight children (my half-sisters and half-brothers). Instead, Bona and Lisette went to live on Marguerite-Bourgeoys in the house that my brother and I had inherited when Serge died. Lisette held it in trust for her lifetime. So I made a trade with Bona: the half of the house that I owned as a down payment on his house. I mortgaged the rest. That's how I got to own the cottage on 1330 de Montmorency. We just called it *Le 1330*.

It would be hard to say which of the two men, Serge or Bona, I consider my father. All through my childhood and adolescence, I believed that Serge was my father. I had some good times with him. But his blood wasn't flowing in my veins. Much later on, I got to know Bona a little better; he was seldom present, and when he was, it always felt as if he was a stranger. Perhaps the man who was more like a father to me was my grandfather, Horace Roy. Because of the somewhat unorthodox family situation I grew up in, with parents who led quite an active social life, I spent most of my childhood with my grandparents.

Patrick didn't really get to know Serge. He was only five when Serge died. To Patrick, Bona was his paternal grandfather, the same Bona who had the magnificent maples planted along the street when *Le 1330* was built in 1936.

Horace lived with my grandmother Blanche and her two sisters, Mathilde and Laura, on the corner of Bougainville and Boulevard René-Lévesque—then Saint-Cyrille. In those days, the government took a less active role in citizens' lives, and families shouldered the burden of lodging and feeding needy relatives. I wasn't allowed to play alone on the street until I was seven. The family was afraid something terrible would happen to me. So from early September until late June, I spent most of my time, when I wasn't at school, playing on a little ten-by-twelve-foot balcony, watching the traffic and trying my best to imitate it with my toy cars. That's how I coped with loneliness and developed a habit of observation and reflection.

Then we moved to Marguerite-Bourgeoys in Sillery. After spending so many years on the little balcony, I had become shy and withdrawn. I didn't mix with others. We lived across from the Bourgault family. Léo Bourgault, an ex-NHLer with the Rangers and the Canadiens among others, was determined to teach the lessons that could be gleaned from competitive sports to his children, particularly his sons, Léo Jr. and Jean. In winter, he set up a rink beside his house, just opposite ours, and installed a powerful spotlight. After school, the kids in the neighborhood would flock to the rink and play hockey until suppertime. Then, the light was switched off and the kids went home. Too bashful to join them, I would watch them for hours from the living room window, racked with envy. When everyone had left and the light was off, I would put on my skates, sneak across the street and romp on the rink, alone in the shadows.

The next summer, I finally worked up the nerve to approach Léo Jr. and Jean. They invited me over to their place. Was I in for a shock! I entered their basement and saw two complete sets of the six NHL team sweaters—kids' size—neatly suspended from coat hangers. Wow! All I'd asked for at Christmastime was a Canadiens jersey, but like the boy in Roch Carrier's famous story "The Hockey Sweater," Santa had left me a Maple Leafs jersey instead!

Noticing my surprise, Léo Jr. tried to put me at ease. "Remember last winter, when you used to come over and skate all by yourself in the evening? Well! We'd turn off the lights in the kitchen and watch you through the window." That just killed me.

His father was a role model: he ignited my love of sports. I could tell he liked me and was impressed when he saw me practicing my skating by myself. He knew that you had to repeat movements over and over if you wanted to perfect them. He understood the importance of encouraging a youngster to develop his skills in sports if he really had the motivation. He was the kind of father I would have liked to have.

—∽—

I hated school. To me, it was just something you had to endure, yet I was good at it. At 13, in 1955, I started classical studies at Collège des Jésuites. My grades, bordering on 90 percent, made Serge and Lisette proud. But the Jesuits were relentless. We studied Latin and Greek. We had Tuesday and Thursday afternoons off instead of Saturday like other schools. There was compulsory mass at college every second Sunday. In two weeks we spent 13 days at school. I didn't get it. I lacked motivation. Sports and music were all I cared about. I couldn't see any point in the academic program. I didn't study. Two years later, in grade ten, it was a struggle to get a passing grade. Father Bourassa was a dedicated teacher. He liked me, but, for the life of him, he couldn't fathom why I was so careless and rebellious.

He used to have us extemporize "serenades" in a notebook. He'd write a subject on the blackboard and give us five minutes to scribble whatever popped into our heads. Then he'd pick up our notebooks, and the next day we'd get them back with his written comments. He wanted to get to know us better and send a message. One day he gave me a warning.

Dear Michel,

You give me the impression that you are a guy who is letting himself go, who is messing up more and more each day. Isn't there anything that interests you besides sports? Your sentences, your style in general and, even more to the point, your ability don't really require comment because it's all so easy for you. What you really lack, but you already realize this, is the drive to make you work, in spite of yourself. Unfortunately, the drive you do have has nothing to do with reality; it is the stuff of illusions, of dreams. Of course, you are aware of all this.

But here is something that you may not know. If you keep letting things happen instead of living your life, you will end up one of those people who are second-rate, frustrated, people who could have had a good professional career and who just gave up at one point. That's a shame.

No willpower, no interests other than baseball. Come on! Unless you want to become another Mantle! Is there anything that could get you out of the rut of mediocrity where you are perhaps in spite of yourself? What should you do? Give up? Accept yourself the way you are? It's your business. But I have the feeling that you are not only wasting your ability, you may be ruining your future. You should be getting between 80% and 90%. You are performing below your capacity.

Think about it. Don't be a victim of circumstances. Master them; use them to your advantage, to prepare for your future. If you don't act, if you don't take the initiative, I don't know what that future will be.

Father Bourassa was right. That year I squeaked through, barely, but before I finished grade eleven, the following April, I dropped out of classical studies. It is one of the episodes in my life that I am least proud of, that I still bitterly regret. I was given a chance to have the best education. I thumbed my nose at it. I was too wrapped up in myself. I didn't see where I was headed. My perspective was very limited. It was a view from the little balcony.

When Serge heard I had dropped out, he blew his stack. He was right to be upset. And when I told him that a scout from the Brooklyn Dodgers showed some interest in me at baseball camp, he tore into me. "You goddamn little bum; you won't be playing squat in the U.S.!"

His reaction was hardly surprising. He was an intellectual whose credo was "the only way to get somewhere in life is by the sweat of your brow." To him, sport was just a pastime. Thus ended my baseball career. I took up tennis. It was simpler; we didn't need 18 players and the ball wasn't as hard.

I eventually went back to school. Several years later, after a number of detours, I earned a master's degree. I'm proud of my career as a public administrator. I have been lucky. But it took me far too long to realize that there's no substitute in life for knowledge. Not even money, and certainly not fun and games!

—◊—

Many Quebecers, on the road to the coast of Maine and all its summer pleasures, drive by Madison, a quaint little village with a population of three thousand, between Jackman and Skowegan, along Highway 201, across the U.S. border. In the early 1980s, I followed the same route with Patrick and Stéphane on our way to the Samoset, a spectacular golf course facing the ocean near Rockport.

Edward "Eddy" Ambrose Miller, Patrick's maternal grandfather, was born in Madison in 1910. He was an American, from a family of Canadians in New Brunswick who had crossed the border to find work in the paper mills. That's also why they came to the Bois-Franc region in Québec when Eddy was a toddler.

Eddy was a born philosopher, a bit of a sage, grateful for what he had in life. He relished the simple things. He paid attention to his health and his diet. White flour and refined sugar were banned from the menu. He was ahead of his time. He loved to walk. He could cover three to seven miles a day. It's not surprising that he kept slim.

When I met him, he was 50 years old and looked 60; when he was 80, he still looked 60. Sometimes I'd have Sunday dinner at the Millers' when I was dating Barbara and even early in our marriage. While Anna was getting the meal ready, I played checkers with Eddy, in his Sunday best. Often he wore a white shirt with gray stripes under a navy blue woolen sweater, crisply pressed gray flannels and black shoes you could see your face in. He played a mean game of checkers.

He could understand Morse code and convert it into English. Shortly before the outbreak of World War II, a job as a telegraph operator with the Canadian Pacific railway drew him to Québec. That's where he met and married Anna Peacock. Their first home was on Fraser Street in the Montcalm district, where Barbara was born in 1941. Eddy didn't own a car, so he walked all the way to Old Québec every day. Along the way, he would chat with acquaintances he bumped into. Eddy was a gregarious soul. He regaled people with all kinds of yarns, sometimes a bit risqué, which he often accompanied with a loud guffaw. He was a voracious reader of reviews and magazines on various subjects, had a phenomenal memory, and when he decided to entertain us, he could go on for hours. I always believed he liked testing our patience and probably did it on purpose, burying us in a mountain of details.

"Oh, Eddy, that's enough now, stop that!" Anna would say with a shy smile. And when he sawed away on his violin to "serenade" us—wow!

He lived to 93 years of age. The most moving part of the funeral came when my son Patrick paid tribute to him.

My grandfather was born in Madison, Maine, on June 10, 1910. The eldest of three children, he spent his childhood in Cap-de-la-Madeleine with his brother John and his sister Margaret. Friends called him Ed or Eddy, but his parents called him Deb.

His first job was with the Canadian Pacific Railway in Montréal. Next he worked in Grand-Mère, then in Québec City, where he met and married my grandmother Anna. Their marriage produced two daughters, my mother Barbara and my aunt Patsy, five grandchildren, including my brother Stéphane and my sister Alexandra, Tim and Tom Fisher, the sons of Patsy and Harold Fisher and seven great-grandchildren.

His love of rail transport never wavered. Benefiting from the privileges granted retirees of the railway company, which became eventually the Canadian National Railway, he often traveled by train along the Québec-Montréal-Toronto corridor to visit friends and relatives. For his own pleasure, he would spend hours studying train schedules and routes, and he would often amuse his grandchildren with a miniature train he kept, it seems, just for them.

He liked walking along the streets of Québec City all the way to Château Frontenac. He also loved to reminisce about the past down to the slightest detail, including the exact dates. He described his trips, giving the names of the stations and the numbers of the routes he had traveled. He was full of life, often wrote letters and loved joking with his family and friends. In a troubled, competitive and sometimes cruelly unjust world, where it's hard to recognize true values, he had the heart of a child. He was filled with awe about the simple things in life: the family, a nice meal, a good walk in the fresh air, a phone call, a postcard.

His other grandchildren and I deeply loved and appreciated our granddad. As far as he was concerned, I never made a mistake. What I did was always perfect. He was my number one fan. My grandfather was a humble man and that's why I loved him so much.

Farewell, granddad!

—m—

Barbara attended St. Patrick's High School. On weekdays after school and on Saturdays, she walked down Grande-Allée, passed by the Provincial Legislature Building, went through Saint-Louis Gate and along rue d'Auteuil, glanced at the skating rink on the Esplanade, continued along rue Saint-Louis, turned onto Sainte-Ursule and continued all the way to Sainte-Anne, where the YWCA was located.

She was a member of the YWCA's synchronized swimming team. There were three other Barbaras on the team: Malenfant, Monaghan and Lamontagne. In the 1940s, many an English-speaking girl was named after figure skating champion Barbara Ann Scott. Sandra Marks and Denise Courteau were also on this remarkable team.

The Y's team was truly unique. Synchronized swimming was a little-known discipline in the late '50s. Even so, American, Mexican and Canadian teams held competitions at a high level. The Y team had won a number of Canadian Championships and would undoubtedly have earned medals if synchronized swimming had been an Olympic discipline.

The training was intense and rigorous under coach Suzanne Éon, the team's visionary founder and inspiration. For over a decade,

Barbara worked tirelessly every day, year round, to learn the rudiments of competitive synchronized swimming. The only time off she took was for the annual three-week summer vacation in Dalhousie, New Brunswick, with her grandfather Miller and her uncle John.

Her efforts were rewarded in the summer of 1959 when the YWCA team went on a six-week tour in Europe to promote synchronized swimming. The swimmers gave demonstrations in five countries: in Paris and Nice, France; in London, England; and in Germany, the Netherlands and Austria.

In 1961, two members of the YWCA team presented their candidacy to represent their respective duchies in the seventh edition of the Québec Winter Carnival. They fulfilled every requirement by the selection committee: Barbara Lamontagne was crowned Duchess of Laval, and Barbara Miller was crowned Duchess of Champlain.

The Québec Winter Carnival is the biggest winter celebration in the world and the third largest carnival, behind Rio de Janeiro and New Orleans. It's also the engine that drives Québec City's winter activities.

That year, 15,000 people attended the coronation of the Carnival Queen at the Québec Colisée. At the end of the selection process, Barbara Ann Miller was crowned Carnival Queen as the crowd roared its approval.

The Queen-elect approached the throne steps, where the Bonhomme Carnaval was waiting for her. After donning a blue velvet ermine-trimmed cape, she was crowned by the Bonhomme Carnaval to the hearty cheers of her subjects and the sounds of the carnival theme song. The carnival had its queen: Barbara Ann I.

—ᵒᵒ—

I had chosen a queen, too. We scheduled the wedding for September 26, 1964, at St. Patrick's Church, but I insisted that part of the ceremony be conducted in French. I also visited Father Ouellet, an old friend of Horace and Blanche, to ask him to say Mass at the wedding. In those days, Father Ouellet was the priest of Saint-Joseph's parish. There had been a time in my life when I called all my parents' friends "uncle" or "auntie," so I called Father Ouellet "Uncle Aurèle." He had baptized me 22 years before. We were having a chat in his modest living quarters in the rectory when he made a surprising request:

"Would you have any objection if I baptized you?

"What?"

"I would like to baptize you again."

"Uh! No . . . I don't mind, but may I ask why?"

"When I baptized you the first time, it was at Église des Saints-Martyrs Canadiens, and I was a little unfamiliar with the instruments. When the time came to pour water over your forehead, I didn't want to drench you, so maybe I was overly cautious. A drop fell from the ewer onto your forehead and remained there like a pearl. I was too timid and cautious to add more. Yet, it says in the Holy Gospel that for a baptism to be valid, 'water must be poured onto the forehead.' So if you don't mind . . ."

"Have you often thought about it since then . . . not to the point of being remorseful about it, I hope . . ."

"It hasn't kept me awake at night, but I've thought about it off and on . . . It's like an idea that is inside me, that haunts me; I had doubts. But now that there is an opportunity . . ."

While he went for a pitcher of holy water in the back, I unbuttoned my shirt collar. This time he didn't miss. I left the rectory, drenched . . . but as pure as an angel, and that's how, a few weeks later, Barbara and I were wed.

The queen and the angel.

CHILDHOOD 4

"Wake up. My water broke."

"What?"

"The baby is coming. We have to get to the hospital."

"Are you sure?"

"Yes, I'm telling you!"

"What time is it?"

"It's early."

"Let's go! Quick!"

We dressed quickly and silently, a bit tense. The first time is always more stressful.

It was the dawn of another October day: October 5, 1965, to be exact. We were renting a three-and-a-half in the Québec City suburb of Sainte-Foy. The Appartements du Jardin was a complex consisting of four fairly modern red brick buildings in Place Mackay, a dead-end street that led onto Chemin Sainte-Foy (there wasn't any Chapdelaine St. at the time) near Avenue du Séminaire, the entrance to Université Laval.

It was barely 15 minutes from the Jeffery Hale Hospital. We checked in a little before 7:00 a.m. A few hours later, at 11:07 a.m. Dr. Jean-Paul Roy delivered Patrick. Name of child: Patrick-Edward-Armand Roy; birth weight: seven pounds one ounce; height:

21 inches. It wouldn't be the last time we recorded statistics about Patrick.

I can't help thinking about the Lemieux family, who were giving birth to Mario in Montréal on the same day. Two of the greatest players in hockey history were born at nearly the same hour.

That day, the astrologist for *La Presse* wrote:

Children born today will be of a passionate nature that will expose them to numerous adventures. They will revel in these challenges as if they were in their natural element and they will always land on their feet. They will be equipped with the knowledge to help them achieve their desires.

This was particularly prophetic as far as Patrick and Mario were concerned.

That same year, 1965, in the hockey world, Terry Sawchuck became the first goaltender to reach the 400-victory plateau in regular season play, and Jean Béliveau won the first Conn Smythe Trophy awarded by the NHL. The newborns were already in the hunt.

—⚬—

Barbara and I didn't want to miss anything about Patrick's development, so at first we set up his crib in our bedroom. And at the slightest peep, we rushed to his side to find out what was wrong.

"Do you think he's cold?"

"No, I think he's too warm."

"Maybe he's hungry."

"I can try to feed him a little."

At first Barbara tried to breastfeed him, but the results weren't conclusive. We had to wake up several times a night, and the baby's hunger showed no signs of abating. Bottle-feeding solved the problem.

A few months later, we moved from 2206 to 2208 Place Mackay, where Patrick could have his own room, until Stéphane was born, 20 months after him.

Patrick had a normal, happy childhood. He was a beautiful baby with blond, almost white, hair and beautiful blue eyes . . . like Bona's. Even when Patrick was tiny, we could tell he was a little athlete. He was a *Jolly Jumper* champion. The *Jolly Jumper* was a sort of harness that we attached to the kitchen doorframe with an elastic. He could bounce up and down in it for hours on end. Little wonder he started walking when he was only ten months old!

He was a handful. When Patrick decided he needed more room, he unglued the bars in his crib one by one. One Sunday morning, while we were fast asleep after a long night, he sneaked out of bed, found some oil paint under the kitchen counter and proceeded to redecorate the chest of drawers in our bedroom, including the mirror.

We installed a gate at his bedroom door.

I found a note I had left for a babysitter when Patrick was not yet two.

1. *Take him to play outdoors until noon.*
2. *At noon, give him his lunch, making sure he doesn't stand up in his highchair.*
3. *After lunch, put him to bed with his bottle. Close the door and close the gate.*

When he plays:
<u>*In the house:*</u> *fasten the safety chain so he won't run into the hall;*

On the back balcony: keep a close watch on him so he won't cross over to the neighbor's place or throw toys off the balcony;

Outdoors: keep a close watch on him so he won't run into the street or fight with other children.

GOOD LUCK

N.B. He is very restless and requires constant surveillance.

Behind that angelic little face and blue eyes there slumbered a volcano ready to erupt at a moment's notice. He reminded us a little of *Dennis the Menace*.

—⁂—

We weren't rich, but we didn't lack for anything either. At the time, I was the public relations director for the Conseil des oeuvres et du bien-être de Québec, Centraide's precursor, and Barbara was teaching swimming at Collège Sainte-Foy. To help pay the bills, I gave guitar lessons on Saturday from time to time. There were a number of couples with small children in the Appartements du Jardin and during the day the kids could play outdoors in complete safety because it was a dead-end street and a quiet neighborhood. It was an ideal place for raising children.

In the summer we gathered on the lawn around the immense pool, which was much bigger than the ones you usually see in a complex like that. Many of the couples had named their baby girls Nathalie, probably inspired by Gilbert Bécaud's hit song; it must have been the name of the year. There was greater variety among the boys' names, but many of them ended in "ick" or "ic." like Éric, Frédérick and, of course, Patrick.

A few years later, when Barbara was appointed the swimming coach for the Québec City team, she gave our boys a taste of competitive swimming. Patrick turned out to be good at the breaststroke.

In fact, around age six, he was one of the best breaststrokers in his age group in the province. Later, Stéphane became every bit as good at the backstroke.

"I beat Pellerin!" said Patrick one evening when he and his mother joined me at work. But his enthusiasm was short-lived. He loved to compete, but he wasn't crazy about swimming.

"It's freezing cold at the pool. I want to play hockey," he said.

One day, the city swim team had a meet in Philadelphia and Barbara couldn't make the trip. She wondered whether Patrick's lack of enthusiasm stemmed from the fact that his mom was the coach. So she asked the coach accompanying the children to take Patrick along. When he got back, she was eager to hear what he had to say.

"How was the trip?"

"Great!"

"No! Don't tell me you're starting to like swimming?"

"Nah, but we drove by the Spectrum!"

All Patrick remembered was seeing the home of the Philadelphia Flyers after he'd bugged the driver non-stop to detour past the Spectrum.

Patrick's indifference to swimming didn't bother me. I recall one lovely Sunday in May when we had to spend the whole day in the stands of an indoor swimming pool in Tracy. The place was damp and dark and reeked of chlorine. Not to mention the four-hour round trip to watch a race that lasted a few seconds. A moment's inattention and we would have missed the whole thing.

He was good at tennis, too. He entered a few tournaments with tennis pro Jack Hérisset's development team. The late Jean Marois, who belonged to the same tennis club as we did, really liked him. In the early 1950s, Marois backstopped for the Québec Aces in the senior league when Jean Béliveau played for them. Marois liked Patrick's competitiveness, his fighting spirit and his fire. But Patrick didn't play tennis for long. I don't know whether Patrick realized it, but he already had a penchant for team sports. We would respect his choice.

—〜—

Because Patrick was born in October, he started grade one at Saint-Joseph Elementary School before he was six years old. It was a private school run by the Missionary Oblates. We thought he'd save a year. What a mistake! He wasn't ready, didn't pay attention in class and had a hard time keeping up with the others. He was off to a bad start. Asked to do a drawing with a snake in it, he sketched a pair of glasses on his snake. That was too much! A psychologist, called in to make sense of this bizarre behavior, considered the snake a bad omen. But we figured that, as he spent a lot of time at the pool where the swimmers wore goggles to protect their eyes, he had concluded that his snake, which was also in the water, should do the same.

In the fall of 1972, we moved to 1330 de Montmorency Street. I rented *Le 1330* for two years before I could buy it. Patrick started playing for an organized team as a forward. He was seven years old. The games were at Club Belvédère, an outdoor rink on rue Calixa-Lavallée run by Robert "Bob" Chevalier, opposite the Millers' place in Saints-Martyrs Canadiens' parish.

In 1973, Barbara registered Patrick, at his request, as a goalie at the Parc Victoria arena in Québec City, where he played for the Cléopâtres, a novice house league team. That year, Coach Jean-Guy Moisan wanted to find out a little more about his two netminders. He rotated them between goalie and forward during the first half of the season. By the time the holiday season rolled around, Patrick was determined to play goal, and when he got up very early on Christmas morning, a new set of goalie gear was waiting for him under the tree.

Some people become writers because they like the feeling they get when they move the pen across the paper; others become musicians because they love the feel of a guitar or a piano. Patrick loved goalie pads. I'd taken him to a Canadiens game at the Forum. That evening, the visitors were the Los Angeles Kings with Rogatien "Roggie" Vachon in goal. I think that outing might have been a turning point. Vachon and Daniel Bouchard became Patrick's role models, two goalies with very different styles.

"I want to be a goalie when I grow up," Patrick announced. Does an eight-year-old really know what he wants to do in life? How many of us have dreamed of becoming a police officer or a firefighter? But with Patrick, we had a feeling it wasn't an idle fancy. He finished the season itching for his turn in the net.

When summer arrived, he attended the Sainte-Foy summer hockey school. There he really sweated under the direction of Michel Lachance, who had played with the Québec Remparts in the Québec Major Junior Hockey League (QMJHL). Patrick was a healthy kid but on the small side for his age. The competition was stiff; it was a big step for him. Some of the kids already had a year of mosquito AA under their belts. They were bigger, stronger, faster. Their shots were harder than the ones Patrick was used to handling when he was with the novices. It was a rough start. Fulfilling the prediction of the astrologist for *La Presse*, he coped and adapted to the level of competition. He loved hockey; he adored the challenge. He would soon find out whether he could make it in mosquito AA.

THE APPRENTICESHIP 5

At the start of the 1974–75 season, the Inter-City Hockey League, in operation since 1969, selected the best players in the Québec City region and grouped them in category AA in the following divisions according to age: mosquito (9 and 10), peewee (11 and 12), bantam (13 and 14) and midget (15 and 16). Only midget AAA had a higher caliber, with teams from all over Québec.

There were seven franchises in what the parents called "the major minor hockey circuit." Each one represented a group of municipalities or districts in the Québec City region with about equal population densities: Beauport (Orléans zone), Charlesbourg (Jean-Talon zone), DSNCO (Duberger, Les Saules, Neufchâtel and Charlesbourg-Ouest), Lévis-Lauzon (South-Shore), QCHV (Québec-Centre-Haute-Ville), Québec-Limoilou and Sainte-Foy (Sainte-Foy, Sillery and Cap-Rouge).

Québec-Centre's impact player was Claude Lefebvre, a rugged, fast-skating forward, who was physically imposing, a valuable asset in those days when body checks were legal at every level. Michel (Michou) Maranda, the manager's son, a "little speed merchant," also wore the red and white uniform of the QCHV. When the season got under way, Martin Matte, who already had a year's experience in mosquito AA, was coach Guy Lafond's number one goalie. He would be minding the net in most of the games. Nearly nine years of age, Patrick, who wasn't very tall or strong, would be the backup.

Patrick didn't know it yet, but he was embarking on a career in competitive hockey that would last for years. Barbara and I were also embarking on a long-term commitment to the wonderful world of hockey arenas. As sports were a way of life for us, we were determined to help our children develop the skills they needed, provided that they had first the desire and then the talent. This idea is very important: parents are duty bound to help their children realize their dreams and not the reverse. With both Patrick and Stéphane, it was up to them; we would support them. Did they have the talent? The best way to find out was to test them and give them every opportunity to develop. At any rate, so far, things were going well. As long as the boys were in category AA, they'd be among the best in their age group.

At the beginning of the season, Guy Lafond let me get on the ice during a practice. I'd worked out a way of showing Patrick how to cover his angles. I took a rope about 30 feet long, slipped a shower curtain ring over it and then attached each end of the rope to each goal post about three feet high. When I tightened the rope pulling on the ring and moved away from the goal, directly in front of it, the rope formed a triangle with the goal as its base.

I asked Patrick to stand inside the rope, which then formed an angle in front of the goal and illustrated the possible trajectories that a puck could take towards the goal. This allowed him to see that the deeper he stayed in the net, the greater the space that separated him from the rope and the more likely it was that pucks taking that trajectory would beat him. By moving out of his goal and heading toward the apex of the triangle (the ring), he nearly managed to touch the rope, which meant that the pucks would strike him instead of entering the goal. When I moved from left to right, letting the rope slide in the ring, Patrick had to follow me to remain equidistant from the two sides, but he noted that the angle closed and that he no longer needed to move out as far from the goal to block a shot perfectly.

In the first few years of his apprenticeship, the focus was on three points. Patrick was told, keep your stick on the ice, stay on your feet and close the angle. Though he still had a lot to learn about technique, he innately possessed the temperament of a champion: the love of the game, the will to win, and an amazing ability to focus on what had to be done and to stay in the moment, making a total abstraction of the people around him and the consequences of his actions. In other words, when a shooter was bearing down on him, he wasn't concerned about what would happen if he didn't make the save, what the fans, his coach, his teammates would think, or what the consequences would be at the final outcome. Intuitively, he stayed in his cocoon, saw himself from the inside rather than the outside, and concentrated on what had to be done at any given instant. Throughout his career, this allowed him to be at his best when the tension was at its greatest.

Patrick's official debut in competitive hockey came on October 12, 1974, at the Parc Victoria arena, a week after his ninth birthday. He relieved Martin Matte, who had gotten off to a shaky start in the game. Beauport won 11 to 6. I attended the game, hardly a goalie's contest, with Pierre Mourey, who didn't know a thing about hockey. He had drawn the fluorescent dragons on Patrick's mask.

A routine was gradually settling in. We attended all of our sons' games. Stéphane played for the Panoramix in the novice division. We often took Alexandra along. She was getting her initiation into arena atmosphere in the first few months of her life. The mosquitoes played one or two games a week and had about the same number of practices. The novices' workload of one match and one practice was considerably less demanding. Barbara and I shared transportation duties. She did the driving during the week and I took care of it on the weekend.

We enrolled our sons in the École Permanente de Hockey set up in Sillery by Claude Malenfant, the father of two Québec-Limoilou players, Dany and Luc. So Patrick and Stéphane had the benefit of an extra practice on Friday evenings, which accelerated their progress. Michel Morin, an excellent skating coach, managed the school. His assistant was Michel Després, who became Minister of Labour in Jean Charest's Liberal cabinet in 2003 and Minister of Transport in 2005.

Later that year, when the Chicago Cougars of the now defunct World Hockey Association (WHA) visited the Québec Nordiques, Patrick's teammates Claude Lefebvre and Michou Maranda were asked to put on a shootout exhibition between periods. Undaunted by the Colisée's intimidating atmosphere, Patrick stopped four of the six shots, conceding a goal apiece to Claude and Michou. Player-coach Pat Stapleton's assistant behind the bench was none other than future Habs coach Jacques Demers.

Before the season ended, the excellent instruction Patrick had received helped him catch up with the second-year goalie, an oft-repeated scenario in his career. Québec-Centre finished fourth, a satisfactory result given the opposition.

Not surprisingly, Patrick easily won the Number 1 spot the following season. There had been a few rule changes. First, the mosquito division was now called the atom division. And body checking was banned in categories below bantam. But the change that suited us the best was the one concerning Stéphane: although he was novice age, he was considered good enough to play atom because of his size and skating ability. We were happy for him because he'd have a chance to play against stiffer competition. There was an added bonus: with both boys on the same team that season, we'd have considerably less driving to do.

The star of the mosquito division was Sylvain Côté. The DSNCO defenseman's skating skills and powerful shot reminded people of Bobby Orr. In fact, Sylvain went on to enjoy an illustrious NHL career with the Hartford Whalers and the Washington Capitals, as well as with Toronto, Chicago and Dallas. Patrick started most of the games in the 1975–76 season and played in the tournaments in Montréal-North and Richmond, among others.

Patrick was making steady progress. He was getting excellent training in winter and summer. But this edition of Québec-Centre wasn't a bumper crop. It was hard to find players to replace the boys moving up. Québec-Centre had roughly the same population density as the other territories, but because of its aging population, it had fewer children than the municipalities in the suburbs. So the reservoir of players was drying up as the years went by. With two scant wins all season, the team ended up mired in last place, and Patrick's goals-against-average teetered on eight. Still, someone must have spotted something in him because he was invited to the all-star game in January. Even so, it was hardly enough to build a future on!

That didn't matter. Hockey made Patrick happy; that's what counted. And God did he love it! He ate, slept and breathed it! No sooner did he get home from practice than he'd race out onto the street or to the Bank of Montréal parking lot for some ball hockey with Stéphane, Sylvain "Ti-Pote" Doyon and their pals in the neighborhood. And in foul weather, Patrick simulated games in the hall or on the landing. He pretended he was a forward, a defenseman and a goalie. He did the play-by-play like renowned Canadiens broadcaster René Lecavalier. He mimed the action with a mini-stick, a rubber ball and cushions for pads: "Lafleur picks up the puck, crosses center ice, passes to Shutt, to Lemaire. He's over the blue line; he drops it off to Lafleur, who fires a cannonading shot . . . but Vachon makes A FANTASTIC SAVE!"

This could go on for hours. In fact, it would go on for years . . .

—⁂—

Cut kitty-corner across the lane behind *Le 1330* and you got to the Doyon family's back yard. The two houses were back to back. With three daughters and three sons, the Doyons were a big family for the time. The late Mr. Doyon, whom the kids affectionately called Ti-Guy, was a bus driver for the Québec Metro-Urban transport company. A dyed-in-the-wool Nordiques fan, he detested the Canadiens.

Sylvain was his youngest, hence the nickname Ti-Pote (Little Buddy). The three brothers endlessly invented games in their back yard. Naturally, all the excitement fascinated Patrick and Stéphane. The Doyon brothers and Roy boys quickly became friends. Ti-Pote was a little older than Patrick and he was also taller. He was slightly overweight. He had the timid look and bashful smile of a boy who was shy but well brought up. He lived and breathed sports. But competition wasn't his thing.

The Roys and Doyons got together with other kids in the neighborhood to form the "Saint-Sacrement" Gang. Claude Lefebvre, from just three streets over, also joined them. In the winter and the off-seasons, they played road hockey; in the summer, they played baseball behind Holland School or in the municipal park. Pick-up games gave Patrick, Stéphane and Claude a breather from competition, since in the summer their Québec-Centre squad in the Inter-City Baseball League vied with the same kids they faced in hockey. The pick-up games were all the sport Sylvain and the others played.

Patrick's head teemed with ideas nonstop. The Lefebvre's phone would ring at 7:00 Sunday morning. Everyone knew who was calling: Patrick with some plan or other. Maybe he was organizing a road hockey tournament, a Canada Cup for nine o'clock. Had to call all the kids. No time to lose.

It was always related to sports. Inclement weather? No problem! The gang crowded into the Doyons' basement for some "small ball," a game Sylvain's brothers had received as a gift. About the size of a card table, it consisted of a miniature baseball stadium made of wood, canvas and plastic with a roof covering the red, white and blue bleachers, an electronic scoreboard for marking the runs after every inning, a lighting system and the baseball diamond, of course—everything you'd see in a real baseball stadium. The game was played with a plastic marble for a baseball. They spent entire evenings playing that game.

Sometimes the boys caught a movie. One day, they saw *Rocky* at Place Québec. Exhilarated at the sight of Rocky Balboa running up the steps of the Philadelphia Museum of Art, on the way back they bolted off the bus at Belvedere, a good mile and a half before their stop, and ran the rest of the way home.

They traded hockey cards, baseball cards. They even invented games with the cards. Once, I gave Patrick money to run an errand to Pomerleau's convenience store. He pocketed the $2.25 in change he got and didn't breathe a word. After school the next day, he used the money to buy his first set of hockey cards. But when he got back home, Anna, his maternal grandmother, lit into him:

"Where'd you get the money for those cards?"

"They gave me change when I went to the store for Dad," Patrick confessed, a little ill at ease.

"That's not right, *cherr*," his grandmother scolded him in her English-Canadian accent. "You'd better go and clean the garage, pick up any empties you find, then take them to the store for refunds. That way you can pay your dad back!"

I never saw the money, but that's how he developed another passion: collecting hockey cards.

The kids were Nordiques fans even before the team entered the NHL, when they still belonged to the WHA. One rainy morning, they wrote some letters in English using a dictionary and sent them to three WHA clubs to ask for souvenir pucks: the Cincinnati Stingers, Indianapolis Racers and Birmingham Bulls. They were just kids, so they thought they'd treasure the pucks forever. But, of course, as they were just kids, as soon as the pucks arrived in the fall, they ran outdoors and played with them in the street.

The Roy boys' routine was interrupted for a few weeks when the family went on a seaside vacation to Bona's Villa Acadia in Bonaventure on the Chaleur Bay. That's where Patrick and Stéphane got to know their half-cousins.

—m—

Of course, life wasn't all fun and games. There was school as well. And school wasn't a game, so Patrick wasn't too interested. In fact, he wasn't a good student. He was easily distracted and hyperactive. He daydreamed in class; he lacked discipline. The teachers plunked him down in the front row to keep an eye on him. Thank goodness for his grade three teacher, Mrs. Bélanger. She took him under her wing. She probably found his impish little face appealing. She salvaged him for a while. Patrick liked Mrs. Bélanger; she probably reminded him of his grandmother Anna, who was always there for him when he got home from school, since Barbara and I worked during the day. Barbara had a job with the Québec City Recreation Department as a lifeguard at the Palais Montcalm pool, and she gave swimming lessons as well. She also coached the city team. After going through a competitive hiring process, I had just been appointed marketing director for the Québec Ministry of Tourism. We were designing the first marketing plan in the history of Québec tourism.

In the evening, Patrick practiced reading and we did our best to help him with his math homework. That, too, could go on for hours.

JUST LIKE
THE PROS

Another baseball season had come and gone. The family took a few days' vacation in Bonaventure. The end of summer meant Patrick was going to start playing peewee. Those were the days, as far as I'm concerned. Eleven- and twelve-year-olds are still children, wide-eyed and full of wonder. Free of adult foibles and failings, they're easier to talk to. At that stage of their development, they may emulate the pros, but they're still passionate, sincere and innocent. Those were the best years because the peewee division was the most famous category in minor hockey. The Québec International Peewee Hockey Tournament, which is part of the Québec City Winter Carnival, had won worldwide recognition for the division.

The tournament has been privileged to include many boys who would later become illustrious NHL players. It suffices to mention Wayne Gretzky, Mario Lemieux, Guy Lafleur, Mike Bossy, Steve Yzerman, Gilbert Perreault, Marcel Dionne, Paul Coffey, Ron Francis, Brad Park, Daniel Bouchard, Steve Shutt, Adam Oates, Doug Gilmour, Scott Stevens, Pat LaFontaine, Sean Burke, Jeremy Roenick, Brendan Shanahan, and of course Patrick, to name just a few. Other stars have registered their sons in the tournament: Maurice Richard entered Normand; Gordie Howe, Mark and Marty; Bobby Hull, Brett. And but for his tragic accident in 1981, Valery Kharlamov would certainly have crossed the Atlantic and accompanied his son Alexandr to the event. Alexandr was a member of the 1989 Soviet team.

Imagine how a kid feels when he skates in those superstars' footsteps, when he plays for ten days in an arena that stores the memories of so many feats. Crowds, possibly exceeding the 10,000 mark, roar at the slightest opportunity. TV cameras are locked onto the action. A boy can read about his game in the papers the next day or his admiring host family can translate the articles for him if he can't read French. Look at the faces of the kids as they head to the Colisée for the first time. You can see the dream in their eyes that fills them with awe. But to play in the Peewee Tournament, you have to be on a team!

For Patrick, it was easy. He was making such steady progress that he made the Québec-Centre AA team in his first year. Directing the squad was the man who had coached him as a first-year atom, Guy Lafond. Patrick was also rejoining his "old" teammates, Claude Lefebvre and Michou Maranda.

Stéphane played atom AA. The practices alternated between atoms and peewees every Saturday and Sunday morning and the players had to be at the arena by 6:00 a.m. That winter, with a son in each division, I had won the booby prize.

So two days on the weekend, at 5:30 in the morning, the little silver-gray Renault pulled away from de Montmorency, took Holland, cruised down Saint-Sacrement, hung a right onto boulevard Charest and detoured through rue Anna to pick up Coco on the way. The little guy from the Saint-Sauveur district was a bit of a devil. He didn't talk much, probably because he didn't get much sleep, but he proved to be a very effective defenseman. Then we drove along Marie-de-l'Incarnation and took des Oblats, turned onto Saint-Ambroise and took Parent to the Parc Victoria arena.

On the way back, we retraced the route except for the obligatory stop at the Royaume de la Tarte, on the corner of des Oblats and Durocher, where we stocked up for the week on the best home-baked pies in the city.

It was as if the Renault ran on automatic pilot. Friday evenings I played in the Metropolitan Tennis League. After-tennis activities often went so late into the night that I had to decide whether it was worth trying to get a little sleep before waking up Patrick and Stéphane at 5:00 a.m. Sometimes a few of my fellow merrymakers would be kind enough to keep me company if I decided to stay up.

We were half-asleep when we arrived at the arena in pitch darkness. The arena was asleep, too. The rink's lighting system wasn't turned on completely until the players jumped onto the ice. We shivered in the cold and dark for an hour while the players donned their gear and listened to Mr. Lafond's instructions. Parents who lived close by could go home. Some looked for a restaurant open early to grab a bite of breakfast. Others dozed in their cars with the motor on and a window open. Sometimes I'd sit in the stands alone in the shadows and savor the tranquility of the arena. It was a place of contemplation, like an empty church.

—〜〜—

The Parc Victoria arena was a dilapidated building with wood floors and stairs, a wire screen instead of Plexiglas, an analog clock and an exterior of asbestos shingle cladding. Yet the building had historic significance. It had originally been built in 1913 with natural ice and a seating capacity of 4,500. The Québec Bulldogs played their home games there in the NHL, which was founded in 1917. The Bulldogs, representing Québec City, had won the Stanley Cup in 1912 in the National Hockey Association. An ice rink refrigeration system was installed in 1933. It was one of the few arenas in the country then with artificial ice. (The brothers Frank and Lester Patrick had built the first two in 1911 in Vancouver and Victoria.) The Québec arena was destroyed by fire in 1942 and rebuilt ten years later.

Until the arena construction boom in the late 1960s, the Parc Victoria rink was one of very few places in the Québec City area that amateur hockey players could rent. The Colisée, built in 1949, was reserved for junior and professional teams that drew paying audiences. Bona Arsenault had something to do with the arena construction explosion in Québec. In the mid-60s, the governments in Ottawa and Québec allocated millions of dollars to municipalities for the construction of cultural and community buildings to mark the Centennial year celebrations in 1967. Of course, arenas were not admissible, but Patrick's paternal grandfather, the Québec minister responsible for administering the program, found a loophole in the regulation. So a number of Québec municipalities took advantage of Bona's shrewdness to build arenas by listing them as "multi-purpose community centers." A network of fashionable hockey temples was born.

In Québec, the 1960s were marked by significant upheavals in public affairs management, notably involving the nationalization of hydroelectric power, the implementation of a province-wide educational system, leading to the creation of comprehensive schools and CEGEPs (colleges of general and vocational education), and the setting up of a modern public service. The 1970s would see the launching of vast hydroelectric projects and the rise of Québec "entrepreneurship" in the business world, along with unprecedented developments in the health-care sector. In barely 15 years, Québec underwent a transformation from a religious, agricultural, rural and closed society to a secular, industrial and urbanized society, highly receptive to new currents of thought. Expo 67 (the 1967 World's Fair) in Montréal dramatically symbolized the opening of Québec society to the world. Furthermore, with the support of the State and its institutions, Quebecers changed from servants of foreign capital to dynamic entrepreneurs and innovators of industry.

This awakening pervaded every stratum of a society in which the dreams of its citizens were now within reach.

—⁂—

The practice routine remained essentially the same. First the players did some laps around the rink to warm up. Then they did a few flexibility and stretching exercises, followed by acceleration drills from blue line to blue line, to the coach's whistle. Next, they practiced puck carrying around cones and shot on the goalie. The players dubbed my favorite exercise "the banana." Divided into two groups, the boys lined up along the boards, diagonally, at each end of the rink. At a signal, they took off one after another at top speed, received a pass at center ice and headed on a breakaway toward the goalie. The sequence got the kids really energized; it also warmed up the atmosphere for the spectators. Patrick had to do essentially the same set of exercises for the next 27 years of his career, with his teammates bombarding him with tens of thousands of pucks.

After the workout, I often watched the start of the next practice while the players changed out of their uniforms. The bantams followed the atoms, and the midgets followed the peewees. I couldn't get over how big and strong the midgets were. I had a hard time imagining my sons in that category. From one year to the next, I found that my perceptions changed. When your son graduates to a higher age group, you're surprised to find that his teammates seem normal-sized. Yet the year before, players in that division looked like giants, and now, the kids in your sons' previous category seem tiny. This is true all the way to the NHL. But there was still a long climb to the NHL.

Québec-Centre had a lot going for it. Mr. Lafond's dedication, the parents' support, the rigorous practices, the players' determination and offensive dynamos like Claude and Michou and a good playmaker named Yves "Boubou" Boulanger. But it was clear, from the beginning of the 1976–77 season that the roster still lacked the depth to get out of the basement. Sometimes, with an all-out team effort and Patrick's sparkling performances, the team produced some spellbinding matches, yet sooner or later, powerhouses like Sainte-Foy, Beauport and DSNCO prevailed.

In late January, just before the 18th Québec International Peewee Hockey Tournament got under way, Québec-Centre was struggling along a notch above last place. Coach Guy Lafond was toiling away at home devising strategies when the phone rang. It was bad news barely three days before the tournament.

"Mr. Lafond, this is Guy Lefebvre, Claude's father."

"Oh! Hello, Mr. Lefebvre."

"Listen, I have some bad news, Mr. Lafond. Claude is in the emergency ward at the hospital. You'll have to get along without him for the whole tournament, even longer."

The coach was stunned.

"But … what happened?"

"Ah! What can I say? He caught a cold he couldn't shake. It turned into the flu, and then degenerated into pleurisy. The doctor came over this morning and ordered him to be taken to the hospital immediately."

In fact, Claude would be hospitalized for over three weeks, and his convalescence would last at least five months. His season was over.

"Listen, wish him the best of luck with his recovery," Lafond stammered, "and tell him his teammates are behind him."

"Thanks, Mr. Lafond. I'll give him your message."

Mr. Lafond hung up the phone. It was like being hit over the head with a brick. Not only was Claude his top goal-scorer, he was the captain, the leader, the heart and soul of the team. But the coach had to turn adversity into opportunity, to energize and motivate the players. For the official tournament photo, the team placed Claude's number 7 jersey in their captain's vacant spot.

A weakened Québec-Centre faced off against the team from Havering, a town just outside Philadelphia. The first match was no contest. Québec-Centre scored 15 goals, and Patrick recorded a shutout in his first appearance. But little could be inferred from a match against weak opposition. Sure the rout made the players feel good, but what did it prove?

The second round matchup promised to be a different story. The opponents were the powerful Raiders from the Ottawa suburb of Nepean. Hockey connoisseurs gave Québec-Centre little chance. Were they in for a surprise! The Michou-Boubou combo dominated the game. Michou scored five goals and Boubou assisted on every one. Patrick, left dangling until the last moment before learning he would be starting his second straight game, turned aside many dangerous Raiders' attacks. It was one of the outstanding goaltending performances since the tournament began. And his team won 6–4.

Québec-Centre played its third game before a packed Colisée. Not that the 10,000 spectators had come to watch a floundering local team; they were there to see Winnipeg's Brett Hull in the previous match.

In those days, the Winnipeg Jets were the Nordiques' fiercest rivals in the WHA. Bobby Hull, who had carved out an illustrious career with the Chicago Blackhawks in the NHL, was their franchise player and Bobby Kromm was the coach. And each had a son—Brett and Richard—playing for the peewee Winnipeg South Monarchs. Tournament organizers feared the reactions of parents or other fervent Nordiques fans.

The behavior of most parents attending their children's games is beyond reproach, but a few parents are far from reasonable. Over the years, I've identified a few species:

The vigilante doesn't follow the game; he studies the referee so he can bellyache about the way the game is being officiated: "Hey, ref, you're missing a good game!"

The screamer hollers about everything: the game, the referee, the linesmen, the opponents, the coaches, the clock, and so on.

The instigator tries to provoke the opposing team's parents, insults rival players and incites his son to violence in subtle terms like, "Smash him! Hit him! Kill him!"

The worrywart only has eyes for his son and is mortally afraid something terrible is going to happen to him.

The loser pushes his son to the limit, hoping to realize his own boyhood dreams through his son.

The stoic observes a game poker-faced.

The analyst gives us the benefit of his expertise throughout the contest, much to our exasperation.

The specialist "coaches" from the stands and has a solution for everything.

The accountant spends the game calculating his son's ice time.

Finally, the whiner takes a very narrow view of things; the penalties his son's team gets are never deserved and the other team's infractions, are never punished.

Fortunately, the crowd at the Colisée gave Brett Hull and Richard Kromm a good reception. Of course there were a few jerks that actually booed the twelve-year-olds. During the pause between games, Patrick was photographed with Hull. He never would have guessed that they would meet as opponents ten years later.

After Winnipeg's victory, most fans stayed in their seats to watch the game between Québec-Centre and Oshawa, a city on the shore of Lake Ontario, just east of Toronto. They didn't regret it. In a scintillating game, the local squad, spurred on by the surprisingly large crowd, got off to an early 3–0 lead. Unfortunately, luck abandoned Québec-Centre as the second period wound down, and Oshawa tied the score and went on to win 5–3. It was the first time Québec-Centre had reached the third round in its history. Not bad for a near-cellar-dweller deprived of its top player!

The Peewee Tournament was the high point of the year. Without Lefebvre, Québec-Centre garnered few victories during the rest of the season. The team was unable to move up in the standings, unlike the Montréal Canadiens who, that year, became the first team in NHL history to rack up 60 wins in a season.

But playing on a weak team has its merits, especially for a goalie. For Patrick, every game was a challenge, and most of the shots he faced helped him develop his technique. Providing he wasn't discouraged by the many defeats!

At a modest reception marking the end of the season, the team managers handed each player a letter with a personal comment. Patrick's read as follows:

Patrick is a proud competitor who hates losing. A spark plug, sometimes he lacks concentration. Can't miss in the coming years, it will be interesting to watch him as he moves up to higher categories.

For someone who hated losing, he had more than his fair share of setbacks in the following season, 1977–78. Coached by Jocelyn Belleau, the team managed only one victory and a single draw in 36 games, earning a meager three points out of a possible 72. There was little optimism about the squad's participation in the Québec Peewee Tournament. They won the first game 4–2 against a club from San José, California, where hockey is certainly not high on the list of children's pastimes, and lost the second 5–1 to Beaconsfield, a Montréal suburb. Even so, Patrick was picked for the all-star game again. He was making steady progress.

Québec-Centre was no longer competitive in the Inter-City League. Changes were needed.

THE MOVE 7

I've always thought of the bantam division as a transitional category. At 13 or 14, people change. It's a passage from childhood to adolescence on their way to adulthood. They graduate from elementary to secondary school. Friendships form. They become a little more independent from the family. They want to assert their autonomy, to be free. Patrick was no exception.

Teens also undergo growth changes. But the growth rate varies from child to child. Some boys shoot up to six feet tall; others barely grow beyond five feet. Some become as strong and sturdy as adults very early on; others remain as scrawny as children.

The bantam division lends itself to a kind of natural selection. Body checking is permitted in competition. Boys at a physical disadvantage often quit. Others, previously involved in recreational hockey, suddenly show an aptitude for competition. They replace the boys who quit. Finally, some acquire other interests and abandon hockey. Patrick was changing too, but not his passion for competitive hockey.

On the eve of the 1978–79 season, the Inter-City League decided to balance the circuit by greenlighting the merger of the Québec-Centre and Québec-Limoilou franchises. The teams of the new franchise, wearing the blue uniform of the NHL's New York Islanders, were named after the famous Québec Citadelles of the disbanded Québec Junior A League. The legendary Jean Béliveau played his junior hockey with that team in the late 1940s. The Citadelles' home games and practices were split between the Parc Victoria arena and the Parc Bardy arena in Limoilou. The merger was good news. With the infusion of the best players from the two squads, the Citadelles could offer a competitive brand of hockey. But it also meant our family would have to make adjustments.

For Patrick, the merger presented an even greater challenge than for us. In his first year at bantam, he would have to earn a spot on the team to have any chance of moving up in AA. The merger meant fiercer competition for the two goalie spots. At the same time Patrick was transitioning from elementary to high school. He was leaving Saint-Sacrement School, where he could join his neighborhood friends every day after a couple minutes' walk. He was now attending Académie Saint-Louis, where he would have to get to know new boys and girls. We chose the school because of its reputation for being effective with study-averse kids. Finally, Patrick would have to ride the bus, and it would take him longer to get to the school at the corner of des Érables and chemin Sainte-Foy.

Meanwhile, my career was on the rise, and I was totally absorbed in my work. The previous year, in the fall of 1977, I had been appointed Assistant Deputy Minister for Tourism, and our team of trailblazers was setting up the network of Regional Tourism Associations.

Barbara was still doubling as swim team coach and swimming monitor.

Now, there were some practices and home games in Parc Bardy in the heart of Limoilou, quite a bit farther from our home than Parc Victoria. This was going to eat into the little time we had for transportation. To further complicate things, Stéphane now played for the peewee Citadelles and attended Saint-Joseph-de-Saint-Vallier Elementary School, and Alexandra was in kindergarten. We'd have a daily regimen of driving kids back and forth!

As the summer of 1978 wound down, the Québec-Centre peewee baseball team qualified for the provincial championship. Patrick was their shortstop. And he loved baseball. All summer, he and his teammates had worked hard to earn the right to qualify. He was thrilled at the prospect of playing in a provincial championship. After all, he had never won anything in hockey. But there was a scheduling conflict. It was just before the Citadelles tryout camp. If he took part in the competition, he would miss the first week of hockey camp and risk hurting his chances of playing for the Citadelles in bantam AA. It was a painful choice. After a long discussion, he decided to sacrifice the baseball championship. It wasn't an easy decision. But if at eight years old, Patrick already knew what he wanted to do when he grew up, at 12 he was even more certain. He kept his eye on the prize. He would do whatever it took to achieve his goal. In the end, he'd made the right decision! Not only did he make the team, he earned the Number 1 spot before training camp was over.

The result of the merger between two moribund clubs, the Citadelles weren't about to sweep aside everything in their way. Far from it. In fact, the team gave the lie to optimistic predictions by parents and supporters. No more Michou, no more Boubou, no more Coco. Claude Lefebvre and Patrick were among the few Québec-Centre players to make the cut in bantam. The nucleus of the team was mostly from Limoilou. The Citadelles floundered about in second-to-last place during the season. In the first round of the playoffs, Sainte-Foy trounced them 6–1 and 8–1 to win the best two of three series. It was getting to be a broken record for Patrick.

—⁂—

Nestled high on a hill overlooking the St. Lawrence, over a mile and a half wide at this point, the Cap-Rouge golf club was a strip of green among the clusters of fairly new houses that made up this Québec City suburb. It hadn't always been like that. Sixty years back, it had been really out in the country. Serge, Patrick's other paternal grandfather, had built a modest house there. Since then, it had been spruced up. And next to the house sat a golf club that wasn't there at the time. Patrick's grandmother, Lisette, seldom went out to Cap-Rouge. The place was out in the boonies, she felt. But it had always been a magnificent site. That's where somebody took the earliest pictures of me, as a newborn in my mother's arms. The famous Québec City painter Francesco Iacurto was a frequent visitor. A friend of my parents, he often went there to work. His oil paintings were inspired by the verdant landscape stretching as far as the eye could see, all the way to the Appalachians, interrupted only by the majestic blue St. Lawrence flowing between the red cliffs of Cap-Rouge and Saint-Nicolas.

We had been club members since the early 1970s, but not to play golf: the fees were too high. Our budget could afford tennis and swimming. It was ideal. While some of us played on the four courts, sheltered from the wind, others bathed in the pool or luxuriated on the immense lawn surrounding it. On weekends, when we could tear Patrick and Stéphane away from the Saint-Sacrement boys, we'd head to Cap-Rouge. Each time it was as if we were moving, what with Alexandra's toys and playpen, all the bathing suits, towels, tennis rackets, spare clothes, diapers, and so forth. I remember Patrick putting on his goalie gear by the pool while we were preparing to drive him to hockey school in Sainte-Foy. It was heartbreaking to gather up the whole kit and caboodle late Sunday afternoon and head back to town when we could have enjoyed the loveliest time of the day in the peace and tranquility of this bucolic setting. That's when an idea began to form in my mind.

When the heart desires, the will chooses and the mind justifies. Right between the front of the golf club and the cliff overlooking the river, a developer was selling lots. I had always dreamed of property with a view of the river. What a coincidence! Suddenly, *Le 1330* had lost its charm. Too big, too dark, too old. The only view we had was the neighbor's house across the way. Our home required frequent costly repairs, and property taxes were high. In contrast, Cap-Rouge seemed to offer every advantage. We could actually see the horizon. We would have a panoramic view of the river. Tennis and swimming were just across the way. And we'd have a house built to our taste and specifications. Above all, Patrick and Stéphane would be living in Sainte-Foy hockey territory, which boasted one of the best Inter-City League organizations. An added advantage was that the Sainte-Foy Gouverneurs of the Midget AAA Hockey Development League were located there. Finally, the proximity of the Sainte-Foy arena would ease our transportation load substantially. No more weak teams! Hurrah for suburban life!

Things moved fast. In June 1979, we bought the property. In August, we sold *Le 1330* and started building our new home. However, the late October delivery date was somewhat inconvenient: an Inter-City League regulation stipulated that a player's place of residence as of September 1 determined the franchise he would belong to that year. So we found a solution! We rented an apartment in Sainte-Foy on rue Grand-Jean, and stayed there from August 28 until we moved to Cap-Rouge. We were ready for the season.

Just before leaving Saint-Sacrement, I was rummaging around in my old things when I found my 1950–1951 NHL card collection. Knowing how much Patrick loved hockey cards, I gave him the set. There were only about 50 cards, but I remembered that when I was nine I must have chewed a hundred packs-worth of gum and carried out some tough negotiations with classmates to get the complete set.

Amid the summer hustle and bustle, Patrick went to École de hockey de la Capitale, run by Andy Dépatie, Marc Tardif and Charles Thiffault at Université Laval Sports Centre, where Nordiques goalie Richard Brodeur shared some advice with him. That year, the Nordiques joined the NHL. Years later, Patrick confessed he hadn't been thrilled about attending summer hockey schools. He believed he learned far more from watching his role models, Bouchard and Vachon, on TV. He much preferred playing ball with Ti-Pote and the Saint-Sacrement gang. But he didn't make a fuss. They were sacrifices he felt he had to make to reach his goal.

Would all that effort pay off? Not a chance! Sainte-Foy ended the 1979–80 season dead last with an identical record to … Patrick's former team, the Québec Citadelles: 8 wins, 21 losses and 1 draw. The more things changed, the more they stayed the same. Still another season plagued with defeats. Still not enough to build a future on.

Was it bad luck, misfortune, a twist of fate? Or was Patrick the problem . . . or was it a combination of the above? Recently, I got in touch with his old bantam coach Robert Fiset to get his point of view.

"When I think about that season," he said, "the first thing that comes to mind was the game we lost 1–0. Patrick must have stopped at least 70 shots. I said to myself, 'the little guy's going to go far, if only he can get a bit bigger.' "

In fact, at five feet, six inches tall, Patrick was about average height for a 14-year-old. But at 114 pounds, he was rather skinny. That year, Stéphane's performance was some consolation. He finished first in scoring in the peewee division. More good news: the move from elementary to secondary school saw Patrick doing better and better, not because he liked school more but because he was studying more.

For the first time, his grades were above average. The Académie Saint-Louis teachers deserved the credit. We had chosen the right school.

Overall, moving to Cap-Rouge was a fiasco for Patrick and Stéphane. I had underestimated their attachment to *Le 1330* and the neighborhood. There's a price to pay for uprooting teenagers. The friendships they form last a lifetime. It wasn't obvious right away because the heavy winter schedule of practices and games, which along with school, left them little spare time. But then summer came, and we realized that Parc Saint-Sacrement, the dusty baseball field and the Doyon's house meant a lot more to them than tennis, swimming pools and Cape-Rouge greenery. A certain form of alienation began to emerge. It was difficult to handle. The anticipated hockey benefits failed to materialize, and Patrick's situation hadn't improved one iota. And Stéphane could have won the scoring title with any other Inter-City League team.

But the worst was yet to come. In the summer of 1980, a disaster was about to take place that would add to the already heavy burden caused by the move.

THE MORASS 8

Robert "Bob" Chevalier, now retired, had made his mark in hockey in the Québec City region. He was powerfully built with a personality to match. He had a piercing gaze beneath his bushy eyebrows and enjoyed chewing on a good cigar. He was a no-nonsense kind of guy. Hockey was in his blood. He was born in Cap Blanc, a rough Québec City neighborhood that had produced more than its share of dockworkers. When Cap Blanc squared off against Saint-Pie X parish, it took the cops to break up the brawls on and off the ice. One man recalled a game in which 14 squad cars had to be brought in to restore order. Chevalier captained the Québec Frontenac junior team. Then, after an unsuccessful trial at the New York Rangers training camp, he finished his career in various senior leagues in Chicoutimi, Victoriaville and Ontario. This hardnosed rearguard wouldn't back down from anyone.

Back in Québec City, he turned up at the Belvédère club on Calixa-Lavallée, in Saints-Martyrs Canadiens parish. He ran the outdoor skating rink in the winter and the tennis courts in the summer. That's where Patrick learned how to skate, as I had 20 years earlier. It was a popular haunt for the youth in a quiet neighborhood.

When I was a teenager, we went there in the evening for a skate and to check out the girls. We never wore hats, even in temperatures of zero degrees Fahrenheit. They would have cramped our style under the rink lights swaying in the breeze. As you walked over to the rink, you could hear the huge speakers belt out, "It's Only Make Believe," the Conway Twitty hit, from ten blocks away. Paul Anka, the Everly Brothers, Fats Domino, Elvis and others saturated the entire neighborhood. But they weren't the problem. The hangout was a magnet for a handful of troublemakers who terrorized the neighborhood. Chevalier's task was to establish order. He did.

And if you wanted to learn a thing or two about hockey, Chevalier was your man. He could be an entirely different person from the tough-guy persona he projected. He'd often go over to a player on the rink, lean down and say, "Don't hold your hockey stick like that. Here's how you do it. Straighten your shoulders a bit. Now, take a few turns around the rink and get used to it." Or he would blow the whistle during a game he was refereeing and say, "This doesn't make any sense, guys. You're all over the place! You, what're you doing over there? You'll never get a pass if you stay over there! And if you do get the puck, what'll you do with it? And you, you're a center. You should always stand in front of the goal unless a winger needs help in the corner." Chevalier never raised his voice. He didn't have to.

In the humble but well-kept shack where we put on our skates, he could be intimidating. Needless to say, no one dared cause trouble. One look from Chevalier was enough to silence the bravest among us. And you couldn't leave anything lying around. No wrappers on the floor. He greeted kids by their names, but as soon as they came in, he told them to wipe their boots so they wouldn't dirty the floor. He wanted to make men of them, to educate them, in his own way. Based on the values he'd learned in the Marines, he insisted on politeness, kindness and respect. He was a guy with a good heart who had grown up in a milieu where fighting was second nature.

His good work earned him a promotion to Hockey and Arena Supervisor for the town of Sainte-Foy a few years later. His duties included managing the blue and red indoor rinks of the arena, as well as the outdoor Gaétan-Boucher skating rink. Since then, the blue rink has been renamed the Robert-Chevalier Rink and the red rink, the Roland-Couillard Rink. The latter was named in honor of one of the rink's benefactors, an important construction entrepreneur who owned several buildings in Sainte-Foy.

Chevalier represented the City of Sainte-Foy in every league in which its teams were entered. He also managed the recreational and competitive leagues in the municipality's parishes. In 1976, he helped found the Midget AAA Development Hockey League. He was justifiably proud of this. At first, the League consisted of five teams. Sainte-Foy's team was named Couillard, to underline Roland Couillard's sponsorship. When Couillard died, Chevalier sought out Roland Dubeau, who was on the board of the Auberge des Gouverneurs. Dubeau stepped in to provide the funding. That's why the Sainte-Foy teams were called the Gouverneurs from the 1979–80 season on. That year, the AAA division already numbered eight teams, and another team was added the following season.

The Midget AAA Sainte-Foy Gouverneurs were a model organization, well ahead of their time. The head coach could count on two assistants behind the bench. A goalie instructor attended the practices and sat in the stands every game. Few teams in the NHL had a comparable setup. That came later on. The Gouverneurs played their home games in the Robert-Chevalier Rink, where they had a permanent dressing room. At a special eight-week training camp in the summer, coaches trained, evaluated and selected players likely to make the team in the coming year.

Once the season started, the players had four practices a week, from Tuesday to Friday, and two games on Saturday and Sunday, one in Sainte-Foy and the other out of town. There was a Bluebird bus to drive the players for away games. All in all, the youngsters skated six days out of seven. If the bantam division represents a transition on the personal level, the midget division is an equally important phase. At midget level, hockey is still a game, but there is more at stake. QMJHL and NHL scouts attend AAA games. In the Québec City region, playing for the Gouverneurs was a rite of passage for any aspirant to a hockey career.

—m—

In the summer of 1980, Chevalier had intended to propose the expansion of the Sainte-Foy territory at the general assembly of the Inter-City League. This would have allowed him to recruit at least three players in Portneuf County for each of his AA teams. Québec City had made a similar request two years earlier and had been allowed to merge Québec-Centre and Québec-Limoilou. For the proposal to come before the assembly, it needed the backing of another franchise's representative. Chevalier warned that if they refused to listen to him, he would withdraw from the League. They thought he was bluffing. He wasn't. No one deigned support his proposal and hold the debate. Chevalier and his loyal lieutenant, Florent Boily, walked out, slamming the door behind them. Sainte-Foy had just withdrawn from the Inter-City League.

For any AA caliber player in Sainte-Foy, this was a disaster. The territory went from having one team in each of the four divisions to eight teams in each. Imagine how much this watered down the competition. Imagine the impact on the coaching quality, practice time and the schedule. There was also a sharp decline in the quality and intensity of the workouts. For 15-year-old Patrick, entering his first year in midget, there was only one hope: to earn the Gouverneurs' AAA red and white jersey.

—ᴍ—

Patrick showed up at the Gouverneurs' camp after a few weeks' vacation with the family in Bonaventure. He had undergone a growth spurt in the last year. He was now almost six feet tall. The Gouverneurs were guided by two principles in selecting goalies. The first was related to a goalie's age. I had learned this from Guy Lafond with the atoms: choose a "16-year-old," a goalie with experience, who would get most of the ice-time, and a "15-year-old," who would be trained for the next year. Stéphane Fortin, the Gouverneurs' 16-year-old goalie, was already guaranteed his position from the start of the camp. The second tradition was related to goaltending style. Ideally the coaches would select a goalie who was compact, not necessarily tall, but rather thick, one who stayed on his feet as much as possible and moved quickly, mirroring Rogatien Vachon's style. Stéphane Fortin fit the mold.

Under the Gouverneurs' head coach, Fred Dixon, the training camp and selection process began in August. It was a big camp with more than 90 players. Among them were a dozen goalies, mostly from the immediate Québec City area, but also from other regions. The first few days were devoted to physical conditioning, skating and other basic drills. The coaches cut players with glaring weaknesses as quickly as possible. Goalie coach Jacques Naud schooled his charges on basic positions in various game phases—stick and glove placement, lateral movement, harpooning and working behind the net. In other words they worked on all the details goalies need to master. Some youngsters were eliminated early on, paving the way for the remaining few to compete for the backup goalie spot.

Two things soon became obvious. The choice would boil down to Patrick or Yves Martel, from Alma, Lac-Saint-Jean. Martel's more conventional style seemed much closer to what the coaches were looking for. Because of his size, Patrick used the "butterfly" style, dropping to his knees and fanning his legs on either side. He merged the contrasting approaches of his two role models: Roggie Vachon's "standup" style, and Daniel Bouchard's "butterfly." Bouchard didn't invent the technique. Glenn Hall pioneered it in the '50s and '60s, and later, Tony Esposito used a modified "butterfly" with the Chicago Blackhawks after a brief stay with the Montréal Canadiens. But Bouchard employed it whenever he had a chance. He was constantly on his knees, contrary to the tenets of the day: a good goalie stayed on his feet as much as possible and, more importantly, never made the first move.

Jacques Naud wasn't a purist. He didn't reject the "butterfly" or any other technique on principle, as long as a goalie respected the fundamentals and made the save. During the camp, Patrick stopped the puck as often as Martel did. But his size, slenderness, teenager's uncoordinated gait, and unorthodox style were worrisome.

Practical considerations accelerated the decision-making process. As it was already September and Martel came from outside the territory, he needed to know his status so he could find lodging, prepare for moving and enroll in a school. The coaches mulled over the dilemma. They had to make up their minds about Martel before settling on their final choice. At the last minute, they picked Martel. His style appealed to them. There were also strategic reasons. Martel came from Lac-Saint-Jean, a region whose players were considered up for grabs by the Development League. If he was cut, he could sign on with any team in the league and come back to haunt the club that had released him. On the other hand, as Patrick came from Cap-Rouge, if he played AAA, it would have to be with the Gouverneurs.

They could recall him at any time. He belonged to them for the next two seasons.

Reality hit Patrick hard. He had never failed to make a team in training camp before. As he lived in Saint-Foy territory, which had withdrawn from Inter-City, he couldn't join a team in AA. He had to try out for the Sillery/Cap-Rouge team in CC, the parish league founded by Bob Chevalier. Our troubles had just begun.

—ᴡ—

On Wednesday, September 10, Barbara accompanied Patrick to the Jacques-Côté arena where Sillery/Cap-Rouge trained under Réjean McCann. A "parish coach," McCann had no idea what had happened at the Gouverneurs camp and didn't follow AA hockey. So he wasn't familiar with Patrick's track record. He didn't know who Patrick was or what he had accomplished so far in hockey. On top of that, his training camp was almost over, and he had already picked his squad. The previous year, he had piloted the Sillery/Cap-Rouge bantam team and had decided to take his two goalies up to the next division with him. Patrick took a few turns in the net. A few players practiced some shots on goal, but the coach didn't pay attention. When the practice was over, Patrick was informed that he was cut and that he would have to try out for the B level team. Cut twice in the same week! He couldn't sink any lower. From AAA to B where hockey was a pastime to keep youngsters occupied. As things stood, Patrick could forget about a career in hockey. It was over. The end of a dream to which he had devoted over seven years.

Huguette Scallon coached the Quartier-Laurentien team in the CC parish league. She was familiar with Patrick's bantam AA performances in Sainte-Foy, and had followed the Gouverneurs selection camp closely. She couldn't believe he'd been cut, given his performance at the camp. By the time Scallon found out that Patrick had been dropped by Sillery/Cap-Rouge, Quartier-Laurentien already had a goalie. But knowing how good Patrick was, she told us that she would like to have him on her team.

I found out what steps I had to take so that Patrick could play for Quartier-Laurentien. I sent a letter to Marcel Bergeron, Vice-President of the Sillery/Cap-Rouge minor hockey committee, to ask for Patrick's release. I assumed this was a formality because the team had dropped Patrick, and after all, these were only 15-year-olds playing at CC level.

I wrote him a letter requesting Patrick's release from the team. Five days later, I got a reply, a letter signed by Édouard Lacroix, the committee secretary.

Dear Sir,

I am writing to inform you of the decision taken by the Sillery/Cap-Rouge minor hockey committee about your request for your son's release.

In accordance with a rule that was adopted last year and renewed this year, the Committee refused the request for release.

Indeed, it is important to understand that such a request would be unacceptable to any serious hockey organization. If your son failed to qualify in the first midget category, he should normally be integrated into the second providing he shows the ability and desire required to make it.

Our organization can no longer afford to let players leave for other organizations. Can you imagine what would happen if this were allowed: any disappointed player who wasn't selected for the "big club" would try his luck with a team owned by a rival organization? What would happen to lower-level clubs?

Best regards,

The inference I drew from the letter was that a "serious hockey organization" is more concerned with its own development than with that of its youngsters.

I went to see Chevalier. After all, he was the one who had withdrawn Sainte-Foy from the Inter-City League. He had his share of responsibility for this mess, and as the head and founder of the CC league, he undoubtedly could fix it.

His answer? "The kids should have fun: tell Huguette to let him play." That's how Patrick joined Quartier-Laurentien.

Meanwhile, Barbara rang up Fred Dixon. She was courteous but she told him he had made a mistake in letting Patrick go. That wasn't the thing to do, and she knew it, especially since she was a swimming coach. She dealt with parent-coach relations on a daily basis. Barbara and I didn't believe in interfering with a coach's decision about our children. Still, this was a mother's cry of desperation. Perhaps she also felt she was a coach talking to another coach. She had the right to give her input. Dixon replied—we could have guessed his answer—that she had a right to her opinion, but that he had made his decision in good faith with the backing of his assistants and in the interest of his team. Several years later, Dixon admitted to me that he had suspected Bob Chevalier had not been very happy with their choice of goalies the year they cut Patrick. This is just a feeling because Chevalier, who didn't meddle in his coaches' decisions, never broached the subject with Dixon. Chevalier never discussed it with us either. Nor did he ever indicate whether he was favorably or unfavorably disposed towards Patrick.

As fate would have it, the season opener pitted Quartier-Laurentien against Sillery/Cap-Rouge, at the Sillery arena. Before the game even started, Sillery/Cap-Rouge representatives filed a protest, claiming that Quartier-Laurentien was using an unauthorized goalie. But Chevalier must have pulled some strings, because as soon as the game started, one of their managers, André Rémillard, approached Scallon, looking to make a deal. He agreed to lend Patrick to Quartier-Laurentien, but only for the season in progress. In return, he requested that the head of hockey for Quartier-Laurentien confirm in writing Patrick's release and that his contract for the 1981–1982 season be returned. Was he hoping to have him in his line up the next season? Scallon hurriedly accepted the deal, and the protest was withdrawn a few days later, once the agreement was confirmed in writing. At least Patrick could play in CC.

—m—

"Ti-Guy" Doyon occasionally drove the Number 15 Bus. On this route, he was scheduled to leave Place d'Youville at 3:20 p.m. He made sure it took him at least ten minutes to reach the corner of des Érables and chemin Sainte-Foy. Meanwhile, the bell signaled the end of the school day for the grade nines at Académie Saint-Louis. Ten minutes was just enough time for Patrick to grab his books, rush downstairs, put on his coat and boots and run to the bus stop. On the bus, he sat on the front seat and chatted with "Ti-Guy" during the one-hour commute to Cap-Rouge. They talked about this and that, the weather, the Canadiens, the Nordiques.

Patrick had yet to develop an interest in school. Even CC hockey took precedence over studies. To earn pocket money, he sometimes worked evenings or weekends as a scorer at the Sainte-Foy arena for two dollars a game. Despite his hectic schedule, he maintained slightly above-average grades, which I found acceptable, given the circumstances. But I was at a loss as to how I could ignite his interest in schoolwork. I would also have loved to spend more time with him, discussing subjects other than hockey. But he was loyal to his Saint-Sacrement friends and preferred spending the little free time he had with them. I didn't have much time for leisure either. Jean Labonté and I were busy preparing the bill that gave birth to the Société du Palais des Congrès de Montréal.

—⁂—

That year, Patrick and Quartier-Laurentien rolled over the opposition. On their way, they captured the regular season title and the Beauport midget championship, in which Patrick was chosen the outstanding goalie. They suffered their only loss in the playoff final. Quite an improvement on the previous years! Still, these results were achieved at CC level, where there was only one game and one practice a week. Meanwhile, Martel laced up his skates six times a week under the tutelage of much more qualified coaches. Patrick's only advantage was that he played in all of his team's games that year, whereas Martel, as a backup goalie, started only six matches and won four of them. There was one small consolation: to monitor his progress, the Gouverneurs invited Patrick to train with them during the Christmas break, while the players from out of town went back home for the holidays. Finally, at the end of the season, he was invited to the Gouverneurs' special training camp, an eight-week training and evaluation session. Patrick could see that while making the team the next year would be a tremendous challenge, it wasn't impossible, with a lot of work . . . and a little bit of luck.

A NEW BEGINNING

It was an August day. The kind of August day when everything seems alive. Trees, flowers, grass. Lazy lakes and rivers. Blue skies and verdant grass . . . Monet's palette. When the days still encroach on the nights. I have come to remember that "August day when everything seemed alive" as the day Patrick's career got off to a new start.

August 1981: another Gouverneurs camp. Patrick's second tryout. His last chance. Again there were 90 players, including several goalies. Among them, Yves Martel, of course. Patrick had a few questions on his mind. "Has Martel got the spot locked up? If not, can I beat him out of it? Will they do something different and pick two 16-year-olds? But there's no time to think about that. Concentrate on what you can do and show them what you're made of! Don't let them cut you. You've got to make them keep you on the team."

Patrick was taller but wiry. He still felt comfortable flopping to his knees in the "butterfly" position, especially since his role model, Daniel Bouchard, had been traded from Calgary to the Québec Nordiques. Patrick's style was not what the Gouverneurs were looking for. Jacques Naud was an exception. He prized performance over style. When the camp got under way, he gave Dixon a glowing report about Patrick. Dixon wasn't impressed. "You're going to have a tough job selling him to me!"

Of our three children, Alexandra adapted to Cap-Rouge the best. We had enrolled her at St. Vincent Elementary School in Sainte-Foy and she had already made new friends.

Stéphane attended Séminaire Saint-François in Cap-Rouge, but at every opportunity, he'd hang out with Patrick in Saint-Sacrement. Stéphane played for the Sillery/Cap-Rouge bantam CC team. What a disaster. One day, I went to the arena to pick him up after practice. As I was sitting there on a bench waiting for him, I spotted cigarette smoke billowing out of the dressing room door. Outraged, I marched over to find out which coach had the gall to smoke around 13- and 14-year-olds. To my dismay I found most of the players happily puffing away. Hardly my image of elite sport. Poor Stéphane! A Ferrari in a jalopy race!

Barbara had quit her job teaching swimming in Québec City. For her, it was the start of a brilliant career as a real estate agent, and eventually as a real estate broker. Her new job gave her more free time. Her schedule was more flexible and she liked the challenge. I had been offered the post of Québec Delegate in Los Angeles, but California was hardly an ideal location for a developing hockey player, so I turned down the offer to avoid hampering Patrick's progress.

—⁂—

The coaches had evaluated the team to prepare for the 1981–1982 season. The offense was their principal asset. They would center their explosive attack on Patrick Émond and Claude Gosselin, two prolific 16-year-old goal scorers. The Trois-Rivières Draveurs of the QMJHL had invited both of them to training camp. The boys had indicated they would return to the Gouverneurs when junior camp was over because they planned to study in Québec City. The blueline corps was another matter. Except for captain Mario Carrier, the defensemen were 15-year-olds without midget AAA experience. True, the coaches could count on Sylvain Côté, the star of the Inter-City League, but they would still have to work with a talented but inconsistent and young defensive rearguard crew. One key question: who would be in goal? Yves Martel had spent most of the previous year with the Gouverneurs, but he had had few starts and he hadn't made the expected progress. Even so, Jacques Naud had tutored him during practice throughout the whole season. So the team was counting on him to start the year as the Number 1 goalie.

Jacques Naud had never bought into the policy of having a 15-year-old goalie as a backup and preparing him for the next season. To progress, a kid needed game experience, he thought, not just practice. Early on, he cut a few netminders who were clearly not AAA level. He worked on fixing technical details with others. For example, he encouraged Patrick to hold his glove higher and keep his elbow tucked into his hip to close the gap under his arm. "A puck that touches a goalie should never get into the net," he insisted.

Barbara and I attended most of the training sessions and the intra-squad games. During the camp, Patrick improved. He seemed to be making an impression. We felt he was better than the other goaltenders, including Martel. But the decision wasn't up to us.

Fred Dixon and assistants Simon Robitaille and Jean-Louis Létourneau focused on the other players, giving the goalies a glance now and then. Jacques Naud worked exclusively with the netminders, jotting down his observations in a small black notebook.

After practice, the coaches huddled to evaluate the goalies. By consulting his notes, Naud was able to say how many shots on goal a keeper had faced and how many saves he had made. Day after day, Patrick stood out from the pack. Maybe he lacked the orthodox style Dixon was looking for, but Naud's statistics showed Patrick was making the most saves. It was an irrefutable argument. He could go through four game simulations without allowing a goal. What more could anybody ask? In the end, the coaches had to choose him. They broke tradition and started the season with two 16-year-olds. Martel still hadn't proven himself as a Number 1, so they were keeping their options open.

This was Patrick's second chance to achieve his goal; it was a new start. It had been a long uphill struggle. He stuck a Daniel Bouchard hockey card in his locker in the Gouverneurs' dressing room. It reminded me of the way seminary students used images of saints as a source of inspiration.

—⁂—

On the eve of the new season, the Gouverneurs suffered a setback. Émond and Gosselin decided not to return. They chose to stay with the Draveurs in Trois-Rivières, a slap in the face for the Gouverneurs. The team had lost its two best players.

Even so, the Gouverneurs bolted out of the gate with five victories in a row. Martel was in goal for three easy wins: 9 to 2, 9 to 7 and 5 to 3. But Patrick's victories were remarkable: identical 5–1 scores against Claude Lemieux and the Richelieu Éclaireurs, who hurled 43 shots on goal in the first contest and 32 in the second. Patrick had given up just two goals in 75 shots. Not bad for a backup! And that was just the beginning. With Patrick in goal, the team tied twice against league favorites Lac-Saint-Louis Lions, who outshot the Gouverneurs 49 to 37 in the first game and 53 to 31 in the second, then blanked the Estrie Cantonniers and whipped the Lac-Saint-Louis Lions 4 to 1. The Lions were in first place at the time. Martel lost his next five starts, including a resounding 11 to 1 defeat to Montréal Concordia.

By mid-November, two months into the season, the coaches had to acknowledge that the team was turning out to be a very different club from the one they had expected. They had anticipated an explosive offense, but the departure of Émond and Gosselin had left the squad with an average attack that relied on team play. The only star they had was Martin Bouliane, whose scoring ability lifted him slightly above the others. Surprisingly, the Gouverneurs boasted the best defensive record in the circuit, largely thanks to Patrick. He was gradually becoming the backbone of the club. The coaches had to use him as often as possible. Realizing that he was loosing his starting job, Yves Martel decided to leave. Martel's stay in Québec was a considerable financial burden for his parents, so they suggested he come back home to Alma.

—∭—

Attorney André Blanchet, a brother-in-law of one of Barbara's colleagues, knew Daniel Bouchard well. He lived close to Bouchard's house in Sainte-Foy. One evening, Patrick was sitting around after supper when he received a phone call. Daniel Bouchard was willing to meet him at Blanchet's place. Patrick hopped on the next bus to go and meet his role model and inspiration. So far, Patrick had only seen him on television. They spent nearly two hours discussing the art of goalkeeping.

Bouchard has always been gracious and easy to talk to. Patrick wanted to learn everything about Bouchard's approach: game preparation, stretching, the splits, stick and glove placement. Patrick asked him how he dealt with game situations, how this, how that, how the other . . .

Bouchard told Patrick that tending goal for weaker teams had its upside. A goalie can learn from facing many shots. This had been Bouchard's experience in the minors. He predicted a great career for Patrick. And Bouchard even autographed one of his Louiseville sticks in the Nordiques colors for him. When Patrick went to the bus stop with the precious stick, he was walking on air. He kept the stick in safekeeping for a while. But finally he gave in to temptation and used it during his games.

—⁂—

Since none of the Gouverneurs players were dominant enough to build the team around, it was easy to sell a team concept. And when the going got tough the players relied on Patrick to bail them out. The Gouverneurs went on a 22-game winning streak. By the end of the regular season, they had climbed to the top, one point ahead of defending champions Lac-Saint-Louis Lions. Patrick realized that a goalie can make the difference. And that's what he intended to do.

Patrick became the team's uncontested leader, inspiring confidence and enthusiasm. In practice, the coaches focused on breakaways, a common occurrence in the league. Patrick would often face all 17 of his teammates without allowing a single goal. Players who managed to beat him would raise their arms in triumph as if they'd accomplished a great feat.

—⁂—

Patrick's ability didn't go unnoticed in the circuit. On Monday evening, January 18, he played in the midget AAA league All-Star Game at the Montréal Forum before 6,000 spectators. Several QMJHL and NHL scouts were in attendance. Still a game, but an increasingly serious game.

We drove through a blinding snowstorm along Highway 20. With the blowing snow and the whiteouts, it took us four and a half hours to make the 150-mile journey between Québec City and Montréal. But nothing could have stopped us from getting to the Forum. Patrick turned in a sub-par performance that day. Usually solid in goal, he seemed nervous and edgy as the starting goalie on the all-star team, conceding three goals in the showcase event. Alain

Raymond of the Estrie Cantonniers replaced him mid-game, as was the custom. Raymond's sterling play earned him goalie of the game honors.

Patrick and his six Gouverneurs teammates on the all-star teams received a letter of congratulations signed by Marcel Bergeron the chairman of the Sainte-Foy minor hockey committee, the same Marcel Bergeron who, as Vice-Chair of the Sillery-Cap-Rouge minor hockey committee had refused my request for Patrick's release the year before. He wrote:

> *Your selection, entirely justified, proves that you meet the criteria set by the Midget AAA Development League and are an example for youngsters in minor hockey. I am certain that, in the future, you will continue to be guided by the principles that you have been taught and that we will have reason to be proud of you and what you accomplish.*

Had he made the link with Patrick?

—⁂—

In the forty-eighth and final game of the regular season, the Gouverneurs edged out the Lac-Saint-Louis Lions by one point in the standings to claim the season title. On their way to the top, they had conceded a league record low 152 goals. The team finished with 27 victories and 10 draws. Patrick also earned a place in the record book with a 2.63 goals-against average. He was proud of this accomplishment, but he had another objective in mind: the Air Canada Cup, emblematic of the national midget hockey championship, to be disputed in Victoria, British Columbia, in April. There was one more obstacle: the Gouverneurs had to get past the Lac-Saint-Louis Lions in the best-of-seven provincial final.

A crowd of 1,000, the largest attendance ever for a midget AAA hockey game, poured into the Sainte-Foy arena for the opening game. The home team gave the fans the money's worth with a 3–0 shutout, in which Patrick stopped 27 shots. In game two in Valleyfield, the next day, a trivial but costly incident was a cause for concern in the Gouverneurs' camp. The Gouverneurs were leading 2–1 with six minutes remaining in the third period. The teams fought for every square inch of the rink. The crowd oohed and aahed with each spectacular hit. In a scramble near the crease, a Lac-Saint-Louis player gloved a pass ahead to a teammate who slipped the puck behind Patrick. Referee Réal Travers signaled a goal. Patrick, with his accustomed fire, stormed towards the official to protest. The play should've been blown dead, he thought, when the illegal pass was made. Travers, retreating as Patrick bore down on him, tripped and fell backwards. Did Patrick push the official? Or did he even touch him? Some, including Travers, claimed it was a push in the heat of the moment. Others disagreed. But when all is said and done, the man with the whistle has the last word. Patrick was ejected.

The incident threatened to have disastrous consequences. Sainte-Foy would have to go the rest of the way with a 15-year-old backup goalie who hadn't started a single game in the regular season. Worse still, he had a scant 42 minutes of experience in midget AAA hockey. After Martel's departure, the Gouverneurs had picked up Alain Couture, ironically dubbed "Colosse" by his teammates because of his frail stature. He wasn't the next best goalie to Martel; he was the best one available. Given Patrick's outstanding performance and the team's anemic offense, "Colosse" had only played when victory was assured.

The players returned to the bench, heads down, aware of the gravity of the situation. Captain Mario Carrier shot a look at the coach as if to say, "What miracle are you gonna pull off now?" It looked as if the tide had turned. The score was even at 2–2. The Gouverneurs would have to play the next seven minutes with a man short—and with a rookie goalie facing the fire. Every single player stepped up. The defensemen blocked shots and the forwards stayed home and checked furiously. "Colosse" displayed remarkable poise. The team held on until the end of regulation time. The first minute of overtime was more of the same. Having killed the penalties, the Gouverneurs turned tiger and went on the attack until Donald Deschênes scored the sudden-death goal at 8:32 of overtime. Having snatched victory from defeat, they led the series 2–0.

On the bus ride back to Sainte-Foy, despite the victory, the look of concern on the players' faces told the story. They needed two more wins to earn a spot in the Air Canada Cup. The Lac-Saint-Louis Lions wouldn't be rolling over. The Gouverneurs had eked out two wins with the best goalie in the league playing for them. What would happen now?

Speculation was rampant. Patrick's expulsion meant he would miss the next game, at least. That was a league rule. As the incident involved a referee, the disciplinary committee of the Québec Ice Hockey Federation, not the league, would deal with the issue. The committee could well mete out much stiffer punishment. Earlier that season, a player had received a three-game suspension for assaulting an official. But the player had a well-deserved reputation as an enforcer. His 128 minutes in penalties made him the most penalized player on his team. Patrick was entirely different. He had never gotten a misconduct penalty in his career and he had picked up only five minor penalties that season. Besides, it wasn't clear that Patrick had even touched the official, never mind assaulted him! Even if the committee were to decide that he had touched the referee, they would be obliged to conclude that it was an accident. What would Travers write in his report? Who would be asked to testify and what would they say? What would the committee decide?

Two days later, Fred Dixon and manager Normand Pruneau took Patrick to Montréal for the disciplinary committee hearing. As they drove along Highway 20, the subject was scarcely broached. They didn't see any reason to prepare for the meeting as Patrick had maintained his innocence. Jacques Naud always sat in the stands near Patrick's goal. He had seen everything. He corroborated Patrick's version. He was sure that Patrick hadn't pushed Travers and the referee had fallen on his own. They would simply have to tell the truth, about what they had seen and heard, and that would be the end of it. Neither Dixon nor Pruneau had ever been to this type of hearing. Nor were they familiar with the disciplinary committee.

When they arrived at the Federation's offices in downtown Montréal, the three of them made their way to the conference room where the hearing would be held. Before entering, Dixon asked whether he and Pruneau could attend the hearing. They got a chilly reception. They could sit next to Patrick, but they could not intervene on his behalf. The only welcome they got was a perfunctory fingertip handshake.

There was a large table in the middle of the conference room. The members of the disciplinary committee sat enthroned on one side, a jury of five appropriately dour, gray-haired middle-aged men. Presiding over the committee was Henri Neckebroeck, a man seemingly predestined for the job. Hardly a barrel of laughs, he meant business and so did his colleagues. The tension was unbearable. Dixon and Pruneau realized they could do little to lighten the mood. Patrick would have to manage on his own.

The hearing was more like an interrogation. The members had obviously read the referee's report, which stated that Patrick had pushed him. There was no reason for them to believe that a federation referee was mistaken, or even worse, lying. The concept "innocent until proven guilty" would carry no weight. They pummeled Patrick with questions, with only one goal in mind: dragging a confession out of him to support the referee's contention.

First they asked Patrick what he had seen. Dixon and Pruneau were astonished to hear him describe in detail where everyone was on the ice at the time of the incident: the players, the referee and the linesmen. He even pinpointed the position of the puck.

I had always thought that he had some kind of radar that enabled him to track his opponents on the ice and anticipate their plays. But I didn't know that he also had a photographic memory. He concluded his testimony by asserting that he had never laid a finger on the referee. The questioning took various forms, but the intent was the same.

"Are you sure you didn't push the official?"

"Yes, I'm sure."

"Then why did the referee claim he was pushed?"

"I don't know . . . he tripped."

"Why did he trip then?"

"I don't know."

"Were you mad at the referee?"

"I was mad because the goal shouldn't have counted, but not at the ref."

"But you disagreed with his decision?"

"Yes."

"So you must have been a little annoyed with him, right?"

"A little, yes . . . but especially with his decision."

"But things happen in the heat of the moment. Could you have pushed him without realizing it?"

It was the same aggressive tone for over an hour. They kept firing questions at Patrick, hoping to trap him, to corner him, make him doubt his version of the facts until they extracted a confession. They grilled him. Even to the end, though he was worn out and mentally exhausted, he refused to confess.

"I know what you're trying to get me to say, but I can't say it because that's not what happened. I didn't push the referee down."

"But could you have touched him without realizing it?"

Patrick knew they were going around in circles, and it was an uneven playing field. He gave up and told them what they wanted to hear to put an end to the inquisition.

". . . I might have touched him . . . but I didn't make him fall . . ."

It was over. The committee let out a collective sigh of relief. The session ended with a curt dismissal. "Our decision will be communicated to you in due course."

Even as adults, Dixon and Pruneau had found the experience painful, troubling and intimidating. Think about how Patrick, a 16-year-old, must have felt. The three of them picked up their coats, went to the car and drove back to Québec. There was little conversation. Dixon was incensed.

"I don't ever want to go through that again. We don't need it. Hockey doesn't need it. How can adults be so cruel to a teenager for a whole hour? They treated him like a criminal! Patrick didn't hurt anybody. And we don't know if he even touched the ref. He definitely didn't knock him down. And even if he did touch him, it was an accident in the heat of the moment, during the provincial midget hockey final. That is unacceptable!"

The verdict was announced the next day. A five-game suspension for assaulting an official: a very harsh decision. Patrick was banned from the remaining provincial final games. And in the event that the Gouverneurs won the final in fewer than seven games, he would miss the first few games in the Air Canada Canadian Championship.

For the next game, 1,200 frenzied Gouverneurs fans flocked to the Sainte-Foy arena. Patrick's teammates ground out a 4–2 win with

Colosse in goal, limiting the Lions to 17 shots. It was his first start in midget AAA hockey and he played commendably. In Valleyfield the next day, the Lions squeaked out their first win in the series. The Gouverneurs had to wait another week, until March 26, to earn a pass to Victoria. Before a record-breaking crowd of 1,300 spectators in Sainte-Foy, the Gouverneurs won 5–4 on a dramatic goal in the first overtime period after a fiercely contested game. Colosse had done the job. The Gouverneurs had qualified to represent Québec at the Air Canada national midget championship in Victoria from April 12–18, 1982. This was Colosse's moment of glory. He died tragically in a motorcycle accident a few years later.

The Gouverneurs appealed the length of Patrick's suspension by the FQHG and they won. The ban was reduced to three games, which allowed him to play in their opening match of the national midget championship. Still, in Patrick's absence, the Gouverneurs had expended a lot of energy in their quest for the league championship and in the series against the Lions. Had the Gouverneurs peaked too soon?

—w—

Victoria is a jewel of a city set on the south shore of Vancouver Island. Double-decker buses, Victorian houses, afternoon teas at the Empress Hotel and the British Columbia Parliament buildings attest to its deep British roots. This was the least of the players' concerns, however, as they deplaned on Sunday, April 11. Their focus was on the 5,000-seat Victoria Memorial Arena, where their first test would take place the next day. They feared it would be rusty from so much time away from competition. After all, it had been more than two weeks since their last game, almost a month for Patrick. They couldn't wait to get back on the blades against a real opponent. True, the coaches had put them through their paces. But how would they handle the long layoff?

Proudly wearing the red, white and blue of the Montréal Canadiens to represent Québec, the Gouverneurs were competing in the DC-8 division with Saskatchewan, Manitoba, Ontario, Alberta and Nova Scotia. This was by far the strongest group. The DC-9 division consisted of Prince Edward Island, Newfoundland, New Brunswick, the Ottawa district, Thunder Bay and the Burnaby Winter Club, representing the home province.

It was a strange week. The Gouverneurs began like an engine restarting after a long period of inactivity. It starts, sputters, stalls, starts again, races; never runs smoothly and steadily. It took ages for them to get going.

Two lackluster victories against Nova Scotia and Alberta, while the Gouverneurs were recovering from jet lag, were followed by a routine win against Manitoba. In that game, one of the Manitoba coaches went over to Naud and inquired whether his goalie was hard of hearing. Naud made a point of sitting in the stands near Patrick's net. He had devised a system of signs to communicate with his goalie during key phases of the game. Naud's repertoire of gestures made him look like a baseball manager. To tell Patrick to stay on his feet more, Naud gave him a thumbs-up sign. When Patrick saw him point his index finger at his eye and then touch his left ear like the witches on the sit-com *Bewitched*, it meant look out for the left-winger. If Naud touched his right earlobe instead, the right-winger was the one to watch. When Naud pointed to his nose, Patrick would check out the center. To remind Patrick to calm down and take a few breaths, Naud would spread his hands out in front of him. They had successfully employed the unusual routine throughout the season.

On April 15, the Gouverneurs faced a daunting challenge, tournament favorites the Saskatchewan Notre Dame Hounds. Unlike the other teams, the Hounds recruited players from across Canada. Some observers even questioned their eligibility for the tournament.

That evening, the real Gouverneurs showed up—the team that had defeated the Lac-Saint-Louis Lions. They got their engine humming and they trounced the Hounds 4–1, outshooting them 48–13.

After four games, the Gouverneurs were the only unbeaten team. Suddenly, it looked like easy sailing. Some players opined that the competition was a piece of cake. The coach had his work cut out for him. He had to bring his 15- and 16-year-old charges back down to earth.

Still feeling pretty cocky on the Friday of the Ontario game, the boys went down to a meaningless 3–2 defeat. Ontario needed the win to qualify for the next round. The Gouverneurs were safely ensconced on top of their division. The motivation wasn't there. But in the quarterfinal the next day, the Gouverneurs avenged the loss with a 7–4 triumph against Ontario. A few hours later, they narrowly defeated Ottawa District 4–3 in overtime.

The table was set for the Sunday final, which would be televised in Québec on TVA. The contest pitted the Québec representatives against the home-team Burnaby Winter Club. It was difficult to evaluate Burnaby, as they had played in the weaker division all week long.

The Gouverneurs stormed out of the gate with 18 shots against Burnaby goalie Dave Roach in the first period. But he held the fort. It was the same story in the second period: the Gouverneurs unleashed 18 shots, but only Joël Guimont put the puck in the back of the net. Roach was nearly unbeatable, and Cliff Ronning was a one-lad wrecking crew on offence. He had assisted on Pretzer's goal in the first period, and it seemed as though he was going to take care of the rest on his own. In the second period he crafted a superb play. Stealing the puck from Sylvain Côté, he scored on a blistering drive into the top of the net. Early in the third, he netted another goal, putting paid to the Gouverneurs' chances.

Ronning was named the tournament MVP. He had beaten the Gouverneurs almost single-handedly, bagging two goals and assisting on the third in Burnaby's 3–1 win. Asked to comment on Ronning's performance, Fred Dixon admitted the youngster was in a league of his own. "At selection camp last year, Ronning was rated the Number 1 midget player in Canada, and he proved it in this tournament. He's probably the best I've seen all season." Four Gouverneurs players joined Ronning on the tournament's first All-Star team: defenseman Mario Carrier and Sylvain Côté and forwards Donald Deschênes and Martin Bouliane.

It was a bitter defeat for Patrick. For a born winner like him, it was galling to see victory slip through his fingers once more. He had led his team to the midget AAA development league title, but his three-match suspension had prevented him from suiting up for the final victory and the on-ice celebrations. The Gouverneurs had outshot Burnaby 45–31 in the last game; they should have won. Roach and Ronning had made the difference. Patrick hadn't been able to do the same.

Yet, he had every reason to be satisfied with his year. At the start of the season, it seemed there was little chance that he would get to play for the Gouverneurs, who were considered "a good small-time team" in the midget AAA development league. He had led his team to the Canadian midget hockey championship final. And he was tabbed the Number 1 goalie in the league. He couldn't bet his future on that, but he could start to think about it.

—⁂—

On the ferry back to Vancouver from Victoria, I wandered out on the deck for a little air. When I got there, I saw Cliff Ronning leaning on the railing by himself, his long blonde hair flowing in the wind, his eyes gazing at the ship's wake. He was on his way back home to

Burnaby. He seemed lost in thought, most likely reflecting on the honors he had earned in the tournament. But I guess he was also wondering what the future had in store for him. I had a strong feeling that he and Patrick would cross paths again.

—m—

The next month, on May 29 to be exact, the Québec Major Junior Hockey League (QMJHL) held its annual draft at the Maurice Richard Arena in Montréal. The 11 clubs spent four hours selecting 214 players. Among them were 106 youngsters from the midget AAA Hockey Development League. Patrick was rated the best available goalie, but he wasn't the first netminder chosen. For the eighth pick in the second round, the Hull (now Gatineau) Olympiques selected Alain Raymond of the Estrie Cantonniers, whose performance had been absolutely scintillating in the league All-Star game at the Montréal Forum. Patrick was selected two slots lower by the Granby Bisons. He would be joining former Gouverneurs teammates Martin Bouliane, Carl Vermette and Bernard Carrier. Patrick was moving along nicely in his quest. But what about Major Junior Hockey? What about the Granby Bisons?

PURGATORY 10

August 17, 1982, I still recall the time, when we drove Patrick to the Bisons' camp. Endless cornfields stretched along winding Route 137 from Saint-Hyacinthe to Granby. I thought Patrick would be better off playing hockey in Québec City. He was almost 17, a good age to solidify the bond between father and son. You can discuss things that really matter. It's your last chance to affect your son's education. But it's also an age when your son wants to affirm himself, get some distance from the family and live his own life. Patrick would have to deal with pressure from coaches, teachers, teammates, opponents, fans and the media. He would have to cope with the dictates of under-20s, with very little guidance.

A billet family provides room and board for a junior player. You can't expect the family, however well-intentioned, to act like surrogate parents, making sure that the young man does his homework, pays attention in class, eats properly and hangs out with the right crowd. That's not their job. For all sorts of reasons, most billet families are too preoccupied with the benefits that accrue to them for hosting the athletes to risk antagonizing their meal tickets. They do everything to make the player's stay comfortable.

I would have liked to be present for my son, but during the hockey season our relationship was carried on mainly by phone or mail.

In Canadian junior hockey, the best players aged 16 to 20 play in one of three leagues: the Western Hockey League (WHL), which, in addition to the Canadian clubs, has five U.S. teams; the Ontario Hockey League (OHL), which also includes three U.S. teams; and the QMJHL, to which teams from each of the Atlantic provinces and the state of Maine were eventually added.

Most of the teams are SMEs (small and medium-sized-enterprises). True, they are concerned about player development, but they also have to survive. Ticket sales account for most of their income, providing for operations, salaries (employees, players, coaches and support staff) and rentals (ice time and office space). Added to these are expenses related to promotion, transportation, administration and sundry other things. These organizations rely for their survival on game attendance, which in turn depends on the quality of the spectacle offered by the team.

To offer quality entertainment, the team relies on players, most of whom are minors. In another industry, the young men would be considered interns. The player's host family receives about $100 a week to pay for the player's subsistence. The player also earns a weekly stipend of between 40 and 60 dollars, depending on his age, for various expenses. Each team can have a maximum of three 20-year-olds, whose salary is negotiable, providing it exceeds $150 a week. A relative pittance, but players find junior hockey worthwhile because it gives them a chance to develop, train and make their mark so they can achieve their goal: the NHL.

In exchange for the access to players under advantageous conditions, the club should make a commitment to their development. This should be the team's fundamental mission. But a team must be viable. No team, no development! And to survive, the team must be profitable, and for that, it must fill the stands as often as possible by giving fans their money's worth with an exciting show by a club that has a fighting chance to win. Profitability, though theoretically secondary to player development, does not always go hand-in-hand with the team's mission. So more often than not, in the daily whirlwind, the tension between the development mission and the profit motive creates a gray zone that blurs the team's *raison d'être*. To further complicate things, the income is derived almost exclusively from the spectacle rather than from player development, with the exception of a few thousand dollars that a team may receive from the NHL when some of its players are drafted.

It is worth noting how junior players are recruited. The teams select them in the league's annual draft, which resembles the NHL process. Players can't choose the team they'll play for. A player from Rouyn-Noranda, for instance, may find himself in St. John's Newfoundland, and vice versa.

Given their age, players are well advised to pursue their studies while developing their hockey skills. The QMJHL has made considerable progress in this regard in the last 15 years. It helped set up sport-study programs, and supports tutors for the players.

But education is not a priority for every team, or for every player. Given the 72-game calendar, intense training and long-distance bus travel, it is not easy to balance sports and studies. In fact, with the obvious exception of salaries, working conditions typical of the NHL are emulated as much as possible. Players find themselves in much the same situation as the pros, in a miniature NHL with the same pressures, so scouts can see how well they cope with the regime. If a player has the talent, Canadian junior hockey is the fast track to the NHL.

Yet NHL teams decide on a junior player's fate very early on. Players can be drafted the year they turn 18 and reach the age of majority before September 15. Then the team must sign the players within two years. If not, the players become available again in the draft. Quick decisions about their future are taken based on an assessment of their potential before they reach age 20, which is before most of them finish developing physically and intellectually. It certainly happens before they finish university. A player who fails in his quest for a hockey career can make up for lost time, provided he has maintained contact with an academic institution. And if he has played a certain number of years in the QMJHL, the league will help finance his university education.

Bobby Smith owns the Halifax Mooseheads of the QMJHL. He starred with the Minnesota North Stars and the Montréal Canadiens in the NHL. He earned an MBA after he retired as an active player in 1993. According to Smith:

> A 16-year-old hockey player can look forward to two challenges in the years that follow. If he manages to make the National Hockey League, there's every chance he will succeed in life. And if he has a good education, his chances of success are excellent. But I think it's impossible to do both at the same time. . . . My 16-year-old son is a good student and he's going to play Junior and do everything he can in the best environment possible to earn a place in the NHL. If he doesn't succeed, he'll become a full-time student at 20 or 21 years of age. . . . There are 730 university hockey players in Canada, 500 of whom are receiving bursaries from their former junior team.

Given this reality, the junior team has an obligation to guarantee that its players maintain contact with their academic milieu.

In 1982, when Patrick began his junior hockey career, the Canadian system accounted for 63.5% of the first 200 players selected by the NHL, compared with 23% from the United States and 13.5% from Europe. By 2005, the year Sidney Crosby was drafted, these proportions had changed to 54.5%, 24% and 21.5% respectively. The Europeans had increased their share at the expense of the Western and Ontario leagues, while the QMJHL had gone from 8.5% to 11.5%.

—w—

The Granby Bisons were just beginning their second season in 1982. The previous year, a group of business people had made an excellent acquisition, the Sorel Éperviers, and had moved the team to Granby. The club wore the black, yellow and white colors of the Pittsburgh Penguins. But the team was a shadow of what it had once been. To cut acquisition costs, the group had been obliged to release some of the best players. After choosing the top two Épervier players, they had to let the next eight players go; they were then distributed among the other eight teams in the league.

So, somewhat hobbled after a botched draft, the Bisons began their first season in 1981. Gaston Drapeau from Québec City coached them. He'd spent the two previous seasons guiding the Remparts' destinies and had run into some problems. The Bisons general manager did his best to justify hiring Drapeau. "He's a leader of men who loves a challenge and has lots of potential. But more than anything else, it's his aggressive pursuit of victory that makes him ideal for us."

Team executives chose Drapeau over Claude St-Sauveur and Jacques Martin. Martin went on to have a stunning career in the NHL with the Ottawa Senators and then the Florida Panthers. He was also one of the few coaches to win the Memorial Cup, emblematic of Canadian junior hockey supremacy, in his first season with the Guelph Platers in 1986.

After a mediocre first season with only 14 wins in 64 games, the Bisons drafted four players from the Sainte-Foy Gouverneurs in their first five picks in May 1982 at the annual QMJHL draft held at the Maurice-Richard Arena in Montréal. By adding winners to their roster, the Bisons started the 1982–83 season on a note of optimism.

But the organization wasn't out of the woods yet. The team had its contingent of administrators and board members, but many of them had insufficient major junior hockey experience to manage the Bisons' affairs, oversee the budget and deal with the fear of defeat and empty stands. This obviously created tension and discord, which had an impact on the mood in training camp. To make matters worse, there was a good deal of coming and going among the team's veterans. Some attended Canada's National Junior Team training camp, others went to the camps of NHL teams with which they had signed a pro contract. And then there was the Sylvestre "case." The net result was that players had difficulty concentrating on their mental and physical preparation for the season.

Jacques Sylvestre was the best player at the Bisons camp. The previous season, he'd been their only ray of sunshine. He had scored 50 goals and earned 70 assists. He was also a model student, who at age 18, finished high school and grade 13, the equivalent of two years of college in the United States.

The league had awarded him the Marcel-Robert Trophy as the Scholastic Player of the Year for best combining on-ice excellence with academic success. Sylvestre was enrolled in Université de Montréal's law school. He was delaying signing with the Bisons until they agreed to pay indemnities for his numerous 90-mile roundtrips between Granby and Montréal. He didn't want it to cost him more to play in Granby than in the Montréal region. The Bisons should have been proud to have such a brilliant young man in their lineup. Instead, they haggled over the issue for weeks. They were afraid that granting him special status would set a dangerous precedent.

The ticket sales staff, goalie coach and chief scout were fired, and then the educational counselor handed in his resignation with the following explanation: "I cannot accept being told to see that the students enroll in only a few college-level courses so that the team doesn't end up with another case like Jacques Sylvestre." The message was loud and clear. It certainly got the attention of Jean Rougeau and Jean Trottier, president and educational counselor of the QMJHL respectively. They paid the Bisons a visit, urging them to acquire the services of a new educational counselor ASAP.

Amid all this hullabaloo, Patrick beat out Claude Kirouac, the previous year's backup goalie, and Ron Montaruli, the former netminder of the Lac-Saint-Louis Lions in the midget AAA league, and won the Number 1 spot for the start of the season. By September 2, he was confident. "I think I'm the one who's done the best so far. The three of us get along well together, but we realize there are only two spots, and one of us will have to go."

Kirouac, still recovering from an ankle injury, was the one to go.

The season opener on September 18, 1982, was especially significant for Patrick. It was his first official QMJHL game. The Bisons would be playing in Québec City against the Remparts under Fred Dixon and Jacques Naud, his former coaches with the Sainte-Foy Gouverneurs. Dixon and Naud had moved up to junior hockey. And the game would take place at the Colisée, home to his favorite NHL team the Nordiques, before his friends, "Ti-Pote" and the others, who would have to divide their loyalties between Claude Lefebvre with the home team and their good buddy Patrick with the visitors.

The game set the tone for Patrick's junior hockey career. Even in defeat, he made his mark, facing a 40-shot onslaught. Over the next three seasons, making 40 to 60 saves a game would become routine. So would the losses.

Some defeats were more remarkable than others. One of them makes you wonder about the tricks fate can play. I've already mentioned that Patrick was born on October 5, 1965. As it happened, on his seventeenth birthday, Patrick conceded five goals on 65 shots in a 5–3 loss against the Longueuil Chevaliers under Jacques Lemaire, who was beginning his coaching career. When the game ended, Patrick received a standing ovation from the 1,065 spectators (a figure that could also be interpreted as the tenth month of 1965), even though they supported the other team. Of course, they had no inkling of the numerical coincidences.

A few weeks into the season, coach Gaston Drapeau was dismissed and replaced by Roger Picard. The burly Montréal Urban Community policeman was a member of a famous hockey family in the Montréal area. He had the curious distinction of having been drafted by the St. Louis Blues at the ripe old age of 34. Had he been named rookie of the year, he would surely have made the NHL record book, but he played only about 20 games in the big league. One of his brothers, Noël, had also played for the Blues. Another brother, Gilles, had a son, Robert, who played for the Montréal Canadiens.

According to Roger Picard, the Bisons were in woeful physical shape. Their speed of execution was lamentable, their team play was poor and several veterans were dragging their feet. But he wasn't born yesterday, and things were going to change on his watch. The team had the potential, he insisted, to finish in the middle of the pack. After his charges lost 13 of 14 games, his arguments seemed less convincing. The Bisons' trajectory was as tortuous as Route 137, the path to victory as cluttered as Granby's cornfields.

—⁂—

My wife Barbara and I often attended Friday evening games at the Palais des sports in Granby. It was a painful experience to drive two and a half hours after a long workweek to see our son face a barrage of shots before highly partisan fans. There was one consolation, however. We got to spend a bit of time with Patrick. We tried to see him as often as possible. After a meal at a restaurant, we'd drive back to Québec late at night or stay overnight at a motel in Granby.

One day in November, we found Patrick nervous, tired and thin. He was having a hard time handling his workload: 40 hours of hockey including practices, travel and games, and 20 hours of classes. That was 60 hours without counting time for study. He would wake up in the middle of the night, wondering if he had done his English or math assignments for the next day. As he was born in October, he was almost a year behind his age group, which meant he hadn't done grade 11 (the final year of high school in Québec) before starting his junior year in hockey. Some of his teammates were in college but he was still in high school, which isn't as flexible as college. Worse still, the high school forced him to earn 12 credits, when he only needed eight to get into college the following year. This course load could have been reduced. He even had to do physical education, though he spent most of his time playing hockey. Aware that players in other cities benefited from a reduced course load, I requested a meeting with the person in charge of grade 11 at Polyvalente Joseph Hermas-Leclerc.

My appeal fell on deaf ears. I was greeted courteously but coldly by the administrator, who was waiting for me in his office, his hands spread on his desk.

"What can I do for you?"

"Well, you know, it's not for me, but for one of your students ... I think we can do something to help him."

"And who is he?"

I described the situation in detail, pointing out that Patrick needed only eight credits to be admitted into college and that I knew a few QMJHL players who had been granted a course reduction in other Québec cities.

"Look, Mr. Roy, over 500 students attend our school. If we start making exceptions . . ."

"Tell me, sir, of your 500 students, how many of them have already chosen a career?"

"Very few. You know, at their age, it's a little early."

"That's the point. You see, Patrick already knows what he wants to be. He wants to be a professional hockey player, a goalie. It might be an ambitious choice, some might find it pretentious, it might surprise us, we might even be somewhat skeptical, but it's his ambition in life. My son and I would like him to pursue his education while he is playing for the Granby Bisons. We would appreciate your help. I think it would be possible."

"Mr. Roy, it's a shame there isn't a hockey team in this high school, isn't it? Then Patrick could play here. That would be so much simpler!"

"Sir, I don't think we understand one another."

It was hopeless. I gave it my best shot for nearly an hour. A few years later, some Bisons players were given a less demanding course load. The trail had been blazed to implement the sport-study program, which had the whole-hearted backing of QMJHL authorities. But in the meantime, Patrick was left to cope as best he could. His education was on a slippery slope.

—⚉—

Patrick was ticked off with the way shots on goal were recorded for home games. The statistician would often lop off about 20 shots by the opposing team and add several for the Bisons to create the statistical impression that the home team was doing just fine. But the same didn't apply when the Bisons were on the road. When Pat Lafontaine scored in overtime to give the Verdun Juniors a victory before the elated home crowd, having dominated the game by 62 shots to 29, Montréal Canadiens GM Serge Savard, an attentive observer at the game, took due note.

Others were also paying attention. Though Patrick was a callow youth of 17 and in his first season in the league, he was invited to play in the All-Star game on January 16, 1983, at the Montréal Forum before 6,000 spectators. The fans also got to see the Midget AAA Development League All-Star game just before the QMJHL match.

It was a double bill for Barbara and me, too. Stéphane, now with the Sainte-Foy Gouverneurs, was in the midget AAA All-Star line-up. Only 15 years of age, he was already rated Québec's top midget player according to the QMJHL central scouting system. Vincent Damphousse was next in line and Stéphane Richer was fourth. Did I say "double bill?" I could have said "triple bill." Were we in for a shock! Patrick, who had always worn his hair as straight as a goal post, showed up with curly hair. I guess it was in style. Gary Carter of the Montréal Expos, ex-Habs great "Boom Boom" Geoffrion, and countless others favored the same hairstyle. In Patrick's case, it was a passing fancy.

Maybe it was the intimidating surroundings, or the ghosts of the Forum or his brother's new hairstyle, but Stéphane, like Patrick before him, had an off day. On the other hand, Patrick made up for the previous year's disappointment with a brilliant performance and was named goalie of the game. "I've been getting ready for this game for a long time, he told a *Journal de Montréal* reporter. "I was absolutely focused. I wanted to redeem myself because last year in the midget AAA All-Star game, I didn't step up. I'm also going through a tough season with the Granby Bisons. We're young, but look out for us next year."

The Remparts' fan club, the Rem-Pops, in collaboration with a restaurant, Le Manoir du Spaghetti, had organized a promotion for the return of the Bisons to the Québec Colisée at the end of January. It was a two-for-one deal offered to any ticket holder, providing the Remparts won. The Rem-Pops had gone all out: a crowd of 4,435 fans, all craving a second plate of spaghetti, a trumpet player louder than he was good, and "Charlie," the restaurant's mascot. And to top it all off, there was a weak opponent. In short, the stage was set for a huge promotional success. One small detail, however, had been overlooked: Patrick. Perhaps the promoters hadn't realized that promising this orgy of spaghetti would be just the thing to motivate Patrick to rain on their parade. And that's what he did. He stopped 43 of 47 shots. The Remparts suffered a 6–4 loss. Patrick certainly deserved a plate of pasta at Le Manoir du Spaghetti for all the free meals he'd just saved them.

Remparts coach Fred Dixon sang the blues. "We controlled the game from start to finish, but we couldn't do a thing with Roy, and I didn't expect him to be any easier in the third period. I was sure that he'd be even tougher in the last 20 minutes. It's quite simple; his miraculous saves in each period broke our backs. But he could have chosen another day to come up with the performance. I could've done without it!"

Jacques Naud, who had helped polish Patrick's technique with the Gouverneurs, had this to say, "Patrick Roy is a goalie who's at his best when the pressure's on. The more fans in the stands, the more he likes to work and the better he gets. I expected this kind of performance from Roy."

Patrick made a few comments to the media. Shortly after that, I wrote him a letter.

February 1, 1983

Bonjour Patrick,

Here is the article from Le Soleil. *You can put it with the one from the* Journal de Québec *that I sent you yesterday.*

I must admit I much prefer the comments you made in the Journal.

It is important to be modest in victory, and especially not to humiliate an opponent more than he has already been by the defeat. I'm pleased you're happy that the Bisons won and that you are expressing it, somewhat exuberantly, but in that case, celebrate your victory, rather than your opponents' defeat . . . do you see the distinction? It's important.

In the end, you weren't hoping to "hurt the Remparts on their spaghetti day," but to see the Bisons enjoy themselves before a large crowd. You didn't want the Remparts to lose as much as you wanted the Bisons to win. That should be the spirit of your post-game comments in victory and in defeat. The sports world, and particularly that of the goalie, is so full of ups and downs that it is important to be careful about your relations with everyone, including your opponents. In this regard, your remarks to the Journal *were perfect. It is important to reserve your aggressiveness for the game. Once it's over, human feelings should take over, especially respect.*

In regard to your studies, I talked to Gabriel Gagnon this morning about the possibility of returning to the Académie Saint-Louis in April. He didn't foresee any problems. I will meet him tomorrow to finalize the details. I'll let you know about the decision as soon as I find out.

Meanwhile, don't neglect your schoolwork. Do your best. I know it's hard for you to realize now how important it is to get through school no matter what happens in your hockey career. Believe me, you won't regret it.

By the time you get this letter, I hope you'll have defeated the Chevaliers Longueuil and that you'll be on your way to doing the same against the Voltigeurs Drummondville. That will give you some practice with press relations.

Bye and good luck.

See you soon,

Dad

The Bisons didn't beat the Chevaliers. In fact, despite Roger Picard's good intentions and a few more exceptional performances by Patrick, the Bisons continued to struggle, picking up only 20 wins in 70 games. They finished tenth in a group of 11 and didn't make it to the playoffs. Patrick pursued his studies, but he only attended the classes he needed to get into college.

Back in Québec City after the season, he attended Académie Saint-Louis until he realized that he had fallen too far behind. So he decided to wait until the next year to finish grade 11. His excellent results in core subjects didn't prevent Polyvalente Joseph Hermas-Leclerc authorities from digging in their heels and again refusing to lighten his course load. They wouldn't consider his particular situation. Patrick had one objective. He had set his priorities and made his choices, but he also wanted to go to college. The school didn't see things that way. He had to quit the regular program and register in adult education. But this was tantamount to dropping out of school because he didn't have a tutor to monitor his progress.

—⚒—

On August 8, 1983, after a short stay with the family at Wells Beach in Maine, we drove Patrick to Granby for his second training camp with the Bisons. Once more, the Bisons coaching staff waxed enthusiastic about the coming season. With the addition of their first draft choice, Stéphane Richer, Roger Picard predicted a fourth-place finish for the squad. The team's flying start with four straight victories seemed to fulfil Picard's predictions. But the squad soon reverted to old habits. By mid-October, the team had seven wins and seven losses. Their record was eight wins and 14 losses at the beginning of November and 11 wins and 17 losses in mid-November.

The Bisons weren't a bad team—on paper. They lacked depth but they had good players in every position. Apart from the management's inexperience, there were two reasons for their poor results. First, Picard wasn't a full-time coach. He still lived in Montréal, where he worked as a police officer. He shuttled daily between Montréal and Granby for practices and home games. On the road, he didn't travel on the bus with players, but headed directly from his home to the game, so he was unaware of his team's off-ice activities. He didn't live with them. In junior hockey, given the players' ages, it is essential for the coach to be present as much as possible. Picard wasn't there, so he didn't have control of his team. Next, as a direct consequence of Picard's absence, it was the law of the 20-year-olds that ruled and empowered a bully among the older players, the kind of foul-mouthed ignoramus who destroys team morale and poisons the atmosphere for the younger players. He terrorized them.

In junior hockey, as in the pros, there is a ritual: the rookie initiation. The ritual can lead to obscene and perverse acts. Just how far it goes depends on the people organizing the activity. For example, some make kids race each other to the wall, pushing raisins across the floor with their penis, shave their pubic hair, or stand naked in a hotel elevator and punch all the buttons so the elevator stops at every floor. Hardly an edifying experience! Usually a rookie had to endure this type of treatment once, at the beginning of the season. After that, he had earned his place in the group and that was the end of it. But that year was the worst of all in Granby. The harassment wouldn't stop. The bully, with amused veterans looking on and too immature to intervene, forced the kids into acts of masturbation and fellatio. The bully made the kids think the initiation was still going on and they had to submit to his perverse schemes. Needless to say, this created tension in the team. The youngsters would rush to take their showers before the bully took his, so they wouldn't have to scrub his back . . . and his buttocks. And they hurried out of the shower stalls when he showed up. It was a climate of terror. The rookies didn't dare revolt, intimidated by some of the veterans, who if they didn't enjoy the sexual harassment, tolerated it. The kids didn't even complain. It's a well-known fact that hockey players as a breed never complain! Patrick, who wasn't a rookie but didn't belong to the clique of influential veterans, went about his business as best he could.

Given the circumstances, it was impossible to build a real team. They were 20 individuals trying to play hockey under conditions that made showing up at the arena increasingly unbearable. It got so bad that Patrick expressed the desire to be traded to the Chicoutimi Saguenéens, his brother Stéphane's team in the QMJHL.

Picard took the fall. The absent are always guilty, that is also a well-known fact! When he was fired, Picard revealed who was responsible for the misdeeds. "All the players are afraid of him, especially the youngsters, and he's hurting team morale," he said. "I should have gotten rid of him a long time ago. But I didn't have any choice; I needed a physical defenseman."

Claude St-Sauveur succeeded Picard. St-Sauveur had seen duty with a few teams in the WHA. He had also had a tour in the NHL, with the Atlanta Flames in 1975–1976, scoring 24 goals and earning 24 assists for the season. The Bisons now had their third coach and their fifth president, hardly a model of stability. But St-Sauveur had a considerable advantage over Picard: he lived in Granby and would be a full-time coach.

—⚞—

Meanwhile, after playing a season with the Sainte-Foy Gouverneurs—they had lost in the Air Canada Cup final for a second consecutive time—Stéphane was the Chicoutimi Saguenéens' first choice, the seventh pick overall in the first round of the draft. He was in good company. Some of the players selected in the first round had brilliant NHL careers: Stéphane Richer was chosen second by the Bisons, Luc Robitaille fourth by the Hull Olympiques and Vincent Damphousse eleventh by the Laval Voisins.

Patrick's brother was also wooed by Colgate University, near Syracuse, New York. It was a tough decision. Colgate offered the possibility of studying in an ideal setting while developing as a hockey player. But there was one disadvantage. As he was still of midget age and hadn't graduated from high school, he would have to play an extra year in Sainte-Foy before moving to Colgate. Since he was considered to be one of the best players in Québec in his age group, pro scouts had their eyes on him and experts thought he was ready for major junior hockey. We were concerned that another year in midget would hamper his hockey development.

Michel Parizeau, an ex-Nordique, was the coach in Chicoutimi. Some years before, he had accomplished the rare feat of completing his studies and playing junior hockey at the same time in Drummondville. He seemed like a good guy and we trusted him. What's more, as Chicoutimi traveled more than any other team, the Saguenéens management had arranged with a high school for its players to enroll in an adult education program in which they benefited from an individualized approach and the support of a tutor. This gave players more flexibility and allowed them to pursue their education despite a heavy hockey schedule. Stéphane chose Chicoutimi. We supported his decision.

Hockey was becoming a serious option for the two brothers. Patrick would be eligible for the next NHL draft, and Stéphane's future seemed promising. The time had come to find them an agent, a competent adviser who would represent them, guide them and look out for their best interests until the end of their junior career. When the time came, he would counsel them in contract negotiations, public relations and sponsorship deals. He would also help manage their finances and provide legal advice.

After looking into the available resources, I met with two firms and asked them to make us an offer. I recommended the Jandec group, headed by Pierre Lacroix, to Patrick and Stéphane. Lacroix had selected his company name to reflect the fact that the group was available 365 days a year, from *Jan*uary to *Dec*ember.

Three facts about Jandec caught my attention. First, Pierre Lacroix's personal qualities. He was dynamic and competent. He never touched alcohol or tobacco and he led an exemplary family life with his wife Colombe and their sons Martin and Éric. In addition, Jandec's business strategy impressed me. Lacroix made a point of providing individualized service for all of his clients. To do this, he limited the number of clients he took on. I insisted that the agreement would be valid only as long as Pierre Lacroix continued to take a personal interest in the affairs of Patrick and Stéphane. My sons could terminate the agreement if this changed. Finally, Lacroix was considered one of the best agents in professional hockey. Robert Sauvé, Mike Bossy, Normand Rochefort and Richard Sévigny were among his clients. He was also responsible for negotiating the Stastny brothers' contract with the Nordiques.

Patrick signed with Jandec on February 19, 1984, never suspecting that this agreement would last until the end of his career.

Claude St-Sauveur's arrival did little to change the hapless Bisons' fate. History was repeating itself. Defeat followed defeat, despite some outstanding performances by Patrick. One example was the 5–4 loss to Laval before a number of NHL scouts. The Voisins, led by Mario Lemieux, overwhelmed the Bisons, firing 62 shots on goal compared with the Bisons' 18. Before the game, Patrick had a little talk with "Charlotte," his catching mitt. He had nicknamed his catching mitt "Charlotte" and it could, at times, perform miracles. In another game, in Verdun, Serge Savard and his brain trust looked on as the Bisons edged in the Junior de Montréal by a score of 4–2, despite being outclassed and outshot 42 shots to 32. Patrick's opposite number that evening was 17-year-old Troy Crosby, who later had a son named Sidney.

Despite Patrick's exploits, the experts, scouts, reporters and even the fans were getting fed up with the Bisons' chronic mediocrity. The bad atmosphere at the club was starting to influence the assessment of Patrick's work. They'd given him the benefit of the doubt, but they'd finally run out of patience. So Patrick wasn't invited to the league's All-Star game. And as the draft approached, his name tumbled down the list of NHL prospects in Québec. The timing was bad.

Prognosticators had penciled in the Bisons for fifth or sixth place. The club finished eighth, a point ahead of Chicoutimi, just enough to qualify for the playoffs. Their relatively low finish meant they would be facing regular season titlists Laval Voisins and their star Mario Lemieux in the first round. The Voisins demolished the Bisons in four straight games.

Despite a disappointing season, Patrick managed to register the third-best goals-against average in the league among starting goaltenders, just behind Laval's Tony Haladuick of the Laval Voisins and the Shawinigan Cataractes' Dave Quigley. Given the Bisons' porous defense, Patrick had accomplished quite a feat. But his 4.44 goals-against average was not likely to impress the scouts. All we could do was cross our fingers and wait for the June 9 NHL draft.

THE LIGHT AT THE END
OF THE CORNFIELD

11

In April 1984, soon after the passing of Barbara's mother Anna, whom the kids loved dearly, we left on a two-week family trip. We could take Patrick and Stéphane along, since their teams had been eliminated. Given their age, Barbara and I felt that it might be our last chance to go away with all three of our children. Bona and Lisette had rented an apartment in Clearwater Beach on Florida's west coast. Barbara, Alexandra and I were going to share a room there. The boys would stay in the nearby Golden Beach Motel on Gulfview Boulevard.

Our Plymouth Reliant K plodded along the 1,750-mile trek from Cap-Rouge to the Gulf of Mexico. Of the two days it took to reach our destination, we were on the road for over 30 hours. Both there and back, Alexandra found herself squeezed between her two brothers, who spent their time teasing her and commandeering legroom. Patrick loved playing tricks on her like pretending that she was adopted or studiously reading her palm and declaring that she was fated to die when she turned 26. To this day, Alexandra recalls breathing a sigh of relief on her twenty-seventh birthday. In competition, Patrick was concentration and determination incarnate, but in his downtime he was a bit of a merry prankster.

Our vacation was just what we needed. We filled our days with fun family activities like swimming in the ocean, jogging on the beach, playing shuffleboard or tennis and watching glorious sunsets over the Gulf of Mexico. After supper, we played cards with Lisette. I can still hear her telling Stéphane, who was taking forever to make up his mind, "Tonight, Stéphane! How about laying down some cards tonight?" Patrick wasn't fluent in English at the time, but he could get what he wanted. At McDonald's, he cheerfully gave his order while the waitress struggled to contain her laughter.

"One big frritts, please!"

"You mean one large fries, dear?"

"That's it! With a soda, please."

Gilles Léger, the Nordiques' Player Development Director, was vacationing with his family a few miles south of us, in Indian Shores. We took in a Tampa Bay Bandits football game with them. We also visited the Epcot Center and Walt Disney World's Magic Kingdom in Orlando, where the family had a good laugh at my expense when a theater troupe randomly plucked me from the crowd to take part in a scene out of Romeo and Juliette, improvised outdoors.

After a Sunday brunch at The Bank Restaurant, we spotted an entertainment machine that purported to tell a person's lucky number for any given day. We dropped a coin in the slot to find out Patrick's lucky number for June 9, 1984. The answer: 51.

—m—

The NHL draft is quite a spectacle and much of it is televised. In 1984, it was held at the now defunct Montréal Forum, perhaps the most prestigious hockey shrine. A large stage had been set up where the ice normally was. Representatives from the 21 NHL teams occupied tables next to the stage. There was enough star power to turn a simple business session into a big show. There were coaches or former players who had become household names, such as Scotty Bowman, Serge Savard, Jacques Lemaire, the late John Ferguson and Rogatien

Vachon, to name a few. They huddled with scouts and administrators in an atmosphere of palpable tension and excitement. One moment, they pored over bulging files and engaged in spirited discussion with their entourage. The next, they wended their way through the tables to initiate negotiations with their counterparts from other teams. In one of these talks, Serge Savard brokered a deal that sent a regular goalkeeper, Rick Wamsley, to the Saint Louis Blues in exchange for a first-round draft choice just as the session was about to start.

The entire proceedings took place before cameras, journalists and hundreds of spectators who had come to watch the draft live. Many more fans had their eyes glued to their TV screens, eager to learn which exciting prospect "their" team would select. It is fascinating to see that so many fans consider the team they support to be "theirs" despite having no control over it beyond choosing whether or not to attend or watch the games. That draft session was a case in point: all the fans could do was look on in helpless anticipation.

There were spectators in the stands, but the vast majority of the people in attendance were players, their families and their agents, all doing their best to hide their anxiety as they waited for the general manager of some NHL team to call out the name they were waiting to hear.

That year, the first pick went to Pittsburgh; they chose Mario Lemieux, destined to become the most celebrated player in Penguins history. There was an awkward moment or two, however, when Mario temporarily refused to don the Penguins jersey in protest against the slowness of negotiations with the team. New Jersey drafted second and selected Kirk Muller. As their two first-round draft choices, the Canadiens chose Petr Svoboda fifth and Shayne Corson eighth. Patrick's Sainte-Foy Gouverneurs teammate from Québec City, Sylvain Côté, went eleventh to the Hartford Whalers (now the Carolina Hurricanes). Côté was also Pierre Lacroix's client.

Stéphane Richer, Patrick's Bisons teammate was selected 29th by the Canadiens. Two goalkeepers, Craig Billington and Daryl Reaugh, had already been selected. Craig Billington was picked 23rd by the New Jersey Devils. Daryl Reaugh was chosen 42nd by the Edmonton Oilers.

Patrick wasn't the least bit nervous. NHL Central Scouting ranked him the fourteenth-best goalkeeper in the draft, fourth in Québec. He wasn't expecting to go before the fourth or fifth round. Curiously enough for someone who had worked tirelessly for so long, Patrick didn't seem to realize how close he was to attaining his objective. It was as though reality was exceeding his dreams. He couldn't believe that he could soon be playing with the giants of the sport on *La Soirée du hockey* (the French-language version of *Hockey Night in Canada*). Television does tend to make people appear larger than life. Patrick still saw professional hockey as an illusory and unattainable world. He just hoped he'd be selected before the draft was over. Any team would do.

Then came the 51st pick, which the Canadiens had secured by trading Robert Picard to Winnipeg. Ironically, Robert was the nephew of Roger Picard, Patrick's former coach in Granby. We couldn't help remembering when that strange machine at the restaurant in Florida had given 51 as Patrick's lucky number on draft day and our hearts started pounding. "No! This can't be true. Pinch me. I must be dreaming!" Serge Savard picked up the microphone at the Canadiens' table. "The Montréal Canadiens are proud to select, from the Granby Bisons, **Patrick Roy!**"

Unbelievable! Destiny had come calling! I shook Patrick's hand and Barbara gave him a big hug. And then he headed off to the Habs' table. As the cameras clicked away, he pulled on his new team's jersey. He immediately began assessing his rivals for a spot on the team. First-string goalie Steve Penney was guaranteed his job, but it seemed to be open season for the backup position. Patrick's strongest competition would come from Richard Sévigny, Mark Holden and Greg Moffett. Patrick openly admitted, "I really admire Steve Penney, a Québec boy like me, who's earned the Number 1 slot. It will be strange to compete against him because he once taught me at a Sainte-Foy hockey school. I'm honored and overjoyed, and I'll give everything I've got at the Canadiens training camp. . . . It won't be the end of the world if I have to go back to the Bisons to further my development because it's a wonderful hockey town."

Long after Patrick had finished answering the journalists, posing for the photographers, and accepting the flood of congratulations, while we sat eating at a terrace in Old Montréal in 88-degree Fahrenheit weather before driving back to Québec City, some players were still cooling their heels in the almost empty stands, desperately hoping that their dreams wouldn't evaporate that day. Luc Robitaille, the most prolific left-winger in NHL history, had to wait until the Los Angeles Kings picked him 171st in the draft. Even for those who consider themselves world-class experts, it is not always easy to assess the talent of players that age.

—m—

Richard Sévigny became a free agent when the Canadiens didn't offer him a contract by the July 1 deadline. The next month he joined the Nordiques. Patrick was now one step closer to Montréal. Only Holden and Moffett stood in his way.

The Canadiens presented Patrick with a contract soon after Sévigny's departure. It was a three-plus-one deal, which meant that they were committed to him for three years with an option on a fourth. His salary would be $75,000 for the first year and then $85,000, $95,000 and $100,000 for the following years. The agreement included a base annual salary of $30,000 if he was sent down to the

(Barbara Miller-Roy collection.)

At age two, beneath pale blond hair and behind beautiful blue eyes, sleeps a volcano ready to erupt at any moment.

(Author's collection.)

Patrick at three and Stéphane at a year-and-a-half.

(Barbara Miller-Roy collection.)

Patrick, age six,
already in a goalie
stance.
(Barbara Miller-Roy
collection.)

Early Christmas
morning in 1973,
Patrick discovers
brand new goalie
equipment under
the tree.
(Author's collection.)

Nine-year-old
Patrick leaves for
the arena in the
morning.
(Author's collection.)

"Le 1330," where Patrick lived between the ages of 7 and 14. When the mid-summer morning sun breaks through the leaves and licks the red-brick facades of the houses, no one would wish to be anywhere else.

(Photo by Pierre Mourey - author's collection.)

One Saturday morning in 1974, Patrick is just back from hockey practice with Stéphane and his parents.

(Author's collection.)

Patrick is easily distracted in grade 3. It's obvious what's on his mind.

(Author's collection.)

Barbara, Québec City's swimming team coach, introduces Patrick and Stéphane to competition. At about seven, Patrick is one of the top breaststrokers in the province in his age group. Stéphane is just as outstanding at the backstroke.

(Barbara Miller-Roy collection.)

Patrick, age 12, in the Québec-Centre-Haute-Ville uniform at the Québec International Pee-Wee Hockey Tournament during the Québec Winter Carnival.

(Author's collection.)

Park Victoria Arena in Québec City, the dilapidated building (now disappeared) where Patrick made his competitive hockey début.

(©Bibliothèque Gabrielle-Roy, 1981. Québec City archives ; série loisirs QC4, cote F8 520.5.1.)

In the summer of 1975, Patrick attends Sainte-Foy Summer Hockey School under the direction of former Québec Rempart Michel Lachance. Stéphane, just behind Patrick, and to the left, is the captain of the team.

(Author's collection.)

The Québec-Centre team at the Montréal-North Atom Hockey Tournament in 1976. Patrick is right beside the coach, Alain Samson. Stéphane is the fourth from the right in the second row.

(Barbara Miller-Roy collection.)

The Peewee All-Star Team of the Intercity Hockey League in 1978. Sylvain Côté is the seventh from the left in the second row.

(Author's collection.)

In 1981-82, Patrick leads the Sainte-Foy Gouverneurs to the Québec Midget AAA League championship and the final of the Air Canada Cup, the Canadian midget hockey championship, in Victoria, British Columbia.

(Author's collection.)

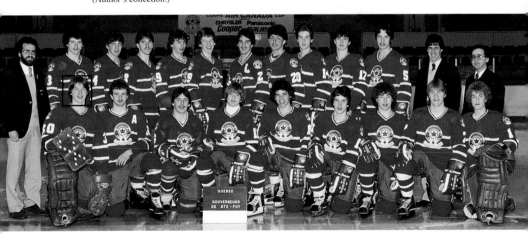

The Sainte-Foy Gouverneurs, representing Québec at the1982 Air Canada Cup. Sylvain Côté, who will have a brilliant NHL career as a defenseman, is the second from the left in the second row.

(Author's collection.)

Before turning professional, Patrick plays junior hockey
with the Granby Bisons from 1982 to 1985, routinely
facing 40 to 60 shots a game.

American Hockey League. If Montréal shipped him back to the juniors, he would earn $5,000. The package also included a signing bonus of $35,000 and several bonuses tied to his performance and to the performance of the team.

Negotiations went swiftly and smoothly. The proposed amounts were within the guidelines, given the round in which he was drafted. In those days, the highest-paid NHL goalkeeper earned $325,000 and only four players in the entire league made more than $400,000. Patrick was only 18; he had never seen so much money. In comparison, I had just been named Vice-President at the Québec Automobile Insurance Board. In this capacity, I oversaw more than 1,300 employees. I also had 20 years of experience. My annual salary was under $68,000.

Patrick signed his first professional contract on July 26, 1984.

—◊—

A few days later, Patrick dropped by a Honda dealership on Charest Boulevard in Québec City with Claude Lefebvre. A charcoal Honda Prelude caught Patrick's eye. A middle-aged sales rep noticed the two teenagers but wasn't too impressed. He chose to detour toward the coffee machine rather than serve them. Then a younger representative, no doubt hungrier than his colleague, came over:

"Can I help you?"

"Yes, I want to buy a car."

"Have you seen our used car lot?"

"No, I have already decided on the car. This is the one I want."

"Oh! But this car goes for nearly $15,000. Are you sure that …"

"Yes this is the one."

"But, who'll be paying?"

"Me!"

"Please step into my office."

Patrick and Claude followed the salesman and sat down in his office.

"Let me show you our financing plan ..."

"That won't be necessary. I can write a check for the amount right now."

"Oh! . . . Very well . . . Of course, I'll have to get confirmation from your bank."

"Of course!"

This certainly wasn't the hardest sale the rep had made in his career. His colleague was still sipping on his coffee when the deal was concluded. Once the call to the bank was taken care of, Patrick was informed that the car would be ready the next day.

He walked into the dealership at the appointed hour to take possession of his car. He could hardly wait to show off his spanking new car to the Doyons and the "Saint-Sacrement gang." But there was one thing he'd overlooked: the tank was almost empty. Just before he got to the Doyons, the car stalled as he was driving up Saint-Sacrement Hill. He managed to turn right onto chemin Sainte-Foy and let the car roll down the street on its own; he just barely made it to a gas station, conveniently located, to save his pride.

In mid-August, Patrick drove to his last Bisons training camp in his new Prelude.

—⁊⁊—

In Granby during the previous season, Patrick had often hung out with his Sainte-Foy teammate Carl Vermette. After Carl was traded to the Saint-Jean Castors just before the holidays, Patrick had started spending a lot of time with Stéphane Richer and had tried to encourage him. They would follow parallel paths for some time.

On September 10, 1984, the two young men left Granby to travel to the Lemoyne Manor on boulevard de Maisonneuve, a few steps from the Montréal Forum. The Canadiens had reserved a room for them for the rookie training camp starting the next day. The camp was designed to prepare them for the "real" training camp that would get under way a week later. They were allowed to play for the Bisons on September 14 in the season opener against Chicoutimi at the Palais des sports in Granby.

Attending that game, I realized the fans' fervent support was a matter of jersey color and that there was a special dynamic associated with being a goalie. Patrick was guarding the net for the Bisons, and my other son, Stéphane, was a forward for Chicoutimi. I wanted Patrick to stop every shot and Stéphane to score on every shot. What a dilemma! What should I do? Should I cheer if Patrick made a save on Stéphane? Stéphane wouldn't forgive me. And what should I do if Stéphane scored? The situation couldn't be more awkward. I couldn't favor one team over the other. If both of my sons had been forwards, I would have cheerfully encouraged them to bag as many goals as they could. As a goalkeeper's father, you feel the game can't end too soon. Ideally the game would last five minutes. A shutout and we'd all go home. If your son plays in any position but netminder, the games are always too short. You want him to score as many goals as possible. I decided to remain neutral and keep my emotions to myself. It was impossible for me to react like a normal fan.

In the worst-case scenario, Patrick would have allowed several goals while Stéphane failed to score. Fortunately, that did not happen. The Bisons won 2–1 on Stéphane Richer's overtime goal. With 32 saves on 33 shots, Patrick earned first-star honors. At age 17, my Stéphane still had time on his side.

—⁓—

The Canadiens regular-team training camp began on September 18. Patrick was awestruck when he thought of the great players who had been in the Habs dressing room over the years. An excerpt from John McCrae's poem *In Flanders Fields*, written above the portraits of his illustrious predecessors, captured his attention: "To you from failing hands we throw/the torch; be yours to hold it high." Soon he would be sharing the ice with such legends as Guy Lafleur, Steve Shutt, Larry Robinson and Bob Gainey, all of whom he only knew from watching television. He was living his dream. He took it all in. Despite Serge Savard's positive comments about him in the media, Patrick was under no illusions about his chances of making the team on his first try. He would savor every moment.

In fact, the Canadiens were not planning to keep Patrick in Montréal that season. The team lacked depth in goal. First-string netminder Steve Penney had been a sensation in the playoffs the previous spring—but it was to everyone's surprise. Management had called him up from the Canadiens' AHL farm team, the Nova Scotia Voyageurs, because they did not want to interfere with the development of Holden and Moffett, who were more highly thought of in the organization. Come the playoffs, a decision had to be made about goaltending before the Habs faced the Bruins. Jacques Lemaire, who had taken over as head coach from Bob Berry in February, queried Savard:

"What do you think of Sévigny?"

"We can't beat the Bruins with Sévigny."

"Wamsley?"

"Wamsley? Not certain."

"Well, since we're not sold on either of them, we might as well give Penney a try. What do you think?"

"Why not? . . . We have nothing to lose. Let's try Penney."

So they decided to bet the farm on a rookie. And Penney rose to the challenge, helping his team sweep the Bruins and defeat the Nordiques before falling to the powerful New York Islanders. But consistency and perseverance are the metrics by which a goalie's value is measured, and Penney had played only 19 games in the NHL. Savard and Lemaire agreed that though Penney had earned his job as the Number 1 goalkeeper, they felt he wasn't well established enough for them to risk choosing an inexperienced junior goalie, no matter how talented, to be his alternate for an entire season.

Even though the odds were stacked against Patrick making the team, the coaches wanted to get a good look at him in a few pre-season games. That way they could see how he reacted under pressure and assess his development. Things went quite well for Patrick right from the start of the rookie training camp: he recorded three straight shutouts in intrasquad games. In one of these games, he thwarted Richer, his roommate, on a breakaway, prompting the forward to declare, "Patrick and 'Charlotte' robbed me. He's fantastic." Then Patrick continued to impress at the regular training camp. He wasn't just turning aside Richer's blasts. In a shootout drill, he raised eyebrows by stopping Lafleur and Carbonneau. Then, an intrasquad game saw Patrick rob Steve Shutt on a breakaway. Some veterans including Larry Robinson were beginning to sing his praises. Gradually, Patrick's confidence grew. He started to believe he could make it. "The game is faster and the shots are harder and more accurate than in junior hockey. I've got to be alert and aggressive. But it's going better than I expected. I thought it would be harder to adapt because I was a bit in awe of all those veterans."

Patrick's comments provoked media speculation about his chances of making the team on his first attempt. Savard did nothing to discourage the talk—quite the contrary. He had little to gain by dampening Patrick's motivation. In fact, he said, "No one disputes that Penney is our Number 1 goalie. The second position is up for grabs, and Roy is in the running, especially since we are considering keeping three goalies with the club. . . . We're definitely going to give him a try to see how he handles playing against pro teams." Lemaire was on board, too: "Wamsley and Sévigny are gone because they weren't getting the job done. We got into a habit of conceding two soft goals a game. . . . I'd rather develop an 18-year-old goalie like Patrick Roy. If he makes two costly mistakes in a game, we'll be where we were last season. No better, no worse."

There was one hitch, however. There was no goalie instructor at the Canadiens camp. It wasn't very common to have one in those days. Savard and Lemaire were old school when it came to netminders. "A goalie should stay up and cover his angles," they thought. "If he goes down, it's because he's in trouble." Like Fred Dixon four years earlier, Lemaire didn't cotton to Patrick's "butterfly" style. That was one strike against Patrick, and Lemaire shared his concern with the media.

Patrick made his views known through the media, too. He wasn't out to challenge authority, but he felt that he was on the right path. He was employing a technique that felt natural, and the results were quite good. Determined, he started showing the characteristic confidence he would display throughout his career: "Maybe I go down a little early, but I come up with the saves."

Lemaire had to agree. He admitted that "Charlotte" was very quick and skillful at catching the puck. So Patrick and his friend Richer were included on the camp's first trip, an excursion out West to Edmonton and Winnipeg. But before leaving, Patrick was given a video so he could study Philadelphia Flyers goalkeeper Pelle Lindbergh and his standup style.

Patrick had only flown once in his life, when he played in the Air Canada Cup with the Sainte-Foy Gouverneurs in Victoria. Then, the organizers had taken care of everything. This was Richer's first flight. Canadiens staff were responsible for the hockey gear, but every player obviously had to look after his small carry-on containing his personal effects. When Patrick and Richer went through the airport security gate, they left their bags behind and headed straight to the embarkation gate, assuming their valises would follow them onto the plane. Fortunately, Claude Quenneville, the Radio-Canada commentator caught them in time:

"Hey guys! You better go back and get your luggage if you want your change of clothes!"

"Oops!!!"

They did their best to hide their embarrassment and doubled back to retrieve their personal effects. That's called getting experience.

—⁓—

Patrick was given the nod for the first pre-season game against the Edmonton Oilers. Facing the Stanley Cup champions before 13,000 spectators was a daunting task even though none of the stars on either team suited up. Patrick didn't play as well as he would have liked. The Habs lost 6–5. He didn't make the big saves that would have swung defeat into a victory. He had hoped to surprise everyone and make a big impact in the game. He conceded six goals on 26 shots; his performance was about as good as the team could expect from an 18-year-old rookie. Once again, "Charlotte's" agility was most impressive; to a certain extent, it saved Patrick's first appearance.

Lemaire's post-game comments were reassuring: "He was nervous and I won't make a final decision after just one game. The only way we'll know whether he is ready for the National Hockey League is by playing him." The next day, Greg Moffett turned in a worse performance, and the Habs suffered a 7–2 loss to the Winnipeg Jets. So, ironically, Mark Holden, left behind in Montréal, made the most progress in the competition for Sévigny's old spot.

Jets scout Charlie Hodge, the former Canadiens goalie who brilliantly bridged the transition between Jacques Plante and Rogatien Vachon, predicted great things for Patrick: "We had also put Patrick

Roy's name on our list because, in my eyes, he was the best junior in Canada during the 1983–84 season. This young man will have an excellent career. He is quick as a cat and never goes down needlessly. I think he is the greatest junior I have watched since Grant Fuhr." Now we know that Hodge had it right, but his enthusiasm seemed a little excessive at the time, given Patrick's unimpressive outing on the previous day.

Lemaire was as good as his word when the Oilers arrived at the Montréal Forum on the following Saturday. This was a chance for the Canadiens to exact revenge for their loss to Edmonton. An unlikely development, most observers agreed, since the Oilers had brought their big guns. Wayne Gretzky, Mark Messier, Jari Kurri, Glenn Anderson, Paul Coffey, Kevin Lowe were all in the lineup and Grant Fuhr was minding the net. The Canadiens announced that Patrick and Greg Moffett would share goaltending duties. In the pre-season matchup, the stakes were not very high for either team. But for Patrick, it was a huge game. He knew that a shellacking by the Oilers would be a major setback for his career, even though he was only 18.

Standing behind the Plexiglas during the Oilers' morning skate on game day, he confided to *La Presse* journalist Richard Hétu, "I hope Gretzky plays." Patrick wanted to compete against the very best so that his performance would really mean something. "But I know that I'm not immune to a bad night," he added cautiously.

While he watched Grant Fuhr turning aside his teammates' shots, he carried on the conversation, somewhat distractedly:

"Did you know that Charlie Hodge said that Fuhr was the best junior goalie he's ever seen in this country?"

"Is that so?" said Hétu, pretending he didn't know. "And who'd he rate second?"

"Me," said Patrick, pointing to his chest with a proud little grin.

"Do you actually know who Charlie Hodge is?"

"No . . . but it doesn't matter."

His attention was drawn back to Fuhr. "This guy made the team at 19, and he's already been playing in the league for three years." As far as Patrick was concerned that's what really mattered.

Patrick already had part of his gear on by 5:30 p.m., and he was raring to go. He wanted to be ready. He wanted to win. He knew what the game meant.

I could hardly keep still. I attended the game with Barbara. It's strange to say, but, in Patrick's whole career, and lord knows there were situations where he had far more on the line, there was never a game when I felt more stressed out. Something curious and unexpected occurred that evening. I said that there wasn't much at stake for either team, but that was without counting on the pride of the most recent Stanley Cup winners who were icing their best lineup and that of an organization with 22 cups to its credit.

And yet the match began like most pre-season games. The two teams felt each other out and scored two goals apiece in the first period. Then Deblois netted an early goal in the second period for the Canadiens, and the Oilers responded with a Kurri tally within a minute. The Oilers then went full throttle, deploying their entire arsenal to establish superiority. But Patrick wasn't having it. Gretzky's gang took 12 shots to the Habs' six in the second period, but Montréal outscored them 2 to 1 and led 4–3 at the end of the period. Lemaire had forgotten to put Moffett in for Patrick halfway through the game. Now there was too much at stake, and Patrick was doing too well. My torment was to continue.

By the third period, everyone in the Forum, players and fans alike, had forgotten that it was only September. The tension on the ice was palpable; it was like a playoff game. There were 15,386 fans sitting on the edge of their seats. It felt like April. Analyzing squad strengths no longer mattered. Both teams were desperate to win. And Patrick was in his element, in his zone. The Oilers tested Patrick 12 more times, but only Kurri succeeded, notching his second goal of the night. As the third period ended, the score stood at 4–4. The game was going into overtime. I went for a beer.

I got back to my seat just in time for the start of overtime. It's a good thing that I did because only 48 seconds into the period, Mario Tremblay grabbed a loose puck in the Oilers zone and rifled a shot past Fuhr. The Canadiens had won the game. What sweet ecstasy! The fans were delirious. Tremblay, nicknamed the *"Bleuets" Bionique* because he came from Lac-Saint-Jean, renowned for its blueberries, slid on his knees as though he had just scored the most important goal in his career. The players jumped on him and Patrick in celebration as if they'd won a playoff game. Patrick had stopped 30 of 34 shots from one of the most potent offences in modern-day hockey. He had been fabulous.

He had proven to himself that he could make the difference, even in the NHL. "I was very tense at the start of the game, but when I saw I could stop Gretzky, I knew I could stop anyone." He was referring to a shot at point-blank range by the Great One early in the game. "You don't realize how much confidence that save gave me. The fans cheered. I could feel their support. It really gave me a boost." Soon after that save, he made fantastic up-close saves on Messier and Anderson. After this performance, he certainly wouldn't be sent to the minors any time soon. "They gave me a big test with a lot of pressure on Saturday night at the Forum. I think I'm in a better position than I was before."

The euphoria lasted at least until the next day. On that beautiful Sunday morning, with the sunlight filtering through the leaves of the tall trees on boulevard de Maisonneuve, the Anglophone neighborhood felt like de Montmorency. We sat down for breakfast in a typical restaurant in the area near the hotel, surrounded by the morning papers, which recounted the Canadiens' triumph. Patrick figured prominently in the articles. *The Sunday Express* had a photo of him on the front page as he slammed the door on Wayne Gretzky. The *Dimanche-Matin* headline read: "ROY AND TREMBLAY beat the Oilers."

After Richer's return to Granby, Penney and Patrick each gave up three goals in a rather insignificant game in Boston. Then, the Canadiens traveled to Québec City to take on the Nordiques at the Colisée, a pressure-packed challenge for Patrick. The contest had personal significance for him since his opposite number, Richard Sévigny, had been Penney's backup barely a few months earlier. It was imperative for Patrick to outperform Sévigny to show the bosses that he was up to the job. He also wanted to vindicate Serge Savard, who was maligned by some for trading away an experienced goalkeeper. Ironically, Patrick was given Sévigny's old number, 33, for the game. Both goalies faced 24 shots, and the Canadiens won 4–3.

Patrick threw his arms in the air at the end of the game. "For me, this was THE game. I was facing Richard Sévigny; I didn't want to let Serge Savard down."

Just when Patrick seemed to have outdistanced his rivals for the coveted post, Savard took a step that showed he had no intention of changing his plans. Well aware of Patrick's abilities, Savard still saw him as a future Number 1, but not right away. Savard traded Mark Holden to Winnipeg for Doug Soetaert. The Canadiens' GM, who had played the final season and a half of his career with Winnipeg, had a good idea of what Soetaert could do. Savard's good friend John Ferguson, the Jets general manager and his old teammate in Montréal, had convinced Savard to come to Winnipeg to finish his career there in 1981. The Jets had two goalkeepers; Soetaert was one of them. He was no Number 1, but he was a reliable goalie, with eight years in the NHL. His inclusion on the team reassured Savard, who was troubled by Penney's lack of experience and thought Patrick was too young. Soetaert gave the Habs something the other two couldn't offer them: solid NHL experience. It was settled. Penney and Soetaert would spend the season in Montréal. But what about Patrick? Would Montréal elect to live with a trio of goalies? Patrick's immediate future would depend, for the most part, on the performance of the other two goalies at the start of the season.

The season began with a 4–3 loss to the Buffalo Sabers, with Penney in goal and Patrick as the backup. Then Penney pulled a muscle in his knee so Patrick backed up Soetaert for a few games. Of course, this gave Patrick valuable experience. He practiced with NHL players and got to see game situations up close: "Watching a game from the end of the bench is much more interesting than watching from the stands or on TV," he said. "On the bench, we know the coach can call on us at any moment. We pay much closer attention." But Patrick was desperate to play. "I'd like to get my chance. I know that if I turned in a bad performance, I could be sent down to Granby. But I just feel ready to take on any team."

After riding the bench for two weeks, Patrick couldn't take it any more. He was both disappointed and relieved when Lemaire took him aside after practice on October 24 and told him that he'd be going back down to Granby, without having played a single regular-season game. Acknowledging that Patrick was the third-ranking goalie in the organization, Lemaire said, "I would have liked to give him an opportunity to start a game before sending him to Granby. But Steve Penney and Doug Soetaert played well. . . . The team has been doing fine since the beginning of the season. We're winning and I don't see why we would risk playing an inexperienced goalkeeper. ... Above all, Patrick needs competition; we couldn't keep him here any longer."

Patrick was dying to play. It took him barely a few minutes to throw his heavy hockey gear, his hockey sticks and his personal effects into his Prelude. After going around the dressing room to thank each of his teammates, choking back his disappointment, he headed off to Granby, where he led the Bisons to a 10–4 victory against the Québec Remparts, that very same evening.

—⁓—

The last season in Granby was very similar to the previous two, but for a few events.

Patrick and Richer were invited to the Team Canada selection camp in Belleville, Ontario, on December 10 for the World Junior Hockey Championships, scheduled for the end of the month in Helsinki, Finland. Terry Simpson and the late Ron Lapointe had been chosen to coach the team by Hockey Canada.

Three days later, without having played a single exhibition game, Patrick was cut from the team. The decision followed an intrasquad game in which one goalie recorded a clean sheet, Patrick and another netminder each allowed three goals, and a fourth goaltender gave up six. Lapointe had this to say about the decision: "Patrick Roy is very good, but he goes down too often. The other three goalies didn't do any better than he did, but they stay on their skates and are more in tune with the style of team we're trying to build." Once again, Patrick's "butterfly" style was the point of contention. Certainly, in a situation where the coaches have to cut players in a hurry, the slightest issue can be enough. But Patrick had employed his "butterfly" style to beat the Edmonton Oilers in September. How many goalkeepers at the Belleville camp could claim as much?

Patrick had his own explanation: "I think I've just realized why Mario Lemieux didn't want to have anything to do with Junior Team Canada last year. I understand him and share his opinion. I came here thinking everyone was equal, but I was mistaken. I now see that Québecers must stand way above the pack to even be considered by the English-speaking organizers. I'm disappointed because I wasn't given a chance. Management came up with weak reasons for their decision, poor excuses: they said I lacked intensity, perhaps because I was playing for the Bisons. I discussed this with the Canadiens' scout Claude Ruel, who said he thought I was the second best goalie there. Why cut me instead of a guy from Ontario who let in six goals? We Francophones are at a disadvantage. I thought that Ron Lapointe could hold his own, but on the other hand, he's by himself and the further we went, the more we could see that the players from the West and from Ontario had an edge."

This was not the first time that a Québec athlete who had been dropped from a national team or not even invited would make such statements. It would not be the last.

A few months later, the highly reputed magazine, *L'Actualité économique*, published a study titled "Francophones in the National Hockey League: an economic analysis of discrimination" in their 61st issue, shedding light on the issue. The authors, Serge Coulombe and Marc Lavoie, economics professors at the University of Ottawa, drew an analogy between the treatment of Francophones in the NHL and that of African-Americans in baseball. They argued that there were entry barriers, which meant that Francophones had to outperform their Anglophone peers to have any chance of plying their trade in the NHL. It should be noted that this study was conducted some 20 years ago and that the situation has evolved since then, especially with the arrival of so many talented European players, particularly from Eastern Europe. Nonetheless, a few passages are still relevant.

The issue of discrimination against Francophones in sporting activities is obviously not a new one. In amateur sports, the most flagrant and most frequently cited example is the national handball

team, which was almost entirely composed of Québecers, and which
Sports Canada refused to sponsor until 1984. There were only two
Québecers on the Canadian hockey team at the Sarajevo Winter
Olympics. In reference to this, the word "racism" was often heard.
In every annual NHL amateur draft, the media raise the issue in
more or less veiled language.

Based on an analysis of draft results over a number of years, the authors concluded that "Francophone Quebecers constituted fewer than 13% of the Canadian players in the NHL from 1950 to 1978 and only 12.9% of the Canadian players drafted in the first two rounds between 1969 and 1977, although they represent 40% of the 20 top scorers of all time."

The study also showed that the entry barriers were inversely proportional to the objectivity of criteria used to measure performance by position. That is, the easier it is to objectively analyze the performance of an athlete, the harder it is to discriminate against him. For example, since it is hardest to evaluate defensemen objectively, the authors concluded:

> *Our statistical results suggest that it is harder for a Francophone*
> *to make his way in a position for which productivity is subjectively*
> *measured, as is the case for defensemen. Therefore, only a*
> *Francophone who was a star would manage to make a place for*
> *himself on an NHL club in this position. . . . Francophones are,*
> *indeed, [taking inspiration from the title of Pierre Vallière's book*
> Les Nègres blancs d'Amérique] *the white niggers of hockey!*

Yvon Pedneault's article in the *Journal de Montréal* the day after Patrick was cut expressed the idea in other terms: "With equal talent, a Francophone has no chance." Even Jean Perron, who had supported Dave King in rejecting Mario Lemieux the previous year, felt uncomfortable: "Listen, it's always the same thing. [The late] Sam Pollock forced Team Canada to take me on board. Dave King did not want me there. He's the one who told me that he had to accede to Mr. Pollock's demand."

Patrick might not have been wrong after all!

The Coulombe-Lavoie study concerned the NHL, but as we have seen, Canadian junior hockey saw itself as the NHL in miniature, and so if cases of discrimination had also been noted among Canadian national teams, it is safe to assume that the same behavior could be found in hockey in general. In the years that followed, Jean Perron, Terry Simpson and Ron Lapointe all made the leap to the NHL. Canada's junior team won the gold medal in Helsinki with Craig Billington in goal. Hockey Canada thus avoided criticism.

—⁂—

In January, the Bisons acquired Patrick's brother through a transaction with the Saguenéens. Stéphane Richer, who had requested a trade a number of times, and Greg Choules went to Chicoutimi in exchange for Stéphane Roy, Marc Bureau and René L'Écuyer. Even though he would be separated from his good friend Richer for a time, Patrick felt that this was a good trade for the Bisons. Stéphane and Bureau were performing well, and L'Écuyer was a rugged defenseman. Above all, the Bisons were obtaining three players who could play regularly in the league, which was certainly not a negligible advantage for a team that lacked depth. Stéphane had mixed feelings about the deal. Happy to join his brother, he regretted leaving a top team where everything was going well for him to become a bottom dweller.

Whatever the positive effects of the trade, they didn't last long. The Bisons' defeatist attitude was too deeply ingrained. A few days after his arrival, Stéphane said, "Team spirit is good. Now we have to instill a winning attitude in the team. The players need to start hating defeat." A couple of weeks later, Marc Bureau's remarks indicated that some players didn't give a damn: they were just waiting for the season to end and didn't care whether the team made the playoffs.

Patrick shed further light on the situation: "The players here are too comfortable; their hearts aren't in the right place. . . . It's not so much the partying off the ice as much as the lack of discipline and aggressiveness, that is letting us down." Commenting on the impact of the trade with Chicoutimi, since he had expected a significant change in the dressing room atmosphere, he said, "Some Bisons players had other ideas; they ended up trying to lure the newcomers into taking the easy way out. We're going nowhere, and it will be hard to change course."

He was right. Sometimes the situation verged on the ridiculous. One evening, the Hull Olympics, coached by Pat Burns, bombarded Patrick with 82 shots. At one point, Patrick stopped one player on a breakaway. Then, out of sheer frustration Patrick gave him back the puck and yelled, "Go ahead. Take another shot!" One save more or less, what's the difference?

The season ended in a tailspin. The prevailing attitude could best be described as total indifference. In early February, Claude St-Sauveur kept his job as general manager but was replaced behind the bench by Yves Robert. Robert survived until mid-March; then Renald Gagné took over. At the end of the season, the club announced that Georges Larivière would be taking the reins the following season.

Meanwhile, Patrick recorded his first NHL win as the Canadiens downed the Winnipeg Jets 6–4. Steve Penney was injured, so Patrick was given Number 33 and designated as Doug Soetaert's backup. But the veteran goalie gave up four goals on only 11 shots in the first two periods. Shortly before the third period, Jacques Lemaire entered the dressing room and said, "Roy, take the net!" Then the coach left, slamming the door behind him. Patrick, whose English was still very rudimentary, turned to Carbonneau and asked, "Did I hear him right?"

"Yeah, you're in the net."

The score was 4–4, so in case of a victory or a loss Patrick would be the goalie of record.

Incandescent, Soetaert was fuming on the bench. TV analyst Gilles Tremblay mistakenly announced that Soetaert had suffered a concussion. But a few minutes later, he said, "Another correction, René [Lecavalier], we apologize, I am told that it is a tactical substitution. Lemaire has decided to play Patrick Roy. It's Flockhart. We got the name wrong. It's Flockhart who has suffered a slight concussion."

Patrick had to handle only two shots, one of which was difficult. The Canadiens, on the other hand, fired 15 shots at Brian Hayward, who was unable to stop the winning goal from Kurvers and the insurance marker by Chris Nilan. It was Nilan's second tally of the game and he earned the first star. On that Saturday evening, Patrick registered his first NHL victory. No longer was he watching *Hockey Night in Canada*; he was in it.

He expected to get the start the next day against the New York Islanders, but that didn't happen. He had to be content with the pre-game warm-up. Nevertheless, he still managed to stand out. The approximately 5,000 spectators settling into their seats before the opening face-off couldn't help but applaud Patrick's superb save against one of his teammates. Nonetheless he was disappointed. Now, in hindsight, Patrick understands Lemaire's decision. The coach was trying to light a fire under Soetaert. Patrick was sent back to Granby after a ten-day road trip out West, during which he did not start a single regular game because Penney was back.

—ɯ—

One night, after a game and a good meal, Patrick and Stéphane couldn't get to sleep, so they decided to make an early drive to Québec City. They had the next day off, and they planned to spend it back home or in Saint-Sacrement. They woke up their Sainte-Foy teammate, Éric Castonguay, and invited him along. Traveling that night turned out to be a nightmare.

Snow started falling more heavily in the middle of the night. Blowing snow drastically reduced visibility. On Highway 20, near the Victoriaville exit, the road was a skating rink. The Prelude suddenly lost traction, went into a spin and then plowed tail first into a snowbank by the side of the road. The force of the impact sent the front of the car into the air, and the car rolled over. The three boys found themselves stuck in the car, upside down. After considerable effort, they forced a door open and extracted themselves from the vehicle. Fortunately, they were all right: more scared than injured! So they brushed the snow off their clothes and started walking toward the road, looking for help, when Stéphane said, "Hey! The motor's running. We're not going to leave the car like this!"

"I'm not going back in there," said Patrick.

"Wait a second," replied Stéphane.

Calmly, as though nothing had happened, Stéphane slid back into the car, switched off the ignition and retrieved the keys.

"There you go big brother. Here are the keys."

At five in the morning, with the storm raging, they got lucky. A Good Samaritan stopped to help them. He took them to Laurier Station to report the accident to the Québec Provincial Police, who later had the Prelude towed to a garage in Victoriaville. Then he drove the lads to Québec City.

During the trip, their benefactor told them that he had lost his son in similar circumstances.

—◆—

On March 19, the Montréal Canadiens assigned Patrick to Sherbrooke of the American Hockey League for what remained of the season.

The Bisons had two games left on the calendar but were mired in the basement, so nobody objected to the move. Patrick was leaving Granby for good.

It also marked the end of Patrick's minor hockey experience, which for the most part had been a hodgepodge of losses and a relentless onslaught of shots with a series of losing teams, game after game, season after season, from the atoms to the juniors. In his 11 years in hockey, he had never won anything, except during the one year he played for the Sainte-Foy Gouverneurs. And even then, a suspension had kept him out of the provincial final, and the team had lost in the national championship final. One could well wonder how he avoided getting discouraged and packing it in. Nowadays, Patrick is quite rightly considered a winner, someone who hates defeat. But do people really know him? He had learned to lose long before he learned to win. Looking back, who would ever have bet that he would be selected in the 1984 NHL draft?

THE INNOVATOR, THE MACHO AND THE GURU

12

During a hockey game, a team normally uses up to a dozen forwards and six defensemen, but only one goalie. The netminder is the only one responsible for making saves on shots from all angles and keeping the puck out of the net, four feet high by six feet wide. To a certain extent, this thankless task isolates him from the flow of the game and from the other players. They make the plays; he reacts. They're in the heat of the action; his role is reaction.

He isn't part of the play. He stays at one end of the rink, and the game goes on in front of him. He is a spectator until danger strikes. In fact, the play stops with him. Either he gives up a goal or he makes the save, and the puck takes off in the opposite direction. He is so little involved in the rest of the play that at the limit he could be replaced with a hockey target. His role is that of an accessory, but oh how important!

He is vulnerable, fragile and often left to his own resources. He is the last bastion against the opponent's attack. And often, he's made the undeserving scapegoat for a defeat because a perceived mistake or weakness on his part is irreparable.

To make matters worse, every error becomes an indelible part of his record. A forward may flub a scoring chance; a defenseman may miss a check. They can try again; they get another chance. Their errors don't appear anywhere. But when a goalie is scored on, it is written in his record and affects his goals-against average and his save percentage forever. Ironically, though he is not part of the play, the netminder is the one whose personal record is most closely linked to team performance. While he is said to work individually, the key metrics for assessing his performance are based on data related to team performance, such as wins and goals-against average. By contrast, to assess forwards and defensemen, who are said to work collectively, we calculate their points, body checks and face-offs won—a whole lot of individual data independent of team performance.

As recently as the 1980s, goalies were the neglected figures of hockey. The kid with the least athletic ability was stuck in goal. The slowest, weakest, smallest kid was put in the net so he wouldn't be in the way. In the higher age categories, organized hockey had no particular provision for training goalies. Practices were not designed for them. In skating drills, goalies lumbered along in their heavy equipment behind their teammates, from one line to another and around the face-off circles or cones. For a goalie, the rest of the practice primarily involved facing shots from every conceivable angle. In short, there was little regard for goaltending despite the pivotal role it often plays in a game. Yet, throughout hockey history, there have been illustrious goalies.

History also tells us that the first official hockey game in which goalies took part was played in 1875 at the Victoria Skating Rink in Montréal, based on rules set by McGill University students. Simple posts served as goals, and that was the case until 1900 when cages first appeared. The hockey sticks of the time made it difficult for players to lift the puck off the ice. That's why a goalie received a two-minute penalty for dropping onto the ice to make a save. He was not allowed to sit, kneel or lie on the ice. The reason was quite simple:

if a goalie stretched out along the goal line, it would be impossible to score. A goalie could use his hands to stop the puck, but he was penalized if he covered it with his glove or threw it to another player. A penalty to a goaltender could prove costly because, until 1940, a netminder had to leave the ice to serve his penalty. However, from 1917 on, goalies were allowed to go down to block shots—shooting had improved—and, beginning in 1922, they could freeze the puck to stop play.

The rules stipulated that goaltenders use the same equipment as other players. But gradually, goalies began to wear cricket pads and a fur helmet attached to the front of their pants for a cup (an athletic supporter). To catch pucks, they were allowed to wear gloves with a little more padding than the ones worn by other players. By 1918, goalies were permitted to use a stick with a blade that could be three-and-a-half inches high. Then in 1924, a goalie by the name of Emil "Pop" Kenesky widened his cricket pads to 12 inches, creating a model that goalies would employ for decades to come.

In 1893, Frederick Arthur Lord Stanley of Preston, then the Governor-General of Canada, donated a trophy bearing his name to be awarded to the best hockey team in the country. Of course, only amateur clubs were involved: the first professional league did not come into existence until 1907 in Ontario. Today, only NHL teams may contend for the Stanley Cup.

Two of the greatest goaltenders in the first quarter of the twentieth century were Clint Benedict of the Ottawa Senators and the Montréal Maroons, and Georges Vézina of the Montréal Canadiens. Born in Chicoutimi, Québec, Vézina tended the net for the Canadiens from 1910 until he succumbed to tuberculosis at age 39 in 1926. The following season, to pay homage to his remarkable willpower, courage and excellence, a trophy bearing his name was introduced as an award for the best goalie in the NHL. George Hainsworth, Vézina's successor with the Canadiens, was the first recipient of the trophy, with a 1.52 goals-against average (GAA) compared with Benedict's 1.54. Hainsworth won the honor three years in a row.

Until the early 1980s, the Vézina Trophy was awarded to the goalie with the lowest GAA, but since then, a vote by the NHL general managers determines the winner. This seems far more equitable. The best GAA actually reflects the overall defensive effort by the whole team, including the goalie, but the Vézina Trophy is intended to reward individual performance. As the NHL had yet to achieve parity, goalies on the strongest teams had a better chance of garnering the prestigious trophy, even if they hadn't played a critical role in their team's success.

Just think of the squads the Canadiens iced in the '50s, '60s and '70s. Before 1960, the universal draft system had yet to be instituted in the NHL. So the teams sponsored junior teams, known as farm teams, which supplied and developed most of their players. For example, the Canadiens could take all the best players in Québec: the Richards, Béliveau, Geoffrion, Moore, Harvey, Plante, etc. In the decade that followed the implementation of the annual draft system, the Canadiens still had the right to protect the two best players from Québec before taking part in the selection session. To give an idea of the immense advantage the privilege represented, if it had been maintained beyond 1970, Guy Lafleur could have played with Gilbert Perreault, Marcel Dionne, Richard Martin, Denis Potvin, Mike Bossy, Raymond Bourque, Denis Savard and Mario Lemieux. It's the sort of formation that makes goalies and coaches look good. And when the privilege was finally abolished, the crafty Sam Pollock, the late general manager of the Habs, had accumulated enough players to trade, without weakening his team, assets that were attractive to new expansion clubs for top draft choices. That's how he got his hands on Guy Lafleur in 1971 after he traded two dispensable players to the California Golden Seals for their first round draft choice. It wasn't until the beginning of the 1980s that this privileged situation no longer had an impact. Finally the Canadiens, despite their glorious past, were obliged to line up at the same starting line as their competitors.

Not to take anything away from the talents of Jacques Plante and Ken Dryden, who were among the best in the trade, they started with a huge advantage over Al Rollins of the Chicago Blackhawks, Ed Giacomin of the New York Rangers or Denis Herron of the California Golden Seals in the race for the Vézina Trophy. Dryden acknowledged this in his book, *The Game*, published in 1983. He writes:

It makes my job different from that of every other goalie in the NHL. I get fewer shots and fewer hard shots. … Each year, I find it harder and harder to make a connection between a Canadiens win and me. … But as the team's superiority has become entrenched, and as the gap between our opponents and us, mostly unchanged, has come to seem wider and more permanent, every save I make seems without urgency, as if it is done completely at my own discretion, a minor bonus if made, a minor inconvenience, quickly overcome, if not.

In fact, the save percentage, a ratio obtained by dividing the number of saves by the number of shots on goal, would have been a much fairer indicator of a goalie's individual performance to determine the recipient of the Vézina Trophy. Now it's the best metric, providing, however, that the number of shots are calculated and recorded accurately, which wasn't always the case, as we have seen in Granby. Some may argue that shots vary in difficulty. That's true. The same applies to baseball batting averages. But by the end of a season the different degrees of difficulty even out, given the large numbers involved.

From 1942, the first year of the modern era of the NHL when there were six teams, until 1980 when there were 21, there was little evolution in the art of goaltending. Jacques Plante was the most innovative goalie during that period. He had original ideas and didn't hesitate to put them into practice. He was one of a kind. He wore a tuque (knitted hat) when he played for the Montréal Royals in the Québec Senior League, just before joining the Canadiens. He had knitted it himself on the team's road trips. He wasn't allowed to continue that eccentricity in the big league, but some of his innovations have had a significant effect on the goalies of his time.

He was the first goalie to skate out of his crease to stop the puck behind his goal and make it easier for his defensemen to launch a counterattack. It was his way of getting involved in the play. He also popularized the wearing of a mask, which he himself had perfected. Before Plante, Clint Benedict with the Montréal Maroons had worn a leather mask in the last five games of the 1929–30 season, after suffering fractures to the nose and jaw. But as the equipment obstructed his view of the puck when it was at his feet, he discarded the mask.

Plante's two great innovations were entirely justified, but they made coach Toe Blake break out in a rash. Blake went apoplectic when his goalie wandered out of his net. Nor did he approve of Plante wearing a mask even in practices. In short, he didn't like Plante. The two were at daggers drawn.

Someone would have to be obtuse and a bit macho to forbid a netminder to wear a mask to protect his face against a frozen puck shot at over 90 miles per hour. Besides, at any moment, the puck can deflect off a stick or a player in front of a goalie whose view is obstructed.

On November 1, 1959, at Madison Square Garden in New York, Plante was struck in the nose by a powerful slap shot by the Rangers'

Andy Bathgate. He collapsed with his face bleeding and was carried by teammates to the infirmary where it took about ten stitches to close the gash. That evening, Plante categorically refused to go back to the fray without a mask. As the Canadiens didn't have a backup goalkeeper, Blake had no alternative but to accept. Plante returned and helped his team win. He swore that he would wear a mask from then on. Blake dug in his heels: "He can wear it until he's completely healed and he's got to remove it after that."

But Plante stuck to his guns. Given his team's success and his superstar goalie's performance and popularity, Blake had little choice. He gave in eventually. During that period, the Canadiens won five Stanley Cups in a row, from 1956 to 1960.

Wearing a mask became widespread, not only in the NHL but throughout hockey. Andy Brown of the Pittsburg Penguins and Lorne "Gump" Worsley, then with the Minnesota North Stars, were the only holdouts until the 1973–74 season: the last two goalies to play without a mask. Of course, Worsley was reluctant to play in the Chicago Stadium where he had to face shots by Stan Mikita and Bobby Hull. After Andy Bathgate, Mikita and Hull were the first to use a curved hockey stick, which propelled the puck at terrific speed in a nearly unpredictable trajectory. It became almost unthinkable for a goalie to play without a mask. Improved equipment and teaching methods were bringing about an evolution in the game.

Not only is hockey a rough sport, it is steeped in a macho culture; the unwillingness to protect themselves is not new among players. But braving fate has its limits. In 1968, Bill Masterson of the Minnesota North Stars died after his head violently hit the ice. Wearing a protective helmet became increasingly widespread in the NHL, but to deal with the resistance by the stonewallers, it took a rule, in 1979, to oblige new players to wear a helmet. Before the rule came into force, a player who wore a helmet risked being called soft by his colleagues. Veterans who played in the league prior to 1979 benefited from the grandfathered right to play bareheaded. Craig MacTavish of the Saint Louis Blues, the last NHLer to play without a helmet, retired in 1997.

Professionals playing hockey for a living may contend understandably (if not convincingly) that wearing a helmet or visor may hamper their performance. A similar claim from amateurs in oldtimer or garage leagues, who derive little out of hockey except a night out with the boys and a chance to stay in shape, are unconvincing. Most amateurs protect themselves, but there are still too many "warriors" who don't wear a visor and grumble about the mandatory helmet rule, even though injuries to the face or the eye region are far from rare. But not one of them would risk playing a game without a jock to protect their balls, which they apparently prize more highly than their brains.

This macho culture often manifests itself in locker-room banter. Of course, there is the nonsense men engage in to ease pre-game jitters or make the post-game beer flow freely. But many guys regale their pals with descriptions of their bumps and bruises or tales about the hits they heroically suffered during the game. As my friend Jean-Guy used to say ironically, "An ordinary man would never make it!"

I hope my fellow old-timers won't resent my lifting the veil off the goings-on in the sanctuary known as "the locker room." It is the male's last refuge since the disappearance of taverns, from which women were once excluded, and since the Canadian Charter of Rights and Freedoms has obliged golf clubs to stop practicing an insidious form of discrimination. Though women are not forbidden access to old-timers' dressing rooms, I have never seen a woman venture into one. The spectacle of sagging flesh, aging bodies and bloated paunches, men drenched with stinking sweat, and talk that rarely rises above the waist is probably not worth it.

From the 1940s to the 1980s, most goalies were not very tall, between five feet, six inches and five feet ten. Stars like Johnny Bower, Lorne Worsley, Rogatien Vachon, Roger Crozier and Bernard Parent were in that category. They all favored essentially the same style. They stood on their feet as much as possible to guard the upper part of the net—we can understand why—and they advanced towards the puck carrier to cover their angles, keeping the blade of their stick flat on the ice. Terry Sawchuck (five feet, 11 inches), Jacques Plante (six feet) and especially Ken Dryden (six feet, four inches) were much taller than average, but they used essentially the same basic technique. However, Sawchuck got into a slight crouch, so he could see the puck between the players' legs.

Other goaltenders had the height and athletic ability to achieve considerable success with the "butterfly" style: Glenn Hall, the acknowledged inventor of the style, Tony Esposito and Daniel Bouchard. They employed the technique in different periods, but it did not become widespread. It had few takers. The conventional wisdom was that their acrobatic skill and great flexibility allowed them to use a style that was considered almost idiosyncratic. Everyone agrees that Ken Dryden was an excellent goalkeeper. But imagine what he would have accomplished at his size with today's goaltending technique.

Of course, the approach didn't exist at the time. Goalies were locked into the classic NHL model. Some like Hall, Esposito and, later, Bouchard and Patrick, instinctively tried something different, but when they displayed the slightest weakness, they were forced to return to the "true" style: to stay on their feet, keep their stick on the ice and cover the angles. The credo had the force of law for decades.

Meanwhile, as playing technique and equipment improved, the

shots became harder and more accurate. Jacques Plante noted in his book titled *On Goaltending* that when he started out there were only one or two players per team with powerful shots. But the situation had evolved to the point that nearly 50% of the players in the National Hockey League could score from 50 feet out if the goaltender wasn't alert. Plante made these observations in 1972. Just imagine what it is like today!

On the eve of the 1980s, there needed to be a radical change in basic goaltending technique and training methods—and fast.

—∞—

François Allaire is tall and thin, with short hair clipped around the ears. With his little round glasses, he exudes the air of a university professor. His icy blue eyes give you the impression he knows what he wants and where he's going.

He was born in 1955 in Mirabel, northwest of Montréal. He got his start as a goalie in the town's minor hockey organization. Then he played for Collège de Saint-Jérôme, where at the age of 17, he noted with chagrin that the technical training goaltenders received was sadly deficient. He had received practically no instruction, and the little coaching he got wasn't always good. He was made to do things that didn't make sense to him. The sole reference Allaire had was Jacques Plante's recently published book. At the time, it was the only work available in French on the subject of goaltending. Allaire considered it advanced for the time.

He read the book over and over. Jacques Plante had played in an era when netminders were left to develop on their own. He had learned on the job, instinctively, by himself. He was gifted with an analytical mind, permitting him to discover why, in a given situation, it was better for a goalie to do one thing rather than another. Every action was based on principles. Plante's book served as a kind of introduction to the subject, but for Allaire it didn't go far enough. Besides, at the rate hockey instruction and the game itself were evolving after the Summit Series between Canada and the Soviet Union in 1972, Plante's theories, in many regards, were becoming rapidly outmoded. And so were his methods. When Roger Picard brought Plante to Granby to check out Patrick at training camp in the fall of 1983, it was a disaster. Plante lived in Switzerland at the time and came to Montréal only a few days a year to monitor the Canadiens' goalies. But hockey was changing too quickly and Plante was out of touch.

"He wanted me to do things," said Patrick, "that didn't make sense to me. I told him, 'I have a lot of respect for you. You're one of the greatest goalies of all time, but I don't believe that what you're asking me to do is right.' That annoyed him, and after the practice, he told Mr. Picard that I would never make the National Hockey League."

When Patrick, age seven, was deciding he would become a goalie, at exactly the same time François Allaire, ten years his elder, was dedicating the rest of his life to training and developing goaltenders. He was absolutely clear about what he wanted to do.

In 1975, Allaire enrolled in the University of Sherbrooke's physical education program. He tended goal for the university hockey team, which competed in a league with clubs from the Eastern Townships, located in south-central Québec between Montréal and Québec City. But the following year, the school withdrew from the league, and he had to play intramural hockey. However, the change was of little consequence to him, since he had never intended to play hockey as a career. He had gone to university with one thing in mind: to become a goalie coach.

At university, most of Allaire's work and research in education, psychology and other fields of interest was related to goaltending. From the age of 15, he had been observing goalies, often taking notes even for games he watched on TV. He recorded his observations in a notebook without really knowing what he would do with them, but he analyzed, broke things down and mulled over the best possible ways to stop shots.

When he graduated from university in 1978, Allaire toured European hockey schools, observing practices, taking notes and analyzing teaching methods. He also exchanged knowledge with instructors and gathered documentation. When he returned to Québec he reviewed all of the available literature in the world on the art of goaltending, using National Library of Canada resources. For two years, he pored over some 200 works from North America, Europe and Japan.

His findings revealed that teaching and training methods in many countries were not necessarily more effective than those employed in Canada, but they were very different. Allaire concluded, therefore, that the NHL credo for training and developing goalies wasn't the only way. This encouraged him to develop his own principles, training methods and prototype for goaltending.

While employed as a sports coordinator for the city of Mirabel, Allaire began coaching minor hockey teams and directing goalie schools to test his theories.

A basic observation on which much of Allaire's thesis rested was that it was easier for a goaltender to move, push off, stop and face the puck than to stand motionless and be obliged to stretch or do the splits to make a save with his pads or glove. Allaire's approach was less spectacular but a lot more effective than the prevalent NHL model. So, whenever he had a chance to work with young goalies, he focused on skating techniques: pushing off, stopping, backing up; pushing off, stopping and backing up. Traditionally, goalie skates were kept rather dull or the blades were given a convex form so they would slide better laterally. Allaire, by contrast, had the skates sharpened until they were like razor blades to facilitate stopping and starting. Since the "butterfly" style required fair-sized goalies with a great deal of agility, few young guys could successfully use the technique. Allaire opted for a hybrid approach, combining the stand-up and "butterfly" styles.

Goaltenders coached by Allaire soon outperformed other goalies. In 1983, he published the results of his research and experiences in his first book, *Devenir gardien de but au hockey (Hockey Goaltending for Young Players* in English*)*. The book provided a four-year development plan detailing everything a coach needed to teach: basic techniques and skating fundamentals; training methods on and off the ice; the assessment and correction of goalies; the role of the coach; the choice of equipment.

The book caught the attention of Pierre Creamer, who coached the Verdun Junior Canadiens of the Québec Major Junior Hockey League. The Montréal Canadiens owned the club. Creamer invited Allaire to join his team and tutor the goalies. The following year, Montréal transferred its American Hockey League farm team from Halifax, Nova Scotia, to Sherbrooke, Québec, and Creamer became the Sherbrooke Canadiens' first coach. He asked Allaire to assist him. Allaire was granted leave without pay from the City of Mirabel and accepted the invitation in order to test his training methods with professional goalkeepers.

Not enough can be said about how much persistence and audacity it took for Allaire to introduce, at the professional level, a goaltending model that went against the grain. Though his work had left him in no doubt about the effectiveness of his approach, he still had to demonstrate that his prototype was the best. But Sherbrooke's goalies lacked the physical stature to put his model into practice. Paul Pageau was small and Greg Moffett was not tall enough to do the "butterfly". Both netminders swore by the traditional style. For the "butterfly" style, they also lacked flexibility and skating skill. Besides, they loved to stay on their feet.

Pierre Creamer gave Allaire the latitude he wanted. Creamer had complete confidence in him. But Allaire was a rookie coach. Diplomacy was called for when suggesting technical changes to the goalies whose resistance he clearly sensed. Given the situation, he established a *modus vivendi*, a compromise that allowed him to begin working and test run his theories with pros.

On the eve of the AHL playoffs in the spring of 1985, everything changed. Allaire was asked to coach a tall (nearly six feet, two inches) 19-year-old from Granby. The youngster loved to drop to his knees in a "butterfly" to make saves. He was fast and, above all, he was eager to try anything that would help him improve. It wasn't the first time Allaire had seen the goalie. The lad had played against the Verdun Juniors in the QMJHL and had performed brilliantly a few times. Creamer considered him the best goalie in junior hockey and told the Canadiens organization as much at a meeting.

Allaire worked with him for two days in Sherbrooke, and then he told Creamer, "Pierre, this is a different caliber goalie. We've gone up a step." Clearly, Patrick was better than the other two. Patrick had powerful legs and good hands. He was fast, flexible and could push off and stop effectively. When he set up properly, he could make saves from every possible angle. It was the first time Allaire was able to put his model into practice with a goalie who possessed the requisite mental and physical qualities. He had found the kind of athlete he'd spent years looking for. But Creamer had other concerns. "Perhaps, François, but look, we're going into the playoffs, we can't start with a 19-year-old rookie in goal! We have to get the other two goalies ready for the playoffs."

Creamer was right. Imagine the criticism he would have faced if the team had flopped with a teenager in net, especially one who hadn't played a single game in Sherbrooke. Allaire didn't insist. In his first year of coaching professional goalies, how could he be absolutely sure of himself? What if he was wrong?

But as training progressed, he could see that he was on the right track. Out of 100 shots, Patrick stopped twice as many as the other goalies. The guru had found his disciple. From the outset, not only did Allaire let him go down to make saves, he encouraged Patrick to do so. Thus, Allaire was freeing Patrick from the constraints hitherto imposed on him, letting him develop a style that came naturally to him. And Patrick gave Allaire the liberty to test his theories at will. Their partnership would revolutionize the art of goaltending and help raise it to the level of other aspects of the game.

From the outset, Allaire assigned Patrick specific training exercises. Patrick no longer had to trudge around behind his teammates in skating sessions or stand mindlessly stopping shots. Creamer even put a few players at Patrick's disposal to simulate game situations. They worked on Patrick's movement in his crease so that he would always be facing the play, no matter how fast the players and passes moved. This was the bedrock of Allaire's thesis. If the goalie is not part of the play, he might as well stay ahead of it so he can make the save. Patrick's skates were sharpened so they would dig into the ice when he pushed off or stopped quickly.

Gradually, they developed a process of trial and error, enabling them to make progress together and formulate a new "gospel" of goaltending. When a problem arose, they found an answer. Allaire's challenge was to suggest a solution; Patrick's was to put it in practice. If Patrick wasn't comfortable with one remedy, the onus was on Allaire to find an alternative until the problem was solved to their mutual satisfaction. That's the way they worked until the end of the playoffs in Sherbrooke.

During the 1985–86 season, Patrick was in Montréal; Allaire was in Sherbrooke. Allaire occasionally headed to the Forum to observe his protégé and offer him some pointers, especially when Patrick watched the games from up in the press box. When Jacques Plante stopped instructing the Canadiens goalies, the team announced that it would be asking Allaire, now and then, to work with the Habs' goalies. As it turned out, they had to manage on their own. Jacques Lemaire had made the announcement in October 1984 to calm a brewing goaltending controversy. Journalists had reproached Canadiens brass for not hiring a goalie instructor, especially to help Steve Penney, as he had little NHL experience. But Lemaire didn't want extra attention focused on his goaltenders to disrupt the practice routine he'd crafted for the rest of the team. So, the occasions when Allaire actually met with Penney and Soetaert were few and far between.

But three weeks before the 1985–86 season ended, Allaire got a call from Habs coach Jean Perron. "François, you're coming to Montréal, and the only goalie you'll talk to, the only one you'll be working with is Patrick Roy."

Allaire headed to Montréal.

Patrick and his personal instructor viewed match films to identify problems Patrick encountered and try to solve them. During practice, they focused on testing solutions; then they went back to study the films again. A week before the end of the season, Perron informed Allaire, "We're going to start the series with Patrick in the net. Don't breathe a word to anybody. Don't say anything."

François Allaire was on a mission. He was going to prepare the starting goalie on the most prestigious team in NHL history for the Stanley Cup Playoffs.

Patrick parked his Prelude behind Motel Le Baron, overlooking the Magog River in Sherbrooke, Québec. He had suffered through an excruciating season in Granby with 16 wins, 23 losses and a 5.48 goals-against average, but on March 19, 1985, the Canadiens had called him up. He had gone through a bit of training. Then the club had sent him to their farm club for professional seasoning. Canadiens management hoped he would be their AHL team's regular goalie for the next season. The stay would familiarize him with a superior caliber of play and acquaint him with his new coaches and teammates. Georges Guilbault, a well-known businessman in the area, was the president of the Sherbrooke Canadiens. I had gotten to know Guilbault some years back when he played junior hockey with the Victoriaville Bruins. He was quite a good player, a bit of a celebrity in the little town. Sometimes, he would drop by Hotel Central for a bit of dancing to the music of Les Mégatones.

After Patrick checked into the hotel, he went to see Pierre Creamer at the Palais des sports on rue du Parc. Coach Creamer introduced him to a few staff members, showed him his place in the dressing room and told him to suit up for a practice.

Patrick found some familiar faces among his teammates. He had played against Bobby Dollas of the Laval Voisins in junior hockey. He had trained with Serge Boisvert, Claude Larose, Thomas Rundqvist, Brian Skrudland, Ric Natress, Gaston Gingras, Mike Lalor and Michel Therrien at the Canadiens camp.

He went through a few on-ice, warm-up and stretching exercises. Then he met François Allaire, who told him to get in goal. Allaire watched Patrick handle some routine shots by his teammates. Next, Allaire went over to have a word with him. Patrick expected Allaire to tell him to stay on his feet more. On the contrary, Allaire encouraged him to drop to his knees in a "butterfly" style and urged him to abandon two-legged pad slides. Instead, he was to execute lateral "butterfly" glides. Allaire had him push off and move so that he would be constantly ahead of the play, facing the shooter. Then, Patrick only had to drop to his knees in position to stop the puck. What a relief! Ever since Jacques Lemaire had complained that he flopped to the ice too soon, Patrick had been a bit puzzled. He had tried his best to change his style, but the results were disappointing. He had been losing confidence. Allaire was the first since Patrick's midget coach, Jacques Naud, to encourage him to make natural, instinctive movements. He already felt more comfortable. He was happy.

—ᴍ—

Greg Moffett was not so happy. Already dissatisfied with sharing ice time with Paul Pageau, he naturally took a dim view of Patrick's arrival. Moffett vented to the media. In fact, his remarks made headlines in Sherbrooke's daily, *La Tribune*. "What do you want me to say? This is shit! No, I'm not happy because it isn't necessary for Patrick Roy to be here. I'm not happy."

Then he took aim at Serge Savard. "If he's giving up on a player, why doesn't he say it to his face instead of going through the papers, as he did with Ric Natress? I've been playing in the Canadiens organization for four years, and I still don't know where I stand. If Savard thinks I'm not good enough to play in the NHL, I'd like him to tell me."

Moffett was an American from Bath, Maine, a journalism graduate from the University of New Hampshire. He had gotten married the previous year. At 26 years of age, he was eager to have a clear picture of his future. His criticism of Serge Savard may well have been his way of accelerating things. But with a regular-season save percentage of 0.860—he stopped 86% of the shots directed at him—his remarks were more likely to pave the way to a career in journalism than a job as an NHL goalie. And the reply from the Habs' boss was not long in coming: "Moffett is paid to stop pucks; I'm paid to manage the team. Let him do his job!"

Pageau took a more diplomatic tack. "We'll need to get some rest before the playoffs. In the end, it's not so bad that he's here."

Patrick trained exclusively with François Allaire for 12 days. Meanwhile, his friend Stéphane Richer had joined the club after the Saguenéens were dispatched in the QMJHL playoffs. Then before a road trip, Pierre Creamer had Patrick play the last game of the season at home, and Sherbrooke downed the New Haven Nighthawks 7–4. Creamer was queried about his decision because the Canadiens were locked in a bitter struggle to make the playoffs. "We brought him to Sherbrooke to play him. He's part of the organization and we wanted to see what he could do, in case we need to call on him."

—⁓—

On Thursday, April 11, the Sherbrooke Canadiens began the playoffs against the Fredericton Express, an affiliate of both the Québec Nordiques and the Vancouver Canucks. At least three players in the series would eventually become NHL coaches: Michel Therrien of the Sherbrooke Canadiens, as well as Claude Julien and Mark Crawford of the Fredericton Express. Michel Therrien would later become better known as a coach than as a defenseman. Crawford was a little pest as a player, the kind of guy who instigates fights and then runs away—the player most detested by his opponents. While playing for the Vancouver Canucks, Crawford ended the Boston Bruins Normand Léveillé's career with a check on October 23, 1982. It wasn't a cheap shot, and Crawford never accepted responsibility for the hit, which was tough but within the rules. In fact, Léveillé played one or two shifts after the incident. But he suddenly collapsed from a brain hemorrhage after intermission. It was later discovered that Léveillé had a congenital malformation, leaving him vulnerable to that kind of injury.

The first two games were played at the Aitken Center in New Brunswick. The Canadiens won both of them. Moffett, impeccable in goal, (Pageau was his backup) went up against Clint Malarchuk. In the third encounter in Sherbrooke, the tide turned quickly. The 6–2 trouncing by the Express dampened the enthusiasm at the Palais des sports. Moffett had nothing to be ashamed of, however. He had faced 34 shots and Malarchuk, only 18.

After the game, François Allaire's comments were surprising but prescient. Acknowledging that Moffett had done a good job so far and that he had the ability to play in the NHL, Allaire nonetheless added, "I wonder, however, if that's his objective. I know he would like to have a career in journalism. So, he needs to make up his mind sooner or later." Then, to everyone's astonishment, he added, "Patrick has all the assets to become the goalie of the next decade. He will have to polish his style and technique, but as for the rest, he has all the qualities to make it in the National Hockey League. I particularly like his aggressiveness and speed of execution." Don't forget it was 1985. Patrick had played only one period in the NHL and, for that matter, only one game in the AHL. Was Allaire clairvoyant? How could he be so sure of his assessment and judgment?

Something occurred in game four that might well have changed the course of the series for the Canadiens. It certainly moved Patrick closer to his destiny. He had been assigned to back up Greg Moffett. During the day, Paul Pageau's wife, Carole, had given birth to a baby daughter. Pageau had spent the day at the hospital; he didn't have his mind on hockey.

Midway through the game, riding their momentum, the Express had already established a 3–0 lead. Suddenly Moffett skated over to the bench. A leg-pad strap had broken. This was the chance Patrick had been waiting for. He stepped in for Moffett, buoyed by the cheers of the crowd. Within minutes, the atmosphere in the Palais des sports changed, and the momentum swung in the Canadiens' favor. The Express stepped up the pressure to expose the rookie, but Patrick stood tall, making save after save. Eventually, it was the Canadiens who scored. Twice.

With the score 3–2, Moffett emerged from the dressing room. The strap had been repaired and he was eager to get back in the game. Behind the bench, Creamer glanced at assistant coach Jean Hamel and then spoke to François Allaire over the headphones. What do we do, François? Moffett is ready to go in." This wasn't the first time Moffett's equipment had broken at an opportune moment when things were going badly. Allaire recalled that it had already happened a few times that season. He knew it was an incredible opportunity to use Patrick in the series without the coaching staff incurring criticism. The young man, Allaire reasoned, was the club's best goaltender, despite his youth and inexperience. "We keep the kid. He hasn't given up a goal, he's making the saves, he's doing well: we keep the kid." That was a turning point, not only in the game, but also in the series. Moffett didn't get another start.

In the third period, Patrick wasn't content just to make many spectacular saves. He did everything he could to goad the Express into taking penalties. First he needled the huge Yvon Vautour. Then, he got under Grant Martin's skin so much that the left winger slashed him right in front of the referee and was promptly banished to the penalty box. With Martin off, the Canadiens tied the score. Before regulation time ended, the teams traded goals, so the teams remained level. The Canadiens had tallied three of their five goals on the power play. It took 31 minutes and 20 seconds of overtime for the Habs to score again and notch their third victory in the best of seven series. In the winners' dressing room, Patrick was beaming. "The crowd cheered for me when I went into the game, and that gave me confidence. In the third, I wanted to make the Express take penalties to throw them off their game, and I think I succeeded." Now, the Express were up against the ropes. The mood in the Canadiens' dressing room was buoyant. Pageau, sporting a smile a mile wide, handed out cigars.

The Canadiens needed two more games to oust the Express. Sherbrooke lost 3–1 in Fredericton but won game six in overtime by a count of 4–3 on April 22 in Sherbrooke.

On May 1, the semifinal got under way between the Sherbrooke Canadiens and the Maine Mariners. Patrick didn't play the first game. The Montréal Canadiens had called him up for a series with the Québec Nordiques. It was a precautionary measure necessitated by Steve Penney's doubtful status due to back spasms.

On his day off after knocking the Express out of the playoffs, Patrick went to the Saint-Sacrement recreation center in Québec City to see a show by some friends who did comic impersonations. He told us how to contact him in case the Canadiens' management tried to reach him. The call came around 11:30 p.m.

He felt up to the task. "I think I can help the club if they need me," he said. "I'm ready to give 100%. I made a lot of progress last month in Sherbrooke, more than I had all season. We've just beaten the Nordiques farm club, we need to do the same to the big club!"

In the end, Penney returned and Patrick didn't get to play. He left Montréal as quickly as he could, but rejoined the farm club too late to work the first game of the series at the Portland Civic Center. Paul Pageau subbed for him in a 5–2 defeat.

The second and third games belonged to Patrick, who was chosen first star in each. Although he faced nearly twice as many shots as his opposite number, Sam St-Laurent, the Canadiens won decisively by the scores of 9–2 and 7–3. When a reporter remarked that he had gotten used to handling a blizzard of shots with the Bisons, Patrick said, "There's no comparison. In Granby, I was getting bombarded; I didn't stand a chance. Here the shots are coming from different angles or from the slot. I make the save and the defensemen jump on the rebound. It's easier that way."

Others waxed enthusiastic. *"Lui, y goale en tabarnak"!* ("He's one hell of a goalie!"), said John Ferguson in his colorful mixture of French and English, pointing to Patrick, who was setting up in goal. Ferguson was the General Manager of the NHL's Winnipeg Jets, who co-managed the Sherbrooke farm club with the Canadiens. He had come to see how some of his players were progressing. Poor "Fergie"! He would have liked to get his hands on Patrick in the last amateur draft, but he had traded his third-round choice, the 51st overall, to his old pal Serge Savard. Ferguson had only himself to blame. He had known the Canadiens were the only ones who could select Patrick before the Jets. After scouting him in Granby, Ferguson had been itching to draft him. He went on to say that Sherbrooke fans should take advantage of the opportunity to see Patrick play in the series because, next year, they might have to be satisfied with watching him on TV.

Mariners coach Tom McVie had a few words of praise for Patrick. After losing 7–3, in a game in which his charges outshot Sherbrooke 51 to 19 (23 to 5 in the first period alone), he said, "I must admit that this young Roy is fantastic. They called Ken Dryden an octopus, but

I've never seen a guy sweep up the puck like Roy. If we'd switched goalies, we would have won 15–1."

Even Greg Moffett, who had lost his number one slot to Patrick after starring in the beginning of the series against the Express, modestly admitted, "Patrick is playing amazing hockey. He's made me acknowledge his talent and swallow my words. It's a bit difficult to accept, but when you see him play, you have to admit that he deserves to be where he is. I no longer have any doubt. He's a heck of a goaltender. Just look at how talented he is at 19 years of age; I was starting college at that age … some years back. … As long as he keeps playing like that, I can't be unhappy."

Sherbrooke hosted game four. The Mariners played the intimidation card. Alan Stewart gave Patrick a cheap shot behind the Sherbrooke goal, hoping to knock him out of the game. But the tactic failed, and the Mariners went down to their third straight defeat. They had tried everything, but to no avail. The series ended on May 8 when the Canadiens won 6–5 in Portland.

Meanwhile, the Nordiques' Peter Stastny beat Steve Penney in overtime to eliminate the Canadiens at the Montréal Forum.

—◊◊◊—

Against all odds, the Sherbrooke Canadiens reached the Calder Cup finals against the Baltimore Skipjacks. I say "against all odds" because in the regular season, the Canadiens had finished sixth, 19 points behind Baltimore.

The Skipjacks could be intimidating. They had just swept the first-place Binghamton Whalers, who had topped the Canadiens by over 33 points. And they had a few players who could stir things up. To give some idea of the picture, Steve Carlson was Baltimore's captain. He had played one of the not-so-subtle Hanson brothers in the movie *Slapshot* with Paul Newman. Carlson's comrades-in-arms included Bennett Wolf, with 285 minutes in penalties, Marty McSorley, Phil Bourke, Dean De Fazio and Ted Bulley, all of them considerably less sophisticated than Paul Newman. The Skipjacks also had solid goaltending. On loan from the Minnesota North Stars, Jon Casey combined the best goals-against average in the American Hockey League with an excellent 0.908 save percentage. His backup was the veteran Granby native Michel Dion, who had acquired a few years' NHL experience with the Québec Nordiques and the Pittsburgh Penguins. The Skipjacks were affiliated with the Penguins and wore their colors: ironically, it was the same uniform that Patrick had worn with the Granby Bisons.

Even before the cup final got under way, coach Gene Ubriaco made a statement that did nothing to dispel his team's reputation for arrogance. He opined that he wouldn't be surprised if his charges needed more than four games to beat Sherbrooke. This undoubtedly "detailed" and "profound" analysis underestimated the presence of Stéphane Richer and Patrick, who not only strengthened the squad but also helped spark the veterans. It wasn't the same team. Ubriaco didn't have to wait long to see his assessment disproved. The Canadiens won the first two games in Baltimore by the identical score of 4–3. It was Sherbrooke's first victory at the Civic Center in two years. Ubriaco could have invoked the rule preventing a goalie called up from the juniors from playing, unless a regular netminder couldn't play because of sickness or injury. He didn't. He was so confident! What could the Canadiens do against his powerhouse with a rookie in the net?

The rookie courted disaster in the first game as the result of a rookie mistake. The previous day, in Sherbrooke, after the morning workout, his catching mitt and blocker had been put in an unusual place—behind the dryer—so they would dry faster and thoroughly. In Baltimore the next day, equipment manager Pierre Gervais, looked sheepish.

"Pat, I have to talk to you."

"What's the matter?"

"Your gloves are back in Sherbrooke."

"What?"

"Yeah, the guy who packed your gear before we left didn't realize your gloves were behind the dryer. We forgot to go and get them before leaving."

"What do you suggest?'

"Look, I got the Skipjacks to lend us some old pair of gloves that belong to Michel Dion. Would you like to try them out in practice this morning?"

Patrick held the mitts, examined them, felt them. They looked like a pair of dusty old slippers from a garage sale. In the end, he decided to borrow Greg Moffett's gloves.

It was something to see Patrick and Moffett passing the gloves to each other as they went into the net to take shots during the pre-game warm-up. For a game in the AHL finals, it was surrealistic. Imagine Patrick in Baltimore without his catching mitt "Charlotte." It forgave him because he was almost as good with Moffett's mitt, earning first star in the match. But "Charlotte" hurried to join him by the next flight.

In the same game, another disaster might have happened. The less-than-elegant Skipjacks winger Dean De Fazio nearly ended the remarkable goaltenders' duel between Casey and Patrick when he charged into the Sherbrooke netminder at full speed. Patrick was bending down in his net. He collapsed under the impact like a sandbag and lost his helmet. As he fell, his head struck a goal post, and he lay motionless for quite a while. Then, to his teammates' great relief, he got up and was able to carry on, though he was seeing stars.

With the Montréal Canadiens out of the playoffs, some of the Montréal brain trust had traveled to Baltimore: President Ronald

Corey, GM Serge Savard, Coach Jacques Lemaire and his assistants, Jean Perron and Jacques Laperrière. At one point, on the catwalk from where he was watching the game, Perron murmured, "He'll be our goalie next year. He's ready for the NHL; we need him."

But there was no way a solid crew like the Skipjacks would throw in the towel. In the first game in Sherbrooke, they stepped up with a 5–3 win thanks to a sparkling performance by Michel Dion, who was relieving Jon Casey. But in the second contest, Stéphane Richer took things in hand and changed the momentum and led the Canadiens to a 6–1 victory.

The Skipjacks had their backs against the ropes. Realizing the championship was slipping through their fingers, Ubriaco belatedly pointed out that according to the rules, Patrick could not suit up with the Canadiens unless Moffett or Pageau were injured. "We have checked and neither Pageau nor Moffett are injured. They say Moffett has a back injury but we've seen him working out with weights. Can you do that kind of exercise if you've got a bad back?" He even contacted AHL Vice President Gordon Anziano, asking him if he could confirm that the two regular goalies of the Canadiens were injured. Dr. Farrar, the Canadiens physician, confirmed that Moffett was indeed suffering from a bad back.

Ubriaco panicked. Nevertheless, his team managed to win the next game in Baltimore 6–2.

—⁂—

The table was set for the Sherbrooke Canadiens. Leading three games to two in the series, they had a chance to wrap it up on Friday, May 24 at home, in the Palais des sports. There was no question of risking losing the championship in a seventh game in Baltimore. They had to win in Sherbrooke. It was now or never.

For the first two periods, the issue was in doubt. Both sides squandered scoring chances. Patrick made 18 saves; Dion made 13.

Neither team managed to put the puck in the net. Michel Dion—Ubriaco was banking on experience—and Patrick were unbeatable.

Baltimore controlled the beginning of the third period. They forced the play and were hungrier than the Canadiens. The Skipjacks were fighting for their survival. Their efforts paid off. Tim Tookey broke free on right wing, then cut quickly to the left in front of Gaston Gingras, who couldn't stop him from getting into the slot, and his hard shot beat Patrick on the stick side. Patrick could do nothing to stop it. It was an important goal, the first of the contest, late in the game at 2:29 of the third period. The fans were stunned.

The Canadiens had no choice. They had to go on the attack, throw caution to the wind, even if it meant neglecting defense. Patrick had to come up with brilliant saves on breakaways by Dan McCarthy, Bob Errey and Arto Javanainen. The saves seemed to stimulate his teammates and, by mid-period, the scoring chances were more evenly divided. At 11:49, Brian Skrudland deflected a Ric Nattress shot from the point, tying the score. Then at 16:28, Stéphane Richer jumped on a loose puck in the neutral zone, streaked into the Baltimore zone, pivoted in front of defenseman Bryan Maxwell, skated back toward Tim Tookey, beat him with ease, and then blazed a slap shot past Michel Dion into the top right corner of the net.

There was slightly more than three minutes remaining in the game. The fans were ecstatic. Serge Savard, attending the game with the other members of the Habs management team, took a puff on his cigar. Sitting beside him, Georges Guilbault breathed a sigh of relief. He had spared no effort and had shown audacity in giving fans in the region a professional team.

The Skipjacks pulled the goalie in favor of a sixth attacker. With three seconds left, Mike Lalor shot the puck from his zone into the empty net, ending the Skipjacks hopes. With their Calder Cup victory, the Canadiens became the first Québec team to win the championship in the 49 years of AHL existence.

The die was cast. As the remaining few seconds ticked away, the fans tossed all kinds of objects onto the ice. Guilbault turned to Savard and held out his hand to thank him for transferring the franchise to Sherbrooke. "Thanks, Serge." Savard could hardly hear him. Powerful speakers blared out "We are the Champions" by the British band Queen, the hit that has become a victory anthem.

Then all the players jumped onto the ice and rushed over to congratulate Patrick. Some fans did the same. It was chaos on the ice. While the players were hugging, high-fiving and backslapping, young people tried to carry off a stick, a glove or a helmet as a souvenir. The fans that were still in the stands were on their feet, shouting, singing, jumping up and down, stomping—delirious. Patrick took a moment to go into the dressing room and put "Charlotte" and his blocker safely out of the reach of the young celebrants. Then he joined his teammates in a victory lap around the rink. A reporter remarked that Patrick had been through some tense moments that season. Patrick said, "Yes, that's true, but at the same time, for me the Calder Cup makes up for the Memorial Cup, which I didn't have a chance to win with the Bisons. In a way, its makes up for my three seasons with the Bisons."

I was at the game with Alexandra. Barbara had also made the trip to Sherbrooke, but a terrible migraine had forced her to stay behind in the motel. I'm always impressed with people who win by surpassing themselves, going beyond their limits, especially if they overcome numerous obstacles on the way. But when it is an athlete, it is all the more dramatic and moving, particularly when it is your son. There was a lump in my throat filled with all the disappointments Patrick and I had endured, all the hopes we had entertained, all the time spent shivering in arenas, the weekends when we had to get up at dawn, the hockey and baseball tournaments, all of it. Only pride kept the tears back. I turned to Alexandra, who squeezed my arm and snuggled up to me. Tears were rolling down her cheeks.

We would have given anything for some sign from Patrick. Anything. A look, a wink, a gesture, anything to acknowledge the bond between us since the long quest began. Sure, it wasn't our victory, but somehow, we felt we had left a little of ourselves along the way, that we had something to do with it.

Not a sign, nothing. Maybe Patrick hadn't spotted us in the stands. Maybe he was too busy sharing his emotions with teammates, answering the reporters who were chasing after him. Or maybe he was too busy eluding fans swarming around him. Though they really had no connection with him, they were grabbing him by the neck, patting him on the shoulder, running their fingers through his hair. We felt lonely, cruelly alone amidst a throng of 5,125 fans whooping it up. We were alone with our emotions that we couldn't share with the fans; they wouldn't understand. Queen kept singing.

Amid the hubbub, a red carpet was rolled out at center ice. Then AHL Vice-President Anziano presented the Calder Cup to Canadiens captain Brian Skrudland. Just before that, Jack Butterfield, the president of the American Hockey League, had awarded him the Jack A. Butterfield Trophy as the series MVP. Skrudland was Sherbrooke's captain; he was a warrior; he had spent the entire season with the team. No doubt, he deserved the honor. But, François Allaire knew, the players knew, and many others knew, that Patrick was the one player who had made the difference.

But for a birth and a busted equipment strap . . .

THE REAL CHALLENGE 14

After a summer of lazing around and playing softball for Auberge Caroussel in Val-Bélair, and being ribbed by the Doyons—Ti-Guy had taped a picture of Nordiques goaltender Mario Gosselin on the fridge—Patrick showed up at the Canadiens training camp in August 1985. The moment of truth would soon arrive. He was determined. "I'm going to Montréal with one aim: to earn a spot with the Big Club this season." But to do so, to become Steve Penney's backup, he had to beat out Doug Soetaert in training camp.

In September of 1985, the team's goaltending situation was as follows: Steve Penney was considered the organization's Number 1 goalie and his position was assured in the short term. Very little attention would be given to him during training camp; he was a known quantity. Yet some of the brass, conscious of Penney's limitations, were reluctant to make a long-term commitment to him. After all, François Allaire had labeled Patrick "the goalie of the next decade" just a few short months before.

Doug Soetaert had just renewed his contract with the Canadiens. He was the insurance policy; he had the much-needed experience, just in case Penney collapsed and Patrick didn't live up to expectations. Soetaert, Penney's backup the previous season, had shown his bosses that he was more than up to the task.

Patrick was in a favorable position. He had displayed great potential at the previous camp, by beating the Oilers and the Nordiques. His play with the Sherbrooke Canadiens in the Calder Cup series had impressed everyone. He represented the future between the posts. But Patrick knew that a young goalie's reputation is only as good as his last performance. When the next game comes, he has to start all over. "Everything will be decided during training camp," he said.

He didn't know how right he was. To add to the pressure, Serge Savard and new head coach Jean Perron had both come out against the three-goalie system. Perron remarked a number of times, "There's no question of keeping three goalies in Montréal. Experience has clearly shown that this approach has never worked. The third-string goalie can't stay game fit and can't be effective when we need him." The message was clear: goalie number three would be shunted off to Sherbrooke in the American League. Patrick had to compete with Doug Soetaert, to see who would stay on with the Montréal Canadiens. And Patrick had to get along without François Allaire, who had gone back to Sherbrooke after rookie camp.

On-ice performance would ultimately determine the winner, but both goaltenders attacked each other through the media. Soetaert said he had heard that Roy had performed brilliantly at the end of the season in the American Hockey League, but he wondered whether the young goalie could do as well in the pros. Soetaert reminded people that the caliber of play in the NHL is much superior to the level found in Junior Hockey and the AHL.

Patrick replied, "Last year, Penney needed to be backed up by an experienced goalie. This isn't the case any more. Penney proved we can have complete confidence in him."

The battle had been joined, and Perron fueled it by setting down a few ground rules. To him, Patrick's youth was not a handicap. "We used to say that goalies took longer than their teammates to develop. But the perception has changed. Today, shots come from every angle, with more puck movement and more power. In this context, a young goalie who doesn't get cold feet can manage quite well." He went on to describe what he expected of a backup goalie. "I want a second goalie who is going to challenge the first. I think that Penney will be better for it."

Soetaert and Patrick had three weeks, the length of the training camp, to show that they had the stuff Perron was looking for.

—⚅—

The team was getting ready for the first road game of the pre-season. Patrick entered the dressing room. He had been out shopping. The year before, he had sometimes been broke. Once, while in Sherbrooke, he had to borrow money from Pierre Gervais to visit his girlfriend in Québec City. He had splashed the cash on the purchase of his Prelude and had nothing left for gas.

So when he received his check from the Canadiens, he decided to treat himself to some new clothes. Though he went shopping by himself, he made some good purchases: a navy blue jacket, steel gray pants, a white shirt and a red tie. This was the same outfit I used to wear, 30 years before, when I went to Jesuit College. Except that, in the Canadiens dressing room, he stuck out like a sore thumb with his goody-two-shoes, wearing-the-uniform-for-the-first-time look. Especially with a jacket that was a size too big for him.

Team trainer Gaétan Lefebvre just had to laugh when he took a look at how this long beanpole was dressed and how he walked. "He looks like a *casseau*," Lefebvre told Larry Robinson, who cracked up. And the moniker caught on. First the Francophones, then the Anglophones, started calling him *Casseau* in the dressing room.

Later, it was said that the nickname was given to him because of the *casseaux* or baskets of French fries that he loved. That wasn't it at all. Gaétan Lefebvre was referring to the awkward or *cassé* manner in which the lanky youth walked. The nickname would stick with him for a long time.

—⁓—

Soetaert was chosen for the first test in his hometown of Edmonton against the mighty Oilers. Even though he gave up six goals he played quite well. After all, he faced 42 shots, and it was thanks to his end-of-game heroics that the Canadiens left Edmonton with a 7–6 victory. Two days later, Patrick got the call against the Jets in Winnipeg. Perron's game-day comments were revealing: "I'm quite excited to see what Patrick can do. He's facing an offensive team, a club that has one of the best players in the league, Dale Hawerchuk. I'm anxious to see how Patrick performs after his impressive work last year in the American League. Will I see the same ability, the same inspiration?"

He did. After 42 shots on goal, the same number that Soetaert faced the night before, including 17 shots in the third period and a Dale Hawerchuk penalty shot that he managed to stop, the Canadiens escaped Winnipeg with a 3–3 tie. It was a reassuring performance for Perron … and for Patrick. Yet the trip hadn't resolved a thing. Both goalies had passed their first test.

According to Canadiens tradition, goalies shared a hotel room on road trips, so Soetaert and Patrick spent a good deal of time together that weekend. It was a peculiar situation: they weren't just teammates; they were rivals fighting for the same job. Of course, Soetaert and Patrick wanted to defeat the Oilers and the Jets, but it was even more important for each of them to beat out his real rival, his roommate. To journalists, who enjoyed this type of situation,

Patrick confided, "We respect each other and our objective is to play the best possible hockey. But in the room, we don't talk about these things. Nothing about hockey, nothing about the situation, no teasing. The competition takes place on the ice, not off it. One of us will have to go to Sherbrooke; I don't want to be the one."

Less than a week after training camp began, the situation evolved. Perhaps Perron was hoping to light a fire under his top goalie, who didn't need to fight for his job and was working relatively stress-free away from the eye of the media. At any rate, the coach certainly caught people's attention when he said, "Penney was the Number 1 goalie before training camp. Now that's all over and done with. We need goalies that are ready to fight to be Number 1. Everyone's position is up for grabs, and Steve knows it." He added, "I don't want a backup goalie who settles for second string. The Number 1 goalie? You'll know who that is when we play the opening game of the season in Pittsburgh." Suddenly, as a result of Perron's strategy, all three goalies were forced to work harder in an atmosphere of intense competition.

Soetaert and Patrick played hard on every occasion. Any sign of weakness could prove fatal to their chances. A brilliant performance would not escape the coaching staff's notice. Soetaert got the call for the next game against the Nordiques at the Québec Colisée. Tensions always ran high whenever the Nordiques and the Canadiens met, even in exhibition games. Reporters lavished more ink than usual. Hockey fans in both cities were feverish with anticipation. They hungered for every tidbit of information about the two teams and would pump themselves up against the other team. Rivalry between the fans attained new heights. And the pressure on the players, especially on the goaltenders, followed suit. A strong performance by Soetaert could help him avoid demotion to Sherbrooke.

Aware of the significance of the game, he was working hard in practice the previous day when Brian Skrudland ripped a hard shot that sneaked between his neck-guard and helmet and struck him in the throat. He crumpled to the ice, writhing in pain. Although he got up under his own power a few minutes later, he seemed dazed and had to leave for the dressing room. Suddenly, it was Patrick who was going to face the Nordiques. "I'm more confident in my abilities this season, and I think that this game will let me prove my worth, and impress those who will be making the decision about my future."

He proved what he could do. The Canadiens were outshot 33 to 24, but they left Québec City with a 6–1 victory. Patrick, the first star of the game, gave an impressive performance and lost the shutout only four seconds before the end of the game. Craig Ludwig, the powerful Habs defenseman, remarked, "For a guy who's trying to win a job, he's sure going about it the right way. You'd have to say he didn't play an ordinary game. Every game we play in front of him, we get more confident. We know he's going to make the first save."

Jean Perron was quick to reply when asked if he would risk putting a 20-year-old in goal, "You can bet on it. If he can prove to me that he's the best, he'll get a lot of ice time." Pleased to see that Patrick had regained the outstanding form he had shown in the Calder Cup series, Perron added, "I don't care what other people say. The guy who led Sherbrooke to the championship was Patrick. He's got talent. A lot of it." Perron went on to say that before the Nordiques game, he had given Patrick some pointers about dealing with the Stastny brothers when the Habs were killing a penalty. A few minutes later, Patrick returned to Perron's office and said he hadn't quite understood. Perron appreciated the gesture. "That shows me that a player wants to raise his game. He doesn't shy away from asking for help. I watched him during the game and I can tell you that he applied everything we talked about."

Patrick didn't assume he had the position wrapped up. "Mr. Perron wants someone to challenge the Number 1 goalie. I've got the message. I don't necessarily want to be Number 1 or Number 2. I want to be part of the 1985–1986 Canadiens. I don't consider myself a goaltender with exceptional skill. My success is a direct result of the effort I've put in. If I work hard in practice, it only makes sense to assume I'll play well in games. I want to prove that I can play for this team."

For the goaltenders, the training camp continued in much the same fashion until the end. Except for one bad game against Boston at the Forum where Soetaert allowed five goals in less than 29 minutes, he turned in good performances. Yet Patrick always found a way to top him. In fact, Steve Penney, who had the least weight on his shoulders, had the most disappointing camp. Given the situation, Perron changed his strategy. It seemed less and less likely that one of the three goalies was going to be sent back to Sherbrooke before the beginning of the season.

On Saturday, October 5, Patrick's birthday, there were very encouraging comments in the media. First it seemed Perron had done an about-turn. He said he was considering starting the season with three goalies after all. "I think, the beginning of the season might last a while …" Perhaps Patrick's rival, Doug Soetaert, was hoping that the favorable light in which Patrick was viewed would reflect back on him, when he said, "I'm happy that Patrick has enjoyed a good training camp. He doesn't deserve to be sent back to Sherbrooke, any more than I do." Finally, Red Fisher, the influential journalist and sports editor of *The Gazette*, complimented Patrick in glowing terms in his daily review. "A training camp doesn't represent a season but there is at least one reason to believe that the Canadiens will be blessed with its best goaltending since the Ken Dryden championship years. The reason: Patrick Roy." Was Fisher just a good analyst or did he possess, like François Allaire before him, the gift of clairvoyance?

The Canadiens had one last game to play before the start of the regular season. A meeting with the Nordiques at the Montréal Forum on Sunday, October 6. It was a contest that Perron was determined to win at all cost to send a message to his main rivals. In a 4–3 victory, Patrick was in goal for the entire game, though Soetaert was supposed to take over midway through the match. "When I saw the Nordiques had gained the momentum after their second goal," Perron explained, "I decided I wanted to continue with Roy. It was a game I wanted to win." Patrick more than rose to the occasion and earned first star honors. He stopped 27 shots, compared with the 19 shots leveled at Nordiques goaltenders Richard Sévigny and Mario Gosselin, whose photo still adorned the Doyons' fridge.

The next day, Perron made the final cuts. Claude Lemieux, John Kordic, Dominic Campedelli and Alfie Turcotte packed their bags and headed to Sherbrooke. Patrick was not part of the group. He had brilliantly achieved his first objective. He would be starting the 1985–86 season with the Montréal Canadiens as a regular player. But for how long? For a young goaltender, a rookie, nothing is certain. If any chinks were found in his armor, he could be shipped back to Sherbrooke, to be recalled later if necessary. His coaches controlled his destiny. Only consistently outstanding performances would ensure his stay in Montréal. But so far, everything was going well.

—⚬—

On October 10, the Canadiens opened the season in Pittsburgh against Mario Lemieux's Penguins. The previous day, before leaving the Forum after practice, the following conversation took place.

"Who's in the nets in Pittsburgh?" Patrick asked.

"I haven't made up my mind," Perron replied.

Later that night at the team dinner, Patrick was told he was Perron's choice.

"There was no reaction from him," Perron said later. "He expected it. From the start of training camp, I said I would go with my best goaltender from game to game, and he was the best. I knew he felt that way when he asked me who would be in the nets. The other two didn't ask."

I've always thought that it was vital for a goaltender to know well in advance whether or not he would be playing. More than any other player, a goalie must get ready for the contest. Just like a boxer, he must carefully analyze the opponent's strengths and weaknesses. He must study on video the style of play of the four lines he'll be facing and the star players' habits. He must also figure out the kinds of shots he'll be facing from the defensemen. This analysis should be done on the day before the game rather than on game day. That way, the brain has time to assimilate the information, and the next day, the goalie can concentrate entirely on the play.

When Patrick was young, I taught him a visualization technique that consists of providing the subconscious with information so that the subconscious continues to prepare for the game while he is asleep at night. Patrick once startled a reporter by saying, "When I lie in bed before going to sleep, I go over in my mind the way my opponent plays and visualize his reactions. I see myself facing the shot, I react to my opponent's dekes, I anticipate what he intends to do, I move, I cover my angles ... as if I was actually playing. Sometimes, in my head, they score on me. I want to see myself react calmly, take the puck out of the net to show my teammates that I haven't been rattled and that I'll come back stronger than ever. I want something positive to come out of every negative situation. And reacting well after giving up a goal can have a positive effect on a hockey team." The next day, on the ice, there wouldn't be any surprises. Everything would seem somehow familiar, like *déjà-vu*.

Starting Patrick in the first game of the season was not a simple decision, especially since Perron had declared that the goalie who played the opening match could be considered the Number 1 netminder. Steve Penney found it hard to swallow, even though he had had an ordinary training camp and had recently been troubled by a slight knee problem. Yet Perron's plan was almost undone by a misunderstanding.

There had been some confusion about the morning skate time. According to the team schedule, the practice was slated to begin at 11:30 a.m., but Perron had second thoughts and informed the team, when it arrived in Pittsburgh, that the practice would start an hour earlier. Some of the players, Patrick among them, hadn't heard the coach. He had gone back to his room after breakfast, and was enjoying a few quiet moments at the start of a day in which he would be playing his first regular-season game in the NHL.

"Where's Patrick Roy?" asked Perron when he arrived at the arena.

"We just called him at the hotel; he'll be on the ice in a few minutes," said André Boudrias.

It was Patrick's first trip to Pittsburgh. The Civic Center was just a 15-minute walk from the team's hotel, but he didn't know how to get to the arena. He was alone in his room, so nobody could take him there. Quite concerned, he decided to go down to the street, hoping to find some indication on how to get to the Center. His superficial knowledge of English made asking directions a last resort. Luckily, he ran into Craig Ludwig and Chris Chelios, who had also missed the change in schedule. The three of them arrived late and were obliged to explain themselves to Serge Savard. The incident was put down to a lack of communication and soon forgotten.

Perron had no reason to regret his decision to start Patrick. He made the difference in a 5–3 Canadiens victory. He had just won his first NHL game. Mike Bullard was the first player to score on him and Mario Lemieux put a shot past him too. With the victory, the team had started off on the right foot. But like the team, the season was still very young.

—⁂—

In 1983, at the request of the Canadiens' president, Ronald Corey, Serge Savard took the team under his wing as General Manager, succeeding Irving Grundman. Savard gave himself five years to build a team that would bring the Stanley Cup back to Montréal. The 1985–86 season was year three of his plan. With a new coach and seven rookies in the lineup, Montréal was in a rebuilding phase. No one in senior management was expecting anything other than continued progress and development. The ultimate victory would come later.

Then, to everyone's surprise, Jacques Lemaire tendered his resignation in July 1985. For Savard, it was as if the sky had fallen. Lemaire suggested Jean Perron as his successor.

The choice did not create consensus among the players, especially the veterans. They had enormous respect for Lemaire; they trusted him. He had an impressive track record as a player. He'd returned from his coaching internship in Europe with modern coaching methods, which he'd tested with the Longueuil Chevaliers in the QMJHL. The players appreciated Lemaire's approach. His resignation meant everything had to start over.

Perron had never played in the NHL. He was from the university circuit, where he had coached the University of Moncton Blue Eagles. He had also served as Dave King's assistant in the Canadian Olympic program. The fact that he had guided a university team to two national championships didn't impress the veterans. They liked him well enough as an assistant and a technician, but having Perron as head coach was something else entirely, they thought. Perron would have a hard time being accepted.

To complicate matters, he had to fill seven regular positions with rookies, something that worried the veterans. It was clear now that it would take time for the mortar to dry, for team spirit to grow, and for the team to stabilize.

Given the situation, Patrick would have to fight to maintain his place on the Habs' roster. It was especially important that he consistently play well. The slightest weakness could dramatically impact his season.

—m—

Yet he lost his next three games, including a 7–2 defeat against the Bruins in Boston. It was only later on that Patrick admitted that the crushing defeat had shaken his confidence. Rattled, he had started to flop down too early. Perron criticized him for that.

As if Patrick didn't have enough pressure on him already, Denis Herron, the veteran 33-year-old goalie, who had been in the doghouse with the Penguins (they were trying to get rid of him), publicly attacked Patrick for no good reason. "I don't understand why Perron has so much confidence in Roy. He goes down too often and you can see the flaws in his technique."

Angered, Patrick replied, "I really don't know what he's trying to achieve with comments like these. Anyway, you can't please everyone. This is my first season in the league and I'm no superman. I have weaknesses and I'm working on them. In the meantime, I have a coach who's encouraging me."

Patrick also found support in Ken Dryden. Passing through Montréal for the unveiling of a statue in his honor at Place Vertu Mall, Dryden talked about his old team's goaltending situation. "As time goes by, my reputation seems to grow. The fans and journalists seem to have forgotten the bad goals I allowed. Maybe it would be best to try and do the same with the current goalies. Let's not forget that I had quite a team in front of me."

Penney and Soetaert were faring little better than Patrick at that stage of the season. The three goalies, used in rotation, gave up 55 goals in 11 games, an average of five per game—a catastrophe in Montréal. Perron had to twist Savard's arm to keep Patrick in the lineup.

"I want to keep Patrick. He needs to stay here," Perron said firmly.

Savard couldn't believe what he'd just heard. "Listen, Jean, we're not amateurs; this is professional hockey," he said. "You can't have three goalies, it's never been done in the NHL."

"We're going to have François Allaire come here from time to time to take care of him."

"All right, but he still won't be used enough."

"How many games does he need?"

"At least 35."

"All right then, I'm going to give him 35 games."

Happenstance sometimes plays a role in situations like these. Often Soetaert or Penney were injured or ill when Perron wanted to start Patrick, as was the case in the opening game of the season in Pittsburgh. So by the end of the season, Patrick played a total of 47 games.

In early November, just before the team was to leave to play five games on a ten-day road-trip, Perron became impatient. "Guy Carbonneau is right when he says that if we make the slightest error, we get scored on. The goalies will have to come up with the big saves, the saves we need to fire up our team. After this road trip, I'll know who'll be our Number 1, Number 2 and Number 3 goalies. We can't wait any longer. We're working like mad and getting nowhere. We have to find a solution. We can't go on like this."

Perron could never have guessed that the trip would go so well, the three goaltenders would shine, and the team would come back with seven points out of a possible ten. Patrick won in Hartford and Long Island; Soetaert shut out the Kings in Los Angeles. And Penney, despite tying in Minnesota and losing in New York, turned in solid performances.

Patrick's victory against the Islanders was particularly significant. The night before, Pierre Lacroix, his agent, had called him to say, "If you're ever going to have a big game, tomorrow would be the time." Patrick understood this to mean that if he had a bad performance in Long Island he would be sent back to Sherbrooke. That's exactly what many people close to the team thought. And that's all he needed to be motivated. The Canadiens had not won at the Nassau Coliseum in ages, and the Islanders were a potent offensive force with players like Mike Bossy, Pat LaFontaine and Bryan Trottier. Perron had said as much: "The Islanders are a huge challenge. It will be harder than the three previous games on the trip. The Islanders are a veteran team, tough to beat at home."

Patrick had a sparkling performance in a 3–2 victory. He made numerous miraculous saves—"Charlotte" never let him down—stopping 30 shots and earning the first star. He had just discouraged any thought of shipping him back to Sherbrooke. But for how long?

Penney and Soeteart, roommates on the entire trip, had a good run. They played well enough to put pressure on the managers to break up the goalie trio. After his shutout in Los Angeles, Soeteart revealed that Penney and he had discussed the roles they could play for the team. "We talked about last year, when we finished fourth in goals-against," said Soetaert. "We talked about what has been going on so far this year … a lot of things. And what it comes down to is that we've become closer as teammates this past week than we were all of last year."

More direct, Penney said, "I'm not the boss. I play when I'm told to play, but when you play only once a week, there's no question that a goaltender loses his rhythm. Another thing, there's not enough work for three goaltenders in practices."

Alone in his room, Patrick had only one thing to do with his time: prepare for the next game.

—⁊⁊—

While all this was taking place, a much more serious event occurred. On November 12, Pelle Lindbergh, the Philadelphia Flyer's goalie, whose video had been given to Patrick so he could study the "stand-up" style, died at the wheel of his Porsche 930. Too much alcohol, too much speed and a curve that came up too quickly. He was 26 years old.

In the Habs dressing room, no one was more affected than Lindbergh's countryman, Mats Naslund, who, at the age of 16, was his teammate on Sweden's national team.

—⁊⁊—

Back in Montréal, Perron confirmed that Patrick's efforts wholly justified his presence on the team. "I'd be dishonest to send Roy to Sherbrooke. I can't do it. I did make a decision, though: no more rotation. From now on, I want one of the three goalies to earn more responsibility."

Larry Robinson knocked on Perron's door. "Hey, coach! The kid's pretty good! I usually score a lot of goals in practice. Against him, I don't! Even in practice, he doesn't want to let anything by." The veteran defenseman's remarks reinforced Perron's decision to use the "kid" more often.

Patrick was told that he could leave Manoir Lemoyne and find a place to live. Teammate Lucien Deblois offered him a three-and-a-half-room apartment in the basement of his triplex where he lived with his wife Lise and three children in Rosemont. This was ideal for Patrick: the apartment was clean and modern. Alone in Montréal, he was comforted by the thought of living near one of the team's veterans and his family.

Deblois liked him a lot. "Patrick is like a brother to me. He's a good kid. I showed him around the neighborhood and introduced him to my bank manager. He often goes shopping with my wife. He usually eats with the family. He loves Lise's delicious pasta. And the kids are crazy about Patrick! He's always playing hockey with them in the house and the twins are delighted. I'm sure he'll make a great dad one day."

Back in action after a shoulder operation, Mario Tremblay was assigned to room with Patrick on road trips. There really wasn't any choice, since few of the other players wanted to room with a chain smoker. Yet despite Tremblay's bad habit, Patrick enjoyed the veteran's company: Tremblay loved to spin a good yarn, entertaining Patrick with all sorts of tales and anecdotes that relaxed the goalie on game day. They became as thick as thieves, and Tremblay took the rookie under his wing. So, Patrick was in good company at home and on the road.

Before the end of December, he won another eight games, giving him a record of 11 wins and three losses since the coach had felt it necessary to take him to task early in the season. Slowly, he was earning Perron's confidence.

In Allaire's absence, Patrick accepted advice from anyone who offered it. He was gaining experience and improving. "Mr. Lemaire (Jacques Lemaire was still close to the team) explained how players hold their stick differently when they're going to shoot than when they're going to pass. This gives me an advantage when I'm facing a two-on-one or three-on-one situation and I'm wondering whether the player is going to pass or shoot. That's what happened in Toronto when three Maple Leafs came in on goal. I was able to make the save on Frycer because I knew he was about to shoot by the way he was holding the stick."

Sometimes, Perron would send videos of Patrick's games to François Allaire so he could study them and correct the goalie's technique the next time he came to Montréal. Other times, Perron relayed Allaire's suggestions to Patrick. He prepared his upcoming games with the utmost attention. The night before a game, Patrick would sit down with his coach and review all the players on the other team, pinpointing their strengths and weaknesses. By watching these videos, Patrick was not only studying opposing players, he was finding out about the rinks where he would be playing—the kind of rebound the puck would take when it hit the boards or the Plexiglas, fan reaction, the scoreboard, and so on. That way, when the game started, he was ready.

Patrick was making good progress in adapting to the NHL. The main changes he had to cope with were related to the power and precision of the shots, the speed of execution in the game, and the much larger crowds making it harder, at times, to concentrate on the game.

He was as intense as ever in practice. "I'm convinced that a hockey player plays the way he practices. I need to give 100% every day. When a player starts taking things for granted, he risks lapsing into mediocrity. To succeed, you've got to be consistent. And to be consistent, you have to give it your best shot every time."

In late 1985, Red Fisher's end-of-the-year review in the *Gazette* graded Patrick and lauded his work:

Patrick Roy (A)—Rookie Roy was the best of the goaltenders during training camp, and he remains the best during the regular season. Roy makes rookie mistakes, but when it's considered that he's been in the nets for 11 of the team's 16 victories, Canadiens management can live with his mistakes … happily. In other words, he's got the No. 1 job because he's played like a No. 1 goaltender.

Red Fisher gave Soetaert a "B," pointing out that although he had not played much, he'd been ready when called on.

Steve Penney got a "C." "He came to training camp as the team's No. 1 goaltender. He left it as the team's No. 3. In other words, it was his job to lose—and he did."

—⁂—

One morning, a dozen players, including Penney and Soetaert, were in the dressing room after practice. They were listening to some music, when the station broke for a commercial. "A goalie clinic will be given next week," blared the radio. "To sign up, just dial …"

The players cracked up. Especially when Penney pretended to be looking for a pen so he could jot down the phone number.

Of course, he was kidding, but the joke had a grain of truth. A few weeks earlier, Penney, demoralized about his performance, had got in touch with Jacques Plante in Switzerland. Penney, who believed in his former goalie coach, was so discouraged that he was ready to offer Plante a plane ticket to Montréal if the situation didn't improve. Yet, he could have called on François Allaire, close by, just 90 minutes away by car along Highway 10. Allaire was more than willing to help him and the club would have picked up the tab. But it was probably a question of confidence. Allaire hadn't proven himself … yet.

—⁂—

It was already January, and all three goaltenders were still in Montréal. For Patrick, it was as if training camp was still going on. When he had a good performance, he was praised. If he had a bad outing, he could be dispatched to Sherbrooke. The situation was no better for Soetaert and Penney.

Then Patrick made a blunder. Delayed by the filming of a TV program about his life as an athlete—the media was starting to be interested in him—he arrived a few minutes late for morning practice. He was supposed to start against the Boston Bruins that night, but Perron wouldn't let him off the hook and replaced him with Penney. A few veterans grumbled. "He just made $150 on TV and he has to pay a $200 fine." The comment was unfair because Patrick was bitterly disappointed about losing the start, not about the fine. He felt he'd let his team down after playing nearly half the games until then. "I made a mistake; I know that. And I can tell you that it won't happen again. Mr. Perron's decision is quite severe, but I'm not offering any excuses. Needless to say I feel very bad, but I guess I still have a lot to learn, don't I?"

Discontent had made its way into the dressing room, and Perron felt the need to call a meeting of "the three wise men": Captain Bob Gainey and his assistants, Mario Tremblay and Larry Robinson. They told Perron that the players, especially the defensemen, found it difficult to get used to three goalies, each with his own style and on-ice habits. So Perron met with the three netminders to let them know what he expected of them.

The result of these confabs was that Patrick was assured that he would not be sent back to Sherbrooke, Penney would be seeing enough action to atone for his lackluster start and Soetaert would be playing third fiddle, but his contract would be modified to include an indemnity as a peace offering. In a very good mood, Perron told the media that the goaltending situation was resolved. "There's no problem any more," he said. "Let's stop talking about it." At least for the time being …

That same evening, on January 15, Patrick recorded his first shutout in the National Hockey League, in a 4–0 win against the Winnipeg Jets. As it happened, the victory was achieved against Daniel Bouchard, the Jets goaltender and Patrick's childhood role model. This was the same Daniel Bouchard whose picture had adorned Patrick's locker when he played for the Sainte-Foy Gouverneurs and who gave the young goaltender one of his sticks, predicted a great career for him, and inspired the teenager to work even harder. "This is my first shutout in four years," Patrick said. "I'd have to go back to the midgets for the last one. That's why this game is so special."

He had done his best, things had worked out well and his teammates had given him good protection: he deserved the shutout. Against Bouchard? Too bad. Maybe Bouchard liked Patrick but he'd made no effort to communicate by word or gesture when the game was over. On the ice, there are no friends. Bouchard had lost; he was disappointed. That was that.

The student had eclipsed the master.

—m—

Until the beginning of March, the Canadiens' play could best be described as a roller-coaster ride. The description applied to Patrick's work, too. Yet every time he had an embarrassing performance, he would bounce back in the next game, in exceptional and sometimes spectacular fashion. That was how he avoided getting the ax.

But the month of March is a turning point in hockey season. That's when a team feels the end of the season is near and the playoffs are around the corner. The pressure on the players, especially on the goaltenders, ratchets up as the race for the championship intensifies. And teams that are out of the running for a division title battle it out to finish as high as possible in the standings to gain home ice advantage in the post-season. Others struggle just to earn a spot in the series.

It's also the time of year when fans start fretting about their team. They worry about the slightest things that affect the club and suddenly become experts in the fine art of prediction. It's also the time when they run out of patience—especially in Montréal where for years "packed" teams have intoxicated them with victory as if winning was an everyday thing. No more experiments; it's time to get down to business. It's all or nothing!

At the beginning of March 1986, the team's prospects looked bleak, especially in goal. Patrick was having a good season—for a rookie— but he had yet to prove he could be consistent enough to give the team a chance of winning in the long post-season. Some said that he gave up one soft goal a game, that he made mistakes when he left the net, that he lacked the stamina to play two games in a row. They didn't care that he was only 20, that he was a rookie who was still learning, and that all season he had been assigned the toughest missions and that Perron counted on him to take on the best clubs in the league.

Looking back, I think that most of the criticism centered on Patrick's style. In Montréal, people hadn't grown accustomed to the "butterfly" style yet. A goaltender with the stand-up style will rarely be scored on between the pads or in the upper part of his net. On the other end, he is vulnerable to low shots near either post. Montréal fans were used to goals being scored that way, rarely blamed the goalies for them and gave the credit to the shooter. By contrast, a goalie with the "butterfly" style will be nearly unbeatable on low shots near the posts, but more vulnerable to shots between the pads (the five hole) or in the upper part of the net, even if the shots have to be perfect to beat him. Unfortunately, goals scored in those spots were generally considered bad goals at the time, and the crowd wouldn't hesitate to show disapproval. Yet Patrick had adopted the "butterfly" style precisely because he had noted that over half of goals were scored on low shots. Statistics were on his side.

It was urgent for Perron to prepare two goalies for the playoffs. With Doug Soetaert on the injury shelf since mid-February with a lingering knee problem, Steve Penney got a start in the Forum against the St. Louis Blues. Though not a bad club, the Blues were certainly not a dominant force in the league. The Habs hoped Penney would once again be the goalie who'd provided stellar post-season work the two previous years, the goalie who against all expectations had stood up to opponents' fiercest onslaughts. Penney could have redeemed himself for the season he'd had, gradually regained confidence and won the Number 1 job on the eve of the playoffs. Instead he leaked goals like a sieve: six goals in 40 minutes in a 7–4 loss. The Blues notched their last tally on Patrick, who had relieved Penney in the third period.

In the next ten days, Patrick played six games, of which the team won only two. He was not used to this type of workload and was exhausted. The last game, at the Forum against the Nordiques, proved a turning point in the Canadiens' season, making it possible to identify a number of problems undermining team morale and to sort them out. The Canadiens suffered the humiliation of losing 8–6 on home territory to their fierce Québec City rivals. Michel Goulet alone scored four goals, including his 52nd of the season. The Nordiques were absolutely jubilant. It was their sixth win in eight meetings with the Canadiens that year. The Doyon household was the scene of divided loyalties.

Yet the Canadiens, pumped up for the match, jumped out to a 3–0 lead in the first eight minutes of play. Nordiques coach Michel Bergeron asked for a 30-second timeout. After that it was a different game. It belonged to the Nordiques. They outscored the Canadiens eight to three. Twelve minutes before the end, Soetaert went in for Patrick.

Soetaert's knee held up. But the same couldn't be said for the team. It had reached its lowest point in the season. The bottom of the barrel. The players felt down, frustrated and powerless. No one escaped criticism. Some veterans pointed their finger at Patrick. Others blamed the rookies. Still others targeted Perron. In short, everyone had a good excuse: a scapegoat. Not even Serge Savard was spared: the fans and the media criticized him for not making trades that would have strengthened the team before the playoffs. And since bad luck never comes alone, Mario Tremblay suffered a broken clavicle in the game. It was a career-ending injury.

Patrick was trying to get a handle on the situation. "Maybe it was one game too many for me. I've played a lot recently. I'm not used to being in so many games in a row. I'm a bit tense. I'm afraid of making mistakes. I feel that if I let in an easy goal, it will discourage my teammates. I never expected all this to happen. I've made errors; I'm well aware of it. Games like that are part of my learning process. I'm learning things every day. I know what I can do. I just need to pull myself together. I know I can do it. I did it before and I'll do it again." He sounded optimistic, but he was rattled. He needed help, three weeks before the playoffs.

He called me to talk about it. I had never been a goaltender, but I'd been carefully observing Patrick in goal for more than a dozen years, long enough to spot any bad techniques that he might have developed in the heat of action. He trusted me. I had noticed that he tended to flop to the ice in a "butterfly" position too early when he was tense, giving the shooter time to adjust his shot. I also found that he was holding "Charlotte" a little too low when he was in his basic ready position. I told him what I had noticed, and he decided to work on these points in practice.

Perron acknowledged that the mood in the club wasn't very healthy. "We need to become a team. Right now, my team's divided in two, the veterans and the young guys. The veterans need to learn that young players have a different mindset today: they are different; they see things differently. I can't understand why some veterans keep criticizing the rookies through the media. It doesn't make sense! Some players on this team are taking it out on Roy, and that's a shame. Because it's easy to blame someone else when things go wrong. Should some players look at themselves in the mirror? I guess you might say that."

Fortunately, the team was leaving for a few games on the road—away from the fans and media scrutiny. It was a chance to sit down and have a frank discussion. Perron decided to talk to eight key players, eight strong personalities whom he could count on to cement team spirit. In his Hotel Westin suite, in Winnipeg, he met with Bob Gainey, Guy Carbonneau, Larry Robinson, Mats Naslund, Ryan Walter, Bobby Smith, Craig Ludwig and Chris Nilan.

Of course, goaltending was one topic of discussion. But Perron also tried to convince the leaders that the rookies needed support rather than public criticism. He also took the opportunity to explain some of his recent decisions and to address the lack of commitment shown by certain players, including some veterans. In short, they laid things on the line.

In St. Louis four days later, a few of the leaders went to Serge Savard, and asked for Perron's head. They claimed that the coach lacked authority—in hockey lingo, he had "lost the bench." Savard wasn't having it. Changing coaches wasn't an option at that point in the season. It must be said that he had just explored the issue with Jacques Lemaire. Savard didn't waste words. "I'm replacing Perron; you're taking the club."

But Lemaire refused. He still believed that the Canadiens were in good hands with Perron as long as he got enough support.

Savard had very little room to maneuver. He told the players, "Listen, it's March, I'm not getting rid of my coach; he's going to finish the year. It's up to you to decide whether you want to play or not."

They decided to play.

Patrick was relaxing in the sauna after a workout at the Forum. Larry Robinson came in. Robinson had just taken a shower, so Patrick guessed that he wasn't coming in for a sweat. Robinson looked him in the eye and said, "No more bad goals!" Then he left just as abruptly as he had entered, without saying another word.

That's when Perron had François Allaire come to Montréal to take care of Patrick, who was taken out of the lineup for nine days so he could work on his technique and rebuild his confidence. Then he was given two starts in two days on the road. He performed well, despite losing in Hartford and tying in Boston.

But a new element had been added to the mix (perhaps it had been the missing ingredient), giving the squad the fire, the fierce determination a team needs to win: Claude Lemieux. In Boston, he hit everything that moved. He was an inspiration.

Cut at training camp, he had joined the Sherbrooke Canadiens. Often discouraged and demoralized, he had come close to chucking it in that season. With Pierre Creamer's encouragement, he persisted. Now back in Montréal, he was hungry. He was ready to rip into anything in his path. With his arrival, it was the rookies' turn to show the veterans the way. Their determination, enthusiasm, spirit and desire to win were contagious.

It was a new dawn.

—ᨌ—

Perron informed Allaire that he was planning on having Patrick start in the playoffs. Patrick won his last three games of the 1985–86 season.

Then the Canadiens got quite a gift from the Hartford Whalers. The Whalers were playing the final game of the season against the

Bruins in Boston. If the Bruins won, they would finish one point ahead of the Canadiens, giving them home-ice advantage in their series against Montréal, and the Canadiens had enjoyed little success in Boston all year. But the Whalers won. The series against Boston would start in Montréal.

To listen to the fans on sports-talk radio and the comments by analysts, the Canadiens' season had been mediocre. They wouldn't go very far in the post-season with a goaltender who gave up one bad goal a game.

Yet the team had finished second in the Adams division, right behind the Nordiques, and Patrick must have made saves that compensated for the soft goals, since his 3.35 goals-against average was one of the best in the league. That year, only one goaltender, Bob Froese of the Philadelphia Flyers, had kept his goals-against average under three, and only three teams had conceded fewer goals than the Canadiens. Goalies with the same average as Patrick's—the Nordiques' Clint Malarchuk, for example—were considered to have enjoyed an excellent season. So the rookie goaltender had actually been a pleasant surprise for Canadiens' management. He had won 23 of 40 matches; Penney and Soetaert shared the other victories, registering 6 and 11 respectively. Patrick was named to the NHL All-Rookie team.

With the playoffs about to begin, Patrick was optimistic. "I know I've been through some rough patches and I was a little disappointed that I gave up too many bad goals. But all the goalies, even the best ones, do. The difference is the best ones find a way to get even tougher mentally and to play better right away. This season, I've shown character. All year, I've had to battle in a goaltending trio to stay in Montréal. Now I've been told that I'm the Number 1 goalie; it's the opportunity I've been waiting for. Don't worry; I'm going to do the job."

Few people believed him ... but they were hoping for the best.

THE CUP OF
INNOCENCE

"Hey! The Canadiens no longer have Dryden, Vachon or Larocque. We have better goalies than they do. And where do you win the playoffs? In goal, right? Do you really think they're going anywhere without a goalie? Do you think any team has miraculously won a series without a top goalie? No way!"

Boston Bruins General Manager Harry Sinden made these comments while his team was traveling to Montréal to start the best-of-five series with the Canadiens. Usually, general managers avoid these kind of statements like the plague, for fear they'll fire up the opposition. But Sinden was so confident of his team's success he couldn't help himself. Or maybe he was using intimidation to try and get inside Patrick's head. At any rate, the Boston GM didn't see the risk. Bruins coach Butch Goring was more circumspect, but everyone knew he agreed with his boss.

Goring had a remarkable career as an NHL player, first with the Los Angeles Kings for 11 years and then with the New York Islanders for five seasons, before ending his career in Boston. In his old taped-up helmet, he was easily recognizable on the ice, a sight to behold. He was one of Rogatien Vachon's teammates when I took Patrick to see a game at the Forum 12 years earlier.

Sinden's remarks may have been a bit over the top, but most hockey observers, including many Montréal fans and analysts, agreed with them. The consensus was that Pat Riggin gave the Bruins a distinct advantage in goal, and they would make quick work of their rivals in the first round of the playoffs.

—⁓—

"*Billets pour ce soir!* Tickets for the game!"

By the late afternoon, the old Forum was springing to life. Scalpers were setting up just outside the building, peddling their tickets to passersby at twice the face value, if not more.

The Bruins, some in blazers, others in suits, but all of them in ties, were strolling over from Manoir Lemoyne to the Forum on Atwater Ave. Their height and bulk made them stand out on boulevard de Maisonneuve. They were in little groups, like college students returning to class after a break.

The Canadiens arrived by bus from the remote Île Charron Sheraton Hotel, where management had kept them cloistered during the playoffs, so they could live together without distractions as if they were in boarding school. The players ironically dubbed the hotel "Alcatraz."

When the players reached the Forum, they headed to the dressing room to prepare their equipment, tape their sticks, bend or straighten the blades with a torch, sharpen their skates, have the physiotherapist iron out any muscle kinks, do a little stretching, chat about the game, and eventually begin to suit up for it.

Then the security agents, souvenir-stand staff and program vendors showed up to receive their instructions for the evening. Next came the ushers and hostesses who would greet 18,000 fans and show them to their seats. The restaurant employees arrived at the same time, gearing up to sell hot dogs, fries, pop, beer, and so on.

Members of the print and broadcast media ambled over to the area or studio reserved for them, tested their equipment and consulted press kits with facts and statistics about the two teams. Based on this information, some reporters started working on their articles, while others prepared interviews, analysis and commentary for the TV and radio broadcasts to an audience of millions. Finally, numerous photographers, whose photos would be seen throughout Canada and the United States, set up their cameras behind the Plexiglas.

The Forum was a veritable anthill in which everyone had a specific task. Strangely enough, the rink, resurfaced after morning practice, stood in sharp contrast: an oasis of calm, under the blazing halogen lights, before becoming the center of activity.

Already some 1,800 eager-beaver standing-room ticket holders were wandering around the place. Some were grabbing a snack at the restaurants or stopping by souvenir stands. Others who had found the spot where they'd be staying until the game was over were leaning on the rail, flipping through the program and gazing, with a twinge of nostalgia, at the banners hanging from the rafters in this hockey sanctuary, recalling the 22 Stanley Cups garnered by the Holy Flannel.

Everything was in place. The show could begin.

—⁂—

No more nervous than usual, Patrick was keyed up, excited. He was anxious for the puck to be dropped. "I know I've got a lot on the line and so has my coach because he's counting on me. But I'm out to prove a lot of things during these playoffs. I want to prove I've got nerve, that I'm not afraid of a challenge. But I'll need the help of the seventh player, the fans. I just hope they'll support me, even if I get beat early on."

He started to put on his heavy equipment for the warm-up. He always went through the same ritual: the left skate first, the left pad first. It wasn't as much a superstition as a routine that helped him concentrate on the essentials. It let him enter what he called his "comfort zone." There's no better way to fight stress, anxiety and nervousness than repeating familiar gestures and movements before plunging into 60 unpredictable minutes of action.

After about a 20-minute pre-game warm-up on the ice, it's back to the dressing room, where he continues his ritual. He only takes off his shirt and gloves. Then he puts on his Walkman earphones and relaxes to the rhythms of Whitney Houston. Finally, at a specific moment, he starts juggling with a puck, the same one since the beginning of the season, bouncing it off the floor with one hand and catching it with the other. Then he puts the puck on the floor, in the corner nearest the equipment people's room. Precisely seven minutes before the opening face-off, he ends the ritual, pulls on his jersey and mitts, and focuses on the game. When Claude Mouton announces "And now, here are YOUR CANADIENS," Patrick is ready.

What's really thrilling about competitive sports is that we never know the outcome in advance, especially when the teams are evenly matched. We fool around with destiny. We try to guess what it will bring; we try to trick it. So when fans proclaim, "The Canadiens in three, no doubt about it!" they're expressing a wish, not a certainty, though they may not know the difference. Nobody really knows.

A winning streak brings a team closer to defeat, and a loss makes a team hungrier for victory. There is a tendency to exaggerate the margin between a winner and a loser. Often the victor is praised to the skies, the loser condemned to obscurity, though, in fact, hardly anything—sometimes a lucky bounce—separates them. Once the contest is over, everything is up for grabs again. The slate is wiped clean. The battle starts anew.

When the referee dropped the frozen rubber disk between centers Ken Linseman and Guy Carbonneau, the past became irrelevant. They were thinking only of the present, hoping the future would take care of itself. Before skating to center ice, Carbonneau exchanged a few words with Patrick to make sure he was ready and would do his best to avoid bad goals at the beginning of the game—he'd given up a few during the regular season.

A team that lacks confidence in its goalie feels its efforts will be to no avail. It plays nervously and without conviction. That describes the Canadiens' performance in the opening period of their first playoff game. Even veterans like Bobby Smith and Larry Robinson made bad plays and sloppy passes.

Then Canadiens John Kordic made a rookie mistake. Thinking he was doing the right thing, he challenged Bruins enforcer Jay Miller to a fight. Miller declined, and Kordic ended up in the box. While Kordic was cooling his heels, Patrick made a sensational glove save on a bullet by Reed Larson, one of the league's premier shooters. But for that save, the Bruins would have taken the lead.

Montréal was so inept that with fewer than six minutes remaining in the first period, the shots were 11–1 in favor of the Bruins. It took the Habs eighteen and a half minutes to mount their first serious attack on Boston goalie Pat Riggin. The veterans bumbled listlessly along. Of the Habs, Patrick was the one who showed the most composure. Despite the outrageous domination by the Bruins, the first period ended with no score.

Patrick's solid, confident work must have gotten a few of his teammates thinking, because the second period was entirely different. The home team, dominant in every aspect of the play, moved out to a 3–0 lead, with Bobby Smith scoring two of the goals.

Both clubs played solid hockey in the third period. Yet Boston desperately tried to disrupt Patrick's concentration. When Gaston Gingras got a tripping penalty, the Bruins asked referee Brian Lewis to measure the blade on Patrick's stick, hoping to have a two-man advantage. A "spy" had probably informed them that the blades of Patrick's sticks weren't regulation width. In fact, they were wider by about an inch. But what the spy didn't realize was that Patrick carefully straightened and filed three sticks before every game so they'd be in conformity with the rules. On top of that, the Canadiens' equipment manager, Eddy Palchak, measured every stick before each game to make sure they were in compliance. The result was that the Bruins ended up with a minor penalty, depriving them of the man advantage that Gingras' infraction had given them.

Nearly halfway through the period, a hard shot by Raymond Bourque found its way under Patrick's shoulder pads, and struck him in the clavicle, rattling him. On the same play, Chris Chelios accidentally struck him in the head with the stick while trying to clear an opponent away from the front of the net. Patrick took some time to get up, after being examined by team trainer Gaétan Lefebvre. Shortly after that, Gord Klusak banged in his own rebound to score the Bruins' first goal.

Sensing that Patrick was rattled and perhaps hoping to finish him off, Louis Sleigher ran into him when he least expected it, as he had gone to recover the puck behind his net. Patrick's mask flew into the air and he crumpled to the ice. Once again the trainer had to come, while Larry Robinson gave Sleigher the thrashing he had coming to him.

Nevertheless, Patrick soldiered on. Despite the Bruins' attempts at intimidation, no other goals were scored. He was solid in goal for the rest of the game, and the Canadiens took the lead in the series with a 3–1 victory. Patrick was selected the first star, and the second went to Bobby Smith, who said that his goaltender's performance had been a wake-up call for the team. "We were playing poorly," he said. "We were having all sorts of problems, but he stopped everything. He gave us time to regroup." Patrick had rallied both his team and the fans. For the first time that season, the Canadiens were a team; the infighting stopped. The players realized they could count on one another. That's when a team undergoes a transformation: it becomes more than the sum of its parts.

—⚏—

The second meeting took place the next day, again on Forum ice. During the regular season, Patrick's recuperative powers had often been questioned. Doubts had been raised about his ability to start two games within a day of each other. The problem supposedly stemmed from eating junk food.

I think this explanation is somewhat inaccurate. Obviously with 165 pounds spread over a six-foot-two frame, Patrick wasn't exactly burly. He would sometimes lose six or seven pounds in a game, since it was much warmer in NHL rinks than in the minor league arenas. Stepping up his water intake during games quickly solved that problem. But I believe that there was an even more important reason. Patrick was in his first year in the circuit and had yet to play against every team and in every rink. That was why he prepared so meticulously for games, especially by studying videos of opposing players. When the Habs' schedule involved two games within 24 hours against different teams in different cities, he didn't have enough time to carry out the analysis he needed. His preparations were less effective for the second match. His play suffered as a consequence, especially since he had not been able to count on François Allaire being there to do the initial spadework during the regular season. It should also be pointed out that Patrick wasn't the only one on the ice, and that some of his teammates might not have had the same bounce in the second game as they had in the first. But in the Boston series, these issues weren't relevant. The second game was in a familiar rink against the club he'd played the previous day.

It was a goaltender's duel. Both Bill Ranford, the rookie whom Goring had sent into action, and Patrick played well. But it was Claude Lemieux who stood out, notching two goals, including the winner late in the third period with the count tied at 2–2. Both times, Lemieux took advantage of the Bruins' attempt at intimidation to score his goals: first when Jay Miller was penalized for roughing John Kordic, and again when Kraig Nienhuis got chased for cross-checking him. With this win, the series returned, a couple of days later, to the Boston Garden, with the Bruins facing elimination.

The Canadiens didn't fret, even though they hadn't won a single game in that rink during the season. They were an entirely different team. Carbonneau expressed it best: "It's always said that you need 20 players to win, but the fact of the matter is that the younger players have a tendency to follow the veterans. Now that kids inspired by Roy and Lemieux are assuming their responsibility, it takes a lot of the pressure off the veterans. We feel encouraged by their play and at the same time we tell ourselves that we don't have a choice. We have to follow their lead." Carbonneau was right. Now, the team's leaders were barely 20 years old. Like their coach, they were in their first season in the NHL.

The following morning, Patrick was one of two players excused from practice; Mats Naslund was the other. In fact, Patrick was not allowed on the ice. Management wanted him rested. Times were changing: a few weeks before, the veterans would have made their discontent known if a rookie earned a break from practice.

Players milled around at center ice, trying to intimidate each other during the warm-up before the third game, but as soon as the puck was dropped both teams concentrated on playing hockey. Goring once again put his trust in Ranford to guard the cage. A surprising decision: Ranford hadn't played poorly in game two, but the Bruins had trumpeted the advantage they had with a veteran goaltender like Riggin. Now they were relying on a 19-year-old rookie, fresh from the Westminster Bruins of the Western Hockey League. He was a few months younger than Patrick and hadn't played a single game in the NHL before his start in Montréal two days earlier.

It was a good contest, the least physical one of the series. The coaches did not call on their goons. Winning was what counted. For the Bruins, victory was essential. A defeat would end their playoff hopes.

The Bruins played with a passion born of desperation. After 40 minutes of play, they had flung 26 shots on goal to the Canadiens' 12. Yet the Bruins held a slim 3–2 advantage.

In the third period, Canadiens captain Bob Gainey took matters into his own hands. Hardly the league's most able sharpshooter—and primarily known for his defensive prowess—he nevertheless managed to score twice and help defeat the Bruins.

It was Patrick, though, who was the star of this series, with Lemieux and Richer also playing leading roles. Butch Goring admitted it. "He stole goals from us in the first period of every game. Our goalies were good, but Roy made no mistakes." Mats Naslund maintained that but for Patrick's extraordinary work in the first ten minutes of the opening game, the Bruins would have dispatched the Canadiens in three straight games. "When the series got under way," he said, "we weren't 100% sure about what we could achieve. Patrick's saves allowed us to regain confidence."

Based on Harry Sinden's own logic, either the Canadiens had wrought a miracle by winning a series without a great goaltender, or perhaps Patrick had just become exactly that.

—⁓—

During the regular season, the Nordiques had beaten the Canadiens six times out of eight. The Hartford Whalers ended up doing the Canadiens another favor when, to everyone's surprise, they swept the Nordiques, the Adams Division champions, in three games. But it would be their last favor to the Canadiens. Heading to Montréal, for the next series they were the hottest team in the league, with only four losses in their last 22 games since the beginning of March. And they fully intended to keep up the momentum.

The Whalers series was a letdown for the fans in the Province of Québec. Obviously, a series against the Nordiques would have fired the passions of fans at both ends of Highway 20 to a far greater extent. The Whalers were certainly a good hockey team, solid in every position: in goal with the veteran Mike Liut, one of the league's premier goalies; on the blue line with Wayne Babych; and up front with Ron Francis, Kevin Dineen, Sylvain Turgeon, Ray Ferraro, John Anderson and Doug Jarvis—the Guy Carbonneau or Bob Gainey of the Whalers. A team of quick, talented, stylish players, a good match for the Canadiens. The Whalers had no fighters and enforcers, and no flamboyant players, but disciplined, methodical and well-organized professionals. Their team reflected Hartford itself: a calm, clean, white-collar city, the cradle of the American insurance industry.

Yet, despite these qualities, the Whalers were a team that lacked flair, a team with a dull, uninspired style. They played a conservative, tight-checking game, given to hooking and interference. Their coach, Jack Evans, a former NHL player and the eldest of the league's coaches, never smiled and looked as boring as the approach he favored. What's more, it didn't help that the team wore a pool-green and white uniform, no more exciting than the club itself. The sole source of interest was the logo. If you focused your attention on the white portion, you could see a "W" over a whale's tail. By looking at the green portion, you could see the "H." It was impossible to see both at once.

The only aspect of this quarterfinal likely to excite the fans was the fact that the teams were evenly matched and therefore the games would probably be close, and viewers of French-language TV would have analyst Mario Tremblay, whose candor and spontaneity would spice up the coverage by Richard Garneau and Gilles Tremblay, looking somewhat stiff in their powder-blue blazers. The comments by Garneau and Tremblay, though apt, hardly conveyed unbridled enthusiasm.

The Whalers were their usual methodical selves, but they had the wind in their sails from the outset, winning the opening game in Montréal 4–1. Liut was clearly the star of the game, with 26 saves, including 14 in the first period alone.

The second game at the Forum saw the Canadiens seize the momentum, triumphing 3–1. The Canadiens demonstrated that they could beat Mike Liut, who suffered his first defeat in the playoffs. The teams headed to Connecticut for the next two encounters.

—⁓—

Hartford's Civic Center is quite an enjoyable place to watch a hockey game. It's a multidisciplinary complex that houses the hockey arena and a shopping mall with boutiques, and restaurants and a movie theater, as well as the Sheraton Hotel. So, visitors can leave their room without putting on a coat or overshoes, grab a bite in a restaurant, and take in a Whalers game—while comfortably installed in a plush seat with armrests—as easily as if they were going to pick up the newspaper in the hotel lobby.

In Hartford, the two teams traded wins: a 3–1 Canadiens victory in the first game, and a 2–1 Hartford win on a Kevin Dineen overtime goal in the second. Incidentally, Dineen was from Québec City, where his father Bill had played for the Aces when they represented the town in the American Hockey League. Interestingly enough, the opening face-off opposed Guy Carbonneau and Doug Jarvis who, 20 years later, would be reunited behind the Canadiens bench.

But the Whalers were hampered by injuries in both games. After only 12 minutes in the first meeting, Mike Liut, due to acute knee pain, gave way to his backup, Steve Weeks. Then their top defenseman, Wayne Babych, suffering a groin injury, joined Liut on the injury shelf and couldn't answer the bell for the second match, which the Whalers nonetheless managed to win.

—m—

The teams arrived back in Montréal with two wins each. So, the battle came down to a best of three series, with the first game to be played in Montréal, the second in Hartford and the third, if necessary, in Montréal.

Up to this point, Patrick's work had been brilliant. Not for an instant did Perron think of replacing him with Soetaert. He never thought of replacing Lemieux, Richer and Skrudland either. And the veterans were in full accord. Claude Lemieux summed up the change that had occurred in the team. "The younger players' contribution has brought everyone closer. Now, we no longer talk about rookies and veterans. We talk about a team."

It was quite a change for a group of players who, a month earlier, weren't really a team. In one practice, Nilan had hit Richer with his stick. The next day, Nilan said he had done it to wake up the rookies. Maybe that's when the veterans began to realize they had been asking too much of the rookies, that they couldn't make the kids more productive by scaring them. Patrick discussed the situation with journalist Bertrand Raymond:

"Maybe the incident helped clear the air, but things didn't get back to normal by themselves. We were in first place when it happened, and then we slipped back to third. We didn't get going until much later. Don't forget that hockey has undergone significant changes over the years, and the arrival of so many rookies this year makes it obvious. The time for kicking around rookies is over. Nowadays, a rookie needs understanding and support."

Certainly, some veterans found it hard to accept that rookies had privileges (such as missing optional practices) that they hadn't had when they were starting out. But now everything was as it should be. Veterans and rookies had to work together if they wanted to win, especially since the Whalers' last victory without Liut and Babych had given them momentum. The Habs would need everyone.

Larry Robinson told reporters he wasn't surprised by Patrick's excellent work. And yet, he was one of those who had openly criticized Patrick at the end of the regular season. When Yvon Pedneault ventured the opinion that Patrick had never strung together seven good performances in a row, Robinson retorted, "Neither have we!"

In the next two games, home-ice advantage was the determining factor: the Habs registered a 5–3 victory at the Forum; then the Whalers recorded a 1–0 shutout at the Civic Center. In the first game, the Canadiens played without passion, but Patrick saved the day. The second game featured the return of Babych and Liut. The goaltender won the goaltending duel, stopping all 32 Habs shots. Once more, Kevin Dineen played a decisive role, netting the Whalers' only goal.

Patrick acknowledged his rival's hard work. "When you only allow one goal in a road game, you hope you'll win. But Liut played well. I wouldn't have thought he could perform like that after sitting out two games with a knee injury." Asked by a journalist to predict the outcome of the seventh and final game, Patrick replied, "We're going to score more goals and win, that's all!"

The die was cast. The winner of the next game at the Forum would move on to the next round.

The tension was palpable. To boost their morale, the Whalers claimed home-ice advantage didn't mean a thing at this point. The Canadiens said that fan support would be pivotal. But the last two times the Canadiens had played a seventh game in a series, they had lost.

"We have to look at this like any other game, and give it all we've got," said Patrick, who had to deal with an increasing number of interviews. "Every key save will be a step forward for the team." When asked to describe Patrick's mindset, Captain Bob Gainey said, "He's showing a calm confidence in his abilities, and I think he actually enjoys the tense atmosphere of the playoffs."

It was a contest marked by cautious play. Another goaltenders' battle. In the first period, Mike McPhee beat Liut on a fine individual shorthanded effort. Neither team scored in the second period, though Guy Carbonneau went in alone on Liut as he had in the first meeting. As the third period wound down, Wayne Babych evened the score on a deflection. Not long after, Stéphane Richer was carried off the ice with what looked like a serious knee injury. Claude Lemieux, one of the stretcher's carriers, promised his teammate he would score the winning goal in overtime.

Now the fate of the two teams would be decided by a single goal. The Canadiens seemed surprisingly upbeat, considering their dismal overtime record: a single victory in 15 overtime appearances since the beginning of the season. Patrick mentioned to his teammates that Liut might be vulnerable to high shots because he stayed deep in the net when the action was going on behind the goal. Lemieux, remembering his promise to Richer, took note.

Just over five minutes into overtime, Ulf Samuelsson viciously crosschecked Lemieux from behind in the Whalers' zone, sending him sprawling head over heels into the boards. The referee ignored the infraction, and the fans' indignation, as they roared their discontent. But Lemieux, rising like an angry bull, shoved an opponent out of the way, skated in front of the goal and then circled behind it, where he out-muscled Tim Bothwell, and somehow lugged the puck in front of the goal and ripped a backhander over Liut's left shoulder into the top shelf. The Whalers were done.

Mario Tremblay whooped with glee, forgetting that he was yelling into a microphone. Meanwhile, arms raised, Lemieux skated aimlessly for a few moments and then dove onto the ice. Jubilant teammates piled onto him to congratulate him. He had just scored the most important goal in his young career—his sixth of the playoffs—and now he had a feeling of exultation.

Calm returned and the teams exchanged the traditional handshakes. Then Robinson was surprisingly unstinting in his praise. "In my 14 years with the Canadiens, I've rarely seen a goalie play as well as Patrick has since the beginning of the playoffs." Coming from a defenseman who had won a few Stanley Cups and who knew the glory years in the 1970s with Ken Dryden in goal, the compliment meant a great deal. Bob Gainey, with his accustomed poise and restraint, added, "We owe Patrick our thanks. He played well against the Whalers."

Yet Patrick accepted the compliments with a certain modesty. "There's no doubt that I'm proud of what I've achieved, but the defense did a wonderful job, and the forwards kept coming back to lend a hand. I would also like to thank the fans whose support gave us the boost we needed when we were exhausted in overtime." Then he praised Mike Liut and Kevin Dineen, who had impressed him all through the series.

Crushed in the losers' dressing room, Dineen had a hard time swallowing his team's defeat. "The Canadiens were no better than us. They just got lucky at the end of the game." Despite the anguish that was written all over his face, he made a point of mentioning Patrick's work. "He was outstanding against us all season. His performances hurt us."

Claude Lemieux, the author of the winning goal and the third star after Patrick and Liut, had a tear in his eye as he spoke about his brother Serge, who suffered from cerebral palsy: "When I scored that goal, my first thought was of him. I don't know him very well. He's in an institution, and we can only visit him once a year. It seems it would be too hard on him to see us more often than that. But he's my brother, and he's always on my mind."

Though running on empty, everyone had found some source of inspiration.

—m—

The Canadiens' opponents in the semifinals, The New York Rangers, were just the opposite of the Whalers. Unpredictable, disorderly and flamboyant in their blue, red and white uniforms—one of the most attractive outfits in the NHL—they could lose 8–1 one evening and win a tight game in overtime the next. They had finished 14th in the overall standings, 19th in defense and 20th in offense, yet they had still found a way to eliminate both the mighty second-place Philadelphia Flyers and the third-place Washington Capitals. An appropriate sobriquet for the Rangers might have been the "Bad News Blue Shirts" because of their propensity for spoiling the lives of other seemingly more "deserving" clubs.

Now they were off to Montréal to do battle for the Prince of Wales conference championship or, far more important, to win the Stanley Cup semifinals. Their principal assets were a young goalie, John "Beezer" Vanbiesbrouck, and a natural goal-scorer named Pierre "Lucky Pete" Larouche.

Larouche, whose indiscipline had given the organization fits, had spent half the season in the American Hockey League, playing 32 games with the Hershey Bears. But he was the Rangers' most natural scorer, so they recalled him just before the playoffs. In his 28 games with New York that year, he had scored 20 times. The only Rangers who had scored more goals were Tomas Sandstrom (25), Bob Brooke (24) and Mike Ridley (22), and they had racked up those results in 73, 79 and 80 games respectively. Larouche was a product of the Québec Major Junior Hockey League, where he had starred with the Sorel Éperviers before their move to Granby. He already had two 50-goal seasons in the NHL: one with Pittsburgh (53) in 1975–1976, the other with the Canadiens (50) in 1979–1980, before being traded to Hartford and then to New York.

The Rangers were ahead of their time in the 1980s with their many European players: four Swedes, two Finns and a West German. This led to a more open playing style with plenty of improvisation. The other members of the team were Canadian except for Vanbiesbrouck, who was born in Detroit.

During the regular season, the Canadiens had not won a single contest out of the three against the Rangers. They had lost twice and tied once. Patrick, who had a 1.78 goals-against average since the start of the playoffs, the best in the league, had not played in any of those games. And the two teams had added new elements that could make a difference: Claude Lemieux for the Canadiens, and Pierre Larouche and the rugged Wilfrid Paiement for the Rangers.

The first game of the series in Montréal ended in a 2–1 victory by the Canadiens. It was a contest resembling the first round of a boxing match, when the two adversaries feel each other out. The Habs were still suffering the effects of the long struggle with Hartford. Yet the game was a goaltenders' contest, with Patrick named the first star and Vanbiesbrouck the third. It was clear that there was more space on the ice—less holding and hooking—than in the Hartford series. Fans were looking forward to fast, exciting hockey with the accent on offense. And that's what happened. During the second period in game two, the Canadiens exploded with four straight goals en route to a 6–2 win.

The Rangers were trailing 2–0 in the series. The time for study and analysis had passed. It was time to use every resource possible, and when it came to that, the Rangers were well equipped. Like Jean Perron, Ted Sator, their coach, was a new wave instructor from the university milieu. He was conversant with physiology, sports psychology, nutrition, work ethic, and more. Counting Bob Johnson of the Calgary Flames, who were battling the St. Louis Blues, three of the four head coaches in the semifinals were considered "hockey intellectuals." Sator made extensive use of game videos. He had no equal in pinpointing another team's weaknesses and devising tactics to exploit them. That's how the Rangers had surprised the hockey world by defeating the Flyers and the Capitals.

And, of course, New York is not Hartford. New York is the biggest city in the United States, with the highest concentration of museums, restaurants, theaters and boutiques in the continent. It is the world entertainment capital and a huge market for an athlete. The New York press is entirely different from the Hartford press. In the Big Apple, sports journalists are accustomed to covering major stars in baseball, football, basketball and boxing. They write articles that appear in dozens of countries. They can be laudatory; they can just as easily be merciless. They're used to covering three NHL teams: the Rangers in Manhattan, the Islanders in Long Island and the Devils in East Rutherford, New Jersey. Nothing like Hartford supporters, Madison Square Garden fans are the most raucous, irreverent and undisciplined in all the circuit. They can intimidate even the most experienced and dedicated veteran. The 20-year-old rookie from Sainte-Foy had to watch out!

Before game two in Montréal, a horde of journalists from the Big Apple descended on Patrick.

"Before the game, you skate halfway toward the blue line, then turn and face your net. Why do you do that?"

"I talk to my goal posts."

"And ... do they answer?"

"Sometimes ..."

"Oh yeah! And what do they say?"

"Sometimes, they say *ping*, when they make a save."

Manhattan journalists thought they were dealing with someone as kooky as Mark "the Bird" Fidrych, the flakey Detroit Tigers hurler, who talked to the ball before throwing it. A glutton for originality, the New York press corps ate up Patrick's comments, and they soon made the rounds throughout North America.

Patrick was having the journalists on. The real answer was that he was performing a visualization exercise. He had begun doing it towards the end of the regular season in a game against Hartford. Since the Canadian and American flags were being raised behind his goal, he had to turn around during the national anthems. He had started observing his net, imagining it so small that he could easily cover it and stop any shot. This reassured him and gave him confidence.

The press tried to get under his skin. But Patrick was as solid in interviews as he was in the net. He never gave an inch and patiently answered all the questions. Only once did he raise his voice, when a scribe informed him that Jack Birch, one of Sator's assistants, had questioned Patrick's technique. "Who is this Jack Birch anyway?" Patrick asked impatiently. "I don't know the guy, and I don't want to know him. I'm not going to start listening to everybody. I don't care what he thinks. I work with François Allaire, and he knows what he's doing." Patrick was sending a message. He was ready to answer any and all questions, but with a 1.71 goals-against average in the series, he wasn't about to waste time on questions that cast doubt on his goaltending abilities and technique, especially if they came from a hack.

He also took advantage of the opportunity to ask reporters to pronounce his name properly. Wherever he went (except for Québec City and Montréal, of course), the announcers would pronounce his name "Rrroye," like the first name of the famous cowboy, Roy Rogers. It was something to see Patrick teach New York journalists how to pronounce his name. "You have to say it as if it were written Roo-Wah!" Not too bad for a period when Francophone players, interviewed in English, sometimes pronounced their fellow Francophone's names the English way: "Morris Rrisharde," "Guy Laflourr," and of course "Mario Lemiew."

Pierre Larouche was also doing some surprising things. During a morning skate reserved for the Rangers, he sat down on the Canadiens' bench for a few moments. He was also doing visualization exercises. "When I sit on their bench, I try to see what their field of vision is like. As our benches are not in the same place, I'm sure they get a different view of the game than we do." He said this in all seriousness; maybe he was trying to find where the Forum ghosts were hiding. He compared the Forum to the lion's den in the Roman Coliseum. "It's a bizarre feeling playing here. It's the building with the most light in the league. Since all the spectators have an eagle-eye view, you feel like you're being offered up as a sacrifice to the home team. I don't know if anyone has studied these things, but I swear it's true."

The day after the Rangers' second loss, Wilfrid Paiement opined that it was easy for a goaltender to stop 20 shots a game. "But let's see how he reacts when we fire 30 or 40 shots at him."

—m—

Patrick had never played in New York. Speaking of a lion's den, a good ten minutes before the players jumped onto the ice, the Rangers fans started roaring, "Go Rangers Go! Go Rangers Go!" Then rink announcer John F.X. Condon introduced each player, starting with the Canadiens. Suddenly, *Go Rangers Go!* morphed into a chorus of boos for Number 1, Doug Soetaert, all the way to Number 44, Stéphane Richer, as well as "Number 33, Patrick Roo-wah," whose name very few people heard anyway due to the deafening jeers.

As soon as a Ranger skated onto the ice, the shouts turned to cheers, "Go Rangers Go!" mixed in with thunderous applause that continued unabated beyond the player introductions, drowning out the *Star-Spangled Banner.*

When the referee dropped the puck, fans started hollering, "Roo-wah! Roo-wah! Roo-wah!" in time with the giant letters flashing on the scoreboard. The obvious intent was to disrupt Patrick's concentration. The ploy failed. For Patrick, all the taunting and jeering was just a stimulant; he heard it all, but transformed that energy to his advantage. He was in his zone. All he saw now was the puck passing from one stick to another, and all he heard was the clack of the puck hitting the blades, the grating of the skates biting into the ice, sliding and stopping abruptly, and the dull thud of checks. Nothing existed but the game.

To say the ploy failed is not completely accurate. In fact, it achieved a much nobler purpose than the one intended. From then on, Francophones named Roy—and God knows there are many of them, especially in Québec—started to have their names pronounced properly all over English-speaking North America.

Whipped into frenzy by the fans, the Rangers dominated the first period, outshooting the Canadiens 16–7. Yet both teams scored only once. The Habs held sway in the second stanza, even though the Rangers tallied the only goal, taking a 2–1 lead. The Broadway Blues seized the upper hand in the third period, but managed to put the puck in the net only once on 12 shots. The Canadiens, whose energy seemed to be melting away in the Madison Square Garden heat, scored two goals on four shots, sending the game into overtime.

Then the mood in the Garden changed dramatically. The fans' excitement turned into paralyzing stress. The stakes were high: if the Rangers lost, they would find themselves on the ropes.

On the other hand, what had been a stressful game for Patrick became an exciting one. He was totally focused on the moment. The pressure that paralyzes even the most experienced and talented athletes in crucial moments comes from fear of failure. Yet, the fear of failure is related to the future, not the present. When the competitor is totally absorbed by the present moment, he doesn't think about the future. Therefore, he doesn't experience fear. He only thinks about the play itself, which becomes exciting and stimulating.

Patrick attained a state of grace. He was invincible, impassive. He anticipated every shot, controlled every rebound. His every movement was fluid and precise; he was relaxed but aggressive, calm but excited. The net felt small and the puck the size of a football. He was enjoying himself.

The Rangers dominated the first four minutes of overtime, and then their control became total. They camped out in the exhausted Canadiens' zone, hurled shots from every angle, tried deflections to screen Patrick. It was like watching a one-way hockey exercise, some

216

kind of Rope-a-Dope on ice. The Blue Shirts fans' impatience grew with every save by Patrick.

After nine agonizing minutes, the inevitable happened. The Canadiens snapped out of their daze, just long enough, like Muhammad Ali against George Foreman in Zaire, a few years before. After a face-off in Montréal territory, the puck bounced towards the blue line, where Rangers defenseman Willie Huber, instead of erring on the side of caution and stopping it with his hand, tried a slap shot, a one-timer in hockey parlance. He missed the puck. McPhee grabbed it, tripped and fell, struggled to his feet, with Huber on his tail, skated to the Rangers' blue line, slipped the puck to Claude Lemieux who, all alone in front of Beezer, like a replay of the "Rumble in the Jungle"—now it was as hot as the African bush in Madison Square Garden—ended the contest with a high hard shot to Vanbiesbrouck's left, just over his trapper. No doubt dumbstruck, the goal judge took some time before flashing the red goal light. But the referee had seen it. Everyone in the Garden had seen it. Defeated and deflated, the fans humbly applauded.

Outshot 47–29, the Canadiens stole a 4–3 victory, taking a stranglehold on the series.

Patrick was lavished with praise—first from his rivals:

John Vanbiesbrouck: "I tip my hat to Roy. He played quite a game tonight. Incredible!"

Bob Brooke: "Roy is exceptional; he inspired his team."

Ted Sator: "I'm proud of my team, they gave it all they had. Roy was amazing."

And from his team:

Coach Jean Perron: "During the playoffs, it's impossible to win if the goalie doesn't come up with the big saves. Patrick played an incredible game. He made some fantastic saves."

Captain Bob Gainey: "We owe this game to Patrick Roy. He's been incredible since the start of the series. But what he did in overtime, I've never seen anything like that in my life."

Mats Naslund: "We will never see a performance quite like what Patrick did tonight. What a performance! As I saw him make save after miraculous save, I told myself that we had a chance. Then bang!"

Chris Nilan: "He was simply sensational. Patrick turned in a scintillating performance."

Patrick's roommate and backup Doug Soetaert, who would have liked to get into the action: "He simply was incredible."

And even some legendary hockey players who had seen so much more.

Phil Esposito: "I've never seen a goalie offer such a performance in overtime. Never!"

Even Jean Béliveau, who had been associated with the Canadiens since the beginning of the '50s and had been the first recipient of the Conn Smythe trophy in 1965, praised him: "I'm trying to think of a performance of that sort in overtime, and I can't manage it. I've thought of Glenn Hall, Jacques Plante, Terry Sawchuk and Ken Dryden. I really have never seen anything like it."

And Ken Dryden, who won the trophy in the 1971 playoffs, said, "It's one thing to be young and promising. It is another to be good. Patrick Roy is finding out how good he is." He then used a jazz analogy, drawing on his own experience to explain what Patrick must be feeling: "It's a mindless energy experience. You don't really have time to feel much of anything, except there's just a sort of building feeling of just feeling good. It's sort of a jazz music riff. All of a sudden the pace picks up and goes higher and higher and you almost know what's going to come next. You don't know where your fingers are going to go, but if you listen, you know what to do to reach the right note. You know it can come crashing down at any moment, but it won't. The right note is going to happen."

Patrick was experiencing one of the best moments in his career: "In the last series, Mike Liut taught me that a goaltender can keep a team in the game. When you feel good, you feel you can stop anything. I've just played the best game of my life, and we won. In the juniors I was used to seeing so many shots, but we'd lose anyway. Tonight we won. I'm in heaven."

—m—

Around two in the morning, I got a phone call. It was Patrick. He was returning from a team supper and needed to share his emotions, to calm himself down.

"So?" he asked.

"It was amazing, you played a great game! Are you tired?"

"I was earlier. I feel better now."

"Do you think you'll be able to sleep?"

"I should. I usually sleep well."

"Anyway, you have a full day of rest ahead of you before the next game. Tonight, you should celebrate. It's normal to be on a high tonight, but you have to remember that tomorrow, you need to put it all behind you, forget everything and come back down to earth. Put your emotions behind you before the next contest."

"I know; don't worry."

I wasn't worried. Patrick could always control his emotions when the pressure was on. Where others keep telling themselves, without ever really succeeding, that they need to calm down and keep focused on what's happening at the moment, he just does it. This is crucial for a goaltender. Other players might be able to use adrenaline to give themselves a little boost, but a goaltender's quality of play is based on impeccable technique: he must remain in complete control at all times.

I was certainly delighted with his performance. Happy, but not surprised. When he played in the minors, he would sometimes reach the same level of intensity. Then, he would be almost unbeatable. I knew he could reach that level under pressure, but what was impressive was his consistency, his capacity to sustain that level for 13 games in a row.

A sports psychologist once told me that an athlete cannot reach his mental or psychological peak more than three times in a season. This was Patrick's third; the first occurred when he had to surpass himself during training camp and the second when word had it that he would be sent back to Sherbrooke and he had to fight to keep his spot on the team.

The next afternoon, Patrick was seen in the lobby of his New York hotel, looking calm and collected. He looked like he had just rolled out of bed, with his eyes puffy, barely open. He was pale, had his earphones around his neck and a copy of an Agatha Christie mystery in his hand. The journalists spotted him, and he was immediately surrounded.

"What does a 20-year-old kid need to remain grounded?"

"Understanding teammates, encouraging coaches, supportive parents and a good agent," replied Patrick.

As an elderly American couple were strolling through the lobby, the lady noticed the young man and wondered who he was. She stopped and took a closer look to see whether he was some Hollywood movie or TV star. Unable to recognize the teenager, she left to catch up with her husband, who'd kept walking, not at all interested in the stranger.

Patrick boarded the team bus heading for the Garden. He wanted to watch the video of the previous night's game, not to congratulate himself about his work, but to identify any mistakes he'd made. "I made some mistakes. A few of my moves were rushed; I wasn't properly positioned for some shots. But, that's the game, right? My teammates saved me by coming from behind three times during the game. If it hadn't been for them, there wouldn't have been any overtime."

The next day, it was back to the drawing board. The Ranger's coaches tried to downplay Jack Birch's comments about Patrick's technique, especially as they had failed to intimidate him. "Roy will become a great goalie one day. When we said that his technique wasn't perfect, we meant that he tries things a veteran wouldn't do. We're trying to take advantage of these weaknesses."

Most coaches didn't realize that Patrick, in collaboration with François Allaire, was inventing a new goaltending style that would inspire nearly all of the next generation's goalies. Coaches had never seen a goaltender whose blades where so sharp, who moved so quickly and so often to face the puck, and who went down so frequently to make saves. The technique violated their netminding credo. It seemed to be a flawed approach; they couldn't understand it.

—⁓—

The Rangers were on the brink of elimination. They did have a final surge in game four in New York with a 2–0 shutout victory. It was Vanbiesbrouck's revenge; he was excellent. But the Rangers' comeback was short-lived. The next day, on Friday, May 9, the New Yorkers were defeated by a score of 3–1 at the Montréal Forum. Their season had come to an end.

By beating the Rangers, the Canadiens became the Prince of Wales Conference champions. But neither the title nor the trophy that accompanied it held any real interest for the Habs. They had their eyes on a berth in the ultimate series, the Stanley Cup final, for the first time since 1979.

The Canadiens would be facing the winner of the series between the Calgary Flames and the St. Louis Blues. But the final would not begin before the following Friday, in six days. So Perron decided to give his team a well-earned rest. They could escape from Alcatraz for the weekend. And there'd be no practices until Monday. A change of scenery would do them a world of good. They had engaged in fierce competition for over a month.

Patrick came to Québec City to see family and friends. He didn't go to the Saint-Sacrement Recreational Center—he was older now—but to a trendy bar on Grande-Allée. He discovered that his growing fame had given him powers of attraction he had never before possessed. People could be heard whispering as soon as he arrived. Everyone recognized him. Guys would congratulate him, try to strike up a conversation, pat him on the back. A little more discreet, girls would try to catch his eye from a distance. He sensed it. He felt like a kid who suddenly could have anything he desired in a candy store.

Then he noticed the bewitching blue eyes of Sophie, a tall, beautiful, honey-blonde woman, and his heart leapt. It was as if the laws of gravity had just been changed and nobody had told him. He only had eyes for her, just as in New York a few short days before—or was it a few months?—when all he could see was the puck.

But the object of this new obsession only had his well-being at heart, and there was no one to blow the final whistle and end the game. He was bewitched, inflamed, consumed with Spring Fever, a terrible virus, more devastating than any flu, when the only Flames that should have preoccupied him were in Calgary, about to polish off the Blues in the other semifinal for the Clarence Campbell Conference title. He was cheating on "Charlotte."

Monday came, and his newfound Eden gave way to practice. Patrick was there in body, if not entirely in mind. The Flames had beaten the Blues. As they had finished a rung higher than the Canadiens in the overall standings, the first game would take place in Calgary, far from any distraction. To get acclimated to the altitude and get over jet lag, the Habs would be arriving in Calgary a few days early.

Most experts prognosticated a Canadiens victory in the Stanley Cup final. They were a formidable new team with no distinctions between rookies and veterans. They were just players, warriors. There was some question, however, about the impact of the long six-day break before the series.

I had the opportunity to see first-hand the incredible team chemistry. Patrick was almost always the last to leave the dressing room, even in the minors, and we'd end up waiting for him for what seemed like hours after every game. I ventured near the sacrosanct Canadiens' dressing room after they had wrapped up the Rangers series. It was a festive mood. From a distance, I watched Patrick answer reporters' questions. Some of the players, mostly veterans, noticed me and came over to give me a hearty hello. Bobby Smith's comments were particularly touching: "Mr. Roy, you must be the only guy in the world more proud of Patrick than we are. All of us are very happy for him." It came from the heart and seemed to represent the feeling of most of his teammates. I knew it was sincere, since I had just heard the big center say the same thing to the media. In fact, he added that the goaltender's impeccable work game after game from the start of the series was the principal reason for the team's unexpected march to the Stanley Cup final.

It was the first time that two rookie goaltenders had met in the Cup final since 1945, when the Toronto Maple Leafs' Frank McCool faced the Red Wings' Harry Lumley. At age 23, Mike Vernon was three years older than Patrick. But Montréal's goalie had the advantage of having played more games: 47 compared with Vernon's 18.

The outcome of the series' first game was decided in the early moments of the third period, when the Flames scored two goals in 79 seconds, garnering a 5–2 victory. Calgary had some big tough players in their lineup, and Jim Peplinski, Joel Otto, Jamie Macoun, Tim Hunter and Nick Fotiu (a former Golden Gloves champion in the New York area) didn't hesitate to rough up some of the Canadiens. Yet the Flames had other assets: they had speed with Lanny McDonald and Joe Mullen; quick hands with Dan Quinn and John Tonelli, as well as Doug Risebrough's tireless work. And what could you say about the shot of Al MacInnis, one of the league's premiere rearguards? However, Patrick lacked the intensity and competitiveness that we had seen in previous series. So did the rest of the team. It's as if the six-day break and the lack of competition had softened the team more than their opponents' hitting. For the first time since the beginning of the playoffs, Patrick allowed more than three goals in a game—the fifth was scored into an empty net.

As the first period wound down, Peplinski scored the Flames' second tally. It was an important goal, giving Calgary a 2–1 lead, but it was also controversial. Peplinski hit the puck in mid-air, with his stick seemingly above his shoulders—back then, the limit was the height of the player's shoulders, not the height of the goal, as it is today, which is much more practical. But Peplinski was tall and referee Kerry Fraser allowed the goal after consulting linesmen Ron Finn and Ray Scapinello.

Despite what was at stake—it was the Stanley Cup final—and the borderline nature of the goal, Fraser failed to consult the video replay. Furious, Patrick hit one of the linesmen on the leg with his stick and lightly jostled the other. Running out of patience, he lost his concentration. Thanks to Scapinello's generosity, Patrick got off with a 10-minute game misconduct penalty for slightly hitting Finn. Scapinello chose to ignore Patrick's action towards him, but if the official had applied article 67 of the regulation to the letter, Montréal's star goalie would have been liable to an automatic suspension of at least three games, and NHL vice president Brian O'Neill could have extended it to ten matches. Patrick had narrowly avoided disaster. Was the referees' leniency based on their uncertainty about the legitimacy of Peplinski's goal? We'll never know. But that doesn't excuse Patrick's actions. The team could've been in real difficulty. Remember that, four years earlier, he had received a five-game suspension, reduced to three games upon appeal, for a much less serious infraction, when the Sainte-Foy Gouverneurs were vying for the Midget AAA League Championship against the Lac-Saint-Louis Lions.

As for the goal itself, Guy Carbonneau was right beside Peplinski when the Flames forward deflected the puck. "The goal should have been disallowed. I was right there; I could see everything. There were three officials on the ice, and they didn't see a thing. They should have taken a look at the video replay. We were doing well until then; that goal changed everything."

Be that as it may, the Flames, coached by Bob Johnson, were leading one game to nothing in the series. Were they too good for the Canadiens? Or were the Habs rusty after the long layoff?

As usual, Johnson resorted to intimidation in an effort to disrupt Patrick's concentration. In addition to mentioning that the Habs' goaltender was not as solid as the goalies the Flames had already met, and that he should have received a suspension for his conduct with the linesmen, he said he had studied Patrick's style. "I've spent a lot of time observing him, and the videos of his games have taught me certain things about him," he said without indicating exactly what he had learned.

The next day, a Calgary newspaper ran a feature story, claiming that the Flames had solved the Patrick Roy riddle. Patrick was incensed. "I haven't read the papers today, but can you tell what great mystery they've solved?" asked Patrick. "They haven't discovered or solved anything. I'll show them what I'm made of. I'll prove a lot of things, you can be sure of that."

He was as good as his word. His teammates showed their mettle, too, in a hard-fought contest, in which the score stood at 2–2 at the end of regulation time. Given how hotly contested the game had been, neither team was expected to put an end to the match anytime soon. But no sooner did the opening face-off take place than McPhee pounced on a bouncing puck in the neutral zone, sped into the Flames zone, faked a shot, drawing both the defenseman and the goaltender over to him, and then fed the disk to Skrudland, who simply redirected it into the net. The dramatic goal left the fans dumbstruck. The whole play took nine seconds. The game was over; the Flames had lost. Still, no one could blame Mike Vernon. He had been excellent: his team had simply been outclassed, 35 shots to 22.

The Canadiens would be returning to Montréal with the home-ice advantage, since the series was tied, at a game apiece. The Habs had regained their composure. But Mike Vernon remained a considerable obstacle, and Patrick would have to be even steadier than the Flames goalie if the Canadiens were to have a chance.

I was concerned about his romance with Sophie. It would've been a pity if a passing infatuation were to disturb a goalie whose total concentration was required to enable the most celebrated hockey club in the world to win its 23rd Stanley Cup. The crucial role that goalies play in the post-season makes teams particularly dependent on their performance. I spoke to Pierre Lacroix about the situation and asked him to keep his eyes open. In the end, there were no consequences to speak of.

—◊◊◊—

Although both coaches came from the university ranks, their teams favored a style of hockey where hooking and interference, with the referees' complicity, ruled. Players had little skating room on the ice. "In this league, if you don't win, you're a dead man. I'm not here to change the rules," said Jean Perron, who admitted he wasn't wild about this type of hockey either.

The third game promised to be like the previous two: a low-scoring goaltenders' duel. It didn't turn out that way, except for early in the match when Patrick had to stop ten shots in less than six minutes, as the Flames had gotten off to a furious start. After that, the two teams scored six goals, four by the Canadiens, before the end of the first period, with three of them in less than 68 seconds. That was it for Mike Vernon: he was lifted in favor of veteran Réjean Lemelin. That was it for the Flames, too: they went down to a 5–3 defeat, despite the addition to their lineup of young Brett Hull, the son of the legendary Bobby Hull.

Vernon returned in game four and redeemed himself by holding Montréal to one goal. Yet Patrick topped him, earning his first post-season shutout. Patrick was proud. "I've always dreamed of winning a 1–0 game," he said. "It's the first time it's happened." And Claude Lemieux came through again, notching his fourth winning tally in the playoffs. He said, "On the goal, I had to go back and play defense since Chris Chelios had pinched in. I stayed in the middle of the ice at their blue line when their defenseman tried a blind pass that their center wasn't expecting. I stepped in and intercepted it and moved towards the goal. I have confidence in my slap shot. As soon as I pulled my stick back, Vernon went down, so I aimed for the five-hole and hit the target."

The game ended in an ugly ten-minute bench-clearing brawl. The Flames, frustrated by the events, decided to vent their spleen on the Habs. The melee, in which a number of fights broke out, lasted a good ten minutes, half the length of a normal period. The Flames were sending a message for game five in Calgary. Leading three games to one, the Canadiens had better be prepared.

Meanwhile, there was considerable speculation about the eventual winner of the Conn Smythe Trophy. Patrick, considered the favorite for the honor, had other things on his mind. "It would be the icing on the cake, but I'm not thinking about it. What I'm concerned about is winning the Stanley Cup. That's the important thing. Game after game, the defensemen clear the traffic in front of the net. When people talk about the Conn Smythe, they should consider it a team award. Everyone makes a contribution. If the Canadiens had not gotten this far, I wouldn't be in the running for the Conn Smythe."

He was right. Had it not been for Bob Gainey who, two months earlier, in no uncertain terms, had put an end to the whining of teammates who were using Patrick as an excuse for not winning, had it not been for Claude Lemieux, whose passion had roused the veterans out of their routine-induced lethargy, had it not been for the methodical and effective defensive work of Carbonneau, Robinson and Green, had it not been for the excellent offensive play of Naslund, Smith and Gingras, or the physical play of Skrudland, McPhee, Lalor, Nilan, Ludwig and Chelios who, game after game, had skated with fire in their belly and sacrificed for the team, and, finally, had it not been for the flair and courage of Jean Perron, who in the worst of the torment had persisted despite everything in inserting an unheard-of number of rookies in the regular lineup, the Canadiens would never have been where they were: one victory away from the Stanley Cup.

Observing how fate can sometimes play a crucial role—that's what happened the previous year in Sherbrooke—Patrick said, "We're forgetting that Doug Soetaert was playing great hockey before getting injured in Los Angeles against the Kings. I was having trouble at the time, but that's when they gave me the Number 1 job and decided to get me ready for the playoffs. I had time to prepare mentally for the challenge. I told myself if I could do the job in Sherbrooke, I could do it here too."

Jean Perron agreed. "I hesitated about starting him in the playoffs. He had won some big games on the road but, on the other hand, he didn't have any Stanley Cup experience. As it turned out, I didn't really have a choice. Sometimes, big decisions are made for you. When you consider that neither Penney nor Soetaert was completely healthy, I had to name Roy as my starting goaltender."

The first two periods of game five featured tough physical play. Curiously, Bob Johnson resorted to intimidation. He insisted on using a line consisting of Sheehy, Hunter and Fotiu. The Habs had a number of scoring chances when those three tough guys were on the ice together. After 40 minutes of play, Montréal led 2–1.

In the third period, play was continuing in much the same fashion when Green and Smith scored one after the other in the space of 19 seconds. Suddenly, the score stood at 4–1. Then, Bozek cut the margin to 4–2 with three minutes remaining.

We know the rest. The Canadiens won their 23rd Stanley Cup, and thus became the most successful team in professional sports, surpassing the New York Yankees' record of 22 World Series victories.

Patrick was the youngest player ever to win the Conn Smythe Trophy, taking his place beside other great goalies: Roger Crozier (1966), Glenn Hall (1968), Ken Dryden (1971), Bernard Parent (1974–1975) and Billy Smith (1983).

THE PARADE 16

Patrick and his blissfully slumbering teammates were soaring over the prairies of Saskatchewan and Manitoba when Barbara, Alexandra, Sophie and I reached Pierre Lacroix's home in Montréal at 3:30 in the morning.

We got a few minutes' rest and then headed to Dorval Airport around 5:00 a.m. to wait for Patrick. We weren't alone. A few thousand fans had already gathered to give the Stanley Cup champions—"their team"—a rousing welcome.

It was a gray and foggy day. The plane circled the airport for over half an hour, trying to find a path through the mist. High above the clouds the players basked in the most glorious sunrise of their lives, while their supporters peered hopefully through the overcast sky. Undoubtedly, among the fans were looters who had pillaged Sainte-Catherine Street boutiques the previous night. This time, the police had come prepared. Members of the Royal Canadian Mounted Police and Montréal's riot squad, equipped with nightsticks and helmets, had been dispatched to the airport.

"There shouldn't be any problem now," the pilot said, before starting the descent. Even so, it took him two attempts to land the craft on the tarmac.

We followed Pierre Lacroix through the dense, excited crowd. Dorval Airport's terminal hadn't been renovated yet, and people were pushing and elbowing their way into the cramped, low-ceilinged arrivals area. Patrick's agent, followed closely by Barbara, Alexandra and Sophie, finally worked his way past the checkpoint and along the corridor to the room set aside for the players' families. Some frenzied fans got in my way, so it took me a little longer to reach the security guard. He eyed me warily.

"You can't go there."

"Listen, I'm with Pierre Lacroix. He just came through here."

"Only the players' families are allowed inside."

"Well, I'm Patrick Roy's father!"

"And I'm Napoleon's son!" he sneered. "Move on!"

While I was fishing through my pockets for my driver's license as proof of identity, Pierre Lacroix noticed I hadn't followed him. He turned around and told the guard, "Let him through; he's Patrick Roy's father!"

The guard underwent a complete metamorphosis. I tried my best to assure him not to worry about it. How could he have known I was Patrick's dad? He was just doing his job. But he followed me down the hall for over 30 yards, fluttering around me like a gentle butterfly, repeating over and over that he was very, very sorry.

—m—

The players finally emerged and armed policemen immediately parted the sea of fans to permit the players to get through unscathed. Yet in the congested quarters, people could actually touch the players, pat them on the head, or even clasp them by the neck, as if they were family or long-lost friends. We were concerned about Patrick.

Slightly claustrophobic, he could become breathless and panic if he felt trapped in a confined space. Pierre Lacroix had asked the police to give him special protection.

Once out of the terminal, Patrick bolted to the car, his shirttail hanging out of his jacket, his tie undone, flanked by a security agent on one side and a panting reporter struggling to keep up while sticking a microphone under his nose. We rushed after Patrick to get to Lacroix's Audi. Patrick plunked down in the passenger seat with his sister on his knee. I sat in the back seat with Barbara and Sophie. Lacroix was at the wheel. Suddenly hundreds of fans swarmed around the car. Some people, who were being squashed up against it by those behind them, banged on the windows and the hood, desperately trying to free themselves. It felt as if we were riding a rowboat on a stormy sea.

Informed of the danger, cops cleared a path to extricate us. With their help, we managed to get to Lacroix's house, where a team from the TV news magazine *Le Point* was waiting for us. Host Simon Durivage was eager to record the first impressions of Patrick and the family.

—⚋—

Patrick couldn't wrap his head around what was happening to him. It had taken him 12 long years to win his first cup in Sherbrooke, and now, barely a year later, he had another: the most prestigious trophy in hockey, every player's dream. It seemed as if he had just finished drinking champagne from the Calder Cup, when he was sipping from the Stanley Cup. The emotions of the previous year were still too fresh to be eclipsed so quickly and so thoroughly by new emotions, no matter how grand the achievement that had stirred them.

Were these triumphs an indication of what the future held? Would every spring end with victory and champagne? Of course not! Many a legendary Hall of Famer had no Stanley Cup to his name. Patrick realized this. But for the time being, it seemed rather abstract and hard to assimilate.

That evening, the players and their families were invited to a banquet at the Queen Elizabeth Hotel, a last chance to get together before the summer vacation. It was announced on TV that the traditional Stanley Cup parade would kick off from City Hall around 11 a.m. the next day. Only in Montréal could a Stanley Cup Parade be referred to as "traditional": some NHL teams have never won the trophy. For example, by 1986, the New York Rangers, an established NHL organization, had not won the cup for 40 years.

—ᴍ—

At eleven in the morning, the players strode up the steps of Montréal's city hall to the cheers of their fervent fans, signed the golden book and chatted with dignitaries. The Habs were in summer attire: short-sleeved shirts and light pants. Many wore the Canadiens' cap to shield them from the sun that would be beating down all day.

After the customary speeches by coaches, management and Canadiens Captain Bob Gainey, the team exited city hall. Gainey led them with the Cup held high. Patrick followed, proudly clutching the Conn Smythe trophy, assisted by Doug Soetaert. Gainey, Robinson and Mario Tremblay were fortunate enough to ride in the trophy car, which would be better protected from aggressive fans. The others sat on the backs of top-down convertibles.

The parade wended its way through the jubilant crowd, which La Presse, a local daily, estimated at nearly a million, about a third of the population in the Montréal area. Organizers had not foreseen the size of the turnout. The players would have to go through a multitude of fans, a situation as risky as it was unprecedented—a four-mile-long expression of fan devotion lasting over five hours. The parade proceeded east from city hall to de Lorimier, then all along Sainte-Catherine to the Forum, where Québec singers and performers including Céline Dion, Yvon Deschamps, Claude Dubois, Pierre Lalonde and Martine Saint-Clair waited to entertain the players and their fans. The price of admission was two dollars. The money raised would be given to charity.

It was a sight to see: the moving mass of humanity, proud fans, strolling under a shower of paper and confetti, which fell like January snow from the tops of buildings, hopping on cars just for a chance to touch "their" players, throwing beer at them, getting sprayed with champagne in return, climbing on the hoods of cars, sitting beside their idols on the trunks, shaking their hands, grabbing them by the neck, kissing them, riding beside them for a bit, just so that, for one moment, they could live the dream in the shoes of *Les Glorieux*. Others scaled lampposts or dangled from traffic lights at intersections so they could see everything—or be seen.

An endless sea of Montréal fans had come to declare their love, out of an overpowering sense of identification with their team. Serge Savard had made sure there were up to eight French-speaking Québecers on the 1985–86 edition of the Canadiens. Players like Lemieux, Carbonneau, Gingras, Richer and Patrick had played a decisive role on the road to the Cup. As well, never had there been such a strong Francophone presence in management with President Ronald Corey, François Allaire, Jean Perron, Jacques Laperrière, Jacques Lemaire, André Boudrias and Claude Ruel. Of course, Montrealers had gone seven long years without the Cup, an eternity for fans accustomed to winning, on average, a Cup every two years. Most of all, the victory had been completely unexpected.

It was beautiful; it was moving. It was unique. At the high point of the parade, many fans brandished posters emblazoned with "incROYable," or *incredible Roy*. With the insouciance of youth, Patrick acted like a master of ceremonies, inviting them to be even more vociferous. Shirtless, he blew kisses at them, climbed onto the car trunk, holding the Conn Smythe up high, howled with joy, waved a Canadiens pennant, and struck a bodybuilding pose to show off his puny muscles to the crowd. He ignited their passion and made their hearts sing, but not without risk. Fortunately, all he lost was his shirt.

At the Forum five hours later, many players had cramps in their hands and shoulders from so many handshakes and so many pats on the back. Some players' shirts or T-shirts were stained with blood after more aggressive fans had fought one another to get close to their heroes.

Gaston Gingras had left the parade a few blocks before the Forum so he could savor the event from a fan's point of view. He arrived at the arena ahead of his teammates and sat in his usual place in the dressing room, exhausted. He'd gone through some difficult times in recent years. He could never really get going after being traded by the Canadiens to the Toronto Maple Leafs in late 1982. He returned to the Habs in 1985, but was promptly shunted off to Sherbrooke in the American Hockey League. Now, he had played a crucial role in the Stanley Cup victory, scoring some important goals.

At city hall earlier that day, Patrick had taken him aside to express his admiration. "You were an inspiration for me. I've followed your career, and I know now that we can always come back from a loss, a setback or a disappointment. You never quit. You have courage and guts, and you've just won two Cups in a row. For young players like me, you're a role model."

Gingras had tears in his eyes. In the silent dressing room before the other players joined them, he broke down. "I've gone through some rough patches." His voice choking with emotion, he said, "During the parade, Patrick came to tell me that he wouldn't have made it this year if it hadn't been for me. He's a hell of a guy. Excuse me." He paused, fighting to regain his composure. "I'm not used to letting it all hang out like this. But I think I've just realized what the Stanley Cup is all about. I didn't know how intense it was. It's as if it suddenly dawned on me."

He wasn't the only one to vent his emotions. The day belonged to the Habs. Any and all excesses and tomfoolery were permitted the players. The fans' celebrations and tribute left them stunned. One by one, they returned to the Forum, exhausted, sunburned, brimming with emotion, beer and champagne, their hair full of confetti and their shirts soaked and disheveled—those who weren't bare-chested by then—riding a high they had never known before. Chris Chelios's mother took one look at her son, who was intoxicated by the sun and beer, mopped his face and said, with a mischievous smile, "Sometimes, I hate being your mother!"

The Forum was the scene of joy and jubilation. After the artists sang a few songs, the fans started chanting "Go Habs go!" as they waited for their idols to be introduced by Claude Mouton, accompanied by humorist Yvon Deschamps and singer Pierre Lalonde.

Patrick made a spectacular entrance. With the exuberance of youth, he pranced around with the Conn Smythe Trophy over his head as the crowd went wild. It was probably the only time that Céline Dion was upstaged.

Barbara couldn't help saying, "On the ice, Patrick shows a great deal of maturity, but off it, he's still a child. Once he has time in a few weeks to sit down a bit and think it all over, I'm sure he'll realize what's happening to him."

And when Bob Gainey appeared with the Stanley Cup, the fans exploded with glee. He raised the trophy towards the rafters, where the 1985–86 banner would soon join the other 22. Thousands of beer cans and bottles rose in unison.

Towards the end of the party, Chris Nilan, inspired by the zany atmosphere, grabbed the mike and conducted the crowd in a mad chorus of: "NA-NA-NA-NA! NA-NA-NA-NA! HEY-HEY-HEY, GOODBYE!..."

—ⵡ—

Patrick was a star. Not yet a superstar perhaps, but a star nonetheless. People recognized him on the street, talked to him when he got the groceries, asked for his autograph when he dined at a restaurant. Now he belonged to the select, incredibly privileged circle that can make a person's day with a simple gesture, wink, handshake or autograph on a scrap of paper.

He had a wonderful, but busy summer. Pierre Lacroix was flooded with offers. Organizers of sporting and social events tripped over one another, asking Patrick to take part in charitable affairs, banquets, receptions, golf tournaments, television and radio shows—not to mention the inevitable visit with Canadian Prime Minister, Brian Mulroney.

Sport magazine saved him one trip, however. Normally, the magazine invited the Conn Smythe winner to the Big Apple for a grand reception attended by the media in a sumptuous hotel, and gave him the keys to a new car. Wayne Gretzky had been fêted the previous year, and Mark Messier had also been honored. For some reason though, *Sport* magazine decided to skip the reception that year. Perhaps their noses were out of joint because Patrick had won the trophy.

Toward the end of July, Patrick and I went to Roberval, where he served as the honorary chairman of the *Traversée internationale du lac St-Jean* (Lake St. Jean International Swimming Marathon). We had left Bonaventure after spending a few days with the family before taking the Rivière-du-Loup ferry to Saint-Siméon, a 90-minute ride. When someone informed the captain that Patrick was on board, we got to tour the ship from stem to stern.

The next morning the event's organizers invited us for breakfast. The meal was presided over by Benoît Bouchard, the MP from Roberval and federal minister of Employment and Immigration in Brian Mulroney's Progressive Conservative cabinet. It was odd to see my son in this company. It was more my milieu than his—I had been deputy minister at the Ministry of Tourism, which had funded the *Traversée*. But all eyes were on Patrick, the 20-year-old hockey hero. I wondered about the disproportionate importance given to stars in our society and about the demands placed on them.

Their influence far exceeds their own field of activity. In the financial community, the Canadian Imperial Bank of Commerce waged a vast advertising campaign with Patrick as its ambassador. He recorded his first TV commercials, in both French and English. The bank thought Patrick would appeal to a younger clientele.

Even high-ranking politicians were aware of his achievements. On May 27, only three days after the Stanley Cup final, the important annual Québec –New York meeting was being held, jointly presided over by Québec Prime Minister Robert Bourassa, and the governor of New York, Mario Cuomo. The meeting took place in the impressive Cabinet Room in Québec City. In attendance were Bourassa's cabinet ministers and New York commissioners who had files that needed to be discussed. Public servants of both sides were also present. All told, there were about 30 of us around the table.

At that time, I was negotiating the first Québec –New York reciprocity agreement on highway-code infractions. Québec 's Transport Minister Marc-Yvan Côté, whose English was somewhat limited, had asked me to accompany him and give the report on the progress of negotiations.

In the solemn atmosphere, the ministers and commissioners presented progress reports on their files. When my turn came,

Mario Cuomo suddenly cut me off, "Monsieur Roy, let me tell you something. Your son might have beat my Rangers, but he won't beat my Mets."

You had to be a hockey fan to appreciate his remark, which certainly wasn't the case for most of the rather sober audience. It also helped to know that Mario Cuomo was not only a powerful U.S. politician, he was an avid sports fan, and he loved baseball, having played minor league ball in his youth. Many around the table looked at each other, puzzled, wondering what in the world was going on. Some may have thought that the governor and I were old friends. Suddenly, I had gained in importance merely because I was the father of someone who had done something important.

In our society, the personality cult has such an appeal that it often completely eclipses the people around the famous person. It was as if Stéphane and Alexandra no longer existed. Henceforth, they would be known as Patrick's brother and sister. Similarly, Barbara and Michel Roy would now be just Patrick's mom and dad. We would be recognized exclusively for our genetic contribution to the NHL. We would exist solely as an extension of our son Patrick, the famous personality.

Patrick had never sought star status. He had no control over the perks of success. All he ever wanted to do was play hockey and win. He hadn't changed: he was still down to earth and close to his family. In February of 1986, I had invited the Québec City lawyer Pierre Jolin to a game at the Forum. We'd been friends in college. When the game was over, we grabbed a bite with Patrick at the *Jardin de Paris*, on Sainte-Catherine Street. It's a restaurant that many players liked to call home after an evening's work. Barbara, Stéphane and Alexandra were also there.

When Jolin and I bumped into each other 20 years later, I was surprised to discover that he recalled that evening in minute detail.

However he seemed to remember everthing but the game. "I was particularly impressed," he said, "with Patrick's attitude toward his younger sister, nine years his junior. There was a feeling of tenderness, friendship and togetherness. He talked to her like a big brother who'd missed his little sister. He inquired about personal things, how school was going, what she did for amusement, or who her friends were, as if he wanted to make sure she was all right, as if he wanted to protect her. You could see a very different guy from the goalie that the media worked so hard to define, and that we believed we knew.

"I was also impressed with the quality of his relationship with you and in the way that he referred to you. He often sought your advice about the way he did things on the ice and in his personal life. He needed support for his beliefs, advice on how to act, think and conduct himself. I was surprised to see that he asked you questions about hockey that he probably didn't even ask his coach. You were his reference.

"He expressed a lot of admiration for you, as a child normally does for his parents, yet it was surprising in his case, given his status as an elite athlete in a sport not known for tenderness and sensitivity.

"Simple, profoundly human family ties seemed important to him, and he seemed comfortable in his skin, not tormented or haunted by fame and not tempted by the lure of material gain. I wasn't expecting this and I was especially pleased because now that he was on the verge of fame and fortune, he could distance himself from his family, especially openly and publicly.

"After the game, he took leave of the media, citing a family dinner commitment. Clearly, he preferred the company of his loved ones to still more media attention. It is rare to see this in a hockey player. I learned a lot that night, and most in contrast to what I had imagined; it rattled my system of values, I'll say that."

Jolin had seen the man behind the image.

The next summer, Patrick met a beautiful blonde with blue eyes who reminded him of Olivia Newton-John, whom he adored. Michèle Piuze wasn't a singer; she played softball. But Limoilou was a lot closer than Melbourne. He was smitten.

THE UNDERTOW 17

"A couple of trophies and a season don't make a career." Patrick was right.

In his *Journal de Montréal* column, Bertrand Raymond listed goalies who had folded under pressure after achieving fleeting glory in moments of high tension. Among them, he mentioned Jim Craig, who led Team USA, coached by Herb Brooks, to a gold medal at the Lake Placid Olympics in 1980, after upsetting the powerful Soviet juggernauts in the semifinals. Dubbed the "Miracle on Ice," the victory made Jim Craig an American hero. The U.S. media hailed his National Hockey League debut as an event of major significance. Yet, Craig never succeeded in the NHL, despite trials with Atlanta, Boston and Minnesota.

Craig was not alone. Don Beaupré, touted as a future NHL superstar, got off to an incredible start with the Minnesota North Stars, then languished in the minors for the next three years before returning to the big time.

The Edmonton Oilers Andy Moog was shunted back to Wichita after eliminating the Canadiens in three straight games with the Edmonton Oilers in 1981. Mike Moffat and Cleon Daskalakis couldn't nail down permanent jobs in the NHL despite heroic post-season debuts with the Boston Bruins in 1982 and 1985 respectively.

In a goalie's first year, everything is fresh; everything is beautiful. He has much to win and nothing to lose. By his second year, opponents have a book on him. They know him inside out and try to expose his weaknesses. Suddenly, fear of failure grips the young man. His confidence is shaken. Doubt is a goalie's worst enemy. It makes him freeze. It makes him lose a split second in reaction time. It can make the difference between success and failure.

In Montréal, because of the winning tradition the fans were accustomed to and the aura of excellence surrounding the temple of hockey, the Montréal Forum, the pressure on the team was unrelenting: they had to win.

The Canadiens' 23 Stanley Cup triumphs involved legendary exploits by their netminders: Georges Vézina, in the 1916 and 1924 victories; George Hainsworth, in 1930 and 1931; Bill Durnan, in 1944 and 1946; Jacques Plante, the architect of the glorious victories in the 1950s, and justifiably considered one of the two best goalies in NHL history along with Terry Sawchuck; Lorne "Gump" Worsley, in the 1960s; and finally Ken Dryden, during the last Montréal dynasty in the 1970s. So Patrick was joining a group of renowned netminders.

In contrast, others had their moment in the sun, then lost their jobs to better goalies: Gerry McNeil, whose career was sandwiched between those of Bill Durnan and Jacques Plante; Charlie Hodge and Rogatien Vachon, between Lorne Worsley and Ken Dryden; and Steve Penney, who dazzled the Nordiques in the 1984 series, but couldn't sustain the level of excellence subsequently. Not to mention Wayne Thomas, Michel Plasse, Phil Myre, Michel "Bunny" Larocque, Denis Herron, Richard Sévigny and Rick Wamsley.

—∞—

Back at the training camp prior to the 1986–87 season, Patrick faced two significant challenges. First he had to prove that his playoff performance wasn't a fluke, that he wasn't a flash in the pan who had played over his head in the playoffs. In other words, he had to determine, consciously or unconsciously, where he belonged. Was he a worthy successor to Durnan, Plante and Dryden, or would he sink into oblivion after a few years like Myre, Larocque and Penney? At age 20, he would have to help maintain the winning tradition of a team with the most illustrious record in NHL history in much tougher circumstances than his glorious predecessors.

He would have to meet these two challenges despite the fact that his performances the previous spring had raised unrealistic expectations. Pierre Lacroix sensed the risk: "How could he improve on his performance in the series? It's impossible. Given that, he'll disappoint the fans, the media and even me."

Patrick was well aware of it. Every day, from the start of training camp, he asked François Allaire to remain on the ice for about an hour after the other players had left. Patrick wanted to improve his play anticipation and increase his lateral speed. "This season, I want to improve night after night, to be more consistent, and to have fewer bad games. I was successful last year, but that's no reason to stop working. I want to go on being successful."

To reassure people who worried he might succumb to the enormous pressure, he said, "That won't happen because hockey is a team sport. My performances are a reflection of teamwork, in victory and in defeat. We'll need to remember the circumstances that led to our success. We didn't solve our late-season problems individually. We won because of team spirit. Everybody pulled in the same direction at the same time." And, gazing at the new banner hanging from the Forum rafters, he added, "No one can ever take away what we achieved last season. We have it for the rest of our lives."

—m—

In the summer of 1986, the Canadiens' front office carried out its yearly team assessment. With Soetaert's departure to New York as a free agent, Patrick clearly emerged as the starting goalie and Penney was his backup. Savard advised Perron to have a chat with Penney: "Look, Jean, now that Patrick is your Number 1 goalie, you have to work things out with Penney. He has to agree to be the backup. We have to take care of that."

A few hours later, Penney showed up at Perron's office and was informed of the decision. The goalie replied somewhat apathetically that he would be leaving on vacation and the subject should be taken up with his agent. Annoyed by Penney's reaction, Savard immediately contacted his buddy John Ferguson of the Winnipeg Jets and traded the goalie with the rights to a relative unknown, Jan Ingman, for Brian Hayward. Case closed.

In François Allaire's opinion, Hayward was a good goaltender, more reliable than Penney, more solid than Soetaert. Hayward, a business management graduate from Cornell University, was acquired by the Jets in 1982, after being selected to the NCAA First All-American Team in the United States.

He did a few stints in Sherbrooke in the American Hockey League between 1982 and 1986. That's where Allaire got to know him. During that period, Hayward also played 165 games for the Jets in the NHL, posting an overall goals-against average of 3.94. In the two seasons before coming to Montréal, he had been very active indeed, making 61 and 52 starts respectively. Hayward would spend the next four seasons in Montréal as Patrick's backup.

—⚬—

Michèle Piuze moved in with Patrick in the fall of 1986. They were engaged the following Christmas during midnight mass at Saint-Ferréol-les-Neiges, in a Québec City suburb. They set up house in

Rosemont, in the triplex owned by Lucien Deblois, and the following year, they moved to Île Bizard, where Patrick had his first house built, on a new housing estate. They soon settled into a routine, based on the team's schedule of practices, games and road trips.

Patrick began the season with a new mask. He had the chin cup lengthened to provide better protection against throat-level shots. Preparing the molding for the new armor was no picnic. His face had to be covered with a kind of paste to make a mold that perfectly fit the contours of his face. Obliged to breathe through a straw, he became claustrophobic. After about 20 minutes, panic set in, and he tore the mold off before it had finished hardening. It took considerable ingenuity to finish the job.

Michel Lefebvre and his son, Patrick, a father-and-son team, who designed Patrick's mask and would later make his pads, had an artist paint the mask in Canadiens colors. The traditional bright red was embellished with blue and white lines. The artist added Patrick's number, 33, the team logo and the name "Roy" on both sides of the mask in stylized letters. The mask became a sort of symbol as if it would permanently bind Patrick to the team.

The mask, made of Kevlar and fiberglass, was surprisingly heavy, forcing Patrick to move his head continually during play stoppages. People wondered about Patrick's constant twitch. With the heat in NHL arenas and the effort he expended, sweat drenched his face and ran down his chin. As a result, the inner surface of the mask irritated his skin. This was the main reason for his odd head twitching movements, coupled with a bit of imitation—Daniel Bouchard twitched, too—and tension.

—∞—

With Jean Perron at the helm until the spring of 1988, Patrick didn't receive the consideration usually granted to a team's Number 1 goalie.

He barely played a dozen more games than Hayward during the regular season. Perron started him in 45 matches, while Number 1 goalies in the NHL usually played 60 or more contests. He was one of two netminders with the Canadiens, and he had to share the chores with his backup. Challenges energized Patrick and he loved dealing with pressure-packed situations, so the two-goalie arrangement was hardly motivating for him. On the other hand, though he worked with François Allaire only occasionally during the 1986–87 season, their partnership helped him make steady progress. Ironically, while the heroic triumph in 1986 proved that he thrived under pressure, he had more problems in the 1987 playoffs than during the regular season.

Yet, things got off to a promising start. In the spring of 1987, the Canadiens again faced the Boston Bruins in the first round, but this time in a best-of-seven series. The Habs dusted off their fierce Bean Town opponents in four straight games. Patrick was solid throughout.

In the next round, the Canadiens met their archrivals, the Québec Nordiques. Hockey fans all over Québec relished the prospect. The first game, at the Montréal Forum, ended with the local club going down to a humiliating 7–5 defeat. The Canadiens, Patrick included, didn't seem up for the game. It was his first bad game in 25 straight playoff starts. He ceded seven goals to the Nordiques, and he wasn't at his best—or very lucky—on some of them. At 7:21 of the third period, he was beaten by a deflection off two players, and Perron replaced him with Hayward.

As in the previous spring, the Habs were sequestered at the remote Sheraton Hotel, called "Alcatraz" by the players, on Île Charron. The day after the Nordiques debacle, Patrick was playing ping-pong with a teammate in the hotel living room; others were playing video games. Brian Hayward walked in, sporting a triumphant smile, and announced that he would be starting the next game.

Patrick hurriedly finished the ping-pong game and went up to his room to call his agent and confidant, Pierre Lacroix.

"Pierre, it's Patrick."

"Hi! How's it going today?"

"Not so good. Hayward is going to play tomorrow. It's the first time since I've been in Montréal that I've been benched during the playoffs. And yet, before the last game, I'd played 24 in a row without giving anyone any reason to complain. I don't get it."

"Did Perron speak to you?"

"No, not a word."

"Well, listen, give him a call and try to meet with him. Ask him to explain."

—m—

Patrick knocked on Perron's door. The coach invited him in. As it happened, Perron had been studying film from the previous game. "Mr. Perron," said Patrick, "I'd like another chance to play the Nordiques. I think I deserve it. If I'm not good, well ... you can bench me." Perron looked him in the eye and said, "Last year, I didn't have any choice; this year I do. I'm going with Hayward."

Appalled, Patrick turned on his heels and left. The coach, who had been amply rewarded for believing in Patrick's ability and giving him his first opportunity in the NHL, was refusing to give him another chance against the Nordiques after one bad match. Perron had some doubts. Frustrated, Patrick returned to his room thinking, "*Tabarnak!* I can never goal for that guy again!"

With Hayward in the net, Canadiens narrowly lost game two by a score of 2–1; then the series moved to Québec City. Perron decided to stick with Hayward. In fact, Hayward played the rest of the series, and the Habs squeaked by in seven games.

In the semifinal, the Canadiens confronted the Philadelphia Flyers and coach Mike Keenan. Perron had initially intended to go with Patrick, but as he thought Hayward was hot—he had performed well against the Nordiques—he changed his mind. He went with Hayward.

When the Flyers jumped out to a two-game lead in the series, Perron suddenly decided to go back to Patrick, to change the momentum, he said. It was May 10, 1987, and Patrick hadn't played since April 20.

He wasn't bad, but he wasn't brilliant in the first two periods, and the Flyers led 3–2. When Philadelphia scored again only 14 seconds into the third period, Perron replaced him with Hayward. It was the last time Patrick played that season. A little over a minute after Hayward relieved Patrick, the Flyers scored another goal, on their way to a relatively easy 6–3 win. They won the next two games and eliminated the Canadiens.

—⁂—

Jean Perron admitted years later that he had made a serious error in benching Patrick in the Nordiques series. "I made a coaching error. I should never have done that. In the playoffs, you live with your Number 1 goalie, come what may. It was my mistake."

At age 21, Patrick was still learning, not only in terms of technique, but also in terms of behavior and attitudes in various situations. He was learning from experience. Today, with the benefit of hindsight, he regrets the way he reacted: "Maybe Perron thought it would be difficult for me to play in my hometown against the Nordiques, that I had too many friends there and that it might distract me. That wasn't the case, but as a coach, he had the right to think so. I should have worked harder in practice and prepared myself better mentally so I could give an outstanding performance when he called on my

249

services again, to show him he had been wrong to pull me out of the series. The way I reacted was wrong. By sulking, I justified his decision."

—◊◊◊—

In August, Team Canada held its training camp in Montréal in preparation for the Canada Cup. Patrick was invited to take part.

He knew that the dice were loaded and that Grant Fuhr of the Edmonton Oilers, the latest Stanley Cup winners, would be in goal for all the games. Fuhr was the goalie with the most experience in international play, and he had a solid reputation in the NHL. Ron Hextall would be his Number 1 backup. Team Canada's head coach Mike Keenan piloted Hextall's team, the Philadelphia Flyers. Keenan also described Hextall as the premier goaltender in the NHL. What's more, Alan Eagleson, who denied being in any conflict of interest despite his numerous functions as the director of the NHL Players' Association, an organizer of the Canada Cup, a member of Sport Canada and an agent of a number of players, also represented Hextall. The New York Islanders' Kelly Hrudey would be the third-string goalie. Keenan didn't breathe a word about it, but Patrick had only been invited because the camp was in Montréal. A fourth goalie was needed for exhibition games and practices, and it would cost less to use a netminder who lived in the city. The final selection was a foregone conclusion.

Yet, as usual, Patrick secretly harbored the notion that if he performed well he could convince the managers and coaches to keep him, if only as a backup. After all, his track record was certainly not embarrassing. Of the four candidates, he was the only one with a goals-against average under 3.00 the previous season (Roy 2.93; Hextall 3.00; Hrudey 3.30; Fuhr 3.44). Of course, Hextall was the most recent recipient of the Conn Smythe Trophy, but Patrick had also won it two seasons earlier. Not only that, but unlike Hextall, he had led his team to ultimate victory.

When the camp opened on August 4, Patrick said, "Grant Fuhr would be my choice, but Hextall's just like me. He doesn't have international experience. The practices and exhibition games should determine which three goalies are kept. Only one will have to go home." He was already starting to put pressure on his competitors. He would have a very good camp.

After 10 days of physical conditioning and intrasquad games, Patrick was in goal, on August 14, in the first of a series of four preparatory games against the United States in Ottawa. Team USA fired 40 shots at Patrick, but he led Team Canada to a 3–2 victory. He was chosen the star of the game.

Three days later, it was Kelly Hrudey's turn to play Team USA and he blanked them 3–0, but the USA had only fired 17 shots. Curiously enough, Hrudey's mask was already painted in Team Canada's colors. Did he know something that the others didn't?

Then Grant Fuhr registered an unconvincing victory of 7–6, and Hextall won 11–2, a game in which the Americans were overwhelmed by 47 shots to 22.

On August 21, after the four encounters, people were extolling the merits of Patrick and Hrudey. This wasn't exactly what Keenan had wished. Then came the game against the Soviets. Normally it was Patrick's turn, but Keenan chose Hextall for a second straight time, hoping that he would prove himself.

It was a disaster. Hextall was awful in the 9–4 defeat, allowing five soft goals. In fact, until then, Hextall was the goalie who had the most difficulty in training camp, not to mention the incident in which he slashed teammate Sylvain Turgeon and broke his arm. The incident occurred during a drill after Turgeon lightly jostled Hextall trying to get a puck between the goalie's skates.

The next day, on August 23, Keenan announced that Patrick had been cut. Apparently, a six-member committee that included Perron and Savard had taken the decision. Perron and Savard had backed Patrick, but the committee was a puppet. Keenan made all the decisions. He was the head coach, and no one dared contradict him for fear of having a negative effect on the team.

The outcome left a bitter taste in Patrick's mouth about how so-called national teams were picked. He remembered how he had been dropped from Junior Team Canada a few years earlier. Not that he questioned Craig Billington's selection. He readily admitted that Billington had been the better goalie during the tryout, but he knew that he'd been dropped so he wouldn't upset the applecart, and that the people who ran the team didn't want him there, no matter what their reasons were. The same scenario occurred three years later. He excelled in the one game in which he was being tested. To make sure he didn't have the chance to do it again, he was promptly eliminated.

Also fresh in his mind was his brother Stéphane's experience at the World Junior Championships earlier in the year. It was one of the darkest, saddest, most disgraceful, most shameful days in the history of international hockey competition.

On Sunday, January 4, 1987, Junior Team Canada, of which Stéphane was a member, faced the representatives of the USSR in Piestany, Czechoslovakia. It was a meaningless game for the young Soviets, who hadn't enjoyed a good tournament. They had no chance of winning a medal. The Canadians were in an entirely different position. Even before the final, they were already assured of at least a bronze medal. But a win would earn them the silver medal and a victory by a margin of five goals would bring them the gold.

As soon as the match got underway, it was clear that the Soviets were on a mission. They abandoned their usual style and resorted to physical intimidation against the Canadians, provoking them with stick work, slashing them, punching them and elbowing them in the face, right in front of the excessively lenient Norwegian referee, Hans-Ivar Ronning. Overwhelmed, he lost control of the game in the first period.

By 13:53 of the second period, team Canada was already leading by two goals, on their way to the silver medal and very confident of winning the gold. But the inevitable happened.

A scrum broke out in front of the Soviet goal. It looked innocent enough. As the referees had lost control of the situation, a number of players dropped their gloves. Suddenly, one or two Soviets left the bench and got involved in the brawl. With that, both benches emptied. Stéphane grabbed an opponent by the sweater, but another Soviet jumped on his back and helped his teammate rain blows on Stéphane for at least a minute.

Overwhelmed, the referees and linesmen fled the rink, leaving the players to carry on to their heart's content. Then something incomprehensible occurred. The lights were turned off. The appalling scene continued another few minutes in the semidarkness before the players ran out of steam and went to their dressing rooms. International Ice Hockey Federation president Gunther Sabetzki disqualified both teams on the spot. The Finns won the gold medal; the Canadiens ended up empty-handed.

This occurred before the collapse of the Soviet Union, when the Eastern Bloc exerted a great deal of influence over the Ice Hockey Federation. Bert Templeton headed Team Canada. Pat Burns was his assistant. When Burns landed at Mirabel, the ex-police officer, pale and drawn, voiced his suspicions. "A lot of strange things happened; we can't explain them. Before the game, the Russian referee, who had worked our game against Sweden, was deep in conversation with [Soviet] coach Vasilev. We couldn't understand what they were saying, but it looked suspicious. Then, at one point, the big boss of USSR hockey, Anatoli Tarasov, walked out of the junior team's dressing room. Vasilev became very aggressive. He was talking loudly. All the Soviets seemed more aggressive than usual; normally they're quite calm." Obviously, the attack on the Canadians had been premeditated.

Burns also had this to say: "What's really unfair is that the two teams got the same punishment. Tournament organizers never took the referee's comments into account—he admitted that the Soviets were the ones responsible for the brawl. They just wanted us to leave Czechoslovakia as soon as possible. As if we were the guilty ones. That's unfair."

Instead of coming home with a medal around their necks, the Canadian juniors had bruises on their faces and shattered spirits. Of course, they would have loved to win a medal, but not at the expense of having five members of the team massacred by the entire Soviet team.

Those events did nothing to increase Patrick's interest in international hockey.

—m—

Negotiations between two parties are always governed by the same principles. One party wants to pay as little as possible; the other wants to be paid as much as possible. The agreement that Patrick had signed, three years before, in the summer of 1984 with the Canadiens was coming to an end. Negotiations were underway.

Pierre Lacroix's strategy was as follows: "My arguments will be entirely based on what Patrick has accomplished since he joined the organization. He was sensational in the Calder Cup series, in the AHL, and he was just as successful in the first Stanley Cup playoffs he was involved in. Those performances cannot be ignored."

The fact that the coach had benched Patrick in the previous playoffs didn't seem to hurt his position. "After he beat the Bruins in four straight games," Lacroix continued, "there was a decision to make a change. From that moment on, Patrick was no longer in control of his destiny. Canadiens made a corporate decision and I respect that. Then, he was sent back into action when his spirit was low. If things didn't work out, it's not my problem."

Serge Savard pointed out that every Canadiens goalie had been successful. In fact many of them had won Vézina or Jennings trophies. In other words, the goalie didn't make the difference; it was the team's overall strength or performance on defense that counted. "There are various ways to assess a situation," said the GM. "I've never tried to belittle a player so I could get a better contract, but I have to take into consideration the team's style when I evaluate an individual's performance. Patrick Roy is a guy of the future, but, above all, he's just one of the many players we have."

Perhaps Savard's argument made sense in the 1960s or 1970s when the Canadiens, enjoying a huge advantage in selecting players, had built hockey dynasties. It no longer held in the 1980s. Savard's remarks were a good illustration of the fact that in those days, NHL goalies' salaries were not yet commensurate with their importance, especially in the post-season. Nevertheless, it must be said that Serge Savard always paid Patrick fairly and equitably.

The parties reached an agreement in late September. The result was a one-year contract with an option year that would earn Patrick a base salary of $150,000 for the 1987–88 season and $175,000 for the next season, the option year. There would be an additional sum of $250,000 deferred over a five-year period between 1992 and 1997, as well as various bonuses, each of which would amount to no more than $10,000, except for one bonus: he'd receive another $100,000 if he won the Vézina Trophy, awarded to the best goalie in the league based on a vote by the general managers.

—∞—

In the autumn of 1987, François Allaire had to make an important career choice. Pierre Creamer, just appointed Pittsburgh Penguins coach, asked the Canadiens for permission to offer Allaire a job with him in Pittsburgh. Savard knew by now how important a goaltending specialist was to his organization. He refused. Instead, he offered Allaire a two-year contract to stay in Montréal.

It was a heart-wrenching decision for Allaire. He had been working with Creamer for five years. Allaire felt as if he was turning his back on him. Creamer had given him his start in professional hockey. What's more, Creamer's request had set things in motion, prompting Savard to offer the goalie coach the chance to move up to the Montréal Canadiens. But Allaire had also thoroughly appraised the goaltending situation in both Pittsburgh and Montréal. Patrick was very good already, but his guru thought it was just a matter of time before he became "*very very* good." Allaire thought that it was a unique opportunity to work full time with a goalie who not only had a burning desire to constantly improve his technique, but who also had what Allaire called sports intelligence.

He had seen him in Sherbrooke in 1985 when, at age 19, Patrick had gotten his baptism of fire in the first round of the playoffs. Patrick did more than make saves. He did everything he could to lure opposing players into taking penalties so he could give his club a chance to come from behind.

He had seen him in the series against the Rangers in 1986 when, after a stoppage in play, he removed his mask and started to examine it. The referee went over to him and asked,

"Do you have a problem?"

Patrick lifted the mask so he could take a look at it against the light of the powerful projectors.

"I don't know," he said, "it looks like there's something in my field of vision, maybe a hair, but I can't find it."

"Let me take a look."

And so the referee lifted the mask and turned it all around, trying to find the hair in question. He did this for a few moments, but he didn't find anything. Then he handed Patrick the mask and told him to put it on so play could resume. Patrick took another look at it and drank a sip of water from the bottle tied to his goal. Then he slipped the mask over his head, giving defenseman Craig Ludwig an ironic grin. Of course, there had never been any hair, but nearly two minutes had elapsed, enough time to cool off the Rangers a few degrees.

In the same series, Allaire had also seen Patrick fall to his knees in pain after being struck by a projectile thrown from the stands, get up a few seconds later and carry on. "I was hit by a paper ball," Patrick later told teammates. "It didn't hurt at all. I just wanted to give Guy Carbonneau a break. He was our best penalty killer, and he'd been on the ice a long time."

Allaire had also watched Patrick at work in Montréal. In the third period of a tough contest, Patrick had left his net several times to speak to a fan near the Plexiglas when play was stopped. Allaire spoke to Patrick after the game.

"Tell me, what were you doing in the corner of the rink? Is it someone you know?"

"No, no. I was exhausted and I asked a fan to throw some coins near my goal so the referee would delay the game and have the ice cleaned."

Allaire chose Montréal.

—⁓—

Allaire's arrival in Montréal on a permanent basis really helped Patrick prepare for the regular-season games, in which, unlike the playoffs, he wouldn't be facing the same opponent game after game.

Allaire broke down the opposing team's play on film and prepared Patrick, the way a trainer gets a boxer ready for a fight. Allaire pointed out, for example, how the opponent entered the attacking zone or organized power plays. He pinpointed a team's strengths and weaknesses. He described the best shooters and where they liked to shoot, and the players who preferred to pass, stickhandle, control the puck, deke. He also used the pre-game practice to simulate the opponent's approach to game situations so Patrick could memorize them.

According to Allaire, Patrick was like a sponge: "He absorbed everything we suggested if he thought it would be useful. We'd identify a problem on tape, we'd talk about ways to deal with it, and, when he felt comfortable with the solution, he'd try it out in practice a few times. The next day, he'd use it in a game as if he'd always done it that way. It was incredible; he was unbelievably quick to adapt."

Every team in the league, for example, found it was a nightmare to deal with the Nordiques' Stastny brothers on a power play. From the corner of the rink, Peter, without even looking, could pass the puck into the slot to Anton, who'd fire off a shot on goal. The Stastnys scored a lot of goals like that.

After reviewing the play a few times, Allaire and Patrick conceived of a way to prevent it. As soon as the puck was in the corner, Patrick would place the blade of his stick perpendicular to his goal line and turn his catching glove toward the passer, ready to catch the puck. This would enable Patrick to put pressure on Peter and cut off a pass to the slot. Patrick went over the maneuver a few times in practice with some reserve players. It later proved effective in a game against the Nordiques.

Now, most NHL goalies use the tactic when the puck is in the corner of the rink, but at the time no one did. That's how the Allaire-Roy tandem functioned for the following eight years in Montréal. Allaire's challenge was to come up with solutions; Patrick's task was to put them into practice.

Meanwhile, Stéphane, who had suffered a groin injury during his third training camp with the Minnesota North Stars, couldn't persuade their new coach, Herb Brooks, to keep him on. Stéphane had been picked 51st (the same place as Patrick) in the 1985 amateur draft. Now he was playing for the North Stars' farm team, the Kalamazoo Wings, in the International Hockey League.

On October 19, the Canadiens hosted the North Stars at the Montréal Forum. In the third period, Warren Babe struck Rick Green twice with his stick in the Canadiens zone and then defiantly skated through Patrick's crease. Patrick was furious because Babe had slashed Rick Green and he also resented the fact that the North Stars had cut his brother in favor of Babe. He slashed Babe behind the legs. Babe could barely limp off the ice.

Herb Brooks screamed bloody murder. The referee hadn't seen the incident, but Patrick was assessed a five-minute penalty for slashing. After the game, the North Stars lodged a complaint with the National Hockey League about Patrick's infraction, claiming that it was similar to Ron Hextall's offence against the Edmonton Oilers' Kent Nilsson in the semifinals the previous spring. Hextall had received an eight-game suspension.

Undoubtedly intending to influence the decision of Brian O'Neill, the NHL executive vice president in charge of disciplinary matters, Brooks maintained the league would do nothing. He claimed that O'Neill would leave the file on league president John Ziegler's desk as usual. Ziegler, he said, would put on his yellow tie, and that would be the end of it. He added, "I'll make sure Roy gets his throat cut next time."

O'Neill met with the officials who had worked the game and insisted on viewing the film of the incident. But as John Kordic and Richard Zemlak were fighting when Patrick struck Babe, the incident had escaped the TV cameras, and no one had witnessed it. Patrick, accompanied by Jacques Lemaire, had to appear before the vice president, who felt obliged to mete out severe punishment, though he would have to rely on hearsay. He argued he couldn't let such an incident pass without taking action. Brooks and Babe complained. Patrick admitted that he had struck Babe, but not violently. The decision was handed down: Patrick was suspended for eight games. It was the only suspension that Patrick received in his entire NHL career.

A few days later, Warren Babe was dispatched to the Kalamazoo Wings. As fate would have it, he was given a spot beside Stéphane in the dressing room. In the years that followed, Babe spent most of his time in Kalamazoo, appearing in only 20 NHL games.

Stéphane returned to the NHL and played in a dozen games with the North Stars in the beginning of 1988. He wore jersey Number 10. He scored his only NHL goal on February 28, against Robert Sauvé of the New Jersey Devils, on a pass from Bob Rouse. Ironically, a few years later, Sauvé became the head of Jandec, succeeding Pierre Lacroix as Patrick's agent.

— ∭ —

Under François Allaire's guidance, Patrick's statistics steadily improved during the regular season. His goals-against average dropped from 3.35 in his first year to 2.93 in the following year, then to 2.90 in 1987–88. Three years in a row, the Roy-Hayward duo won the William M. Jennings Trophy for allowing the fewest goals of any goaltending tandem in the NHL.

During the same period, his save percentage rose from .875 to .900; in other words, out of 10 shots, he stopped nine on average. This was the bar that separated very good goalies from merely good ones. At the same time, the Canadiens also had an excellent 1987–88 season, finishing second in the overall standings with 103 points, only two points behind the Calgary Flames, the Canadiens' rivals in the 1986 Stanley Cup final. The Flames had been a dominant force for a few years, at least during the regular season.

—⁂—

The Warren Babe incident did not impact Patrick's season. For the first time, he was elected to an NHL All-Star team, the Second All-Star team, so he played in the All-Star game, held in St. Louis, Missouri in February. Larry Robinson and Mats Naslund also took part in the match. He was impressed to find himself in the company of Mario Lemieux, Wayne Gretzky, Dennis Potvin, Raymond Bourque and Grant Fuhr. It was also a source of satisfaction that not only had he made the NHL; he belonged to the elite.

On the occasion, the Prince of Wales Conference, mainly consisting of clubs from the eastern North America, with Mario Lemieux as the captain, won 6–5 over the Clarence Campbell conference, composed of teams from the West, with Gretzky as captain. Lemieux was the star of the contest, involved in all of his team's goals. He scored four goals and assisted on two others, setting a new All-Star record with six points. Naslund, who played on a line with Lemieux, earned five assists. Patrick, who relieved the starting goalie, Ron Hextall, was credited with the win since the score was tied when he entered the game and it remained level until Lemieux scored the winning goal in overtime.

—⁂—

It was during the playoffs that things went wrong. Once again. In the first round, the Canadiens met the Hartford Whalers. The teams had to play four games in five evenings and travel from Montréal to Hartford on the third day. The Habs won the first three encounters with Patrick in the net, but bowed 7–5 in game four, in which they were outshot 43 to 30.

Perron started to have doubts again. Just as he had done the previous spring after the slightest sign of weakness by Patrick, Perron replaced him with Hayward for the rest of the series, and the Canadiens finally won four games to two.

The Habs met the Boston Bruins in the next round. Having finished second in the Adams Division, nine points behind the Canadiens, the Bruins were a good team, but Montréal were the favorites, at least on paper. On the ice, it was another story.

Perron opted to start game one with Hayward in goal, relegating Patrick to backup duty. Halfway through the third period, Perron pulled Hayward, after he gave up four goals on only 14 shots. The move was too late. The Bruins won the game by the score of 4–3.

The Canadiens coach went back to Patrick for the second day, but for him, it was too late. His rhythm was broken. He was unable to get into his zone as he had done in 1986. He couldn't recapture the feeling of near invincibility, the state of grace that enabled him to anticipate everything, stop everything and demoralize opponents.

Instead, the Canadiens seemed disheartened, and the constant flip-flopping about the goaltending situation did little to boost the Habs' morale. There was nothing to inspire them with the confidence and zeal they needed to win in the playoffs. They had lost the will to fight. The Bruins swept the remaining games, in which the Canadiens could only score two meager goals. What a disaster for the Canadiens! Scoring a paltry two goals in three games in the playoffs. Not only that, but it was the first time in 19 attempts that the Bruins eliminated the Canadiens from the playoffs.

Perron's days were numbered.

—m—

Perron's departure took place in circumstances worthy of the adventures of Hercule Poirot. Perron was vacationing with his wife in Guadeloupe. His eldest son, age 16, was in tears when he called his father to inform him that on Tuesday, May 10, Mario Tremblay had announced, on *la Soirée du hockey*, that Perron would be fired. Perron couldn't believe it because he was involved in contract negotiations with Serge Savard at the time.

The following day, he telephoned Savard. The GM reassured him, told him not to worry, to get some rest and relaxation. Savard said he would meet Perron on his return. The rumors were swirling, and Savard, in Chicoutimi to watch Memorial Cup games with André Boudrias, Jacques Lemaire and Pat Burns, was swarmed by reporters. Savard issued a blanket denial. Yet, he had been seen huddling with Pat Burns in the corner of a restaurant in town. Maybe the two were discussing the future of Sherbrooke Canadiens players. After all, Burns was their coach. But why wasn't Boudrias also present? Wasn't he Sherbooke's GM?

It was no secret that Perron's failure to rein in his players was a source of concern for Savard. On the eve of the first playoff game against the Bruins in Montréal, three Habs players, Chelios, Corson and Svoboda, had escaped from Alcatraz. They had been spotted in the wee hours of the morning in an advanced state of intoxication with two women at their side, after the vehicle that one of the ladies was driving ran into a lamppost in Boucherville. Sure, the three players had been caught, but had others escaped Perron's surveillance? And there was this nonchalance, this flagrant lack of commitment and combativeness that had resulted in the Habs' elimination by a weaker team. Burns, by contrast, was an ex-cop with a reputation as a stern disciplinarian. What a coincidence!

Meanwhile, unbeknownst to each other, two Montréal radio reporters, Danièle Rainville of CKAC and Jean Gagnon of CJMS, flew to Guadeloupe to interview Perron. Danièle Rainville showed up at the Club Med. She was told it was full. But she didn't give up so easily. Before looking for a room elsewhere, she dropped by the discotheque where there was some lively music being played. She spotted Perron and his wife. She walked over to them. "What are you doing here?" Perron asked. Without giving the reporter time to answer, Perron's wife dragged her husband onto the dance floor. Ms. Rainville waited for the couple to return, but a security agent told her she had no business in the place. The next day and to the end of the week, Perron was nowhere to be seen.

The following Monday, when he returned to Montréal, Perron huddled with Savard. After the meeting, which lasted a good two hours, Perron announced his resignation, explaining that the pressure had become unbearable for his family and him.

A few weeks later, after wild speculation in the media, Savard presented the new coach of the Canadiens: Pat Burns.

THE WARRIOR'S REVENGE

When he took over the helm with the Canadiens, Pat Burns could count on the league's best goalie tandem in Brian Hayward and Patrick. Drawing an analogy with the car world, François Allaire compared Patrick to a Ferrari and Hayward to a Cadillac. "For thrills and excitement," he said, "take the Ferrari, but for a good, calm, comfortable ride, take the Cadillac." It was a colorful and apt metaphor for the coaching staff's view of the two goalies.

This approach sparked a fierce rivalry between Hayward and Patrick, a competition that the team benefited from. Patrick, one might suspect, valued his first-string status; he would have preferred to play 60 games a season. He started only 45. The equally competitive Hayward believed he could be the club's first-string goalie, if given half a chance. He appeared in 35 matches, but he would have preferred more action. He was probably the best backup goaltender in the league, but he wanted to be Number 1.

That wasn't in the cards, not with Patrick on the team. The statistics proved that Patrick was more effective than Hayward. In the NHL, people didn't start paying attention to the save percentage—saves per shots on goal—until the 1980s. And yet, no matter how reliable the shots-on-goal statistics were, Patrick was the only goalie in history with a save percentage consistently above .900. In fact, the goaltenders who managed the feat even for one season could be counted on the fingers of one hand. In 1987–88, only Patrick reached that plateau. Even more remarkably, he was the first to remain above .900 in all the years that followed. In his four seasons under Pat Burns, his save percentage varied between .906 and .914 (he stopped more than 90 of every 100 shots). A .900 save percentage was a kind of psychological block for goalies, much as the four-minute mile had stymied runners until England's Roger Bannister broke through the barrier in 1954. It wasn't until the mid-1990s that the best netminders consistently surpassed the .900 mark.

Hayward's goaltending style fit his size and athletic limitations. He couldn't fully adopt the Allaire technique, but he remained an excellent goalie and was instrumental in the team's defensive success that helped win William M. Jennings trophies. Hayward could be credited with keeping things on an even keel, safe and comfortable, while turning in excellent performances. In extreme situations, however, when the Cadillac and the Ferrari had to be pushed to the limit, the Cadillac couldn't match the Ferrari's incredible speeds. When the chips were down, the coaches turned to Patrick. Patrick and Hayward complemented each other.

Burn's and Allaire realized the goaltending tandem was a marriage of convenience. It couldn't last forever, especially with a latent rivalry brewing between the two, who were roommates on the road. But the coaches took advantage of the situation as long as possible, electing not to cross the bridge before they got to it.

—m—

Patrick loved playing for Burns. From 1988–89 to 1991–92, under Burns's leadership, Patrick enjoyed his most productive four-year period in Montréal. Three times he won the Vézina Trophy, as the NHL's top goalie awarded by the league's general managers. He probably would have won the honor four times in a row but for his injuries in 1990–91. He was a two-time winner of the William M. Jennings Trophy, for the best goals-against average, and the Trico Goaltending Award, for the best save percentage. He would have won the Trico Award for a third straight year, but the league withdrew the honor.

The heavily mustached Burns cut an imposing figure. He was gruff, unbending, withdrawn and distant. He didn't let anything pass; his principal mission was to maintain order. The task had been assigned to him by the general manager and suggested by veterans Smith, Walter, Robinson, Gainey and Green, winners who deplored the lack of discipline and the lax attitude of the club. Burns was an intimidating presence in the dressing room. He made it clear what he expected of the players. Pity the player who failed to heed the rules. Between the stick and the carrot, Burns preferred the stick. It was "convert or die!"

Burns was born in Saint-Henri, a working-class district in the southwestern part of Montréal, not far from the downtown core. Saint-Henri had the reputation of being a rough-and-ready neighborhood with regrettable delinquency and crime figures. The face of the neighborhood was scarred by the long railroad tracks, and marked by overhanging highways carrying, morning and night, a cohort of comfortable suburbanites, who distractedly glanced down on it from on high.

But the district has also given the province of Québec a fair share of notable people. It has given the jazz world the renowned pianists Oscar Peterson and Oliver Jones, as well as bassist Charles Biddle. Celebrities like humorist Yvon Deschamps and author Lise Payette spent most of their youth there. Gabrielle Roy's first novel, *Bonheur d'occasion*, written in 1945, was inspired by the lives of the residents of Saint-Henri.

When his father died, Burns and his mother moved to Gatineau in the Outaouais, where he attended school and played junior hockey. At age 19, he entered the police cadets in Ottawa, when authorities were looking for French-speaking candidates to keep an eye on the Byward Market area. It was the start of a 17-year career in the police force, which brought him back to Gatineau two years later to work for the city, where he registered in a senior hockey league.

One thing led to another: he became a minor hockey coach on outdoor rinks and ran into a number of good players in the region. His work attracted the attention of the QMJHL Hull Olympiques, who offered him a job as a part-time scout. Then, Michel Morin became the coach of the Olympiques in the early 1980s—the same Morin who had taught Patrick and Stéphane the fundamentals of hockey at the École permanente de hockey de Sillery in 1974—and invited Burns to join him as a part-time assistant.

In 1984, Burns succeeded Morin as Hull's head coach, but kept his day job with the Gatineau police force. The next year, Wayne Gretzky bought the Olympiques and personally asked the City of Gatineau to grant Burns leave without pay so he could coach the team full time. Gretzky already considered Burns as a potential NHL coach. The future would prove Gretzky right.

In the first year of Gretzky's association with the Olympiques, which had a number of good players, including Luc Robitaille, the club reached the Memorial Cup finals against the Guelph Platers, coached by Jacques Martin, who had applied for the Granby Bisons coaching job four years earlier but been rejected.

Then, after a year with Junior Team Canada, with whom he went through the nightmare known as the "Punch-up in Piestany" against the Soviets in the World Junior Ice Hockey Championship, Burns was asked by Serge Savard to coach the Sherbrooke Canadiens in the American Hockey League.

Burns's arrival in Montréal had a positive effect on the team from the start, particularly in the first year. In 1988–89, the Canadiens were runners-up in the overall standings, with a remarkable total of 115 points, only two points behind the Calgary Flames, who had enjoyed a phenomenal season.

It was also an extraordinary season for Patrick, who had a record of 33 wins, three draws and only five losses, a goals-againsts average of 2.47 and a save percentage of .908. He went undefeated at the Forum. His 25 home victories eclipsed the former mark of the 23-home-games-undefeated streak set by Bill Durnan back in the 1940s. Patrick equaled Durnan's record on March 15, 1989, the very day when Jonathan, his first son, was born at 6:18 in the morning. Patrick called Burns scarcely an hour later to ask to be excused from the morning skate. He insisted, however, on tending goal against the Los Angeles Kings that evening.

Finally, that season he ran off with every goaltending honor—the Vézina, William M. Jennings and Trico awards—and he made the NHL First All-Star team. It was a very productive year indeed.

In the post-season, the Canadiens made short work of the Hartford Whalers in four games, then proceeded to eliminate the Boston Bruins in five and the Philadelphia Flyers in six, to reach the final against the Calgary Flames. After the team ran up a 3–0 lead in the Whalers series, Burns used Hayward in game four, probably to keep him happy, and came back with Patrick in the Bruins series. Again, Burns opted for Hayward in game four, but this time Hayward lost. That was his last appearance in the series.

The Flames boasted a potent lineup, with Joe Mullen, Hakan Loob, Doug Gilmour, Joe Nieuwendyk, Al MacInnis, Gary Suter, Joel Otto,

Gary Roberts, Lanny McDonald and the excellent Mike Vernon in goal. Coaches Terry Crisp and Pat Burns had never met in the playoffs, but a number of players were members of the 1986 edition. For the Flames, who had been in the final and lost, the defeat still rankled. What's more, on paper they were stronger than Montréal, having scored 354 goals during the season compared with 315 by Montréal.

They were thirsting for revenge when they jumped on the ice at the Saddledome for the first game of the Stanley Cup final. The two teams split the games in Calgary. The Flames won 3–2 in the series opener, in which Vernon sparkled, and the Canadiens responded with a 4–2 victory in the next, in which Patrick shone.

In Montréal, the scenario was repeated in games three and four. Each team won a match. The third encounter was a duel of titans. The contest went into the second period of overtime before Ryan Walter ended the struggle with the goal that gave the Habs a 4–3 victory. Patrick stopped 34 of the 37 shots. In the fourth game, the Flames easily dominated the Canadiens, outshooting them 35 shots to 19 and winning by the score of 4–2. The fourth goal was scored into an empty net after the Canadiens removed the goalie in favor of a sixth attacker. The teams were tied in the series, with two wins apiece. It would now move to Calgary. The Flames had recaptured the home-ice advantage. By far the hungrier team, the Flames took advantage of it to win the next two games: 3–2 in Calgary and 4–2 on the Forum ice. The Canadiens had gone to defeat. The Flames had exacted revenge, winning the first Stanley Cup in their history.

Nevertheless, Burns was awarded the Jack Adams Trophy as the coach of the year. Patrick, chosen the best goalie, won the Vézina Trophy for the first time in his career. This was rather surprising, since he had played only 44 games, just four more than half the schedule. François Allaire thought the decision was justified by Patrick's consistently excellent performance. That year, not a single general manager could recall seeing him play a bad match. He was regularly one of the three best players on his team. As a result, many GMs voted for him.

—⁂—

Before the 1989–90 season got underway, both Rick Green and Captain Bob Gainey announced their retirement. Co-captains Guy Carbonneau and Chris Chelios filled Gainey's role. The face of the team was gradually being transformed. Veterans were leaving; younger players were replacing them.

Burns kept on rotating goalies until late January 1990. Hayward had a losing record of 10 victories and 12 losses. Not only that, but he had to be replaced by Patrick after turning in poor performances in his last two starts. Patrick had racked up 17 victories until then. Patrick was fed up, so he went to see Burns. "Say, coach, I've been putting up with this situation for four years without saying a word. What would it take to play more games [he had swept all the goaltending trophies the previous year], or maybe get the number of games normally given the Number 1 goalie on a team?" Burns understood his argument. Hayward made only four more appearances that season.

As Patrick and Hayward increasingly resembled a grumpy old couple, Patrick told Burns's assistant, Jacques Laperrière, that he wanted another roommate on the road. He remembered that Hayward had once tried to intimidate him. Hayward had said that he'd come to Montréal expecting to start a lot of games and play in the post-season. Hayward was experienced, he knew the ropes, and Patrick was still a raw rookie. And during those years when they roomed together on the road, Hayward went to bed early the day before a game that he was going to play the next day, and he watched television until late at night the day before Patrick's matches. This attitude had sparked a rivalry and fed a cold war between the two men. They were more competitors than teammates. And yet, by 1990, Patrick was no longer a rookie; his game had attained a level that Hayward would never reach. Intimidation no longer worked. Laperrière picked Éric Desjardins as Patrick's new roomie on the road.

Patrick won the Vézina and Trico Trophies for the second consecutive year, and made the First All-Star team. He ended the season with 31 victories, 16 defeats and five draws, a goals-against average of 2.53 and a save percentage of .912, the best in the league. He was the first goalie to win the Vézina Trophy two years in a row since the general managers began to vote for the recipient.

In the first two rounds of the playoffs, teams competed within their division, so the Canadiens did not have home-ice advantage in either of their series, though they finished fourth in the overall standings in the regular season. First, they eliminated the Buffalo Sabers in six games, but bowed to the Boston Bruins in six in the next round.

—⁓—

Much was made of Patrick's pre-game preparations. He always started on the left side when he put on a piece of equipment. He juggled a puck in the dressing room; he visualized his goal after the singing of the national anthem. Some dismissed his routine as superstition, claiming that goalies had always been a race apart. But there was much more to it than that. Much more. His gestures were part of a ritual that helped him cope with pressure, stress and distractions. They also helped him block out negative thoughts and get into a kind of comfort zone before a game. He always went through the same routine, repeating it mechanically, without thinking. It helped fill the time before the opening face-off: the long feverish minutes before the game when there was not enough time to rest, but too much time to do what remained to be done. Then he felt safe, secure and solid as a locomotive on its rails. Everything was in place. All he had to do was follow the same routine he'd done hundreds of times until the game began. He was on familiar terrain, at home, in his domain. He felt good. He was in the zone.

He was certainly not the only one to perform a ritual. Besides other players' individual quirks, the whole team performed a routine just before the game began. Soon after the coach's final instructions, scarcely three minutes before they went on the ice, it was something to see the players lined up at the dressing room door. It was always the same order at the beginning of every game and at the beginning of every period. It never changed. It was like a game before the game.

Carbonneau and Green would high-five just inside the dressing room door. Then Robinson would go ahead of Carbonneau and be the first into the corridor, ahead of Patrick and Skrudland. Next Skrudland would tap Patrick on the pads a couple of times with his stick and give Hayward's pads a couple of taps. Patrick would then go into the hall past Robinson, who would be waiting in a corner to let him by and show his support to all his teammates as they walked by. Hayward followed Patrick, and next came Walter, Desjardins, Keane and all the others, always in the same order, on their way to the rink. Carbonneau and Green would remain behind by the dressing room door and encourage their teammates with a pat on the back. Chelios would come a little bit afterward, and then Gainey, who had left the room ahead of him, would pass by. Chelios and Corson would engage in their own sophisticated mutual encouragement routine with a series of high fives and taps with the stick. Next Corson would walk ahead of Chelios, who would follow immediately behind. Carbonneau waited for Naslund to precede him and then left close behind, followed by Green and, finally, Ludwig always the last one to leave the room.

It was certainly a peculiar routine, but it was as organized as a Mass. It promoted unity, solidarity and collaboration. It fostered peace of mind in a moment of tension. And who could say that it didn't contribute to victory? The margin between victory and defeat is razor-thin. At that level of competition, a slight variation in preparation, routine or emotion can make a huge difference.

And that wasn't the end of it. On the ice, after the warm-up session and just before the national anthems, the players continued their routine. There was nothing haphazard about the way they gathered around Patrick's goal. Ludwig and Carbonneau lined up like guards on his right, while Robinson did the same on his left and one after another, the other players patted him with their sticks on his goalie pads to encourage him. Fifteen feet away, Naslund faced them, directly in front of Patrick as if he were observing the scene. Coming from the left, Chelios and Corson expressed their good wishes to Ludwig, Carbonneau, Patrick and Robinson. Larry Robinson waited until Green tapped him from behind on the shoulder. It was a signal that things were about to start. *Ite, missa est.* Then Robinson skated by Patrick, gave him an encouraging tap on the pads, did the same to Carbonneau and Ludwig, then to Green, and headed over to Naslund, still standing in front. Robinson and Naslund would touch gloves with their left hands. Suddenly, Naslund would take off, and tap Patrick's blocker with his stick. Next came Ludwig, who whacked Patrick's pads with his stick with a great flourish, followed by Captain Carbonneau, who not only provided another whack, but added three other touches with the stick, on Patrick's trapper (Charlotte) left shoulder and head.

The players executed this routine like clockwork, as if they were actors entering and exiting the stage. Everyone had a role; everyone had to respect the others' role or everything would come undone. If nobody got tangled up, they would have a good game. The national anthems were about to begin. As the final few measures were sung,

Patrick would skate to the blue line, turn toward his goal and go through his visualization exercise, race back to the goal, cut sharply to the left corner of the rink and skate back to his net. He was ready to begin.

What followed was much less predictable. The players couldn't control what happened next. They would have to deal with their opponents, who also had their plans.

During commercial breaks or at the end of a period, when he could skate to the bench, Patrick had the habit of skipping over the red and blue lines to avoid touching them. He didn't want to tempt fate by making changes.

—⁂—

One day, during a Canadiens away game, Patrick returned to the dressing room after the first period and noticed the puck that he'd been juggling had disappeared. Alarmed, he asked the equipment manager, "Pierre, what's happened to my puck?"

Pierre Gervais understood the gravity of the situation. He guessed what had happened. It is customary in the NHL for the host team to put an employee at the visitors' disposal to assist their equipment manager. Gervais rushed to see the employee.

"Hey, did you see a puck on the floor, in the corner of the room?"

"Uh, yes ... there was one on the floor."

"Where is it? What did you do with it?"

"I gave it to a friend who's here to see the game. Why? Is it important?"

"Can you go and get it? We've got to have that puck before the start of the second period."

The employee must have thought Gervais was out of his mind. Teams bring dozens of pucks. What was so important about that one?

Usually, the Canadiens equipment manager warned employees in rinks he visited to keep their hands off the precious object. This time, Gervais had forgotten. Fortunately, a few minutes later, after wandering through the seats to find his friend, the employee returned with the puck. Gervais took it and gave him another one. The routine was assured. The victory, too, perhaps.

—◊—

June 9, 1990, was the occasion of a more solemn rite, the wedding Mass of Michèle Piuze and Patrick, celebrated at Saint-Sacrement Church in Québec City. After the reception at the Château Bonne Entente in Sainte-Foy, they flew to Hawaii for their honeymoon.

—◊—

As Mats Naslund had decided to pursue his career in Europe, the Canadiens gave up Chris Chelios in exchange for the Chicago Blackhawks' forward Denis Savard at the beginning of the 1990–91 season. The team was strong defensively, but it had been struggling offensively for two years. It was thought that Savard would help Stéphane Richer, Shayne Corson and Russ Courtnall score more goals. People also noted the departure of veterans Bobby Smith and Craig Ludwig, as well as Claude Lemieux, traded to the New Jersey Devils for Sylvain Turgeon.

That year, at the invitation of the National Hockey League, which wanted to promote hockey abroad, the Canadiens accepted an invitation to hold part of their training camp in the Soviet Union. There were 128 people on the trip, including the cook from the Forum restaurant, *La Mise au jeu*, to compensate for the fare in Russian restaurants, which didn't enjoy the best of reputations. Care had also been taken to bring supplies of water and food sufficient to meet the needs of the team.

The players first flew to Sweden on September 4, in preparation for a first game in Stockholm on September 10. The players' wives joined them the day before the game. The six-day interval was enough time for the team to prepare. After that, the Habs played a game every two days behind the Iron Curtain. In Leningrad on September 12, in Riga on the 14th, and in Moscow on the 16th and 18th, where they played the Dynamo and the Red Army in what could be called the highlight of the trip.

The trip wasn't a great success, at least in terms of hockey. The Canadiens were still in their conditioning phase; they lacked physical fitness and their play lacked synchronization. But how do you explain this to teams that had been training for weeks and were champing at the bit to match skills, before their fans, with the most prestigious team in the world? It was much too much pressure at that stage of the Habs' training camp. The final games of the trip against the Moscow Dynamo and the Red Army were marred by a lack of discipline, frustration, fights and cheap shots. There was nothing remotely resembling friendly exhibition games. Nothing to embellish the image of Canadian hockey players, even if their adversaries, more often than not, were the instigators. Nothing either to remind Canadiens that they were visiting the second-ranking hockey power in the world, the country of Vladislav Tretiak and Valeri Kharlamov, who, in 1972, had amazed the world with an awesome display of skill against Canada's finest players.

Nor did everyone appreciate the tourist aspect of the trip. Of course, the group had a chance to visit cities and internationally renowned places like the Kremlin, Red Square, St. Basil's Cathedral and the Lenin Mausoleum. But it was the swan song of the Soviet Union, barely 15 months before its collapse put an end to 74 years of the communist regime. The economic difficulties were obvious, and the poverty that could clearly be seen in a city like Leningrad, to cite only one example, made many of the visitors uncomfortable. The USSR's economy was undergoing a transformation and was beginning to open up to foreign investment. A McDonald's restaurant, one of the most flamboyant symbols of American capitalism, had recently opened in Gorky Park. The establishment served thousands of meals a day. The Canadiens and their companions were certainly not going to stand in a line of Muscovites 200 yards long, waiting to get a Big Mac.

After two weeks, everyone had had enough, and Burns said it publicly. "No one is calmer and more patient than Patrick Roy. So when Patrick says that he's had enough, I think it's time to go home," he declared.

—∞—

On October 3, a few days before the season got underway, Patrick's contract was renegotiated, making him the highest-paid goalie in the NHL and the top earner in the Montréal Canadiens' history. With his new three-year agreement, which included an option year, he would earn $780,000 in each of the first two years and $1,040,000 in the third. There were generous performance bonuses as well. It was a long way from Leningrad.

Brian Hayward realized his days in Montréal were numbered. He had asked to play at least half of the team's games. As Burns couldn't promise him this, he decided to go on strike and stay home on Nun's Island. It was October 8, only two games into the season. Hayward claimed he had been assured that he would be treated on an equal footing with Patrick when he had signed a two-year contract in the summer and that promise had been broken.

They had reached the bridge.

First, Hayward was suspended without pay, and then he was traded to the Minnesota North Stars one month later in exchange for defenseman Jayson More. Hayward had elected to give up his status

(© Pierre Vidricaire, *Le Journal de Montréal*.)

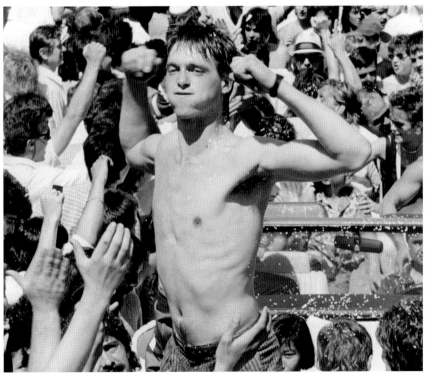

At the height of the Stanley Cup parade in 1986, nearly a million fans give their Canadiens an outpouring of love, stretching over more than 4 miles in the streets of Montréal for over five hours. Shirtless, with the insouciance of youth, Patrick acts like an MC, blowing kisses at the fans, howling with joy, striking a bodybuilding pose to show off his puny muscles to the crowd and making Montréalers' hearts sing.

(© Pierre McCann, *La Presse*.)

Brian Hayward and Patrick, the "Cadillac" and the "Ferrari." The NHL's premier goaltending duo from 1986 to 1990.

(© *Le Journal de Montréal*.)

In the opening game of the 1986 series, the Boston Bruins' Louis Sleigher viciously charges into Patrick, whose mask flies into the air.

(© *Le Journal de Montréal*.)

From 1985 to 1995, François Allaire and Patrick transform the Montréal Forum into a research laboratory to improve the art of goaltending. Their collaboration is unique in the NHL, unique in the world. They are innovating, inventing new ways of doing things and perfecting a prototype that will inspire future generations of elite goalies.

(© *Le Journal de Montréal*.)

Patrick loves playing for Pat Burns. The coach makes it clear what he expects of players. Pity the guy who fails to obey. From 1988 to 1992, under Burns's leadership, Patrick enjoys his most productive four-year period in Montréal, winning the Vézina Trophy three times as the NHL's top goalie.

(© Bernard Brault, *La Presse*.)

Patrick and Jacques Demers are often on the same wavelength because they have one thing in mind: the interest of the team. Demers has confidence in Patrick and the goalie would never let him down, come what may.

(© Bernard Brault, *La Presse*.)

In the spring of 1993, Patrick proudly carries something nobody in Montréal expected to see that season, which he dubs the "Cup of Recognition," with Lyle Odelein, Captain Kirk Muller and John LeClair looking on.

(© Robert Mailloux, *La Presse*.)

On June 7, during the 1993 finals, Patrick gives Tomas Sandstrom of the Los Angeles Kings a wink that travels around North America thanks to an alert TV producer, Jacques Primeau.

(© Société Radio-Canada.)

On Saturday, October 29, 1994, during the NHL lockout, Patrick plays on a forward line for the Chicago Masters with his brother Stéphane and his father Michel, who has brought the team to Montréal.

(© Charles Cherney – author's collection.)

In September 1993, Patrick and Serge Savard sign a $16 million contract. For the first time in hockey history, a goalie is among the highest paid players in the NHL. In the background is Pierre Lacroix, Patrick's agent.

(©Le Journal de Montréal.)

Patrick with his sister Alexandra and his brother Stéphane.

(Barbara Miller-Roy collection.)

In the late 1980s, Patrick's enormous popularity inspired good young athletes to take up goaltending. Eleven-year-old Jean-Sébastien Giguère, who will be the netminder for the 2007 Stanley Cup champion Anaheim Mighty Ducks, proudly poses with his role model.

(© *Le Journal de Montréal*.)

On Wednesday, December 6, 1995, thin and downhearted, Patrick sits in the Learjet chartered by Pierre Lacroix, heading to Denver, Colorado. Bertrand Raymond titles his column the next day in the *Journal de Montréal*, "We're going to regret it!"

(© *Le Journal de Montréal*.)

as the league's best backup goalie and the recognition that came with it in the Canadiens' organization to try his luck as a first-string goalie elsewhere. Plagued by back injuries, he never managed to achieve this objective, neither in Minnesota, nor with the San Jose Sharks, where he ended up the following season when they joined the NHL. He was no longer physically up to performing the demanding role of a Number 1 goalie.

Ironically, the injury jinx didn't hit Patrick until Hayward left. Though goalies are subjected to a daily onslaught of shots both in games and practices, rarely are they seriously injured. True, they sustain their fair share of bruises, when pucks find their way to more vulnerable spots, but in general, their heavy equipment provides adequate protection from serious injury. In the 1990–91 season, however, Patrick missed the most games due to injury. First, he missed nine games after Petr Svoboda and Wendell Clark fell on his left knee on December 12. The diagnosis was strained ligaments. Then on January 27, after being checked by Donald Dufresne, Bruins right-winger Graeme Townshend landed his entire 225 pounds on Patrick's left ankle. Patrick sustained a ruptured ligament that kept him on the injury shelf for 14 games. The mishap had its plus side: Patrick had time to fully enjoy the birth of his second son, Frédérick, on February 26. Finally, he re-injured the ankle on March 16, and had to miss two more starts. Goalies André Racicot and Jean-Claude Bergeron shared relief duties in the 25 games that Patrick missed.

His prolonged absence may have cost him a Vézina Trophy, since he only managed to win 25 games. But he was back in tip-top shape the following year, during the 1991–92 season, with 36 wins, a 2.36 goals-against average and a .914 save percentage. In addition to picking up his third Vézina Trophy, he won the William M. Jennings and was selected on the First All-Star team. He finished second behind Mark Messier of the New York Rangers in the race for the coveted Hart Trophy, awarded to the player deemed most valuable to his team during the regular season. Finally, he chalked up the best save percentage in the league, and once again, he was the only one to finish above .900.

In the post-season, the Canadiens eliminated the Buffalo Sabers in six games before bowing to the Boston Bruins in seven. Boston won the seventh and deciding game of the series by a score of 2–1 in the Boston Garden.

That year, Bob Gainey led his team to a Stanley Cup final against the Pittsburgh Penguins, in his first year as coach of the Minnesota North stars.

—⚏—

Patrick had only one reservation about Burns: the coach feared that the players would take advantage of him. As a consequence, during the 80-game schedule, there were few days off and the practices were intense, so that by the end of the season players were running on empty. But Patrick loved Burns's work ethic, the discipline he imposed, the simplicity and clarity of his system, with its focus on tight defensive play. These qualities have enabled the ex-policeman to carve out an outstanding career, earning him the Adams Trophy as coach of the year three times with three different teams.

Despite a stern exterior, Burns could have fun on occasion. His assistant, Jacques Laperrière, was the champion prankster on the team. Sometimes, he would rub Vaseline on Burns's telephone. Then, Burns would end up with an entire side of his face smeared with grease when he got a call. To get even with Laperrière, Burns asked former police department colleagues for some powder that investigators use to catch counterfeiters or drug traffickers during money deals. The powder was said to have ultraviolet properties that made it invisible to the naked eye when sprinkled on a bank note, for example. But as soon as the powder came in contact with a warm object (such as a damp hand) it changed into a violet liquid that left spots that were extremely difficult to remove.

Burns nabbed Laperrière by sprinkling powder on the telephone receiver. Laperrière's mouth turned blue. Impressed, Laperrière suggested that they spread powder on the inside of Patrick's mask before a practice. Burns was only too glad to agree. He was looking for a little revenge of his own. One day when Burns had put his socks on, his foot had gone right through. Someone had cut off the toes of his socks. He strongly suspected that Patrick or one of his teammates was the culprit. "You're looking for war? Okay!" he told himself. But he was well aware of the effects of the product. "Lappy, don't put too much on; that powder leaves a hell of a stain!" But "Lappy" wouldn't listen. He was too eager for his practical joke to succeed. He gave the mask a liberal dose.

In practice, Patrick was warming up and sweat started to flow under his mask. As he was used to sweating profusely, it took him a while to realize that his sweat was a different color than usual. When Patrick went to the bench and removed his mask to get a drink of water, Pierre Gervais, who wasn't in on the plot, saw the violet streaks all over Patrick's face. Patrick looked like some kind of monster.

He went to the trainer's room, where it took two men a good hour to rub the stuff off his face, using all sorts of products, from soap to turpentine, alcohol and peroxide. Eventually, they succeeded, as best they could, in cleaning his face. Patrick immediately suspected Laperrière, who was still on the ice in his sweat suit. Patrick walked right into Lappy's office and snipped off the pant legs of his suit. Burns got off easy.

But he wouldn't get off so easy in the 1991–92 season. His close-checking, defensive system failed to generate much offense or lift the fans off their seats. The faithful grew disenchanted with a spectacle that could best be described as dull and boring. Canadiens finished the regular season in fifth place in the overall standings, but they were only fourteenth—out of 22 teams—in goals scored. Montréal's top scorers that year were Kirk Muller (36), acquired at the beginning of the season from the New Jersey Devils along with goalie Roland Melanson, in return for Stéphane Richer and Tom Chorske, Denis Savard (28), Stephan Lebeau (27), Brent Gilchrist (23) and Gilbert Dionne (21). To make matters worse, the team had lost its last two series against the Bruins. Things were becoming grim.

Journalists had their own complaints. Burns appeared increasingly impatient during press briefings, especially when the team was in a slump. It was obvious that he was only talking to the press because he was forced to, and media relations were becoming more and more of a burden.

—⚏—

The first round of the 1992 playoffs pitted the Canadiens against the Hartford Whalers. The Habs won by the skin of their teeth on Russ Courtnall's goal in the second overtime period of the seventh and deciding game. In the other Adams Division series, the Boston Bruins surprisingly eliminated the Buffalo Sabers. So for the third year in a row, the Canadiens would be dueling with the Bruins coached by Rick Bowness in the quarterfinal. Boston had sent the Canadiens on vacation the two previous years.

Patrick got off to a shaky start. He had a horrible game, allowing at least three bad goals in a 6–4 defeat. It is difficult to explain his performance. It was as if something was controlling his movements. He was tense and out of sorts. Here was the winner of the Vézina Trophy for the third time in four years, who had climbed to the summit to become the best goalie in the league, fighting the puck as if he'd forgotten everything he knew. He had lost his bearings. He was fumbling around in the dark.

But under the powerful Forum lights, there was no place to hide. The crowd wasn't thinking about Vézina Trophies. They were thinking only about the consecutive post-season defeats to the Bruins; about Patrick's performance which, astonishingly, had had its ups and downs in the last series even though he had been so consistent during the regular season; about the goal given up to Cam Neely on a shot from the blue line which had sent the Canadiens on an early vacation the year before. And Robinson was no longer there to remind him: "No more bad goals!"

Patrick was the team's top wage earner. He was its backbone and its superstar, the one the players counted on to make the difference and lead them to victory, as he had done in 1986. Few thought the Habs could count on their anemic offense to achieve victory. But the unrealistic expectations placed on Patrick gave him little margin for error. His slightest misstep would impact a game's outcome. That evening, he gave up three weak goals: three too many.

Denis Savard's marker near the end of the second period revived the fans' hopes. The score was 4–3 in favor of the Bruins. But barely a few seconds later, Reggie Leach's weak shot from the face-off circle in Canadien's territory eluded Patrick to his right when he uncharacteristically made a belated, tense, awkward movement. He was a shadow of himself. Hoots of derision rained down from the stands. Some fans chanted "Ra-ci-cot! Ra-ci-cot!" urging Burns to yank Patrick and replace him with André Racicot. Patrick was roundly booed as he skated off at intermission, crestfallen.

What the crowd wants, the gods deliver! Racicot started the third period. I wrote, "started" because he lasted only 52 seconds. Burns wouldn't be intimidated; he resolutely stuck to his plan. He wanted to show the crowd that he was the coach, that Patrick was still "his man" and that he would support his Number 1 goalie come hell or high water. The Bruins began the period on a power play. They buzzed around in Habs' territory. Trailing by only two goals, Burns wasn't ready to throw in the towel. He remembered that playing yo-yo with goalies wasn't a very good playoff strategy. There could be nothing worse than to make the players start doubting themselves, especially the player who should be there but wasn't. Burns waited until the first time the referee blew the play to a halt to send Patrick back into action. It was poor timing: Racicot had just made his first save. So some fans booed as Patrick went back into the net, but his teammates on the bench stood up and applauded. The pressure on him was enormous.

He had only been in goal for a few seconds when he made a miraculous, if a bit lucky, save after Joé Juneau jumped on a rebound. Fortunately, the crowd calmed down. The game ended without incident. Both teams scored once in the final stanza. Boston left with the victory. At the end of the game, Patrick was shaken. He couldn't understand what had happened to him. Why had he been unable to make the right move when it was needed? Why had everything seemed so difficult? Still, his teammates supported him. In fact, Denis Savard said, "We've won 41 games this season, and Patrick has given us 36," he said. "What happened in this game was hard on the players; it was even harder on him. He won't have two games like this one. Not him. Never!"

Indeed, Patrick regained his composure. But it wasn't enough to halt the Bruins' momentum. After winning game two in overtime, the Bruins easily won the rest of the series. They swept the Canadiens four games to nothing. Patrick had been solid, but again he hadn't been the inspired goalie we'd seen in the spring of 1986. On the other hand, some players lacked the fighting spirit needed to compete with a team of fiercely gritty muckers like the Bruins. Something was clearly wrong: indifference and discontent were palpable. Burns came under fire; his tenure was called into question. There was a strong sense of *déjà-vu*, recalling the 1988 series with the Bruins, which had led to Jean Perron's departure.

When the siren sounded, Burns knew that he had coached the Canadiens for the last time. The fans would never accept three defeats in three consecutive years against Boston. The front office would have to clean house. And Burns's sometimes stormy media relations had drained him. He had had enough. A few days later, it was announced that he would be coming back in the fall, an obvious ploy to calm things down. Before the end of the month, Burns handed in his resignation, declaring, "Some players let me down!"

As for Patrick, despite three disappointing series against the Bruins, he had managed, during the four years when Burns was at the helm, to establish himself as the best goalie in the NHL through his consistently excellent performances in the regular season.

THE QUEST FOR PERFECTION

19

For eight years, Patrick and François Allaire had been on a quest for perfection. Perfection would demand that a goalie never give up a goal. They realized it was an objective they would never achieve; that perfection isn't of this world, especially not in hockey and even less in goalies. Like knights in the Middle Ages who tested their mettle in the vain pursuit of the Holy Grail, Patrick and Allaire embarked on a quest in which process was more important than objective. Not only had their endeavor made Patrick the best goalie in the NHL, it had revolutionized goaltending and enabled goalies to bridge the technical gap between them and players in other positions in modern hockey.

They had gone far from the beaten path traced by their predecessors. Driven by their instinct and vision, they had explored new terrain and new spaces. They were convinced they were headed in the right direction, and they were not mistaken. Soon, many others would follow.

The Forum had become a research laboratory in the art of goaltending. The collaboration between Patrick and François Allaire in Montréal was unique in the NHL, unique in the world. They outstripped anything done elsewhere. Not only were netminders being prepared for games; innovations were taking place, perfecting a prototype that would inspire the future generation of elite goaltenders.

—⁓—

The bedrock of optimal netminding performance is solid technique, adequate equipment, unshakable confidence and powerful motivation. Whether it was a match day or a practice, Patrick had a routine that he never departed from. François Allaire worked within those established schedules. After each game, he spent two hours viewing films to analyze play sequences that had tested Patrick. Then Allaire showed Patrick, at an opportune moment, a five-minute montage based on what he termed the "sandwich" concept: first came the introduction showing Patrick executing movements effectively; then came the "meat" indicating what he needed to avoid, change or improve; finally Allaire ended the session with sequences that showed Patrick at his best to reinforce what he did particularly well. That's how, game after game, day after day, for a good ten years, Patrick and Allaire devoted thousands of hours, in a room scrutinizing videotapes, and on the ice adapting and perfecting the "butterfly" style, endeavoring to correct any flaws, so that Patrick could employ the technique in every situation, real and imagined, in his quest for perfection. If Patrick had a goal scored on him in a new way, they immediately sought a remedy and experimented with it in the next practice.

As his technique evolved, Patrick noticed that he needed fewer and fewer movements to make a save. Everything seemed easier, simpler, more fluid. In the language of management, he was becoming more efficient.

At first, TV analysts and color commentators failed to grasp Patrick's new art. As the saves seemed so easy, they concluded that the shots couldn't be so difficult after all. When he was caught out of position and he had to make a desperate stab with his glove or pad to make the save, they concluded he had made an incredible stop, when in reality he had been forced to make the move because his anticipation of the play or speed of execution had somehow been inadequate. And when a perfect shot beat him in the basic "butterfly" position, they claimed it was a soft goal and that he had been weak, ignoring the fact that, thanks to the technique, he was stopping many shots that eluded other netminders, especially those along the ice. Of course, Patrick's performance in the 1986 playoffs and his status as the league's best goalie created unrealistic expectations. How many times did a TV analyst exclaim, "He seemed shaky on that save," or "He was lucky to make that stop," or "This isn't the same goalie!" Making a save wasn't enough. He should have done it the way the analyst wanted him to do it. Nevertheless, he was stopping more and more shots, as his steadily increasing save percentage attested. Not only was he the league's premier goalie, he was one of the most consistent in games as well as in practices.

—◊◊—

But equipment lagged behind technique. Initially, goalie pants and pads were designed to protect a netminder with a stand-up style. In the "butterfly" position, the gear left holes that pucks could sneak through, for example between the legs (the five hole). So gradually, Patrick and Allaire put as much emphasis on equipment as on technique. What was the use in performing a movement properly if it was undermined by inadequate equipment? From then on, goaltending equipment was no longer limited to protection against the impact from shots; like the stick, it became an ally in stopping shots, within the limits permitted by the rules.

Michel and Patrick Lefebvre, the craftsmen who had designed Patrick's mask, were asked to design leg pads based on new parameters. They were so successful that Patrick wore their pads throughout his career, except for a few seasons when Koho manufactured them. Goalie pants and body armor regularly underwent adjustments, too. Marco Argentino, a sports equipment repair specialist, performed that function for the Canadiens. He had learned how to modify equipment to the players' satisfaction. Gradually, goaltending equipment evolved to match the new technique, and the goalies who left Montréal to play elsewhere carried the innovations with them.

—m—

Stephan Lebeau was well acquainted with Patrick. He played a half dozen seasons with him in Montréal and roomed with him on the road for a year. He recalled: "What characterized Patrick was his unshakable self-confidence, a confidence few athletes possess, a capacity never to doubt oneself, even in difficult moments, to consider failures as temporary events, accidents that happen. That's why he was always able to turn the page quickly after a poor performance and rebound fast. That's why he had so much success."

Without confidence, the pressure can become overwhelming and paralyzing. With confidence, the pressure becomes a stimulant. That's why Patrick always needed pressure to get the best out of himself.

During an April 1992 interview with Jean-Luc Mongrain on a TV news program called *L'Heure juste* on Télé-Métropole, the host was astonished by one of Patrick's answers. Mongrain asked Patrick whom he blamed when he allowed a goal.

"I blame myself . . . because I'm the last bastion."

"Yes, but you can't stop every shot?"

"Yes. In my head, that's what I believe."

The response typified Patrick's mindset. He was convinced that he could stop everything. And sometimes . . . he did. This wasn't arrogance; it was a matter of confidence. He didn't say, "I'm going to stop everything," he said, "I believe that I can stop everything." The nuance is important. He aimed at perfection, rarely attained it, but came as close to it as possible.

In games, his gestures often seemed arrogant, but that wasn't the case. Arrogance is based on a feeling of disdain or a lack of respect. Patrick hated defeat, not his opponents, for whom he always had the greatest respect. Of course, his tactics were designed to show them that he was in control, on top of things—even when he wasn't. He could also intimidate them, distract them and make them lose concentration. It was all about competition. But his gestures, even if his opponents might have considered them provocative, were really directed at his own teammates, to show them that he had mastered the situation and that they, in turn, could play with full confidence and composure.

—⁓—

Sometimes fans are frustrated with a player's apparent nonchalance. They yell, "You goddamn bum, with the salary you're making, you should move your ass!" Yet, motivation has little to do with salary. It's a basic principle that management faculties teach their students. Salary is a factor of mental hygiene. A player who earns four million dollars a year will be unhappy if he thinks he is as good as players who make six million. A player who earns $800,000 a year will be perfectly content to earn the biggest salary in his class. Motivation comes from something else. The proof? The playoffs are when the players are the most highly motivated to win. Yet, except for a few bonuses that are relatively insignificant compared with their annual salary, athletes aren't paid in the post-season. They receive all of their salary during the regular season.

Motivation is more closely related to accomplishment, the will to achieve that leads to self-fulfillment. In turn, an athlete's desire is fired by the esteem and recognition he receives from his entourage, particularly from his coach. In the spring of 1986, Jean Perron was counting on Patrick and let him know it. Perron charged Patrick with the responsibility, as goalie, of leading the team to a Stanley Cup victory. Patrick had to justify the confidence placed in him. He felt valued. He couldn't let his coach down. He had something to prove to himself and to the others. He felt focused, responsible. He had a personal challenge to meet. He felt invigorated. He had to win. The next spring, the same coach decided that Patrick had to share the responsibility with his backup. The esteem was also shared. It was no longer the same challenge. The desire to achieve was no longer invested with the same intensity, and, I would say without his knowing it, Patrick no longer had the same motivation.

In the regular season, in previous years in Montréal, Patrick was driven by the challenge to produce consistently excellent performances and to become the premier netminder in the league. He was just as intense in practices as he was in games. Later in his career, he found motivation in the pursuit of goaltending records.

—ɯ—

In the early 1990s, when Patrick attained superstar status with the Canadiens, there was a dramatic change in the caliber of athletes attending goaltending schools. Until then, netminders served an unenviable function. To be constrained to preventing goals was hardly an attractive proposition. Thus, it was common practice among kids to put their less athletically gifted friends in goal because they were smaller, weaker, less skillful or poorer skaters.

But all of a sudden, the superstar of the Montréal Canadiens wasn't a Richard, a Béliveau or a Lafleur; he wasn't a forward, a prolific goal scorer, or even a defenseman. This was different. He was a goalie—a goalie who had made a spectacular debut in the league, despite all odds, who turned in incredible performances for a team in a city offering incredible media exposure, a goalie who had his personal trademark, and who had abandoned his white mask, his dull brown leather mitts and pads, and replaced them with hallowed equipment in the traditional red, white and blue of *Les Glorieux.*

Suddenly, good young athletes with the talent and size to play any position on the rink aspired to be goalies and showed up in schools specifically designed for the purpose. Up to then, parents had been lukewarm about the prospect of their offspring tending goal. Now attitudes had changed markedly.

The next crop of goaltenders worked relentlessly on technical skills, pursuing the path traced for them by Patrick and François Allaire. For over a decade, all of the goalies who were selected in the early rounds of the entry draft and earned jobs on NHL teams came from this new crop.

Today, with the benefit of equipment that has greatly improved over the years, this new generation of goaltenders consistently produces save percentages of over .925; similarly, hundreds of athletes in the world have run the mile in less than four minutes (40 did it in the year 2007).

The greatest tribute Patrick and François Allaire could receive for their contribution to the advancement of the goaltending art came in 2004, though it wasn't especially intended for them. It was during the lockout, while NHL authorities asked various workgroups for suggestions on how to improve their products. Patrick was invited to testify before a committee, of which Ken Dryden was a member. The committee was mandated to find ways of increasing the average number of goals scored per game—in other words, to raise netminders' goals-against average—with a view toward offering a more exciting spectacle. The suggestion was even made to redesign the goal, making it bigger to give shooters a better chance and leave goalies more vulnerable.

Statistics showed that during the 2003–04 season, just before league activities came to a halt, 6,342 goals had been scored by the 30 teams, an average of 211.4 goals per team, while in 1983–84, the 21 teams at the time scored 6,627 goals, an average of 315.6 per team. In 20 years, the goalies had come a long way.

THE CUP OF RECOGNITION

20

Saint Patrick, lacking wood to build a boat but knowing that only faith keeps you afloat, sailed off on a stone trough when he left to evangelize Europe. Jacques Demers, the new coach, after a season considered little more than passable for an organization like the Canadiens—they had finished sixth in the overall standings—told his players, "We're going to shock the world of hockey by winning the Stanley Cup."

Faith, we are told, can move mountains, and many mountains and hills stood in the Canadiens' way in the spring of 1993. What would be the greater miracle? Floating a stone trough or bringing the Habs to a Stanley Cup victory?

In the Patrick Division, the Cup winners the two previous years, the Pittsburgh Penguins, were lying in wait. With their three prodigious goal scorers, Mario Lemieux (69), Kevin Stevens (55) and Rick Tocchet (48), and Tom Barrasso in the net, they were formidable foes. In the Adams Division, in addition to the powerful Bruins, the Nordiques seemed dangerous since the resolution of the Lindros affair—Eric Lindros had refused to show up in Québec City for training camp after being drafted by the Nordiques—which helped team president Marcel Aubut land a slew of talented players and add an extra $15 million to the kitty.

Patrick's performance was also creating some concern. Though he had excellent regular seasons, he couldn't replicate in post-season play the feats he accomplished in the 1986 playoffs, when he earned the Conn Smythe. The first cup had come so quickly that he did not have time to fully savor it, but now, he was starting to wonder whether he'd ever lift the trophy again.

What's more, the season that Patrick had just finished was far from his best. In fact, statistically speaking, it was his worst since 1985–86. Nothing to reassure the faithful, unless they were superstitious. How could the lackluster year be explained? There was no particular reason, but there were a plethora of small problems.

Jacques Demers, after winning the coach-of-the-year award twice with the Detroit Red Wings, had moved to Montréal intending to lead a team that would provide a better show and more exciting offense. Serge Savard shared his vision. So he signed two excellent scorers, Vincent Damphousse and Brian Bellows. Damphousse was acquired in exchange for Shayne Corson, Brent Gilchrist and Vladimir Vujtek. The Habs gave up Russ Courtnall to get Bellows. The new additions promised to stimulate Muller, Lebeau, Dionne and Denis Savard, and the team would score more goals—in fact, during that 1992–93 season, the Habs scored 59 more goals than the previous year. The emphasis had shifted to offense. Not that defense was neglected, though it relied on a rather young and inexperienced crew, but the attack became the priority.

Also, at the beginning of the season, Upper Deck made Patrick their spokesperson for the sale of hockey cards. It wasn't a bad idea, especially since Patrick was known as an avid card collector—he has over 150,000 cards. But the ad campaign launch had an adverse effect on Patrick's status and disrupted his season. At his drawing table, the designer came up with the slogan "Trade Roy." Plastered on billboards all over the city, the words had an effect that neither the American company nor Pierre Lacroix had foreseen. The slogan was supposed to encourage kids to trade cards with each other, not to incite Montréal to trade Patrick! But the ad, repeated *ad nauseam*, had an impact on the target audience. Soon sports-talk shows started to get in on the act, conducting province-wide therapy sessions for weeks on end.

The fans who still had the successive defeats against the Bruins stuck in their craw, those who had shouted "Ra-ci-cot! Ra-ci-cot!" in the previous series, and those who despised the team's defensive style and hoped the Habs would exchange Patrick for some prolific scorers jumped on board the "Trade Roy" bandwagon. According to a *Journal de Montréal* poll on January 13, 1993, 57 percent of the respondents favored trading Patrick. But the paper's sports editor, Bertrand Raymond, came to Patrick's defense: "Canadiens fans would get what's coming to them if the trade became a reality."

Patrick's statistics weren't that bad. Curiously, he was the public's choice for the All-Star game on February 6 at the Montréal Forum. But his record of 16 wins, 13 losses and 5 ties suffered in comparison to backup Racicot's (9,2,0). The ad campaign clouded the fans' judgment: they didn't take into account, for example, the fact that Racicot played the league's weakest teams and that the Canadiens had an easy time scoring on them. Patrick, of course, got the harder assignments. On average, he gave up one goal a game fewer than his stand-in, but the Habs scored one goal a game fewer when Patrick played, which explains why he had more losses.

His results weren't bad, but he had accustomed the fans to far better. He realized that. The situation wasn't desperate, yet Patrick was going through the hardest period in his career. He had experienced difficult moments in the playoffs, but this was the first time he was so inconsistent during the regular season. Even Serge Savard, who once said he did not want to trade Patrick, no longer insisted he would never trade him. Patrick, who had just moved into a new home on Île Ducharme in Rosemère, had this to say: "I would never ask to be traded," he said. "I would never ask to be rescued from a bad situation. I'll deal with it myself. I want to spend my entire career in Montréal, and I understand that my general manager has no choice but to talk like this . . . it's a new situation for me. It's a challenge I'm prepared to meet."

François Allaire was trying to keep a lid on things. He reminded everyone that Patrick had made consistent progress for seven years and that this was the first time he'd been through a rough patch. "I know many goalies in the National Hockey League who'd pay a lot if they could be guaranteed they'd just have one slump in seven years."

Even so, the Upper Deck promotional campaign and the incessant trade rumors had hurt Patrick's performances and skewed the poll results.

Jacques Demers, refusing to consider dealing away the teams' linchpin and exasperated with the wild rumors and speculation, brought everyone back to reality. "Patrick can relax; he won't be traded."

Before the beginning of the season, Patrick had signed a contract with Koho. He had never been very demanding about his equipment. When he was comfortable with something, he could keep it for a long time. His first year with the Canadiens, he used the same miscellaneous gear he'd used in Granby and Sherbrooke. He could be seen with his white mask, his Jofa pads (later Lefebvre), a Jofa or Ferland blocker, a Cooper trapper and a Sherwood stick, each one a different color. The Koho contract was the fruit of lengthy negotiations with Robert Sauvé, who had been advising the company on the development of goalie equipment since his retirement from active play. He had recommended that the company propose this deal to Patrick.

So Patrick had to abandon the leg pads he really liked, the ones that Michel and Patrick Lefebvre had designed for him. He was willing to do so because he believed that the Lefebvres would be joining Koho sooner or later. But they weren't ready to hire themselves out to a big company. For the time being, they preferred their independence. A few years went by before they got together with Koho.

So Patrick went through the season in leg pads that he found uncomfortable. They were too rigid, reduced his mobility and interfered with his basic "butterfly" position.

It suffices to note that the difference between a mediocre goals-against average of 3.20 and an excellent one of 2.70 is only one goal every two games to realize how little room to maneuver goalies actually have and how numerous small details can have an enormous effect on the final result. This is what happened to Patrick in the 1992–93 season.

—⁂—

After losing his last five outings in the regular season, Patrick had had enough. At 7 p.m., he dropped by the Lefebvres' with Pierre Lacroix and Robert Sauvé. The mission? To empty the Koho pads of their content and rebuild them from the inside out.

Michel and Patrick Lefebvre toiled away all night. By the break of dawn, the pads were finished. After a sleepless night, they went over to Patrick's home on Île Ducharme to deliver them. Patrick carefully tightened the straps around his legs, took a few steps in the hall and did a few stretching exercises. Then he turned to the Lefebvres and said, "With these, I'll win the Stanley Cup."

He had regained his faith.

—⁂—

After a miserable end-of-season with only eight wins in their last 19 games, the Canadiens could do no better than finish third in the Adams Division behind the Bruins and the Nordiques. This meant they'd be battling the Nordiques in the first round, with the first two games at the Québec Colisée.

Fans and journalists in both cities had long looked forward to the duel. Media-owners and brewers were tickled, too. They stood to make a fortune. It had been six years since the clubs had faced off in the post-season. Back then, Jean Perron regretted replacing Patrick with Brian Hayward after the opening game of the series, in which the Canadiens barely squeaked by the Nordiques in the seventh game.

Since then, the Nordiques had been transformed, especially since the Lindros deal that brought many talented players to Québec City: Peter Forsberg, Mike Ricci, Steve Duchesne, huge Chris Simon, and goaltenders Ron Hextall and Jocelyn Thibault to name but a few. These stars joined the likes of Joe Sakic, Mats Sundin, Owen Nolan, Valeri Kamenski, Andrei Kovalenko and goalie Stéphane Fiset, already on the team. The Nordiques were formidable opponents with a devastating offense.

The Canadiens had also been transformed. Patrick and Guy Carbonneau were the only survivors from the 1985–86 roster. But the Nordiques' ascension seemed more obvious, and most fans in the province thought they'd beat the Habs. The goaltending duel between Patrick and Hextall was also greatly anticipated.

—m—

On the evening of the opening game, electricity was in the air. Many Montréal fans had made the 160-mile trip to the Québec Colisée. The animosity between the two teams' partisans was nearly matched by the tension between sports journalists from the two cities. And coaches Jacques Demers and Pierre Pagé were hardly the best of friends. Québec City streets were empty, the bars deserted. Everyone was either at the Colisée or at home glued to the TV.

Mr. Aubut, a lawyer with an innate sense of showmanship, invited famous Montréal singer Ginette Reno to sing the national anthem. He was taking a leaf from the Philadelphia Flyers, who'd had the celebrated American songstress Kate Smith inspire their players during their 1974 and 1975 Stanley Cup conquests. Accompanied by ecstatic fans, she sang Irving Berlin's *God Bless America*, which she had made popular in the late 1930s. The Flyers made her their good luck charm and called on her each time the stakes were high. With Kate Smith opening the ceremonies, they had a record of 64 wins, 15 losses and 3 ties.

By inviting Ginette Reno, attired in a sumptuous dress of blue and white—the Nordiques' colors—the team was thumbing its nose at the Canadiens. Not only was Ginette Reno a native-born Montrealer, at the time she was the finest vocalist in all of Québec. In so doing, the Nordiques seemed ready to take over, to inspire the whole of Québec, to become the true successors of the most illustrious hockey club of all time. Their fans believed it. There could be no doubt: this would be the Nordiques' year, the year of truth, when they would finally end the domination of their great Montréal rivals, not only on the ice but in the heart of every Quebecer. And their association with Ginette Reno would be as triumphant as the Flyers' relationship with Kate Smith.

The results of the first two games at the Colisée seemed to justify this buoyant mood. The Nordiques won both of them. In the first meeting, they inflicted a painful 3–2 overtime defeat on the Habs, after tying the match with only 47 seconds left in the third period.

The second match was a much less hotly contested affair: a 4–1 Nordiques victory in which Patrick was shaky in the first period, surrendering two weak goals to Scott Young. Patrick played well the rest of the way, but the damage had been done. His opposite number, Hextall, was brilliant.

The series would be shifting to Montréal, but the Nordiques, leading two games to none, took to gloating. They were within two victories of eliminating a singularly unimpressive Montréal squad. Few experts gave the Habs any chance of mounting a comeback. Even the players were starting to have doubts.

The pressure on Patrick was enormous. The day after he got back to Montréal, the fans' criticism of him on radio sports-talk shows and in the newspapers was vicious. Many hoped that Racicot would start the third game. And Daniel Bouchard, Patrick's former role model, now the Nordiques goalie coach, publicly declared that he had found a chink in Patrick's armor.

The day before game three at the Forum, Jacques Demers made a decision that had a crucial effect on the series, and probably on the rest of the Canadiens' progress that year. It was a turning point. He invited Patrick to his office and reaffirmed his confidence in the goalie by saying, "You don't need to worry; I'm going to live and die with you."

Suddenly, Patrick felt as if he had grown; his confidence soared. Demers had given him the chance to show character, and now Patrick had one aim: to justify Demers's trust, not to let him down, come what may. He no longer needed to worry about his job. All he needed to do was make the saves. He'd be the only one responsible for guarding the Canadiens' goal.

Patrick would rediscover the state of grace he had experienced in the spring of 1986. He could feel the adrenaline pumping inside him.

Crippling stress was giving way to the headiness of the challenge. If Bouchard had really found a chink in Patrick's armor, he should have kept it to himself. Like the New York media ploy of 1986, this questionable tactic could backfire on Bouchard's team.

Patrick had fire in his eyes as he spoke to his teammates at the pre-game meeting, projecting his energy and newfound confidence. "Listen, guys, we can't keep on watching the Nordiques skate around us like that! We're giving them too much respect and letting them play their game! Their defensemen aren't the strongest in the league. Let's start by shaking them up a bit. If we step up, we can beat them. We just need to believe!"

On game day, Jacques Demers and Serge Savard spotted a few things that revived their hopes. Maybe they had also found a chink in the armor, but this time the armor belonged to the Nordiques. Observing them during their morning skate, Demers had noted that some players seemed overconfident, as if they didn't respect the Canadiens, as if the series was in the bag. Later in the afternoon, Pierre Pagé, in an astonishing show of contempt, dismissing his adversary's hospitality, dumped all the food and drink out of the reception lounge that had been set up for Pagé and the Nordiques' guests by the Canadiens' organization. Savard couldn't get over it. It was a Canadiens tradition to make this gesture to the teams they faced in the playoffs. Obviously, Savard and Demers used the incident as a motivational tool when they addressed their players just before they took to the ice at the Forum.

The two games in Montréal were like an arm wrestling match between Patrick and Hextall. Both goaltenders excelled; the competition between the teams was lively. But more combative, the Canadiens came out on top with a 2–1 overtime win in the first contest and a 3–2 victory in the second.

With the teams tied at two victories apiece, it was a completely new series, with the games alternating between the two cities. The Nordiques were still the favorites, but the pressure was on them now and the fear of losing began to creep in. If they lost the fifth match at the Colisée, they would be in dire straits. Nor could they hope to win on talent alone; they'd have to grind away and suffer to beat the Canadiens. The Habs had regained their confidence; they believed they could conquer their powerful rivals. After all, with 102 points during the regular season, they had finished only two points behind the Nordiques in the overall standings.

Ginette Reno didn't sing the national anthem at the Colisée at the opening of the fifth game, perhaps the first hint of nonchalance by the Nordiques. The fans were also less aggressive at the beginning of the match. In the opening game, they had booed the Canadiens every time they touched the puck, until Gilbert Dionne quieted them down with a goal after five minutes of play.

Once again, the Habs scored first and finished the period with the lead. In the second, right after the opening face-off, the Nordiques unleashed a furious attack. Nearing the Canadiens' goal, Mike Hough ripped a bullet that hit Patrick on the right shoulder near his neck. He fell to the ice, writhing in pain. The shot had hit him on the clavicle between two pieces of equipment. He remained on the ice until trainer Gaétan Lefebvre attended to him. Patrick got up with difficulty, skated a little around his net, hoping to shrug off the pain. He decided to stay in nets.

Barely 90 seconds later, Andrei Kovalenko went in on goal, circled the net and then slipped the puck past Patrick's stick side. With the period barely a minute and 46 seconds old, the score was tied one all. Patrick had been unable to react. His arm refused to budge. It would have been madness to continue. He left the game. André Racicot replaced him and Patrick headed under the stands to the dressing room. Play resumed.

Pierre Lacroix was sitting in the fifth row, near ice level. He felt someone tap him on the shoulder and he turned around. "Mr. Lacroix, please follow me. You're wanted in the Canadiens' dressing room." Worried, Lacroix followed the security guard. After a short walk through the Colisé catacombs, they reached a door, where there was a man standing.

"Hello, Mr. Lacroix, I'm Dr. Eric Lenczner."

"Hello, doctor."

"Mr. Lacroix, I injected lidocaine into Patrick's shoulder a few minutes ago. Unfortunately, the analgesic doesn't seem to have worked. He has a serious contusion and he has great difficulty moving his arm. He wants me to administer another dose, but I think it might be risky without a more thorough diagnosis of the injury. From a professional responsibility perspective, I really can't do that."

"Just a moment, I'll talk to him. Is he in there?"

"Yes."

Lacroix pushed the dressing room door open and saw Patrick sitting on a bench, holding his shoulder.

"Hi! How're you feeling?"

But Patrick had no time for the niceties. He was fuming.

"Listen Pierre, I have to get back in goal. We're going to win the game, I'm telling you. The doc stuck me in the wrong place; he has to do it again but he doesn't want to. He has to stick his needle right where the puck hit me, where it hurts. I'm sure it will work."

"I understand, Patrick, but this is a serious decision. The doctor cannot take the responsibility. He just won't take it."

But Patrick pleaded with him.

"Tell him to freeze me. I'm going to win the game, I tell you!"

Lacroix went to speak to the doctor in the corridor. "Doc, just do what he says. You won't have any problems about responsibility."

When the teams went to their dressing rooms after the second period, the score was tied 3–3.

Patrick was ready to get back into action. Lacroix later admitted that he had never faced a similar situation or seen such determination in an athlete in 20 years as a player's agent.

As the third period got under way, the Nordiques' skates must have felt heavier when they saw Patrick back in goal. But they had no choice. They couldn't allow themselves to lose the game at home and then return to Montréal, staring down elimination. They had to fight with the strength born of desperation. And that's what they did.

At the end of regulation time, the game was deadlocked 4–4. The Nordiques had outshot the Canadiens 41 to 28. And when it came to real scoring chances, the statistics were even more telling: 25 to 7 for the Nordiques.

After 8 minutes and 17 seconds of overtime, the Nordiques had already fired five shots on goal before the Habs got off their first shot, a seemingly harmless 30-foot effort by Kirk Muller. Somehow the puck managed to slither through Hextall's skates. The Nordiques were beaten just as the pain was returning in Patrick's clavicle. Hextall had cracked. Patrick was named the game's first star.

At his press conference, Jacques Demers said, "I'll be honest with you . . . this evening if it hadn't been for Patrick, we'd have lost. The Nordiques dominated us all night. We've got to be honest: they played better than us tonight."

Yet the most surprising comments came from the Old Capital's best known journalist and radio host, Marc Simoneau, a dyed-in-the-wool Nordiques fan. "The story of this series is Patrick Roy. The

Canadiens would never have gotten to overtime without him. I think the Habs won the series tonight because of Patrick, and that it will all be over Wednesday at the Forum."

Simoneau was right. Nothing is more demoralizing for a team that started out as the favorite than to go all out, absolutely dominate its opponent and end up losing. The Nordiques could never find the energy to turn things around. They bowed 6–2 in the next game at the Forum—a bitter defeat for them.

After the contest Camille Dubé of *Radio-Canada* interviewed Patrick. Calmly leaning on his net as the crowd thundered its approval, Patrick said, "The greatest player in this series was behind the bench. It was Jacques Demers." Patrick acknowledged the effectiveness of Demers' motivational methods, all the small details that he had considered to prepare his club and give it the confidence to beat its great Québec City rival.

—⁓—

In the other Adams Division series, the Buffalo Sabers surprised everyone by ousting the Boston Bruins, who'd finished 23 points ahead of them in the standings. A mountain had been removed from the Canadiens' path; they wouldn't be facing Boston for a fourth year in a row. It also meant that clubs lower down in the standings had eliminated the top two teams in the Adams Division.

Though the Habs faced the best goaltending tandem in the league in Grant Fuhr and Dominik Hasek—Hasek had been traded to Buffalo by the Chicago Blackhawks—and strong forwards like Alexander Mogilny, Pat LaFontaine and Dale Hawerchuk, they swept the Sabres. But in each of the four games, their adversaries had outclassed them in shots-on-goal. An oddity: all four contests ended in the identical score of 4–3, three of them in overtime. Patrick had beaten Fuhr.

Meanwhile, in the Patrick Division, the Pittsburgh Penguins, Stanley Cup champions for two years running, had more difficulty than expected against the New York Islanders, even with superstars Mario Lemieux and Jaromir Jagr. The series was tied two-all. The Canadiens would be dueling with the winners in the Prince of Wales Conference final, the Stanley Cup semifinals.

As the Habs had been cloistered in the Auberge des Gouverneurs in downtown Montréal since the start of the series, Demers used the break to let them spend time with their families. Back at the hotel a few days later, they gathered to watch the final clash in the Patrick Division series and saw another enormous mountain removed from their path. The Penguins, despite their remarkable 119-point season, went down to the Islanders, a team that had garnered a mere 87 points, and their venerable coach, Al Arbour. An opening had emerged for a berth in the final. Now the Habs were riding high.

The well-rested Canadiens, benefiting from the fact that the Islanders were exhausted after their long struggle with the Penguins, took a 3–0 stranglehold on the series. Since Demers had invited Patrick into the office and expressed confidence in him when he was going through a difficult time, the team had racked up 11 straight wins, seven in overtime. Both figures were NHL records. The players had truly taken up the torch held out to them by the battered arms of previous generations. The whole team was on a mission.

After an insignificant loss in Long Island, the Canadiens sealed the deal, wrapping up the series in the following game at the Forum. The team that few experts had thought would be around late in May was heading to the Stanley Cup final.

—ɯɯ—

The Canadiens increasingly resembled *Les Glorieux* of the great years. The final between the Canadiens and the Los Angeles Kings in the Stanley Cup's centennial was worthy of a movie script. The most prestigious, most successful team of the century was only four wins away from its 24th Cup. Standing in the way was Wayne Gretzky, the most prolific scorer in history and hockey's most effective ambassador in the United States. And for once the eyes of L.A. sports fans would be turned toward hockey. The Kings' logo could be seen everywhere: in shop windows, in restaurants, on caps, T-shirts, sweat suits, and more.

Gretzky was far from the only person intending to thwart the Canadiens' plans. Barry Melrose, the Kings' coach, could count on great scorers like Luc Robitaille, Jari Kurri and Tony Granato, as well as solid rearguards like Rob Blake and Marty McSorley—he had faced Patrick with the Baltimore Skipjacks in their series against the Sherbrooke Canadiens—and an excellent backstopper in Kelly Hrudey.

Since they had polished off their opponents faster than the Kings, the Canadiens hadn't played in over a week. The Kings got a two-day break after eliminating the Toronto Maple Leafs and their new coach, Pat Burns, in a series resembling trench warfare that went the full seven games. Two days of rest were just enough.

Enough to surprise the Habs with a 4–1 victory in the curtain raiser. Gretzky was the star of the first game in Montréal. With a goal and three assists, he participated in every one of his team's goals. He even scored the Canadiens' goal when he tried to intercept an Ed Ronan pass and deflected the puck behind his own goaltender.

With the victory, the Kings snatched home-ice advantage.

—m—

As soon as the contest ended, Patrick rushed to the Lakeshore Hospital to attend a blessed event: the birth of his daughter. It was a delightful surprise to have a daughter after two sons. He was following the same path as the previous generation of Roys.

The baby was due on June 10; the birth had been induced because otherwise the child might have been born while Patrick was in California. At 7:50 am on June 2, Patrick kissed his daughter Jana for the first time.

Around 9:00 a.m. after a sleepless night, with his face drawn and his hair a mess, he was sitting in a restaurant over a plate of eggs and sausages when some customers approached him. "What happened last night? Do you think you guys will bounce back?" At that particular moment, the game was the furthest thing from Patrick's mind. Why weren't they asking how his wife and child were doing? They could not know. He answered mechanically.

—m—

The next day, Patrick got back to business. He joined his teammates, who were studying a video of the first game. He gave each of them a card he'd had printed and plasticized. It read, "The real winner does not stick as much to success as he does to the great, the ultimate victory. The remainder is only temporary futility."

After the video session, Carbonneau knocked on Demers' door to make a suggestion. In the first encounter, Demers had sent Muller's trio up against the Gretzky line, matching offense with offense. But Gretzky was unique, and Carbonneau had something in mind: "Listen, Jacques, my entire career I've played against the best players. As far as I'm concerned, Gretzky is the biggest challenge, especially in a Stanley Cup final. It's not a question of ego; I'm sure I can do the job and do even more to help my team go on to victory." Demers, always receptive to his players and open to good suggestions as long as they benefited the team, agreed. "Carbo" would face Gretzky.

Carbonneau checked Gretzky to a fare-thee-well, limiting him to a single weak shot in the entire second game. Still, it took a bit of drama to notch the victory. And Carbonneau had something to do with it. While keeping tabs on The Great One, he noticed that Robitaille's and McSorley's stick blades were sharply curved, perhaps beyond what the rules allowed. At the beginning of the third period, with the Kings enjoying a two-man advantage as a result of the Canadiens' penalties, Carbonneau informed his coach about the sticks in case he wanted to cut the Kings' advantage to one man. But Demers chose to wait.

Toward the end of the game, Carbonneau noticed that Robitaille had made sure to change sticks. But not McSorley. Once again, Carbonneau spoke to Demers about the situation. Since the Kings had a 2–1 lead with only one minute and 45 seconds remaining, and it would have been disastrous to show up in Los Angeles two games down, Demers played his last card. During a stoppage in play, he asked referee Kerry Fraser to measure McSorley's stick. The stakes were high. On the catwalk, tension was etched on the faces of Savard and his management team of Lemaire, Vadnais, Boudrias and Allaire. Demers was playing all his chips. If the stick was in compliance with the rules, the Canadiens would receive a penalty for delay of game, possibly dashing any hope of a comeback in the series.

The stick was measured. It was illegal by almost half an inch. The referee gave the Kings a penalty, and Demers pulled Patrick to give the Habs a six-on-four advantage. Play resumed, and 32 seconds later, Éric Desjardins leveled the score with a shot from the point, his second goal of the game. The match was going into overtime. Up to that point the Canadiens had emerged with seven straight overtime victories. The players were confident.

Fifty-one seconds into overtime, Desjardins completed his hat trick with a goal that sealed the Habs' victory. With its eighth straight sudden death win, Montréal had tied the series at a game each. The

Kings blamed the Habs' victory on the Forum ghosts. But that night, the ghosts had names: Carbonneau, Desjardins and Demers. The first star was awarded to Éric Desjardins. After accounting for all of his team's goals, he deserved it. But had it not been for Carbonneau's alertness and Demers' nerve, Desjardins would never have had the opportunity to score the last two.

—⁂—

Hollywood's jet set were out in force at the Great Western Forum as if the game were a movie premiere. The stars were living the Californian hockey dream, supporting their Kings, who were participating in their first Stanley Cup final in their 26 years of existence. The only thing missing was the red carpet of Oscar night. The stands were bursting with celebrities like the star of westerns and former President Ronald Reagan and his wife Nancy, Sylvester Stallone, Sheena Easton, Michelle Pfeiffer, James Wood, the late John Candy, Heather Locklear, Nicolas Cage, Susan Sarandon and Goldie Hawn, whose spouse Kurt Russell would later play Herb Brooks in the movie titled *Miracle on Ice*. While Céline Dion was singing in Paris, her husband and manager René Angelil was sitting in the stands with some friends, bravely wearing a Canadiens' jersey. The sports personalities included Andre Agassi, Reggie Jackson, Magic Johnson and Craig Stadler.

The fans booed Jacques Demers with gusto when he was announced. They hadn't forgotten his maneuver in the dying minutes of the previous game. Many considered it cheating. But Demers got valuable support from Los Angeles Dodgers manager Tommy Lasorda, who had been Montréal Royals pitcher in the 1950s. Lasorda publicly asserted that he would have done the same if he had suspected an opposing player of hitting a home run using an illegal bat.

The teams played fast, exciting and tough, sometimes dirty hockey in the two games in Los Angeles. In the second game in L.A., the goalies were outstanding, and Patrick earned the first star. Both contests went into overtime. But Hollywood screenwriters hadn't written the script, and Wayne Gretzky didn't show up at the last moment to free the heroine from the train tracks and save her from the oncoming locomotive. Both times, a goal by John LeClair gave the Canadiens the win, their ninth and tenth in overtime, by the scores of 4–3 and 3–2 respectively.

Jacques Laperrière, who sometimes made quick and witty remarks, said later, "This record of ten consecutive wins in overtime will never be beaten, since no team who wins the Cup will ever play poorly enough to be forced into overtime ten times."

With only a minute left in regulation time during the second game in Los Angeles and with the camera trained on him, Patrick looked through his mask and gave Tomas Sandstrom the longest, most media-covered wink—it's still shown today— in hockey history. In the series, Sandstrom had 18 shots on goal without scoring, including seven in the second match. Frustrated, he began pestering Patrick with little slashes. After stopping a shot by Luc Robitaille, Patrick used "Charlotte," to freeze the puck. Sandstrom poked at Patrick's catching mitt with his stick, hoping to knock the puck lose. The referee whistled the play dead, but Sandstrom defiantly circled Patrick like a vulture stalking his prey. It was then that Patrick gave him a wink and a mocking grin that seemed to say, "I'm in total control, and try as you might, there's nothing you can do about it." That added to Sandstrom's frustration and demoralized him. A discerning television producer and a quick cameraman immortalized that look that went by quicker than . . . a wink. It was enough to discourage the Kings just before sudden-death overtime.

Stephan Lebeau recalls the mood in the dressing room. "Just before overtime, it was so intense you could have cut it with a knife. Everyone was in his zone, in his own cocoon; you could practically see Patrick's around him. That day, I was sitting right next to him in the room. When he got ready to go on the ice, I heard him mutter through clenched teeth, 'Score a goal, I'll take care of the rest.' It was brief. That was it. And he didn't say it with bravado or arrogance. It was almost a murmur, a growl of determination. And the dressing room was dead silent, so everyone heard him. And everyone understood. After that, we couldn't be beaten." John LeClair scored his goal at 14:37. Now the Canadiens led the series three to one.

—⁂—

The Kings headed to Montréal, facing elimination in the same city where, only a week earlier, they'd come so close, but for an illegal stick, to taking an insurmountable lead.

On the afternoon of June 9, a crowd had already gathered around the Forum. And when a Montréal crowd smells the sweet scent of victory . . . The Kings were never in the game. The Canadiens had a 3–1 lead after two periods. Then, at 12:06 of the third, Paul Di Pietro, who'd only scored four goals in the regular season, recorded his eighth of the playoffs. The lead was insurmountable. The crowd rose and started to sing and hoot and howl: "*NA-NA-NA-NA! NA-NA-NA-NA!*"

As the minutes ticked away in the final period, the Canadiens' bench was euphoric. *Les Glorieux* had a feeling of invincibility. No one could touch them now. Out of respect for their opponents, and maybe to avoid tempting fate, they refrained from celebrating too soon. But they knew. There were eight minutes left on the clock and they knew they had won. What an incredible feeling! To know they couldn't lose and to sense victory while it was happening, while the game was still going on. Patrick had sometimes felt invincible when totally absorbed in a game, nearly in a state of grace. But now, all the players felt invincible. They couldn't lose. *"HEY-HEY-HEY, GOODBYE!"*

The apotheosis came when Kings defenseman Darryl Sydor shot the puck into the stands at the final siren. He was the last player to touch the puck in the 1992–93 season. It was a gracious act, but one of surrender that marked the end of the hostilities. The Canadiens had just won the 24th Stanley Cup in their glorious history. Players and coaches jumped onto the ice, congratulating each other, giving free rein to their emotions.

The game had been over for a few minutes, yet the fans still stood at their seats, applauding, whistling, hooting and howling, as if they were trying to prolong the moment of pure elation. On the ice, the new NHL commissioner Gary Bettman awarded Patrick the Conn Smythe Trophy as the outstanding player in the playoffs. With his 16 victories, including ten in overtime and only four losses, he had beaten Hextall, Fuhr and Hrudey, the three goalies chosen over him during the Team Canada camp in 1987. Interestingly enough, he went through all 20 playoff games with the same stick, out of superstition. After each match, he gave the stick to Pierre Gervais, who put it in a secret hiding place for safekeeping. Before the last few contests, Patrick had wound fiberglass around the stick so it wouldn't break apart. That's how important it had become to him.

With a 2.13 goals-against average and a .929 save percentage, Patrick was the most valuable player on his team. The most valuable among many others, since every player on this much-underestimated team had surpassed himself. Jacques Demers had built bonds between the players and convinced them that they were one big family that could accomplish anything. Even players whose work had been disappointing during the regular season had stepped up in the playoffs. Jacques Demers had said, "We're going to shock the world of hockey." They had done it.

As Patrick circled the rink in the traditional victory lap with the Cup held high, he skated over to a camera and yelled, "I'm going to Disneyland!" in reference to an original ad showing winners of individual honors in various sports indicating, trophy in hand, that they intended to visit the tourist destination. Then there were the joyous libations in the dressing room, where players sprayed each other with champagne and gave interviews to journalists.

The victory parade took place on the following Friday, along Sherbrooke Street from Lafontaine Park to Guy Street. It was an enormous success. Of the 28 players used by Demers in the series, 14, including captain Guy Carbonneau, were French-speaking Quebecers, as were president Corey, general manager Savard and head coach Demers, who was readily acknowledged to have played a crucial role in the team's success. Montréal's fans identified with the team and great stars named Carbonneau, Damphousse, Desjardins, Roy and Denis Savard. It is also important to salute Serge Savard's great insight: when he had to choose between players of equal talent, he made it a point of honor to choose French-speaking Quebecers. First of all, he needed to promote the Habs at a time when they were being challenged by the Nordiques in the Québec market. Furthermore, Savard was convinced that a player who spent his summers in Québec would have a greater sense of responsibility for the team's success.

A few days later, Patrick held a sumptuous reception at his home for his teammates and their wives. The Conn Smythe Trophy winner also received a sum of $25,000. Since the award was an individual honor, the money naturally went to Patrick. But he didn't see it that way. He believed that all his teammates deserved a share of the trophy.

That's why he used the money to throw the party so everyone could benefit. At some point during the evening, the base of the Stanley Cup was unscrewed, and some of us carved our initials inside the trophy, hoping that it was the real thing, and not a replica.

But beyond the trophies and rewards of all kinds, after a difficult season of highs and lows, during which many fans had clamored for his departure from Montréal, Patrick had regained the confidence of the hockey world, which now recognized him for the athlete he truly was.

FIVE DAYS IN APRIL 21

Before the start of the 1993–94 season, Patrick signed a four-year $16 million contract. He had changed goaltending fundamentals with respect to technique and equipment. Now he was having an impact on salaries. For the first time in hockey history, a goaltender was among the highest paid players in the National Hockey League. A goalie's value to a team had long been recognized, but there was still hesitation about establishing an appropriate wage scale for goalies. Now the situation would change.

—⁂—

With the second Stanley Cup and his second Conn Smythe Trophy, Patrick's status rose from star to superstar. He now joined the club of the excessively privileged few who are admired, even idolized, whom others try to emulate, who are larger than life and whose every comment and action are scrutinized.

Did the fame and money affect his personality? Not at all. He wasn't in hockey for the fame or money. His will to win and his passion for the game were his only source of motivation. "Events have made hockey as much a business as a game," he said, "but I love the game and I'd play it even without the money." Pierre Lacroix told me that Patrick's passion actually became an obstacle in contract negotiations. In the final phases of bargaining, when both parties dug in, Patrick was always tempted to make concessions because, to him, the game was what really counted.

Beneath the appearance of the mature athlete and the confident businessman who knew how to manage his assets, Patrick was a child at heart. In the basement of his new house, he had built a 40-by-32-foot rink with a *dekhockey* mat so he could play with his children and their friends. There were white boards with red edges, face-off circles, nets and goal creases at each end, players' benches, even penalty boxes. On the walls, Patrick had hung his collection of sweaters worn by famous players like Larry Robinson, Chris Chelios and Raymond Bourque, and sticks used by Mario Lemieux and Wayne Gretzky, to name but a few. In the room, he also kept his hockey card collection and replicas of his trophies. It was a miniature hockey temple. "It's a place where I can relax," he said. "I think about hockey, but I can do it while I have fun with my kids."

With friends and teammates, Patrick was simple and friendly. Stephan Lebeau, his roommate for away games that year, recalls those days:

"On the road, he was a real calm guy. He was happy when we ordered room service and spent the night watching TV and talking about the game we'd played or the one we were going to play the next day. In the difficult times after a loss, he'd keep questioning what went wrong and suggesting changes, which we'd discuss from every conceivable angle.

"We didn't go out very often, and when we did, we'd go shopping at a mall during the day, or sometimes we'd go with a few of the guys to a strip joint at night, but nothing would ever happen there. It was a guy thing, and once we got there, we'd talk about hockey anyway. It was one of the few public places where we could have a conversation in peace."

Lebeau also mentioned Patrick's leadership in the dressing room. "Some people claim that Patrick always had a lot to say in the dressing room. That's completely false. He didn't need to say anything. He was so intense that all we had to do was look at him and we understood. I never saw Maurice Richard play, but I watched the movie based on his life. Patrick had the same kind of leadership, the same kind of influence on the team.

"And sometimes he'd light a fire under me. At one point, I was going through a slump; actually the whole team had been for a few games. He didn't climb on a table and make a fiery speech; that's not how he did it. As I was putting on my equipment for the game, he came over to me and said discreetly, "'Bobo,' we need you tonight; it's time to wake up.' No more than that. Brief and to the point.

"That night, I scored two goals."

Until the mid-90s Patrick answered his fan mail personally. And there were hundreds of letters. Sometimes, Lebeau would give him a hand with them.

"He got so many letters," recalls Lebeau, "that, on the plane, I'd often help him stuff autographed photos into envelopes and address them. Unlike what many people think, he was always very accessible. When we'd get off the bus, fans would be waiting for him and he could spend many minutes signing autographs or having his picture taken with some of his admirers. But of course there were too many, and he couldn't satisfy everyone."

Patrick enjoyed fulfilling the wishes of his younger fans. But one thing exasperated him: some adults made a business of using children to ask players to autograph cards and then sold them for a hefty price. This happened in every city he visited, including Montréal. In the end he saw the same faces so often he could recognize them.

His growing fame earned him a four-year deal to promote Gatorade products, and he appeared in a Gatorade commercial with Michael Jordan that was widely broadcast during the 1993 playoffs.

It also enabled him to get involved in important humanitarian initiatives. For example, he teamed up with McDonald's Restaurants and Gillette Canada to add 15 rooms to the Ronald McDonald House that lodges the families of children treated for serious illnesses at Saint Justine Hospital in Montréal.

—⁂—

From a purely statistical perspective, the 1993–94 season was one of Patrick's best. Thirty-five victories including seven shutouts, a 2.50 goals-against average and a .918 save percentage. With Patrick in goal, the Habs registered 35 wins, 17 losses and 11 ties. Without him, they had 6 wins, 12 losses and 3 ties. His record justified his salary.

Carbonneau also had a remarkable season. Unfortunately, the same couldn't be said for the rest of the team. Too many players were coasting on the previous year's Stanley Cup victory. Too many thought they were better than they really were. Too many seemed to have forgotten that it wasn't talent but hard work that had brought them the Cup the previous spring. Among those who'd played a key role in that series and who were now disappointing were Gilbert Dionne, Paul Di Pietro, John LeClair and Stephan Lebeau. Despite Patrick's encouragement, Lebeau didn't survive. Savard lost patience with him and traded him to the Anaheim Mighty Ducks for goaltender Ron Tugnutt on February 20. Netminders André Racicot and Les Kuntar were spinning their wheels, and the general manager wanted to give Patrick a good backup.

Without passion for the work, the Canadiens were a mediocre team. They had an inconsistent season: a terrible start, followed by an eleven-game winning streak from mid-February to mid-March, when they looked like a championship club. They then finished the year on a sour note, with only three victories in their last 12 starts, including a humiliating 9–0 thrashing by the Detroit Red Wings. Jacques Demers was moved to say, "When Patrick Roy doesn't get the first star, the team doesn't win."

—⁓—

The Habs began the playoffs the way they'd played in the regular season, without conviction. Demers tried motivating his troops with the recipe that had worked so well the previous season. He demanded aggressiveness, intensity and unity. But the formula seemed tired now. There wasn't the same team spirit; many players lacked character. There were many inflated egos. A few bad apples caused dissension in the ranks. Players did their own thing without talking to each other. The defensemen acted as if they expected the "Four Million Dollar Man" to carry the load by himself.

The Canadiens lacked conviction in the playoff opener on April 16 in Boston. Mathieu Schneider was particularly nonchalant. After the second period Radio-Canada analyst Mario Tremblay commented, "Patrick Roy doesn't deserve the poor effort the players in front of him are making tonight. They owe him one. They need to work harder and help him out." In fact, Patrick was excellent in the first game and Jon Casey, his opponent, was rather unsteady. But the Habs created few scoring chances and couldn't exploit his weaknesses. The Bruins won 3–2.

The second game, two days later, ended up in the identical 3–2 score, but this time the Canadiens won, thanks to Patrick's stellar performance. He exceeded expectations by stopping 40 of 42 shots, while the Canadiens had 24 shots. He was selected the first star of the game and the Habs returned to Montréal with the series even.

Right at the end of the match, during a scrum in front of the net, Patrick kicked Glen Wesley, who was holding his stick between the goalie's legs. The Bruins didn't appreciate this, and vowed that they'd get even the next game. It wasn't the first time a team had tried to intimidate Patrick. When he returned to Montréal on Monday evening, he wasn't concerned about the threat.

—⚏—

What happened in the next five days would be too farfetched even for a surrealistic movie. Here's how the events unfolded:

ON TUESDAY, April 19, all the players are on a break, as the third game is not until Thursday. While Patrick is on the phone, his son, Jonathan, gives him a playful poke in the lower abdomen. Patrick feels a strange pain, but puts it out of his mind, thinking it will pass. In the evening, the pain gets so intense that Patrick can hardly buckle his belt. He mentions the problem to Dr. Alban Perrier, who has invited his wife and him for dinner.

ON WEDNESDAY, April 20, in the early afternoon, Patrick goes to the Forum with Vincent Damphousse for a practice. The pain persists. He tells the team's trainer, Gaétan Lefebvre about it:

"Gates, my stomach hurts so much, I don't think I can put my cup on."

"Wait, I'll call Dr. Kinnear."

Dr. Doug G. Kinnear, a physician with the Montréal General Hospital, has been treating Canadiens players for more than 32 years. When Lefebvre describes the symptoms, the doctor insists on seeing Patrick immediately.

Drs. Kinnear and Brown examine Patrick and make their diagnosis. Bad news! Patrick has appendicitis, an acute inflammation of his appendix. The infection has nothing to do with the playful punch that Jonathan gave him the day before. It is pure coincidence.

But this is no joke. Patrick can cope with all kinds of attacks, but not one like this. He cries out in frustration. "The Bruins threatened me; they swore to 'get even.' I've got to stand up to them!"

In cases of appendicitis, doctors usually recommend the removal of the appendix. But even with a laparoscopic procedure, Patrick would miss at least two weeks in the best of cases.

He wants no part of this. He asks the physicians whether there is another option that will let him return to play against the Bruins.

There is one, but it has only one chance in two of succeeding. It consists of treating the inflammation with antibiotics strong enough to suppress it. The treatment does involve some risk. If the medication doesn't work, the appendix may perforate and spread puss into the abdomen. It then develops into peritonitis and patients may die of poisoning if they are not treated within a few days. Since Patrick is under constant medical supervision, this is an unlikely eventuality. And since he wants to return to play, he decides to take the risk.

He is kept at the hospital, where he has a sonogram to determine the extent of the inflammation. He is then administered antibiotics and a serum intravenously. He has lost his appetite and is unable to eat. If the medication doesn't take effect by Friday, he'll have to undergo surgery. Until then, Patrick remains hospitalized.

ON THURSDAY, April 21, in the afternoon, Patrick makes a brief escape from the hospital. He wants to go to the Forum and meet his teammates before the morning skate to give them a few words of encouragement, hoping to urge them to win the game despite his absence. "It was brief and emotional," says Vincent Damphousse, "because he was upset about missing such an important game. Patrick doesn't speak often, but when he does, everybody listens."

Patrick shares a few words with Demers, who is more concerned about the man than the player. "I realized what this guy meant to me," the coach said later. "People often point out that I like my goaltender, but when I heard the news, I realized how important Patrick was in my career and, if I may say so, in my life." Demers contacts the Montréal General Hospital to make sure there is a security guard on duty outside Patrick's room so he won't be disturbed.

That afternoon, in a room overflowing with journalists and cameras, Savard describes Patrick's situation. Everyone in the room turns toward Demers as if to say, "You can forget the cup this year, Mr. Demers!"

Up until the last minute, the Bruins' GM Harry Sinden and head coach Brian Sutter think it is a hoax the Canadiens are pulling to disrupt Boston's game plan. Just before the start of the game, Sinden still insists, "Wait a bit before you say Roy is out. There are 15 minutes left." He fears the Forum ghosts. But Jacques Demers would never have used Patrick as part of such a questionable strategy.

People are under strict instructions at the Montréal General Hospital. Visitors have to present an I.D. card with a photo and leave their cell phones at the door before entering Patrick's room. The telephone has been removed from the room.

In the evening, lying on the hospital bed with a needle stuck in his arm to feed him and to fight the infection, dreading an operation, Patrick watches the game on television. His teammates give up the fight from the outset. They end up losing 6–3, with Ron Tugnutt between the posts. Patrick cries out in rage and frustration. He can't take it any more. He begs the doctors, "Give me more antibiotics; I need to play on Saturday!"

ON FRIDAY, April 22, a new sonogram reveals that his appendix is still inflamed, but that the infection around it has subsided. The antibiotics are working. There is a good chance that Patrick will avoid surgery, in the short term at least. The final decision will be made next morning after another assessment of his situation. Meanwhile, he is bedridden and continues to receive antibiotics intravenously.

He is hungry and now able to absorb solid food. To help him recover quickly—he has been fed intravenously for the past two days—now he eats chicken, his favorite dish, delivered from the Laurier Bar-B-Q, for lunch. In the evening, Da Vinci Restaurant brings him some minestrone soup and spaghetti Bolognese. He devours the meal.

ON SATURDAY, April 23, early in the morning, still bedridden, he plays electronic golf with his friend and agent Pierre Lacroix. Bertrand Raymond recounted the scene, the next day, in the *Journal de Montréal*.

> *After 17 holes, both players were tied. The 18th hole, a 245-yard par three, was the kind of challenge Roy likes. The game indicated that he had the wind at his back. The goalie looked at his agent, smiled slightly and chose a three wood.*
>
> *Bang! Hole in one. Game Over.*

Shortly after 9 a.m., the doctor and nurses arrive. The moment is at hand. Everything will be decided in the next few hours. Pierre Lacroix witnesses a sequence of events that boggles the mind.

"They came to his room and rolled his bed all the way to the elevator, with the IV still connected to his arm. We went downstairs to the ambulance. Gaétan Lefebvre met us there. We put Patrick's bed into the ambulance and climbed in. A flock of reporters and photographers were covering every exit, except the morgue exit, which was the one we used. We drove down Atwater to the Forum. The ambulance entered through the garage, which was being guarded by policemen, and drove as close as possible to the corridor leading to the team's dressing room. Corey and Savard had moved their cars to clear the way for the ambulance. The needle was taken out of Patrick's arm, and he walked over to the dressing room to put on his equipment."

At precisely 10:20 a.m., Patrick skates onto the ice. Every photographer and TV camera operator in the building immediately starts shooting. Some Bruins, arriving before their scheduled practice, watch the scene for a while. Patrick skates around the rink a few times with his teammates to warm up. Then he takes his place in net.

Dr. Kinnear sits down behind the Plexiglas to observe his patient. The Surgeon-in-Chief of the Montréal General Hospital, Dr. David Mulder, is at his side. While they assess Patrick's reactions, they answer a few questions from some skeptical journalists.

"Isn't it a bit risky to let an athlete who's been hospitalized for three days, and who's only been able to absorb solid food for a day to get on the ice just a few minutes after he's left the hospital?"

"Probably, a little," replies Mulder.

Kinnear doesn't seem to share the concern. "What surprises me is the rapidity with which he's returned to good health. Clearly, the appendicitis has almost completely subsided. Patrick ate twice yesterday. The blood tests show nothing abnormal. He'll continue to take his antibiotics for five to seven days. The absorption of this medication won't have any side effects. He might feel some pain while playing, or after the games or in practice, but there's no danger. His youth and fitness will help him."

Mulder and Kinnear are especially attentive to any signs of side effects. They want to see whether Patrick seems as strong as usual and whether his reflexes are as quick. Watching him play, it would have been hard to see any drop in his intensity level. The doctors recommend that he go all out to make sure their observations are accurate.

Patrick practices for a good 30 minutes, then leaves the way he has come, his helmet on his head, without talking to anyone. His preparation for the game has begun. He returns to the hospital to get another dose of antibiotics and get the final verdict from the doctors. Their conclusion: if he isn't experiencing any pain, the decision is his.

That night, the broadcast of the fourth game opens with a statement by Dr. Kinnear: "We repeated the sonogram this morning, and the appendix has deflated. He doesn't have a fever, the blood tests are normal and he's still on antibiotics. From a medical standpoint, he can play. So the decision will be between him and his coach."

The camera then turns toward *La soirée du Hockey* sportscaster Jean Pagé, who is posted right next to the gate through which the players will be skating onto the ice, so he can be the first to see whether Patrick or Tugnutt comes out first.

"A few moments ago," says Pagé, "Patrick Roy took part in the pre-game warm-up. He exited the Canadiens' dressing room like a rocket. But it still hasn't been confirmed whether he will play this fourth game of the series between the Boston Bruins and the Canadiens.

"Welcome to the *Soirée du Hockey Molson* brought to you by Radio-Canada. Well, well! Like the 18,000 fans here in the Montréal Forum, we're waiting to see who will be first through the Canadiens' dressing room door tonight . . . and here he is! It's Patrick Roy; he'll be in goal tonight! Listen to the ovation the fans are giving him, a standing ovation for the goalie . . . What an ovation and what an atmosphere for goaltender Patrick Roy!"

The real question is, how Patrick will fare? Will he have enough energy to play for 60 minutes? Will his legs, inactive for three days, carry him through three periods?

Dr. Kinnear describes the situation: "Let's just say it'd be better if he had an easy night. His chances will be better if he doesn't get bombarded with 40 shots." Jacques Demers agrees. "I'll take care of it."

Demers' message doesn't get through. The Canadiens manage only 15 shots on the Bruins' goal; Boston unleashes 41 on Patrick. But he stops 39 of them, and the Canadiens win 5–2. He is awarded the first star of the game and receives another standing ovation when he comes back on the ice. The morning's golf game was a good omen after all. He still has the wind at his back.

He admits that he actually hit the wall in the second period. His face was lined with fatigue when he raised his mask to drink some water. "But Carbonneau's goal toward the end of the period gave me a boost. I've been ready to play since Friday night at the hospital," he points out. From a hospital bed to a win in the playoffs. Amazing, one-of-a-kind!

On Radio-Canada TV, Mario Tremblay says, "We owe this athlete enormous respect. Not only is Roy talented, he's courageous. He's been bedridden for three days, yet he still insisted on coming back to play in nets. He's one of a group of very courageous men, like Bob Gainey, who played in the playoffs despite a dislocated shoulder."

The series was level now, with two wins for each side.

—⁂—

The episode prompted Michel Talbot, the president of the Association of Québec Surgeons, to comment. He publicly accused the Canadiens' doctors of practicing bush medicine. He spoke of the risks of using antibiotics to treat appendicitis and the danger of a relapse with serious consequences. Patrick responded to this assertion and then moved on to things he considered more important: "I don't pay much attention to all those comments because I was looked after by the best doctors in Montréal: Mulder, Kinnear and Brown."

Dr. Mulder, who had a reputation for being a conservative and prudent physician, decided to set things straight. "Every patient is an individual case. To the best of my knowledge, the physicians who commented [in the media] on Roy's case did not examine him. Patrick was informed of the treatment in every detail. There could not have been a more honest description of his case than the one Dr. Kinnear made in his press conference. Medicine has changed. Three years ago, we didn't use sonograms for these types of cases. We would have had to operate."

No fewer than four specialists had given their opinion on Patrick's case before he had been given the green light.

—ᨬ—

On the morning of April 25, the day of the fifth game, Patrick sat in the stands in the Boston Garden, reading a declaration that Bruins' coach Brian Sutter had made the previous day. "Roy better be good," he said, "because we will be better." Patrick took a felt-tip pen, circled the comment and, without saying a word, placed the newspaper near a journalist who was watching the Bruins' practice.

To be on the safe side, the entire Canadiens' medical staff made the trip to Boston: Drs. David Mulder, Doug Kinnear, Eric Lenczer and Claude Clément. Given the way the Canadiens played that night, it might have been better if the doctors had laced up their skates. The Bruins completely dominated the game, with a 61-shot onslaught. But once again, Patrick prevailed. He made 59 saves, and Kirk Muller memorably ended the agony by scoring the Canadiens' third goal at 17:18 of overtime.

The Habs had won their last two games and were now returning to Montréal with a 3–2 lead in the series. But they had been outshot 102 to 51. "The players seem to depend entirely on Patrick Roy," wrote the *Journal de Montréal* the next day. Even Derek Sanderson, ex-Bruin turned radio analyst, lauded him. "Patrick is one of those rare athletes who isn't criticized for making $4 million a season. He's honest. With him, you're sure to get a good show."

The *Boston Globe* wrote that Patrick had become a part of Garden legend, adding his name to a select group that included Milt Schmidt, Rocky Marciano, Gordie Howe, John F. Kennedy, Bill Russell, The Beatles, Bobby Orr, Bob Cousy, Wilt Chamberlain, Frank Sinatra, Wayne Gretzky, Larry Bird and Michael Jordan, who had all written a page in the history of this venerable arena.

Asked to compare his performance in the fifth game against the Bruins with his work in the third game against the New York Rangers in the 1986 series, when he had shocked Madison Square Garden fans in the Prince of Wales Conference final, Patrick said that the Boston game was the best in his career, on a technical level at least. "In New York, I was a rookie and I depended almost entirely on my reflexes. Now, when people say after a game that everything looked easy, it's because I did my job well. When you haven't played for four or five days, it's important to return to the basics. To me, the basics mean strong technique. I try to be as perfect as possible."

It all seemed so easy, but making so many saves, in long games in warm rinks, drained the energy he needed to fight his sickness. If the players did not support their goaltender, the Bruins would sooner or later gain the upper hand.

Despite Patrick's efforts, team spirit did not improve. At one point, he overheard a conversation between some of his teammates. Apparently they thought that the number of shots on goal had been exaggerated in Boston. It was a surprising comment that was more likely to disappoint Patrick and erode his motivation.

—m—

In Montréal two days later, the Bruins were facing elimination. For once, the Habs and Patrick could not overcome the law of averages. Their opponents were stronger, more powerful, quicker and, above all, more determined. They won by the score of 3–2. "I hate to compare us with previous teams, but last year, we would never have lost a sixth game of a series if we'd been leading after five," Patrick declared after the game. He added, "I don't know if it's because we don't want to pay the price, but we're missing the magic touch we had last year."

The table was set for the seventh and deciding game in Boston.

—⁓—

On the morning of April 29, Harry Sinden's latest reflection occupied the front page of Boston newspapers: "ROY SUCKS!" Sinden wanted to make sure Bostonians didn't think that Patrick was some kind of hero. A local merchant printed 5000 T-shirts with the goalie's picture and Sinden's comment. That night, he sold them all at the Garden's entrance.

Before the game, Patrick had clearly lost some of his conviction. "There's no vibe in the dressing room," he said. "Last year, they kept telling us we were the worst team ever to win the Cup. Maybe that got under everyone's skin. I hope I didn't leave the hospital just to play four games!"

François Allaire was furious. "One of the things I most regret in my career," he recalls, "is not protecting Patrick better before that seventh game. Everything depended on him. We knew Boston was a better team, they were playing better hockey than us, game after game. Some of our players weren't playing well, and Patrick was the only reason we were in a seventh game.

"But too many people were talking to him when they should have let him prepare for the game. Jacques Demers met with him to motivate him, President Corey met with him to motivate him. I saw others talking to him that day. Of all the players on the team, Patrick was the least in need of motivation by other people. During the pre-game warm-up, I noticed he wasn't stopping shots. I was so angry that I—his coach—didn't say anything to him. Too many people had played goalie coach already.

"The situation really hurt me since I knew Patrick didn't need that. He had battled sickness to come back; he knew what he was doing. He might not have been 100 percent physically, but mentally he was sharp. He just needed to be left alone so he could prepare for the game."

The Canadiens were never in it. After 25 minutes of play, the Bruins had already given themselves a 4–0 lead, en route to a 5–3 victory. The Habs were eliminated.

Today, Patrick agrees with François Allaire. "But, on the other hand," he adds, "I didn't have any energy left. I'd given it everything I had. I'm not sure it would have changed much, even if I had been left alone. Adrenaline kept me going for the fourth and fifth games. By the last one, I was out of gas. I didn't have anything left. I was exhausted, empty."

—⁂—

That summer, while negotiations for a new collective bargaining agreement between team owners and the National Hockey League Players' Association (NHLPA) were at a standstill, the most talked-about appendix in North America was removed.

INTERMISSION 22

For the first time in 11 years, the Canadiens failed to get past the opening round of the playoffs. The Nordiques fared even worse. Despite their impressive line-up, they didn't qualify for the post-season with a measly total of 76 points in the regular season. So, during the summer of 1994, Marcel Aubut fired his coach and general manager, Pierre Pagé, and replaced him with Pierre Lacroix and Mark Crawford. In the process, Patrick had lost his agent.

Robert and Daniel Sauvé took over at Jandec. Given the additional clause that I had requested be included in his contract with the company, Patrick was then free to pick an adviser of his choice.

Robert Sauvé had been Pierre Lacroix's first client and had helped launch his career as a players' agent. In 1975, the Buffalo Sabers selected Sauvé in the first round of the amateur draft. He tended goal in the NHL for over 11 years in Buffalo, Detroit, Chicago and New Jersey, earning the Vézina Trophy in 1979–80 (with Don Edwards) and the Jennings Trophy in 1984–85 (with Tom Barrasso). His partner, Daniel Sauvé (no relation), had worked as a chartered accountant with the accounting firm of Lanctôt, Lalumière & Sauvé. The two Sauvés were Pierre Lacroix's partners for a year. When Lacroix left for Québec City, they purchased his shares in the company.

Out of loyalty, Patrick decided to maintain his business relationship with Jandec.

Unable to reach an agreement with the National Hockey League Players' Association (NHLPA), the National Hockey League declared a lockout on September 30, the day before the 1994–95 season was scheduled to begin. So, Patrick had plenty of time to play with his children that autumn. The lockout lasted until mid-January. A long intermission . . .

—᚛᚜—

Patrick made sure he kept in shape. He worked out with teammates at the Rosemère Arena every day. In November, he also played for the Québec team in a tournament organized by the National Hockey League Players' Association in Toronto.

A few weeks earlier, he had caused quite a stir among some players from Chicago whom I had brought to Montréal for a weekend of hockey. I had become the Québec Representative in the 12 Midwest States, based in Chicago, in 1994. In my spare time, I still enjoyed a game of hockey, so I joined a recreational league, the Chicago Masters, set up by Steve Demitro, a former player with the Milwaukee Admirals of the International Hockey League. When he got wind that Patrick was my son, Demitro had asked me whether some of our teammates, who were passionate about hockey, could play at the Montréal Forum before the hockey temple was demolished.

I phoned Serge Savard. "Serge, get a team together, and I'll bring a group from Chicago to play them."

He liked the idea. As the NHL was in lockout, he was available, as were several ex-players and the Forum itself. The friendly game took place in late October.

Savard had formed a squad of former pros, Depression League players and show-biz personalities. Jacques Lemaire, Yvon Lambert,

André Boudrias, Serge Savard and his son Serge Jr. teamed up with the likes of Guy Cloutier, Robert Charlebois and Jean-Guy Moreau.

To bolster the Masters lineup, I asked my son Stéphane to join us. I also invited Patrick, but he declined, preferring not to set foot in the Forum during the labor conflict.

The following day, I had arranged to have the Québec Aces Old Timers square off against the Chicago Masters in Montréal. I had played with the Aces before leaving for Chicago. There hadn't been any former Aces in the lineup for a long time, but it did include, among others, an ex-Nordique, Michel Parizeau. The match took place in Brossard, at the Quatre-Glaces complex. An innovative concept for the time, it included four ice rinks around the service area. It was designed and built by Léo Bourgault, my childhood friend from rue Marguerite-Bourgeois, who was the director of the complex. Stéphane joined us again for that game.

We were getting ready in the dressing room when Patrick arrived. He had borrowed some equipment from Vincent Damphousse so he could play up front with us. His arrival astonished my teammates who had only about half an hour to shake it off before the game. Hardly the ideal way to prepare for competition! Fortunately, it was only a friendly match.

That day, Patrick centered a trio with his father on leftwing and his brother on rightwing. It was the most moving event of my career as a "decrepit old-timer."

—⁂—

January 20, 1995, marked the resumption of NHL activities, with each team playing an abbreviated 48-game schedule. The season was a disaster for the Canadiens. To think that the only excitement at the Forum that year was generated by a pickup game between the Chicago Masters and some Canadiens old-timers.

Patrick had an explanation for the Habs' poor showing. "In my opinion, our team was the one most affected by the lockout," he said. "First, for some reason, we usually got much better results against Western Conference teams. But that year, because of the abbreviated schedule, all our games were with Eastern Conference clubs.

"Then, in Montréal, public opinion solidly opposed the players in this conflict. We were considered 'spoilt brats,' who were responsible for the deadlock. A lot of people didn't make the distinction between a lockout and a strike. Several of my teammates were very active in the union and were quite affected by the work stoppage. When the season finally got under way, their hearts weren't in it; their thoughts were elsewhere."

Obviously, the average citizen can't be expected to sympathize with an athlete earning a few million dollars a year who wants to protect his assets and improve his situation through his association. Patrick had a four-year $16 million contract in his pocket, and just before the lockout, Vincent Damphousse had signed a new deal estimated at $10 million for four years.

That was a lot of money. Daniel Doyle, then President of the Québec Association of Cardiologists, declared, in the context of ongoing negotiations with the government, that Patrick earned more money than all Québec cardiologists combined. I would have preferred him to cite another example to pique the public's imagination—there were plenty to choose from—but he was right. From a societal point of view, it does seem immoral to spend $4 million a year on a guy just because he's good at stopping pucks, while others with jobs infinitely more valuable to society earn considerably less.

But our world remunerates heads of large corporations and people in the entertainment industry (including professional sports since the advent of television) more generously than other people.

In the 1994–95 season, shortened by three months, the team underwent significant upheavals. Before the season even began, Guy Carbonneau was traded to the St. Louis Blues for little-known forward Jim Montgomery. Kirk Muller became the 22nd captain in Canadiens history. Vincent Damphousse, Jean-Jacques Daigneault and Mike Keane were named assistants.

On February 9, barely three weeks after play resumed, Serge Savard, irked by his team's lethargy, concluded a major transaction with the Philadelphia Flyers. He gave away Éric Desjardins, the Canadiens' best defenseman; Gilbert Dionne, a 20-goal forward on the outs with Jacques Demers; and John LeClair, an elite talent with 50-goal potential whose lackluster efforts limited him to an output of 20. In return, Savard acquired Mark Recchi, a right-winger who had just produced his fourth straight 40-goal season. Two months later, the GM pulled off another big deal, reeling in Pierre Turgeon and Vladimir Malakhov from the New York Islanders in exchange for Kirk Muller, who was spinning his wheels, Craig Darby, who wasn't going anywhere, and Mathieu Schneider, an increasingly controversial defenseman in Montréal.

In Philadelphia one evening, Patrick had a rumble with Schneider in an intermission during an 8–4 drubbing by the Flyers. Several players in the Montréal lineup were displeased with Schneider's attitude. Looking for a new contract, he couldn't care less about his team's defensive game. He took risks that often put Patrick and his teammates in a jam. He did everything he could to rack up as many points as possible, convinced that it was the best way to persuade Savard to loosen his purse strings. But Patrick really resented Schneider for letting the team down when it was eliminated by the Bruins the previous spring, by "playing soft" or refusing to play with the slightest injury. When Patrick accused Schneider of acting that way because he didn't want to compromise his negotiations for a new deal, the two came to blows.

In retrospect, Patrick regrets being so direct with his teammates in those days. "I should have acted differently and spoken in more general terms instead of addressing specific individuals. That's what J.J. Daigneault told me. He was right. I've learned from these experiences."

With this last transaction, not only did Savard settle the Schneider problem, but he also acquired a gifted player, fierce competitor and prolific goal scorer in Pierre Turgeon. After Kirk Muller left, Mike Keane, a character player and a popular unifying force with his teammates, inherited the captain's C.

—m—

Despite the many changes, the Canadiens missed the playoffs for the first time in 25 years, winning only three of 24 road games. It was the only season in Patrick's career that he had a losing record: 20 defeats, 17 wins and 6 ties. Despite this, he had a goals against average of 2.97 and a save percentage of .906. Not bad. But all in all, it was a season best forgotten.

For the Nordiques, it was a tragedy, even though they had become a powerhouse in the league, having finished the regular season in second place overall, guided by the Lacroix-Crawford duo. During the labor dispute, the team owners failed to convince the players to accept a wage ceiling. At the rate the salaries were escalating, a small-market town like Québec City no longer had the size or the financial capacity to support an NHL team. In the summer of 1995, to the great dismay of Quebecers, the team emigrated to Denver and became the Colorado Avalanche.

THE RUPTURE 23

"We have to play toast to toast with the Maple Leafs!"

He meant *toe to toe*, he said *toes to toes*, but with his strong French-Canadian-Lac-St-Jean accent, it sounded like *toast to toast*. Patrick lowered his head and tried not to laugh.

He remembered his first year with the Montréal Canadiens when he and Mario Tremblay were roomies on the road. Patrick was a rookie; Tremblay was a veteran. Patrick didn't speak much English, and Tremblay would sometimes tease him about it. Nothing mean-spirited, *"Bleuets"* was just joshing him. Now, Tremblay was giving his first talk to the players in the dressing room after being introduced to the media as the Canadiens' new coach. The roles were reversed: Tremblay was a rookie coach and Patrick was a veteran goalie largely responsible for leading his team to two Stanley Cup victories.

Patrick glanced out of the corner of his eye at Mike Keane standing beside him. Keane, a red-headed guy with freckles, was starting to swell up like a pumpkin. He was biting his lips so hard to keep from cracking up that Patrick thought he could see a thin streak of blood escaping from the corner of his teammate's mouth. Finally Patrick lost it and burst out laughing.

Tremblay broke off his talk and walked right over to him:

"What's so funny?"

"It's nothing against you, Mario; it's just the way you expressed yourself . . . nothing against you."

"What do you find so funny, '*s'tie*'? Do you think this is a fucking joke?"

The relationship between the two men was off to a shaky start. Nothing too serious, but things weren't so funny anymore.

—w—

For several months now, Serge Savard had been putting together a blockbuster trade that, he thought, would make the Canadiens serious contenders for a 25th Stanley Cup. With the arrival of Recchi, Turgeon and Malakhov, he thought his team was just two players short of a championship team. He had talked with his counterpart Pierre Lacroix a number of times without either of them mentioning players' names. As is common between seasoned negotiators, each of them tried to size up the other's interest by feigning indifference. Meanwhile, each was convinced that the other possessed the missing piece that could lead his team to the ultimate prize. Lacroix wanted Patrick; Savard, Owen Nolan.

As soon as there were assurances that both players might be available, a deal would be possible. The other players involved in the negotiations would be a secondary consideration and wouldn't preclude an agreement, provided that Savard got a goalie to replace Patrick until the promising José Théodore was ready. The goalie he wanted was Stéphane Fiset.

Patrick was 30 years old now and his performance in the previous season, Savard believed, was a sign that his best years were behind him. The Avalanche could spare 23-year-old Nolan: they had a glut of players of his caliber.

By early October 1995, the two general managers were on the verge of making a trade. They were getting close to the goal. Pierre

Lacroix knew that rumors would swirl as soon as he and Savard started mentioning names and possibilities to their principal lieutenants. He called Savard, hoping to seal a deal as fast as possible.

—⁓—

The Canadiens got off to a rough start in the 1995–96 season.

First, it began amid controversy when Mike Keane was introduced to the media as the team's 23rd captain. The next day, in reply to a question by Mathias Brunet of *La Presse* (a Montréal daily newspaper), Keane tactlessly declared that he had no intention of learning French: "Why learn French? I'm not a spokesman. I just liaise between the players and management. Everyone here speaks English. I don't feel any need to learn French."

When Keane said "here" he was referring to the team and its habits in the dressing room. But it wasn't clear what he meant; "here" might also have been taken to mean "here, in Québec." Now, Québec was involved in a referendum campaign about its political future, and Bernard Landry objected to the remark. Landry—Québec Premier from 2001 to 2003—was then Minister of International Affairs. He publicly took the Canadiens' front office to task: "It's not the captain I reproach; it's the Canadiens' management who hasn't understood, that as a corporate entity, it has a duty to encourage those who come here to speak the language spoken here."

Then the Habs went down to defeat in their first four games of the season, scoring a paltry four goals while conceding 20 to its adversaries. After missing the playoffs the previous spring, the team was taking time to redeem itself. Its potentially formidable offence could best be described as anemic. An average of one goal per game. Demers' motivational methods no longer sufficed.

The Forum crowd was growing restless, and Patrick was taking most of the flack. Increasingly, easy saves were being greeted with mock applause. As much as he stepped up his efforts in practice, leaving the rink after the other players to set an example, the results weren't forthcoming. He made what eventually could be considered a prescient comment to the *Journal de Montréal*—it was only mid-October:

"I can live with criticism and I'll work like a dog to get over this. But I'd like to know what will happen when they get rid of me. Who'll be blamed? My successor? The coach?"

The fans' behavior was reminiscent of the atmosphere two years earlier when some of them entertained the idea of trading Patrick. With Montréal's 1993 Stanley Cup victory a few months later, the demand to trade Patrick had abated for a time.

Finally, the trade Savard had made with the Philadelphia Flyers a year before was working to the Flyers' advantage. John LeClair had chosen this time to blossom into a full-fledged star, and on a line with Eric Lindros, he had become a prolific goal scorer who, to add salt to the wound, filled the Canadiens' net every time the teams crossed paths.

In the early afternoon of October 17, 1995, Savard was called into President Ronald Corey's office. Corey coldly and abruptly informed Savard that he was being fired, along with his principal assistants, André Boudrias and Carol Vadnais. Corey believed that Savard devoted too much time to his personal interests, to the detriment of the team's. The coach, Jacques Demers, and his assistant, Charles Thiffault, also relieved of their functions, would occupy less prominent posts within the organization. Only former players, assistant coaches Jacques Laperrière and Steve Shutt, retained their positions.

Savard hadn't seen it coming. He had spent his entire career with the Canadiens, except for two seasons in Winnipeg in the early 1980s. As a player, he had won eight Stanley Cups with the team. He had been a member of the organization since he was 15, when he played junior hockey. As the Habs general manager for over 13 years, he had won two more Cups and his line-up had lost in the finals once. An enviable track record. The solid base that he was convinced he had within Molson Brewery, the owners of the Canadiens at the time, would make him immune from dismissal.

It's hard to understand why Savard's termination was handled so brutally. Corey had his reasons for wanting to replace him. So be it. But why didn't he have the good grace to allow Savard to make the decision? There are any number of reasons Savard could have invoked, including personal ones, and the parting of the ways could have taken place smoothly. Everyone would have understood. But he wasn't given the chance to save face. He left as an outcast from the organization to which he had devoted more than 32 years and to which he still felt a strong bond.

—⁂—

Savard was hardly out of Corey's office and starting to pack his personal files in boxes when the phone rang. It was his personal line:

"Hello! Serge?"

"Yes, it's me."

"It's Pierre. You know, we'd better finalize our deal before the rumors start spreading!"

"Maybe, but you'll have to finalize it with someone else. Corey has just given me the boot."

Lacroix was dumbstruck. He'd have to wait for events to unfold.

—⁂—

These "events" took place four days later in the form of a press conference in which President Corey introduced a new general manager, Réjean Houle, a new coach, Mario Tremblay, and his assistant, Yvan Cournoyer. It was astonishing news. "I took a shower, a good cold shower to make sure I wasn't dreaming," Patrick said spontaneously.

He wasn't the only one who was skeptical about the appointments. Red Fisher of *The Gazette*, who had seen a lot in his time, leaned toward a colleague and whispered: "Tell me I'm dreaming!"

Columnist Réjean Tremblay of *La Presse* wrote:

> *It's been five hours since I learned that Réjean Houle is the new general manager, and I'm trying to comprehend the logic behind all this upheaval and I don't get it.*
>
> *Peanut, General Manager of the Canadiens? He's spent the last ten years selling beer!*
>
> *. . . But I know that a man as experienced as Serge Savard was replaced yesterday by a communications director for Molson who has never managed anything other than a softball team in his life.*

In fact, Patrick remembered a trip he and some other Canadiens took to Gatineau to play softball. "On the way back," he said, "the bus had mechanical problems. The diesel pump was defective, and someone had to hold onto it all the time. Houle volunteered. But every time he let go of it because he was tired or for some other reason, the bus stopped. It was late and we were exhausted. Most of the players, who were trying to sleep, would yell, "Peanut, *Tabarnak*, hold on to the fuckin' pump!"

Now, Houle was holding the reins of the Montréal Canadiens Hockey Club. Everyone knew he was a generous, warm, intelligent, hard-working and kind-hearted individual. But most people wondered whether he had the stature, the scope and the credibility to fill Serge Savard's shoes and stand up to his tough and, above all, experienced opposite numbers.

Mario Tremblay had spent the last ten years behind a mike. He was a neophyte behind the bench. It showed a lack of consideration for the coaching profession to assume that he could just suddenly take over a team, without any preparation.

North American hockey had evolved since the Summit Series of 1972, perhaps too slowly for some tastes, but it had evolved. A number of physical education specialists had chosen hockey as the subject of their doctoral studies. Among them were Georges Larivière, Gaston Marcotte, Christian Pelchat and Charles Thiffault. Through the Québec Ice Hockey Federation, their knowledge has contributed to the development of teaching in the sport, particularly in the training of minor hockey coaches. It might also be argued that this evolution took place from the grassroots up, as professional hockey was still considerably resistant to the academics and their theories.

To coach a peewee team, for example, a person had to undergo training in theory and take a workshop with the Québec Ice Hockey Federation. To coach in the NHL, no training was required. All that was needed was for the general manager to be convinced he had found "his man." But, the coaching profession had evolved. It was no longer enough to be a "motivator," a cheerleader or a door opener.

Coaching is a demanding job. Coaches need the hockey knowledge to devise game plans for offenses and defenses, at even strength, on power plays and for penalty killing. During a game, they need to be constantly on the alert for changes in strategy by the other team and ready to counter them. They have to organize and implement a fitness program to make sure their players are in peak condition. They must be good leaders, have authority over their players, be credible, know where they are headed, convince their players to follow them and be good psychologists. They must be effective communicators, able to deal with the media on a daily basis. And Montréal is probably the most demanding city in the NHL to practice this profession in, given the degree of attention sports writers and fans accord to professional hockey there.

In the past, coaches like the Nordiques Michel Bergeron and the Canadiens Jacques Demers, aware of their technical limitations, had sensibly associated themselves with a specialist of Charles Thiffault's caliber to make up for their shortcomings.

Now, before announcing Mario Tremblay's appointment as coach, the Canadiens had demoted Thiffault from his job as assistant coach. Tremblay chose to fill the post with Yvan Cournoyer, whom he felt comfortable with, a former player with much the same profile, knowledge and outlook with, but the same limitations and shortcomings as well. He had no more coaching experience, aside from his stint with the Montréal Roadrunners roller hockey team.

A general manager with no experience had hired a coach with no experience who in turn had chosen an assistant with no experience. They all had great qualities; they all had a "CH" tattooed on their hearts; they were all passionate; they had all shown heart, character, grit and determination; but they lacked the knowledge and experience for the task at hand. It was like mustering up the heart and character to throw oneself down an expert ski run without ever having clamped on a pair of skis. In the short term, players usually handle a coaching change well. It stimulates them. But in the medium term, the three ex-teammates were heading straight into a wall. It didn't help that Tremblay, trying to mask his inexperience, showed up in the dressing room with an uncompromising look about him.

Tremblay decided to meet each player individually. A good initiative. When it was Patrick's turn, he apologized for laughing when Tremblay first met the players: "Sorry about Saturday, Mario, it wasn't what you said that was funny. It was just the way it sounded in English. I didn't mean to laugh at you in front of the guys."

Tremblay didn't accept the hand Patrick extended. Unlike Demers and Burns before him, he didn't realize that it would be a good idea to make Patrick his ally in the interest of the team. He replied coldly: "Fine. Now just concentrate on goaltending."

During the six weeks that followed, Tremblay picked on him every time he could. Patrick recalls, "I don't know why, but he was on my case from the start. Yet it didn't stop me from playing well and doing my job. I've never played that kind of game no matter where I've been. I've never asked for favors; I've never wanted any. I just wanted to win."

And win he did! Of his 15 starts under Tremblay, Patrick posted 12 wins, losing only twice, both times by one goal. One game finished in a tie, in Colorado against the Denver Avalanche, and goalie Jocelyn Thibault. Patrick had decided to tread softly, avoid making waves. But some things bugged him, mostly details. Journalist Mathias Brunet's unauthorized biography *Mario Tremblay: Le Bagarreur* (*Mario Tremblay: The Fighter*) sheds light on the subject.

Since his start with the Canadiens in 1985, Patrick liked to get to the Forum early before practices and games. He would stop by trainer Gaétan Lefebvre's medical clinic. Patrick would chat about hockey with his teammates, who were being treated. He preferred this quiet place to the dressing room where the rock music was so loud the floors would vibrate. One day, he was shocked to see a sign on the wall: "Players who aren't injured are forbidden to be in the clinic!" He was told that Tremblay had ordered it be placed there. Patrick removed it. A few moments later, the coach walked in and noticed that the sign was on the floor:

"Who did this?" he asked rhetorically.

"I did," said Patrick. "I've been coming here for ten years, and I'll keep coming. This is junior league stuff . . ."

Furious, Tremblay stormed out.

Another anecdote takes us to Edmonton. *Les Glorieux* had just won three straight games on the road against the Calgary Flames, Vancouver Canucks and Edmonton Oilers. Patrick had earned first star honors in two of the contests and second star in the other.

After stopping 42 of the Oilers' 43 shots and leading his team to victory, Patrick headed to the hotel bar to have a beer with Pierre Turgeon, his roommate, as he had sometimes done with Stephan Lebeau. It was around midnight, and most of the other players had gone out to celebrate in clubs and strip joints. Brunet described the scene:

Roy is sipping his beer, calmly talking to Turgeon and three reporters from Montréal when Mario Tremblay bursts into the nearly deserted bar. He goes over to the goalie.

"You're not supposed to be here, "Casseau"! You know the rule."

Since Bob Berry's arrival in 1983, players on the Canadiens had in fact been forbidden to frequent bars at the hotels where the team was staying. Jacques Demers had made an exception for Roy, who disliked the large crowds that frequent clubs.

"Listen, Mario," Roy said, "we're just having a beer. I don't feel like going out. It's quiet here. I just want to relax. We've won three straight games."

"I said go to your room!"

Roy doesn't budge. Tremblay goes and sits a little further away. No. 33 orders another beer . . .

Mario is fuming.

Fifteen minutes later, the coach calls to his goalie from across the room.

"Come here right now!"

Roy, nonchalantly, like a student who is about to be scolded, walks over to his coach.

"I told you to go to your room!!"

Turgeon and Roy exchange glances and finally go up to their room.

When I described the incident to a former coach, he said:

"Not so long ago, many coaches treated their players like cattle, like slaves. They insisted that their players have character and grit, but the minute the same players manifested these qualities at their expense, the coaches clamped down hard. Mario, for instance, suffered a great deal under Scotty Bowman's domination. Now that Tremblay was in a position of authority, he tried to emulate the model he was familiar with, not taking into account the evolution that had taken place since the players have been represented by an association. The common assumption is that players don't listen as much now that they earn more money. But money doesn't have anything to do with it. They are simply human beings who want to be treated as such.

"Bob Berry's rule made sense. Can you imagine if half the players had a drink in the hotel bar in front of reporters who cover the team and the curiosity seekers who'd certainly be around? Things could easily have gotten out of hand. But a veteran coach with confidence in his abilities would know how to use discretion and judgment in applying a rule. In this case, Patrick and Turgeon were alone with three reporters; there was no one else in the bar. They were talking quietly. Obviously, Tremblay could have been more lenient. It would have been to his advantage. Instead, afraid his authority was being flouted, he put his ego ahead of the team's interests."

—◦◦◦—

It is commonly believed that Patrick's departure from Montréal was occasioned by the irreconcilable differences between Mario Tremblay and him. But François Allaire doesn't share that view. Of course, the conflict between Patrick and his coach didn't help. After a while, their sole means of communication was through the media, even when Tremblay announced that he was using the backup goalie in the next game. But it was bearable. It didn't hamper Patrick's performance. And they both were so hungry to win that they could have patched up their differences, with a little goodwill.

So it took a catalyst.

Mario Tremblay bore a grudge against Scotty Bowman. In Tremblay's first five seasons in the National Hockey League with the Canadiens, he had endured Coach Bowman's tyrannical behavior. Then Bowman left the organization for other challenges. But Tremblay still had it in for him. In a ten-year stint with the media, Tremblay never interviewed Bowman when he visited Montréal with an opposing team. When the two men crossed paths, Tremblay barely acknowledged the coach, who was now in his 24th season.

On Tuesday, November 28, 1995, the Canadiens were playing the Red Wings in Detroit. With all of 16 games behind the Habs bench and 12 wins to his credit, Tremblay saw a chance to settle an old score. He would show his ex-torturer that the lil' *Bleuet* from Alma had come a long way.

On the Monday before the game, pride and inexperience led Tremblay to vent to Mario Leclerc of the *Journal de Montréal*. "He was constantly on my case," he said, referring to Bowman. "He used to ask what I was doing on the team; he said I couldn't skate or shoot. He was constantly threatening to send me back to the minors. . . . I'd go home, crying and enraged. Because of him, I almost gave it all up. . . . The memory of this has faded somewhat but not completely. . . . If we win [tomorrow] *Tabarnak* will I be happy as hell!"

In the same edition of the newspaper, Yvan Cournoyer, hardly more cautious, put his two-cents-worth in, "What I most disliked about him [Bowman] was his lack of honesty. . . . I have no intention of speaking to him before, during or after the game. Maybe we'll have to, depending on what happens in the game, but if we speak to him, I doubt it'll be to wish him Merry Christmas!"

That evening, Marc de Foy, one of Leclerc's colleagues at the *Journal de Montréal*, called Bowman in Detroit to let him know about the remarks by Tremblay and Cournoyer and to get his response. Unruffled, Bowman calmly replied, "I'm sure Mario understands now. If I was tough on him, it's because the situation called for it. There's a reason for everything. When you're in the coaching trade, you can't tell the public everything that happens in the dressing room. The media can't have access to everything."

—⚏—

The next day, the Wings beat the Canadiens 3–2. Hardly a humiliating defeat, given that it was a road game against the best team in the league. On the morning of Wednesday, November 29, the *Journal de Montréal*'s front-page headline read: "BOWMAN HAS THE LAST WORD."

That was to underestimate Scotty Bowman. He knew that the clubs were slated to cross paths the next Saturday, this time at the Montréal Forum. It is not too much to suppose that William Scott Bowman had every intention of making these two greenhorns swallow their pride in front of their own fans. And if the whole Canadiens organization had to pay, so what! Bowman didn't owe them anything. Hadn't the Canadiens let him down in 1978 when GM Sam Pollock chose Irving Grundman as his successor? After bringing Montréal four consecutive Stanley Cups, Bowman had thought he deserved the post. He had been obliged to go to Buffalo to get the position he deserved.

In Detroit, Bowman had the arsenal he needed to exact revenge. The Wings were a powerhouse who had scored an average of 4.28 goals per game and would go on to finish the 1995–96 season with 131 points, 24 more than their closest rival, the Philadelphia Flyers, and 41 more than the Canadiens, who garnered a respectable 90 points. Bowman could bank on a devastating offense with Sergei Federov, Steve Yzerman, Vyacheslav Kozlov, Igor Larionov, Keith Primeau and Dino Ciccarelli; on the league's best blue line unit with Paul Coffey, Nicklas Lidstrom, Viacheslav Fetisov and Vladimir Konstantinov; and on airtight goaltending with Chris Osgood and Mike Vernon. That's how an armed and determined Bowman showed up at the Montréal Forum on Saturday, December 2, 1995.

—ᴍ—

In Montréal, a somewhat fatigued Robert Sauvé decided to take the evening off and not go to the Forum, probably for the only time that year. He watched the game on television in the comfort of his home.

For once, François Allaire was not at the Forum either. He was in Fredericton, assessing the progress of the organization's young goalies. He and Ron Wilson, an assistant coach with the farm team, watched the game on TV. Allaire gives his version of what he saw:

"That evening, Scotty Bowman had decided to settle the score on the ice with Tremblay and Cournoyer. He had two powerful units: the Russian unit, known as the Russian Five, and the Yzerman line. And then it began: the Russians, then Yzerman, the third line briefly, then the Russians again, and back to Yzerman, and so on. A power play, the Russians . . . Yzerman. Bowman used only two lines through almost the entire game.

"Bowman had absolutely no intention of letting up. Detroit's attack was relentless, coming from all quarters. And Patrick was reaping the whirlwind, a response to the media outbursts by Tremblay and Cournoyer. The Canadiens were overwhelmed. The score kept mounting, 5–1, 6–1, 7–1. For some reason, Tremblay decided to keep Patrick in the game. Why? To show who was boss? Maybe. But the way the game unfolded was a result of the comments in the media by Tremblay and Cournoyer. If it hadn't been for their remarks in the run-up to the game, I doubt that Bowman would have used only two lines against the Canadiens. At 5–1, he would have taken his foot off the pedal; he would have rested the Russians. But as it was, he went at it the full sixty minutes non-stop."

—⁂—

On the morning of the game, when Patrick was leaving his house for the team's morning skate, Jonathan and Frédérick handed him a pog to give to Mario Tremblay. They had drawn the coach's face on it. When Patrick arrived at the Forum, he gave it to Tremblay. The coach was pleasantly surprised: "I'll keep it in my pocket tonight; it'll be my good luck charm." Giving Tremblay the pog was a gesture of reconciliation.

That evening, a few minutes before the warm-up, Tremblay was fuming in the dressing room. Vincent Damphousse hadn't arrived yet. He had fallen asleep at home in the afternoon and had woken up late. Damphousse was an important player on the team, one of the best goal-scorers. The Canadiens needed him, particularly in a game against Detroit.

Damphousse showed up in the dressing room less than ten minutes before the warm-up. Tremblay patted him on the back. "Let's go Vinny, hurry up, it's a big game tonight!"

Patrick was annoyed. Damphousse had just gotten out of bed; he was barely awake. How could he give it his best shot? Tremblay had been on Patrick's case for weeks, claiming that all players should be treated the same. If Patrick had showed up late for the warm-up, how would Tremblay have reacted? Patrick couldn't take it anymore. Maybe he shouldn't have, but he walked up to Tremblay and said:

"Mario, we're playing Detroit. If Damphousse's name was Yves Sarault [a fourth-line player], would he be suiting up tonight?"

"It wouldn't be any different. Things happen," Tremblay replied coldly.

—⚘—

Before the game, former stars from the two clubs were introduced: Marcel Pronovost and Mickey Redmond for the Wings, Bernard "Boom Boom" Geoffrion and Maurice Richard for the Canadiens. The "Rocket" received a standing ovation that lasted several minutes.

Then the whirlwind was unleashed. By the end of the first period, Detroit already led 5–1. Patrick couldn't blame himself for any of the goals. Three of them were scored while the Canadiens were killing penalties, one of them with a two-man disadvantage near the end of the period, when Patrice Brisebois was given a five-minute major and a game misconduct while one of his teammates was already in the box. Every goal was a fine piece of work that Patrick was powerless to stop.

It was probably a good time to change goalies. If François Allaire had been there, that's what he would have recommended. But he wasn't, and Tremblay still believed his team had a chance to catch up. It's hard to blame a rookie coach for being overconfident. At the very least, it was necessary to limit the humiliation on a Saturday night at the Forum.

When the second period began, there were two minutes and 39 seconds remaining in Brisebois' penalty. Detroit cashed in on the man advantage. Kozlov, left alone in front of the net, knocked in his third goal on a clever pass from Larionov.

The score was 6–1. In Tremblay's position, Bowman would not have waited any longer to switch goalies: "I usually waited till the fifth goal, depending on the game and the score," Bowman later replied when asked about his strategy in similar circumstances. About that particular game, he added: "We consistently controlled the puck. That was one of the best performances in my [nine-year] association with the Wings."

Detroit was unstoppable that evening. On the blue line, the Habs were springing leaks all over the place, and the game was out of control. Despite that, Tremblay still didn't pull Patrick.

That's what led to the drama that was about to take place. At 4:33, young Mathieu Dandenault went in on a breakaway on Patrick and misfired, but the puck got stuck in his equipment. He kept on skating and the puck entered the net. A lucky goal, but that made the score 7–1. Steve Shutt, up on the catwalk, headphones on, yelled to Cournoyer, standing next to Tremblay behind the bench: "You've got to pull Patrick out of the game now."

Patrick looked toward the bench in desperation. No reaction. He saw Cournoyer talking to Tremblay, who didn't budge.

About two minutes after the goal, Federov let rip a bullet from the blue line, which Patrick handled easily. Some of the fans applauded mockingly. Exasperated and defenseless, Patrick threw up his arms in hopelessness.

The game looked like a meeting between the Red Army and the Fredericton Canadiens of the American Hockey League, and Patrick was paying the price. He looked to the bench again. Tremblay still didn't make a move. Play resumed. Every time Patrick made a save, the crowd cheered in derision.

Finally, Bowman sent his fourth line into the melee. But briefly. Keith Primeau fed a beautiful pass to Greg Johnson, alone in front of the goal. Now it was 8–1.

Patrick stopped looking to his coach. He understood he was being punished and humiliated. They'd abandoned him. Discouraged, he shook his head in disgust. At the bench, Tremblay, apparently thinking the punishment had lasted just about long enough, instructed backup goalie Pat Jablonski to get ready. Slowly. Very slowly. So slowly in fact, that nearly two minutes later, Federov had time to score another goal at point blank range from the slot—the ninth goal on Patrick. He couldn't be blamed for any of the goals, except perhaps Dandenault's tally on a breakaway, on which Patrick had bad luck. Jablonski finally came in to replace him.

Patrick leaned his stick against the wall in the corridor and handed his mask and gloves to Pierre Gervais. He walked by Tremblay on the way to the backup goalie's stool. Once again, he was trying to extend a hand. He would have at least expected Tremblay to make some sympathetic gesture, as coaches normally do when they pull a goalie. He would have liked a sign of encouragement, anything; a pat on the back, like the one Tremblay had given Damphousse before the game. There was nothing.

Patrick realized that it didn't make sense anymore. It couldn't go on like that. He turned around and walked past Tremblay again. Still nothing. Not only did Tremblay not react, he stood stock still with his arms crossed, nose in the air, looking scornful. Patrick got it. It was the end. He realized it. Later, he would say: "If I'd had some word of support from Mario Tremblay, if I'd felt that he wanted to help me, I wouldn't have gone to see Ronald Corey. That's when it hit me." He approached Ronald Corey, sitting right behind the bench, and told him: "I've just played my last game with the Canadiens." He passed by Tremblay again, who hadn't changed expression, sat down on the bench and yelled to him:

"You heard me!"

After the second period, "Bob" Sauvé called up trainer Gaétan Lefebvre on the cell.

"Gaétan, can you give me Patrick?"

"Wait."

Lefebvre went into the dressing room and handed Patrick the phone.

"Sauvé wants to talk to you."

"Hello!"

"Patrick, it's Bob. When the game's over, get dressed quickly, don't say a word to anyone, and come and meet me by the back door. I'll be parked there."

"OK."

Tremblay entered the dressing room and made a beeline for his goalie.

"What did you say to Corey?"

"Listen Mario, we'll discuss it after the game."

"Fuckin' right you fuckin' asshole!!!"

Patrick got up.

"That's enough, you're not going to call me an 'asshole' in this room!"

Tremblay turned and left the dressing room.

Detroit won 11–1.

—〰—

When the game was over, Sauvé picked up Patrick. The two men spent most of the night talking, and then Sauvé drove Patrick home. The next morning, after a short night, the two met back at

Sauvé's house to continue to ponder the situation and explore every possible avenue. The agent wanted to see if the rift with Tremblay was irreparable.

They reviewed the events of the recent weeks: Tremblay's uncompromising attitude toward Patrick even about trivialities, his officiousness, his habit of firing shots near Patrick's head in practice, his determination to put Patrick in his place and break him, as Bowman had done with his players in the past, particularly the "plumbers" and rookies. There was nothing irreparable. To this day, Patrick says, "I can't say that Mario's attitude bothered me much. It didn't stop me from doing my job well. He would have eventually appreciated me because the team would have won. He would have ended up liking me."

But there still remained the humiliation of the previous evening in front of a million and a half TV viewers, and its consequences. Would he still be booed and ridiculed at the slightest sign of weakness? Would Tremblay be wise enough to come halfway and treat Patrick more considerately? Could he get over the fact that Patrick had spoken directly to the team's president in front of a million and a half viewers? Could he accept that his authority had been challenged? What about Corey, who claimed after the game that he hadn't understood what Patrick had said? Where did he stand? With diligence and diplomacy, he alone could put the pieces back together. Patrick and Sauvé agreed to contact Réjean Houle to find out the Canadiens' position on the matter. Houle summoned them to his office in the mid-afternoon.

The general manager didn't mince words. "There's no going back. We're going to make a trade." Both Patrick and Sauvé noticed that Houle was shaken; he had tears in his eyes.

Clearly, he was carrying out someone else's will. In hindsight, Patrick thinks, "Réjean Houle was a good person, maybe too good for that job. If he had been able to stand up to his coach, he would have been more successful in the post. I can't hold it against him. He liked me and was extremely generous."

So whose will was it? If Mario Tremblay had wanted to keep Patrick in Montréal, it would have been easy for him to convince his bosses. If Ronald Corey had wanted Patrick in Montréal, it would have been easy for him to intervene and convince the people he had just hired. But they would have had to put their egos aside in the interest of the team. Patrick would have regrouped and they could have started afresh.

The will just wasn't there.

The beginning of the season ushered in a threefold rupture for the Canadiens. First with Savard, then with Patrick, and soon, with victory.

Behind the rebellious appearance of a guy prepared to take on any challenge, Patrick is a sensitive person who has never liked displaying his emotions in public. But his rupture with the Canadiens deeply affected him.

He had just lived through the ten most intense years of his life in an organization that he adored. In that decade, he had been under constant pressure. Game after game, he'd had to step up, settling for nothing but the best, to help his team win. He had fought tooth and nail to hold the torch of the organization high, and now, not only were his arms battered, so was his heart. Battered because the organization he loved no longer respected him. It was his turn to be banished like an outcast, like Serge Savard before him . . . and like Guy Lafleur before Savard. Yet, he was the only goalie since Georges Vézina to play ten complete seasons in Montréal, thought by many experts to be the most demanding city in the NHL for goalies. He had started more games in the Canadiens jersey than any other goalie in the glorious team's history: 665 matches, compared with 646 for Jacques Plante, 509 for Ken Dryden and 367 for Georges Vézina.

Journalist Bertrand Raymond asked President Ronald Corey, who had expressed a desire to see more former ex-Habs around the

Forum: "Tell me, what's the use of opening the door to former players if you slam it in the faces of the greatest?"

—✺—

In the following days, Patrick was in mourning. He cried at home, alone in his car, and with Bob Sauvé in the Jandec offices. He looked at his house, which had just been built and equipped to his taste. He circled the neighborhood, stopping to look at the residences of neighbors like Pierre Turgeon and Mike Bossy, whom he would have to leave, and the parents of the kids who came over to Patrick's house to play with Jonathan and Frédéric. He and his whole family would have to turn the page on a past that still seemed all too fresh, and move on to a destination yet unknown to him.

The unfortunate episode tore him apart. The tears flowed. So did the ink. By the next day, Sunday, the news was all over the media: the papers, radio, TV. Everyone was talking about it. In shock, Québec sports fans were putting forward theories of all kinds, from the most rational to the most preposterous.

Patrick ignored calls, waiting for the dust to settle. But Bertrand Raymond managed to get through. "I need time to reflect," Patrick told him. "I've devoted the last ten years of my life to the Canadiens. I gave my all to this team. I think I deserve a quiet evening with my family and friends. . . . This wasn't planned. It's hard to believe that some people think it was. I didn't sleep last night. I just had a rough day. I find this real hard, if you want to know. For now, I need to think things over."

And the next day promised to be a big one: two press briefings. One happy, the other sad, was the way he described them. At the first event, he would be turning the sod to mark the beginning of work on the site of the Patrick Roy Wing at the Ronald McDonald House. He would also take the occasion to make a personal contribution of

$500,000. Fifteen new rooms would be added to the building, which, since 1982, had accommodated, for the modest fee of ten dollars a night, the families of children hospitalized at the Sainte-Justine Hospital. Several private companies, including Gillette Canada and McDonald's Restaurants, would also help fund the project, which would cost an estimated 1.6 million dollars. A conversation with the father of a sick child during the Canadiens' annual visit to the House had sparked Patrick's interest in the undertaking. The father told him, "You know, you're lucky. My wife was in the room next to yours when your son [Jonathan] was born. Since then, I've spent my time in hospitals." Patrick had been deeply moved.

That morning, he was concerned that his beloved project would be submerged by the tsunami of media speculation about the incidents of the weekend. He needn't have worried. When the briefing got under way, he asked the media to respect this special day for the children and not to focus on his personal drama. "This is a joyful event for me. This evening will be a sad one," he told them in reference to the explanations he would provide later that day about the events of the weekend. His wish was respected.

François Ouimet of the Fondation des amis de l'enfance accepted Patrick's check and said, "Some might not realize it, but Patrick will make a huge difference in the lives of thousands of children in the coming years." The children were the reason he had chosen to be associated with the project. Children were his friends—they didn't let him down when things got difficult; they would never have mocked him on the Forum ice. He reassured them, "Even when I'm pursuing my career elsewhere, I will never give up on a cause like this."

The media event had been planned for ages, well before December 2. While it was difficult for Patrick to deal with bittersweet emotions, to jump from hot to cold in the same day, all the same, the announcement of his commitment to the project was likely to arouse a wave of public sympathy for him. He certainly would need it to face the attack that was coming his way.

It's important to recall that at the time, Patrick was the most popular athlete not only in Québec, but in the whole of Canada. This had been confirmed in a survey McDonald's Canada had commissioned to assess the popularity of the personality who would be associated with the Ronald McDonald House endeavor. Patrick had ranked far ahead of the others on the list, including Michael Jordan, who was second, and Wayne Gretzky.

The Canadiens' front office was aware of this, and to make sure the break with Patrick wouldn't tarnish the club's image, it would let loose all its ammunition. It was of the utmost importance to the organization that the responsibility for Patrick's departure be placed at Patrick's doorstep in the public's mind. In a column the next day, Réjean Tremblay described how Patrick's second press briefing had been organized:

If you want to know what goes on in the world of the suits, you may have noticed a tall young man with glasses who was standing near Patrick Roy at his press conference. That was Mr. Paul Wilson, a public relations advisor for National, the communications and public relations firm. National handles public relations for Molson and the Forum. When Ronald Corey was about to fire Serge Savard, he called Daniel Lamarre, the head of National, even before he informed Savard, to find out how to release the news to the press. To know which words to use, which points to stress. As incredible as it may seem, National helped prepare Patrick Roy's press conference. On the right National, on the left National, and may the better man win.

It's not hard to guess which of the two clients National prioritized. However, "Bob" Sauvé gave an explanation for what seemed to be a blatant conflict of interest. Sauvé and Patrick had worked with Wilson on the Ronald McDonald House project, as McDonald's was a National client, too. Sauvé insisted it made sense for them to enlist Wilson's services since they had a good relationship with him. National's responsibility was limited to technical support, such as room bookings and assembling journalists. It would not handle Patrick's speech or his communications strategy.

Fair enough. But on one hand Daniel Lamarre and his entire National team was checking statements emanating from the Canadiens' front office, word by word. And on the other, Patrick, in a state of extreme fatigue and tension, found himself alone to prepare his text with the help of friends at Jandec and Lise Végiard, the personal assistant and secretary to the company's president. None of them was a communications specialist. Sauvé recalls those stressful times: "We were in the office, trying to help him with his speech, we had barely slept and all of a sudden, we'd all burst out crying like babies.

Patrick explains: "It seemed impossible to us that ten beautiful years were wiped out just like that . . . it was real tough." He could have used the support of communications specialists. The sides were very unequal.

Fortunately, *La Presse* and the *Journal de Montréal* had assigned their top two sports writers, Réjean Tremblay and Bertrand Raymond, to cover Patrick's second meeting with the media. They were influential professionals of unquestionable integrity.

Faced with about a hundred media people, Patrick handled things fairly well. He spoke from the heart, but it was a tired heart. Réjean Tremblay described the scene the next day in his column:

The man who met with the journalists at the Sheraton Laval was exhausted, shaken, heartsick.

I've never seen Patrick Roy in such a state. Not even when he was carried from the hospital on a stretcher to play the Boston Bruins in the post-season.

The man has lost weight and his skin is pale. Shaken, he spends his time apologizing for Saturday evening's incidents during the game against the Detroit Red Wings, beating himself up in public and seeking to be forgiven.

I hope a good night's rest will allow him to bounce back. I hope he'll realize this morning that the Canadiens got rid of him like a dirty pair of socks.

I hope Patrick Roy will continue to love the Canadiens, but I also hope he'll understand that he was abandoned by people who got richer thanks to him.

Abandoned by Ronald Corey who banished him from the Forum.

Abandoned by Réjean Houle who banished him from the Forum.

Abandoned by Mario Tremblay who banished him from the Forum.

Never, never was Patrick Roy given a ghost of a chance to explain, to apologize, and to reclaim his job as the Canadiens' goalie. When he entered Réjean Houle's office, the trio who run hockey with the Canadiens had already made their decision. Out with this leper, this black sheep, who sullied the Organization.

His voice choking with emotion, Patrick started the press conference by saying, "I apologize to the fans for the gesture I made when I raised my arms. It was a serious error on my part. I was frustrated, humiliated, but that's not an excuse. I deeply regret it.

Throughout my career, I've played my heart out, and I ask you to forgive this expression of frustration."

Apologizing was the appropriate and dignified thing for him to do, especially out of respect to the majority of fans, those who hadn't mocked him. But a true public relations specialist would probably have counseled him to qualify his remarks. The gesture he made wasn't directed at all the fans, but only at the ones who had provoked him.

Ken Dryden broaches the issue of fan reaction in his book, *The Game*:

> *I am a professional, paid to do my job no matter the circumstances. . . . I do only what I can. And by buying a ticket, does a fan acquire a right that a fan in the street has not? Opportunity, yes; access, yes; but any greater right? Does he acquire license to abuse me any way he likes, to say what he won't say to anyone else, anywhere else? Is that what I'm paid for, like a lightning rod, to stand in the place of everyman and attract and purge the resentments from his life? Am I supposed to take it and feel nothing? Is that all part of the game? I hear it all: every 'On veut Larocque,' every angry buzz, the tone in words I don't understand, the meanness in bitter, mocking applause.*

There's a difference between criticizing an athlete's poor quality of play and vilifying the athlete. Some spectators, for whom hockey is a release, fail to make that distinction. They take revenge on a third party for frustrations they are suffering at the hands of a boss, a spouse, a teacher, a colleague, a friend. It's as if the boss, spouse, teacher, colleague, friend is there. They know him well, they see him every day in the newspapers, he visits them through the TV, they call him by his nickname: "Hey! 'Casseau'! You stink!"

With tears in his eyes, Patrick continued: "Today, my career is taking a new turn. I would have preferred to finish on a different note in Montréal. It will most certainly be the biggest disappointment in my career. I didn't want it to end in such an unfortunate manner. I could see myself in the new Forum [now called the Bell Centre]. I could see myself there for a few more years. That's what makes it so hard." In the short term, Patrick's words had a positive effect. But a reaction wasn't long in coming.

First, there was Jean Béliveau's statement. He was my childhood hero when he played for the Québec Citadelles and later for the Aces in the same city. "If the crowd's boos caused him to act the way he did, I think he is too thin-skinned. That's not the stuff of a true professional. . . . I have no sympathy for him."

Obviously, he was overlooking the humiliation Patrick had suffered because of Tremblay. No doubt Béliveau would have accepted it … as a true professional. It's important to note that he had been Vice President for Social Affairs with the Canadiens and was still frequently asked to represent the organization at various events, among them, charity fundraisers. So, he was speaking as a "company man" on behalf of the organization—one who embodied perfection both on and off the ice, who respected authority at all times, who never rebelled. He was the same man who had fully endorsed the nominations of Houle, Tremblay and Cournoyer six weeks earlier. Bertrand Raymond had an answer for Béliveau in his column:

I've always had a deep respect for Jean Béliveau. He knows the esteem I have for him. That said, for once I have to disagree with him. I concur with Claude Lemieux who can't believe that this 30-year-old goalie has held up so long under the pressure of the public, the media, and let's admit it, his bosses. Throughout these years, Roy was frequently left on his own to hold the fort,

Mr. Béliveau. Other athletes can only dream of having as tough a skin as his.

Maurice Richard was contacted for his opinion. While agreeing with the Canadiens' administration, the man who'd had his share of confrontations with authority and had never let anyone step on his toes, was wise enough to add, "There are probably things we're unaware of . . ."

Then Guy Lafleur was reached at the Le Gardeur arena, where he was the guest of honor at a provincial bantam and midget tournament. After describing Patrick's behavior as unforgivable, inadmissible and unacceptable, he made an observation that was surprising to say the least: "Before the major changes brought about by Ronald Corey, Patrick was the one leading the team. Jacques Demers has finally paid the price for that." Certainly, Patrick occasionally made suggestions to Demers. The latter was open to suggestions from his players—from Patrick, Carbonneau and any of the others. If he considered an idea valid, he used it. If not, he rejected it. But he was the one who decided. Not Patrick or the others. He and his goalie were often on the same wavelength because they had one thing in mind: the team's interest.

A few years later, Demers shed light on the special relationship he had with Patrick: "Contrary to popular belief, Patrick and I have never been close friends. We never invited each other to our homes. At most, we played golf together four times, on two of those occasions with Serge Savard. Our relationship was based on respect. It's completely erroneous to say that he had free rein."

For those who—like Tremblay and Lafleur—thought that Patrick chose when he would play, Demers added:

"I planned a monthly schedule for the goalies. People who believe that Patrick Roy picked his games don't know him. If it had been up to him, he would have been in goal every evening. But it was my responsibility to make sure he got some rest once in a while. I discussed the schedule with him, but I made the final decision.

"As to the place he took up in the dressing room, what would you expect? He was the only superstar on the team. Who do you think the journalists went to see after practices and games? That's why we heard about him so often. In the dressing room, he had the space he deserved. He was a leader. He was under enormous pressure in Montréal. Many players would have folded or been crushed in his place. But he assumed his role wholeheartedly. He put the team above everyone and everything. That's the mark of a true champion."

It is worth noting that before coaching in Montréal, Demers had lived in the United States for several years. So he was immersed in the American mentality in which superstars who carry their teams inevitably have a special status. He had seen how Shaquille O'Neal, Barry Bonds, Michael Jordan, Mario Lemieux, Wayne Gretzky and Dan Marino were treated. He had also noted just how much more these athletes contribute to their club than their teammates. He had carried that culture to Montréal . . . where Patrick had enabled him to win a Stanley Cup.

Réjean Tremblay shared this view. In an article on December 4, 1995, he wrote:

No one is bigger than his team or his sport. But Mario Tremblay and Réjean Houle will have to learn, and very quickly, that you don't treat a thoroughbred like a draft-horse. Both have had good careers as "super" plumbers, but their Stanley Cup rings were earned by Guy Lafleur and the other stars in the 1970s, and Patrick Roy in 1986 who made the difference.

The columnist referred to another tactic intended to discredit Patrick. Some portrayed Patrick as selfish and overly individualistic, someone too preoccupied with himself, who put his personal success above that of the team. But Réjean Tremblay had done his homework:

Yesterday, members of the Organization tried to have us believe that Roy may not have been very popular in the dressing room and that many players had grown tired of his leadership and his strong character. I brought up the issue with five players, including an Anglophone. I put the question to them off the record. But the players chose to speak openly in front of the TV cameras. The answer was loud and clear. Patrick was adored by his teammates. He was the kind of guy who was the first into battle; he was the ideal teammate always ready to come to the team's rescue. There were no dissenting voices.

In fact, here is what some of them had to say:

Vincent Damphousse: "Patrick was the first to go to war for his teammates. There is no doubt, and I mean no doubt, that Patrick Roy is a great team player. Stop making up those stories!"

Pierre Turgeon: "I don't agree with that [that Patrick was too individualistic.] Patrick is a winner; he simply didn't like to lose. In the dressing room, he's an incredible leader."

Brian Savage: "To me, Patrick is the greatest team player I've ever encountered. He had only one thing in mind: winning. When he won, he was happy for himself and for the team. He never gave the impression that he thought he was more important than the team."

The *Journal de Montréal* may have employed the most artful means of undermining the fans' confidence in Patrick. In its December 5, 1995, edition, the paper surveyed its readers with the following question: "Was Patrick Roy's idea of leaving the Canadiens premeditated?"

It was artful in three respects. First, as formulated, the question suggested the answer. It misleadingly implied that it was Patrick's idea to leave the Habs, even though he dreamt of finishing his career with the Canadiens. Next, the very fact that the question was asked was likely to sow doubt in the readers' minds. It suggested the question: "Could it be that Patrick Roy was cunning enough to plan his exit from Montréal?" Yet, it's a well-known fact that these household surveys have no scientific value because the sampling is not representative of the overall readership. People could dial the number and give their opinion as often as they wished. But there was every chance that some readers would assume that the *Journal de Montréal's* survey results were as valid as the results of a real survey. And how did the readers respond? Out of 835 calls, more than 566 answers were in the affirmative (68%).

Still, in 2003 and 2005, journalists like Bernard Brisset (*Journal de Montréal*) and Pierre Trudel (*La Presse*), despite the evidence, persisted in writing that Patrick had wished for and orchestrated his departure from Montréal. It's true that Brisset was the vice president responsible for communications with the Canadiens in 1995. He was the one who met with Réjean Tremblay after the game when the journalist had rushed to the Forum, sensing that something dramatic was about to occur: "Ronald [Corey] told me that he hadn't heard what Patrick had said to him. He was too stunned to understand. He has no idea what Patrick muttered," Brisset informed the journalist. The next day, Tremblay pointed out in his column:

Either Corey lied to his Vice-President, or Bernard wanted to protect his 'boss' by making up a story for the journalists. In either case, it's hardly very glorieux.

Trudel had partnered Mario Tremblay for nearly nine years on the radio. He publicly acknowledged that the two were friends. It's admirable that he chose to stand up for his friend, but one might ask on what basis the journalists made the allegations that helped tarnish Patrick's reputation.

At the same time, the Canadiens' front office kept insisting that they had no choice but to trade Patrick because he had said he had played his last game in Montréal and because "with the Canadiens, the team had always been and would always be put ahead of individuals." It was vital to them that he bear the burden of responsibility for his departure.

—ᴍ—

It was 3:00 a.m. on Wednesday, December 6, when the phone rang. Patrick had thought about unplugging the telephone when he went to bed, but had changed his mind. He had the feeling that something important would take place that night. Réjean Houle was on the line: "Patrick, you're going to Colorado with the Avalanche. We've traded you and Mike Keane for Jocelyn Thibault, Martin Rucinsky and Andrei Kovalenko."

Patrick was relieved. During the meeting with Houle on Sunday, Patrick and Sauvé had requested just one favor from the Canadiens' general manager: that Patrick be dealt to a competitive team, if possible. Houle had respected his wish. It was a noble gesture on his part.

Barely a few hours later, Pierre Lacroix chartered a Learjet for the Denver-Montréal-Denver roundtrip. The plane would bring the three new Canadiens to Montréal. After a brief stopover in the city, just enough time for a press conference at Dorval Airport, it would fly Patrick and Keane to Colorado.

"WE'RE GOING TO REGRET IT!" screamed the headline of Bertrand Raymond's column in the *Journal de Montréal* on Thursday morning. The text was accompanied by a telephoto shot of Patrick taken through the window of the plane bound for Denver. The journalist wrote:

> *National has a lot of work ahead. The agency is in charge of putting in a favorable light an organization that has made many more blunders than it has won Stanley Cups in the last 15 years . . .*
>
> *Roy has led the team to victory when it lacked the necessary resources. Thanks to his talent, his intimidating presence in goal and his exemplary behavior off the ice, he enabled the organization to maintain its credibility among its competitors. . . .*
>
> *The greatest leader of the last decade has just been replaced by a young man from a good family and two followers who haven't a clue about the Canadiens' tradition . . .*
>
> *Patrick is far more than a "puck stopper." He's a friend to kids and an idol for true fans. For those in a higher bracket, he symbolizes personal success.*

Bertrand Raymond was right on the mark when he wrote that Patrick's departure would be regretted. More than a decade later, the Montréal Canadiens were still struggling to break out of the rut of mediocrity into which the upheavals of the 1995–96 season had plunged them.

In October 2000, Guy Carbonneau explained in an interview with Mathias Brunet of *La Presse*: "I have to rank him [Patrick] with the great leaders like Gretzky and Jagr. He could win a game all by himself, intimidate the opponents before a game . . .

"Towards the end of his career in Montréal, some suggested that he took up too much space in the dressing room. But leaders need their space, or else the club is in trouble. In fact, the Canadiens have gotten rid of their leaders in the last seven years. Patrick and I complemented each other well. We assumed most of the leadership. We constantly discussed ways of improving the team. We took the pulse of the club. That's not taking up too much space; it's assuming the necessary leadership."

Later, Carbonneau would add: "Patrick and I often talked because we traveled together from our homes to the Forum. I was the guy who had the most to say in the dressing room, but often, I was conveying Patrick's ideas."

Today, when he looks back at his successors' work, Serge Savard asserts, "The deal they made was completely different from the one I'd envisaged. By letting Patrick and Keane go, they got rid of the character of the club. Given that later on, they went out and acquired players I had let go because they weren't doing the job any more, like Richer and Corson, I think they destroyed the team."

On the tenth anniversary of this memorable transaction, the worst in the history of the Canadiens, the *Journal de Montréal* wrote:

On December 6, 1995, the Canadiens, in haste and in panic, traded Patrick Roy and forward Mike Keane to the Colorado Avalanche in return for forwards Andrei Kovalenko and Martin Rucinsky as well as goalie Jocelyn Thibault.

While it sometimes takes time to assess transactions of this scope, this one took no time at all to reveal the incompetence of the Canadiens administration in those days. In exchange for Roy [the King], the Canadiens got three jacks.

—∞—

In his ten-year career in Montréal, Patrick was never regarded as a controversial figure, any more than he was in Colorado in the eight years after that. It was in Montréal, just after his departure, that his reputation as a controversial figure was created. Six months later Bertrand Raymond wrote in his column on June 4, 1996:

> *The Forum then squandered several thousand dollars on a vast public relations operation aimed at giving itself a good image in the 'Patrick Roy' affair. It was done so skilfully that, today, the 30-year-old goalie is nothing more than just another* Glorieux *in exile in Colorado.*

THE CUP OF DIGNITY

25

Early that Thursday morning, Patrick threw the curtains open. Instead of the languid movement of the Mille-Îles River, he saw the rugged peaks of the Rockies and the snow-capped summits of the Front Range. He wasn't home. Everything was foreign to him.

Reality had caught up with him. He had arrived the day before. Late in the evening, he and Mike Keane had been introduced to the local media. The makeshift press conference took place in the Avalanche dressing room. On a hanger behind where he sat, there was a Number 33 jersey, but the colors were unfamiliar. Still, it was his name over the 33. The Avalanche was his new team, but it felt strange. He would have to get used to it. He put on the jersey for the photographers.

He had said to the journalists, "I got two Stanley Cups with the Canadiens and, when you win one of those, you want more. I look forward to helping my new team reach its goal of winning the Stanley Cup." Already, he was starting to be his old self again with the media. It was typical of Patrick to set challenges for himself in public and then have to assume the consequences. That's what Mike Keane had recommended on the plane: "Just be yourself and Colorado fans will love you."

It was so much more exhilarating in Denver than in the pressure cooker atmosphere of Montréal, where playing 0.500 hockey and crawling into the playoffs had become the ultimate goal. Patrick and Keane weren't in Denver just to play hockey. They were on a mission to capture the Stanley Cup. And Pierre Lacroix was elated. Well before Denver fans knew how to pronounce "Roy" properly; Lacroix knew what the name would mean for the club. He knew he was bringing in a warrior who could turn a good team into a championship team.

But for now, everything felt strange to Patrick. It was the first time in his life that he had set foot in the city, the first time in his life that he had switched from one team to another in mid-season. Even in junior hockey, he'd never experienced anything like that. He couldn't wait to get back into a hockey dressing room. He'd feel more at home there. With a few exceptions, all dressing rooms seem alike. The smell, atmosphere, excitement, gestures and objects would be familiar to him. He would recognize the faces, too: his new teammates were his former adversaries with the Nordiques, who had moved to Denver in the summer. In fact, Denver was as close to Québec City as he could have ended up after leaving Montréal. The Canadiens would never have traded him to the Nordiques when they were in the same division.

Over breakfast, in the hotel dinning room, he distractedly leafed through newspapers abuzz with his arrival in Denver. A photo of him with Keane in the background filled the front page of the *Rocky Mountain News*, which devoted six pages to the event. Its columnist, Bob Kravitz wrote, "In six short months, this organization—with laudable support from its ownership—has established itself as the most creative and fearless in town, not to mention the most likely to bring Denver its first real professional sports championship." The *Denver Post* also gave the trade front-page coverage with a photo.

Patrick went back up to his room. As he crossed the lobby, he was surprised that passersby greeted him and bade him welcome, as had several employees at the hotel. He flipped on the TV. His arrival in Colorado was the headline on all the news bulletins.

At nine o'clock, Claude Lemieux came by to pick up Mike Keane and Patrick at the hotel. Patrick felt at home with them. Lemieux, nicknamed "Pepe," had been traded from New Jersey to the Avalanche during the summer for Wendell Clark. He would be their guide. He drove them to the Family Sports Center, in the suburbs of Centennial where the Avalanche practiced. Along the way, he talked about the city, the fans and the organization, and boasted about the beautiful Colorado landscape.

Scores of journalists were waiting for Patrick at the arena. None of the Avs had ever had that happen to them. The media's attention was normally geared toward the Nuggets (basketball), the Broncos (football) or the Rockies (baseball). Events had moved so fast since the previous Saturday that Patrick's mind had trouble keeping up. Asked to comment on his new team, he made a slip that made the reporters chuckle: "Very good team," he said, "they're first in their conference . . . Uh! . . . We're first in our conference."

"It's much more relaxed here," he confided to Mathias Brunet of *La Presse*. "There's less tension. The philosophy is different. There are three other professional sports teams. John Elway, the Broncos' quarterback, is a huge star in this city. Things will be different. I was told he owns five car dealerships. I might drop by and see him about a car . . ."

While his wife was out house-hunting with a real estate agent, Patrick stepped onto the ice in Denver for the first time. Mark Crawford, his new coach, shook hands with him. Crawford was a native of Belleville, Ontario. How could Patrick have forgotten the "little pest" who had played for the Fredericton Express, in the Calder

Cup series in the spring of 1935? How the Sherbrooke Canadiens had detested him!

Then others came over to greet him, including former adversaries, among them Avalanche captain Joe Sakic; goalie Stéphane Fiset, who described how the puck ricocheted off the Plexiglas; Adam Foote, who would be his roommate on the road; Peter Forsberg; Valeri Kamensky; Chris Simon; Mike Ricci and Sandis Ozolinsh, whom Pierre Lacroix had just acquired from the San Jose Sharks in exchange for Owen Nolan. In addition to ex-teammates Mike Keane and Claude Lemieux, there was Sylvain Lefebvre, who had spent three seasons, from 1989 to 1992, in Montréal.

Exhausted—he had barely slept in the last five days and had lost 11 pounds—he nevertheless got the start against the Edmonton Oilers that evening at the McNichols Sports Arena, home to the Avalanche.

In the afternoon, he tried to run through his pre-game ritual. But he couldn't get to sleep. Too much adrenaline and excitement. Thoughts jumbled in his head. It was the same in the evening. Of course, the dressing room was familiar territory, but it wasn't the same work environment. Pierre Gervais wasn't there to prepare his sticks, to hand him his good-luck puck which he juggled a few minutes before the game and to place the puck in the corner of the dressing room as he got ready to head for the rink. He realized that in Montréal so many habits had become part of his pre-game routine that doing without them was more frustrating than donning a strange jersey. The ritual was broken. He couldn't find the "comfort zone" that allowed him to get ready without thinking about anything. He had lost his reference points. He decided that the time had come to break with most of his habits and rethink the way he prepared.

The Avalanche offered little resistance to the Oilers. That was to be expected. A 5–3 defeat. Patrick conceded four goals on 30 shots;

the fifth was scored late in the game after the Avalanche had pulled their goalie in favor of a sixth attacker.

After the match, the exhaustion and stress caught up with him. His head was spinning in the dressing room. Unable to eat, he headed straight to the hotel. He collapsed on the bed, but barely got a wink of sleep the whole night. He spent hours vomiting in the bathroom. He had shivers and crying bouts he couldn't control. The next day, on the plane flying the team to Ottawa, he still couldn't hold back the sobs. He felt alienated from what was going on around him. Like a rookie. His teammates had their places on the plane. Now he had to make his. He was starting from scratch. As he had so aptly said, "You can't erase ten years of your existence overnight."

On Saturday, Stéphane Fiset tended goal against the Senators. Patrick was assigned the next game in Toronto against the Maple Leafs on Monday, December 11. In a much better frame of mind, he produced a brilliant performance with 30 saves in a 5–1 victory, his first in the Avalanche uniform. He was slowly putting Montréal behind him.

Still, he lost the next two games. Bob Sauvé, seeing that his new goalie was going through a rough patch, wrote "Be a Warrior" inside his blocker. Patrick kept that inscription for the rest of his career. He also took to writing the names of his three children on his stick before every game for inspiration. This sign of family attachment recalls an anecdote about Maurice "Rocket" Richard. He asked his coach, Dick Irvin, for jersey Number 9 because he found the number inspiring since his firstborn weighed nine pounds at birth. Irvin agreed to the Rocket's request.

Patrick was aware that the transaction that had brought him to Denver was vitally important to the Avalanche, and he certainly didn't want to disappoint his friend, Pierre Lacroix. But Lacroix felt that Patrick was putting too much pressure on himself. The Colorado

GM had one advantage over other general managers who might have obtained Patrick in a trade. He knew Patrick well: he'd been his agent for over a decade. After a defeat against the Vancouver Canucks at the McNichols Sports Arena, he gave Patrick a lift home, and used the occasion to have a few words with him.

"Listen, Patrick, this isn't Montréal. No one expects the impossible from you. Try to have fun playing the game. No matter what happens, I will always appreciate you for who you are, who you've been and what you're capable of. Only one person can put so much pressure on you that it becomes unbearable: you. You're putting too much weight on your shoulders. It's not necessary. The pressure to win is one thing, but the pressure not to disappoint someone you care about is a whole other thing."

Patrick wasn't accustomed to this kind of pep talk. In fact, he was used to just the opposite reaction. Lacroix's advice did him a world of good. But the turning point of the season came later, on March 22, during a visit to Detroit. Since joining the Avalanche, Patrick had played the Red Wings twice and lost both times, 3–2 and 4–2.

That evening, he was doing some stretching exercises on the ice during the warm-up when Sakic turned to him and said:

"The team went and got you for games like this one!"

"Yeah, but it's in games like this one that you also have to step up," Patrick replied.

The game was a disaster, a 7–0 trouncing by the team the Avalanche would have to beat in the playoffs if they hoped to move on. Everyone had played so poorly that the next day, the players felt they needed a team meeting.

Patrick recalls the situation: "We had good veterans in the lineup. Troy Murray and Dave Hannan stood up and talked. It was excellent. Afterwards, we really started playing well."

Back on February 5, Patrick had played his first game against the Canadiens in a Colorado uniform. It was like a reunion. When the Habs arrived the previous afternoon, Patrick and his wife had invited Pierre Turgeon to their house for dinner. Other players who were former teammates were also looking forward to getting together. But Tremblay got wind of the plans, and decided to nip this excessive hospitality in the bud by holding a team dinner at a restaurant. Needless to say, Patrick was furious.

Journalists from Montréal, where the game was becoming a major event, had arrived in Denver several days ahead of time. After the first period of the game, TV viewers saw a taped interview in which Pierre Houde asked Patrick whether the media frenzy might disturb his preparation for the game. "Not at all," he answered. "It's a pleasure to see Québec journalists again. I have to admit to you that in Montréal I was well treated by the media. So it wasn't difficult at all for me to see them again."

It is common practice among National Hockey League players, for whom money is less of an issue than it is for most people, to pledge a sum of money when they especially want their team to win a game for one reason or another. The money is then used to pay for a group meal in a good restaurant when the team is on the road, and if there's some left over, it's given to charity. The day before the Canadiens game, Patrick had indicated on the dressing room board that he would contribute $4,000 if the team won. With $1,000 from Mike Keane and a few other pledges, the kitty rose to $6,000.

The pledgers might as well have put the money back in their pockets. Even though the Avalanche won 4–2, the Canadiens dominated the game with 39 shots and 28 scoring opportunities compared with 30 shots and 21 scoring opportunities for their opponents. But Patrick was nearly unbeatable: in a brilliant display, he stopped 37 shots. He even tried to score near the end of the contest by shooting at the Habs' goal after Jocelyn Thibault had been pulled in favor of a sixth attacker. If Patrick had succeeded, it would have been the supreme insult, but he missed his shot.

While teammates were crowding round Patrick after the game to congratulate him, Avs defenseman Curtis Leschyshyn handed him the game puck. Out of the corner of his eye, Patrick spotted Mario Tremblay crossing the rink on his way to the dressing room. With the events of December and the previous night's abortive supper in mind, he rolled the puck towards his ex-coach.

It was the kind of spontaneous, impulsive, thoughtless thing that players do on the ice to intimidate their adversaries. But when a player does it to an opposing coach after the game, albeit Mario Tremblay, he risks being accused of being arrogant and showing contempt. Patrick admits it. "To be honest, I was a little arrogant. But I was so happy!" Still with the Canadiens, François Allaire, who often has a particular way of summing things up, noted, "Unfortunately for us, Patrick waited till the game was over to make his only bad move."

In American sports culture, what Patrick did would have been considered trivial; it would have gone unnoticed. But in Montréal, the cradle of hockey, where players learn very early on to show the utmost respect to authority and the Holy Flannel (the Canadiens' jersey), such behavior was considered reprehensible. The scene was caught on camera, and people made a meal of it in Montréal: on TV, on radio and on the talk shows. Tremblay, perceived to be the victim, regained the sympathy of Montréal hockey buffs.

After the game, the Canadiens spent the night in Denver, so Patrick finally had a chance to break bread with his pal Turgeon, whom he'd frustrated on four or five occasions with some of his best saves.

—m—

The Avalanche began the post-season against the Vancouver Canucks, who had trailed them by 25 points in the general standings. Patrick was concerned about the losing mentality afflicting his new organization during its final seasons in Québec City. The Nordiques hadn't gotten past the first round of the playoffs since 1987. Their captain, Joe Sakic, had never gone beyond that stage in his NHL career. Yet, the Avalanche had the potential to go far. Patrick wanted to help the team get out of its rut, but he still didn't feel he was at his best. He was worried about that.

The teams traded victories in their first two meetings in Colorado. Patrick was dissatisfied with his work. He was having difficulty concentrating for the entire game. He would catch himself checking the scoreboard for the results of other games to see how the Canadiens were shaping up in their series with the New York Rangers.

The day before game three in Vancouver, he called me to talk about the problem. I didn't really know what I could say that would help him, but since the problem involved concentration, I suggested that he constantly keep his eyes on the puck and follow it even when it was in the other team's zone. I figured that would keep his mind from wandering.

In game three, he shut out the Canucks in front of their own supporters and the Avalanche won 4–0. The next morning, he called me in Chicago, all fired up. "Hey, Dad! It worked!" The Avalanche went on to eliminate the Canucks in six games. Patrick was relieved, but he believed he hadn't been the one who'd made the difference in the victory, as he was accustomed to do in the playoffs.

—m—

In the next series, as fate would have it, the Avalanche was pitted against the Chicago Blackhawks. So I had a chance to see Patrick a few times, for supper at my house or for breakfast at the Drake Hotel, where the players were staying. Patrick was more relaxed. Getting past the first round, he believed, would be a shot in the arm for the Avalanche, and the team would improve as they moved on in the post-season. It would need to; the Blackhawks would be a formidable test.

The two evenly matched squads headed for Chicago after trading victories in their first two meetings in Denver. It was a closely fought series in which four games went into sudden death. All told, the two squads played 76 minutes and 26 seconds of overtime. The Blackhawks were a solid outfit with Ed Belfour in the net, Chris Chelios and Gary Suter on the blue line, and gifted scorers like Jeremy Roenick, Tony Amonte, Bernie Nicholls and Éric Dazé up front.

In Chicago, the two teams split overtime victories, with the second game ending in the third period of extra time. In the first overtime period, Chicago's Jeremy Roenick could have ended the game when he broke in alone on the Avalanche goal. But Sandis Ozolinsh hooked him from behind and he couldn't make a play. No penalty was called though the referee could easily have awarded a penalty shot to the Hawks' stellar center. The play and the referee's leniency provoked some verbal sparring between the two stars ("PR" vs. "JR") while the interviewer acted as a mediator.

"The reason why he kind of slowed down is because he knew that I was ready for his forehand shot. I don't think he would have beaten me," said Patrick.

"There should have been a penalty shot, there is no doubt about that," replied Roenick. "I like Patrick's quote that he would have stopped me. I wonder where he was in game three [Roenick had beaten Patrick on a breakaway] probably getting his 'jock' out of the stands, out of the United Center rafters."

Asked by a journalist to comment on Roenick's last remark, Patrick said with a big smile, "I didn't really hear what Jeremy said because I had my two Stanley Cup rings plugged in my ears." Patrick's rejoinder made the rounds of North American media. He later admitted that Mike Keane had whispered the line to him.

Chicago failed to win another game. The Avalanche took the series by four games to two. When the last game ended, the journalists kept their ears tuned in as Patrick and Roenick shook hands. "He told me that he respected me," said Patrick. "You know, our little run-in was just words. It's part of the game. He played very well in this series. Jeremy is a great competitor."

—⁂—

Six days later, the Avalanche started the Western Conference final in Detroit against the powerful Red Wings. During the regular season, the Wings had left their closest rivals in the dust—they finished 27 points ahead of the third place Avalanche. Patrick failed to register a single triumph in five matches with them. His record included two crushing defeats, one with the Canadiens and the other with the Avalanche. Yet, Patrick remained confident despite these gloomy results. He felt reassured because two of Detroit's wins had been by the slimmest of one-goal margins. That gave him reason to be confident. Of course, there'd been the 7–0 blowout, but the team had shaped up since then.

Barry Melrose, the Los Angeles Kings' former coach, had lost to Patrick and the Canadiens in the 1993 final. He knew what the goalie was capable of doing. Now an ESPN commentator, Melrose declared, "Patrick hasn't played well against Detroit this year but that was the regular season and it's a different Patrick Roy now, a different Colorado Avalanche also; they are a much more confident team. What I love about Patrick is that he doesn't give any soft goals in the playoffs and that can make the difference. He knows he hasn't played well against Detroit and the press will bring it up every night. Patrick will use this to motivate himself; that's how that man works. The more they will challenge him, the better he will become."

And as Randy Holtz, a *Rocky Mountain News* staff writer wrote in a feature article, there was so much more than his play on the ice.

> *There is that charisma, that nebulous human virtue not easily defined or described that can pull his teammates to the top, make them believe in themselves and make them give their best to achieve victory.*
>
> *When Roy walks into a room, eyes instinctively follow him. It is an almost regal thing, an almost kinglike bearing, a manner and posture that suggest calm and control and confidence.*

Indeed, there was a new wind blowing. To everyone's surprise, the Avalanche eked out a 3–2 overtime victory in the opening game in Detroit. "If the Wings had played against us [the Canadiens] like they're playing in the playoffs so far," said Patrick after the game, "I don't think that they would have led 9 to 1 after two periods, on December 2, 1995. I don't think that Detroit are playing as well as they wish and I think that we [the Avalanche] are playing our best hockey so far. We believe we have a good chance to beat them and we'll have to show them that tomorrow afternoon in the second encounter."

As he had done so often in the playoffs, Patrick had given himself a challenge. And as he had done so often in the playoffs, he met the challenge, making 35 saves and blanking the Wings in a 3–0 triumph in game two. Much to Scotty Bowman's dismay, the Wings were in trouble.

In Denver, however, it was the Wings' turn to rain on the home fans' parade, upsetting the Avalanche by the score of 6–4. Patrick confessed to former Canadiens' defenseman, Brian Engblom, then an ESPN commentator, that he had found it hard to get up for the match. For some inexplicable reason, he had felt too relaxed, and his concentration wavered during the game. It was hardly surprising, therefore, that he underperformed. But he made up for it in the next game with 29 saves in a 4–2 victory. Trailing by three games to one, the Wings now had their backs to the wall.

As expected, the Wings won in Detroit, but they were unable to resist the Avalanche's final surge two days later in Denver. The powerful Red Wings, who had caused Patrick's exile to Colorado, were eliminated. He had out-dueled his excellent rival, Chris Osgood.

Patrick is sure he overheard Scotty Bowman sigh during an interview later on: "If I'd only known . . ."

—⁂—

Meanwhile, in the Eastern Conference, the Florida Panthers, defying all logic, eliminated the Philadelphia Flyers, the runner-up in the overall standings, and ousted the Pittsburgh Penguins, despite the presence of Mario Lemieux and Jaromir Jagr. The success of the Panthers, now viewed as a Cinderella team, was largely due to the skilful coaching of Doug MacLean and the solid play of their experienced goalie, John Vanbiesbrouck. Hockey fans recalled the trench war in the 1986 series between Patrick and Vanbiesbrouck, who was then with the New York Rangers. In the 1996 quarter- and semifinal, he had been an unsolvable enigma for the Flyers and the Penguins.

The Stanley Cup final featured two teams from cities without a long-standing hockey tradition. The Avalanche were in their first year in Denver—the Rockies had played there without much success from 1976 to 1982—and the Panthers toiled in a climate that would never have spawned a winter sport like hockey.

Nevertheless, due to the scope of the event, and also to the presence of numerous European players on both teams, the final series would be telecast to as many as 140 countries around the globe. Teams of commentators from Japan, Sweden, Finland, Norway, Russia and Germany were on site to describe the action and transmit it live to their respective countries in the middle of the night.

In the United States, though the series was on TV, 16,000 Avalanche supporters crammed into the McNichols Sports Arena to watch the game on a giant screen so they wouldn't miss a bit of the action in the games played in Miami. In Canada, no fans were more excited than the hockey lovers in Québec City. Nostalgic, sad and perhaps a trifle frustrated, they would be following the slightest progress of their former beloved Nordiques.

This ultimate series could have been dubbed the "rats' final," much to the chagrin of the National Hockey League authorities. The vilified little rodent had become the Panthers' talisman early in the regular season after an unforeseeable event. Just before Florida's inaugural game against the Calgary Flames, a fair-sized rat with a long tail wreaked havoc in the Panthers' dressing room at the Miami Arena. While his teammates were screaming and hopping all over the place, assistant captain Scott Mellanby screwed up his courage and crushed the intruder's skull with a hockey stick. He then went on to score two goals in a 4–3 victory against the Flames.

Two games later, after another Panthers victory, the fans tossed two plastic rats onto the ice. Soon there were 25, . . . then 50, . . . and 100. In the series against the Penguins, the rat patrol, on hand to pick up the plastic rodents thrown after every Florida goal, estimated that an average of 2,000 rats were thrown onto the ice per game. A few merchants, such as Annie's Costumes and Magic Boutique, sensed a good business opportunity and ordered thousands of rats for the final.

It was, in fact, the most spectacular aspect of the final, as the Avalanche gobbled up the Panthers in four straight games. In the first period of the inaugural game in Denver, Patrick had to hold the fort while his teammates shook off the rust from a six-day break after eliminating Detroit. But the Avalanche eventually got rolling and won two games at home by the scores of 3–1 and 8–1. The show was then on the road to the Miami rat trap.

Before game three, Patrick said, "If the Panthers score, I'm not going to hide in my net, I'm telling you. I'll stand up there and get hit by the rats; I don't care. I have too much pride to hide in the net." It was his way of punishing himself if he gave up a goal and his way of motivating himself, too.

He surrendered two goals in the first period alone, and hundreds of rats rained down on him. Then he shut out the Panthers in the next two periods, forestalling another rat attack. More important, the Avalanche won 3–2 and stood one game away from the Cup.

I previously mentioned that the detestable practice of firing plastic rats on the ice was the most spectacular aspect of the Stanley Cup final. But that's not really true. The most comical perhaps, but not the most spectacular. In fact, NHL commissioner Gary Bettman had already announced that the practice would be banned the next year. Just scooping up the little beasts from the ice unduly delayed the game.

No. The most spectacular event was the magnificent contest between Patrick and Vanbiesbrouck in game four. It was one of the most stunning netminding duels in NHL history.

Patrick didn't wait for Bettman's plan to be implemented. He had decided to put an end to the rat show. How would he manage it? Quite simply, he would shut the door on the Panthers. He wouldn't allow them any goals. This way, the fans would keep their plastic rodents for themselves.

On Radio Canada's *La Soirée du Hockey*, host Jean Pagé began the program in the following way:

> *It's hurricane season here in Miami, but the only thing that the Florida Panthers want to avoid is to be swept in four straight games by the tornado that is the Colorado Avalanche. To them, it's a question of pride, a question of honor. They want to win this evening's game. That's what we'll see in a few moments in this fourth game of the Stanley Cup final. However, facing the Florida Panthers players is a wonderful hockey machine led by an extraordinary athlete, goalie Patrick Roy. He came to our studio at about 6:30 pm to chat about this and that, pass the time and relax. And believe me, he had fire in his eyes. The series could definitely be wrapped up tonight.*

Easy to say, but Vanbiesbrouck and his teammates were determined; they weren't about to give up without a struggle.

After three periods of regulation time, the score was 0–0. After four periods, it was still 0–0. After five periods, still 0–0. It wasn't until 4:31 of the sixth period, at 1:06 a.m., that defenseman Uwe Krupp broke the deadlock with a shot from the blue line that beat Vanbiesbrouck. The residents of Krupp's birthplace, Cologne, Germany, must have leapt out of their beds or spilt their coffee. It was the 56th Avalanche shot fired at Vanbiesbrouck. Patrick had stopped 63 shots by the Panthers, recalling his game three exploits in the 1986 semifinal against the Rangers, when he had also faced Vanbiesbrouck. On top of that, he had shut out his opponents in the last eight periods (a total of 152 minutes and 12 seconds of play), while making 88 consecutive saves in the process.

Realizing the rodents no longer served any purpose, the 14,703 exasperated fans hurled the remaining beasties onto the ice. That didn't prevent Patrick and Mike Keane from setting off the celebrations with an emotional hug. They had come a long way together. "We looked at each other and said nothing," Keane recalls. "There was nothing more to say. Patrick worked so hard to get there. We were on a mission, he and I, as soon as we left Montréal. That Cup is the most beautiful thing!"

When they shook hands, Patrick and Vanbiesbrouck didn't talk much longer. "There wasn't much to say," Vanbiesbrouck said. "He was pretty anxious to grab the Cup, and I was kind of anxious to get out of there."

Then, on a rink only partially clear of plastic rats, Gary Bettman awarded Colorado captain Joe Sakic the two most prestigious awards of the NHL playoffs: the Conn Smythe Trophy and the Stanley Cup.

The next day, columnist Bernard Raymond wrote:

Roy has nothing left to prove. In the Panthers' four playoff series, the Avalanche goalie was the only wall they hit. Florida came into this final with the outstanding goalie in the first three series. It didn't take long for Florida players to discover a better one. Roy limited them to four goals in four games.

And in the last match, he milked the pleasure to the maximum. He forced Ronald, 'Peanut' and 'Bleuets' to stay up late, just to remind them what kind of fighter they let go.

For Patrick, it was a great victory. After a rollercoaster ride of a season full of upheavals and powerful emotions, after being run out of Montréal, denigrated by some, scorned by others, he had won his third Stanley Cup. For him, this was the "Cup of Dignity." Raising it on high, with beads of sweat streaming down his face, he yelled: "Right now, I'm thinking about all the people who didn't let me down!"

THE CONQUEST OF THE WEST

26

Hoisting the Stanley Cup, the former Nordiques now with the Avalanche couldn't help sparing a thought for Québec City hockey lovers. Speaking for his teammates, Uwe Krupp, who had scored the final goal, paid them homage in an interview on *La Soirée du Hockey*, telecast over the Radio-Canada airwaves. In moving and eloquent fashion, he spontaneously thanked the fans of the Old Capital for their support over so many years and assured them that the Avalanche players had not forgotten them.

The Nordiques had entered the National Hockey League in the 1979–80 season after spending seven years in the now defunct World Hockey Association. Patrick had admired and supported them when he was a teenager. They achieved early success by acquiring the Stastny brothers, Peter and Anton, whom they snatched away from Czechoslovakia under the noses of KGB agents. This event—the stuff of fiction—earned Gilles Leger, Nordiques President Marcel Aubut's right-hand man, the nickname "Colombo." With a line-up including Marian, the eldest of the Stastny brothers, who had joined them ten months later, and other talented players such as Réal Cloutier, Michel Goulet, Marc Tardif and Jacques Richard, as well as character players like Dale Hunter, Wilfrid Paiement and Mario Marois, the excellent goalie Daniel Bouchard, and a few strong rearguards, the Nordiques reached the semifinal of the NHL playoffs in 1982, brushing aside the proud Montréal Canadiens on the way.

But a few years later, when Patrick started his career with the Habs, age was catching up with the Nordiques' stars, and the team went through a terrible four-year dry spell from 1988–89 to 1991–92, finishing last in the overall standings of the NHL in every one of those years. Imagine Québec City fans' disappointment. Nevertheless, ending in the league basement year after year allowed the Nordiques to rebuild through judicious entry-draft selections: they landed future stars such as Joe Sakic, Mats Sundin, Peter Forsberg, Owen Nolan, Valery Kamensky, Adam Deadmarsh and Adam Foote.

This long period of travail seemed to pay dividends at the end of the 1994–95 season, the year of the NHL lockout, when the Nordiques claimed second place in the overall standings. However, as we have seen, the new stars didn't blossom with the Old Capital club, but in Colorado in Avalanche colors. And much to the frustration of Québec City fans, they blossomed the year after the team left their city. That's what Uwe Krupp was referring to when he paid homage to the people of Québec City.

It is interesting to note that, more than a decade after the Nordiques' heart was transplanted into an Avalanche jersey, it still drives the new organization and fires Avalanche partisans' imagination, since the same Francophone Quebecers are in charge: Pierre Lacroix, President; Francois Giguère, Executive Vice President and General Manager; Jean Martineau, Senior Vice President, Communications and Business Operations; Michel Goulet, Assistant to the Executive Vice President and General Manager; Jacques Cloutier, Assistant Coach.

This organization gave Colorado its first-ever major championship, all sports included. Its hockey fans were won over. According to the Denver police estimate, more than 450,000 fans showed up the next day to cheer when their heroes returned and paraded through the streets of the city. No other event had attracted such a huge turnout, not even the Broncos' parade after their Super Bowl defeat in January 1987 (100,000) or the Mass celebrated by Pope John Paul II in August 1993 (375,000).

The Avalanche exploits must have spurred on the Broncos, who went on to win the Super Bowl in 1998 and in 1999, just before John Elway retired.

—⅏—

In the summer of 1996, Patrick held the second edition of his golf tournament at the Summerlea Golf and Country Club in the Montréal area to top off funding for the expansion of the Patrick-Roy wing of the Ronald McDonald House, slated to be inaugurated the following September. A number of hockey and golf stars took part in the tournament, including Fred Couples, with whom Patrick became friends.

From Denver, Patrick continued to make donations to support causes that he felt strongly about. For example, he sponsored Dean Bergeron, a wheelchair athlete who set the 400-meter world record at the Paralympic Games, for four years, at the rate of $10,000 annually. Patrick also donated tens of thousands of dollars to the Cardinal-Villeneuve foundation and the Kidney Foundation of Canada. In Parker, where he lived, his financial support made it possible to set up a children's playground.

That summer, Patrick stopped over in Québec City to show the Stanley Cup to a group of friends. But his refusal to invite journalists to the event earned him a certain amount of negative media criticism. He was worried that press coverage might exacerbate the bitterness and frustration he had sensed among a very considerable number of

Nordiques partisans. He was also concerned that this initiative might be perceived as a provocation, especially since some of the fans had regarded him as the enemy in his many years with the Canadiens.

Patrick still maintained his residence in Montréal so he spent most of his two-month vacations in that city. But he felt that he had few ties there. His job took him to Denver ten months a year, and his roots were deeply embedded in Québec City.

He often thought about Québec City. He was born there; that's where his childhood friends lived. It was a city he still felt attached to despite his ten years in Montréal. He hadn't admitted it to other people or even to himself yet, but that's where he contemplated living when his career was over.

He was already thinking of becoming associated with a junior hockey team. He didn't know how, where, or in what capacity, but the idea was growing within him. He discussed this project with one of his golf partners, Julien Gagnon, a dentist from Québec City. Gagnon knew Jacques Tanguay, the vice president of Ameublement Tanguay, the largest furniture retail company in the Province of Québec. Passionate about sports, Tanguay and his father Maurice managed the Rimouski Océanique, a team in the QMJHL.

Gagnon organized a round of golf at the Rosemère Golf Club, where Patrick was a member. Gagnon invited a fellow dentist, Gilles Rompré, and Jacques Tanguay, with the avowed goal of introducing him to Patrick. The two hit it off immediately. They had several interests in common: they were both passionate about sports, hockey in particular; they felt attached to Québec City, which they believed should remain the hub of junior hockey in the Province of Québec; and they wanted to be involved in their community by promoting youth development. That was the type of involvement Patrick wanted to dedicate himself to once his career as a player was over.

This round of golf accelerated events.

For a few years, junior hockey had been on its last legs in the Québec City region. The only team in the area, the Harfangs, in the suburb of Beauport, was experiencing financial difficulties. There was even talk of transferring the franchise to the United States.

Barely a few weeks after the round of golf in Rosemère, Harfangs general manager Raymond Bolduc requested a meeting with Maurice Tanguay to discuss the precarious state of the team and to ask for his support. The Tanguay family decided that Jacques would pull out of the Rimouski Océanique and do his best to save the Beauport franchise.

Virtually at the same time, Patrick, who had sources in Québec City and was keeping a close watch on the developments in junior hockey, rang up Tanguay:

"Jacques, I've heard that the Harfangs are flying a little low lately and that something might happen soon."

"Yes, Patrick, I'm aware of that. I've been working on the dossier for some time and I'm evaluating the terms and conditions that would allow people like us to acquire the franchise and keep it in the Québec City region. Tell me, would you be interested in investing with me?"

"Immediately!" Patrick replied without hesitation.

"Then we're partners. Listen, I have another friend in Québec City, Michel Cadrin, a successful businessman, who also loves hockey and would most likely be interested in investing in the venture. Would it be okay if I invited him to come in with us?"

"Of course! That would be great!"

However, Patrick added, "You understand that for a few more years, I'll only be able to be involved in the team from a distance. But once my career as a goalie is over, I'll be happy to come and take care of it in Québec City."

Right after that conversation, Tanguay contacted his friend Cadrin, a prosperous businessman with a solid reputation in Québec City. Cadrin had already made up his mind to get involved eventually in junior hockey, so it didn't take him any time to decide to get involved in the undertaking.

That's how the partnership between these three men was born. It was just that simple and straightforward. For the sum of $750,000, invested in equal shares, they would become the owners of the Beauport franchise and transfer it to Québec City. They would revive the Remparts, the team of the glorious years of junior hockey in Québec City, when Guy Lafleur packed the Colisée in the early 1970s.

The transaction was concluded on December 23, 1996. Patrick immediately contacted Raymond Bolduc and coach Guy Chouinard from Denver to ask them to provide videos of practices and games to give him an idea about the team's resources. He did the same with goalie coach Benoît Fortier. He also asked them to give him videos of games in the Midget AAA League to familiarize himself with the talent pool available for junior teams. Almost every day during his years in Denver, he communicated with one member or another of the organization to follow the team's development. He wanted to know everything. During telephone conferences with Bolduc and Chouinard between Québec City and Denver, the three of them would sometimes watch the video of a game simultaneously as Patrick gave them his input and advice as the tape played. He knew every team in the league inside out and was aware of the strengths and weaknesses of each player on the Harfangs/Remparts. He traced their development on a huge board he had installed in his Denver home. He updated it almost on a daily basis.

Even though he often thought about Québec City, his immediate future lay in Colorado, for another few years, especially given the success in the 1996 series, which had resulted in him signing a three-year contract worth $14 million in American dollars.

—m—

Denver's elevation of 5,280 feet has given it the nickname of the Mile-High City. Sitting at the foot of the Rockies, with 200 municipal parks, it's a true paradise for enthusiasts of outdoor sports. Nearby tourist destinations like Aspen, Vail and Colorado Springs are natural four-season playgrounds.

Denver is the only major city in west-central United States, situated halfway between the major Midwest urban centers like Chicago and Detroit and those of the West coast, including Los Angeles. This situation has made it the most important commercial and financial center in the Rockies region. It is a prosperous urban area of nearly three million residents, including its metropolitan region, which encompasses the cities of Aurora and Boulder. It is not surprising that its downtown core—known as the Central Business District, with its forest of skyscrapers that sprouted in less than 15 years—exudes prosperity and affluence. It was the pursuit of wealth that led to the foundation of Denver in 1858. At a time when the territory was principally occupied by Native Americans—the Arapaho, Cheyenne, Comanche and Kiowa—the discovery of gold deposits at the confluence of the South Platte River and Cherry Creek gave rise to a great gold rush. Colonies settled on the sites and became suppliers of prospecting material. In response to burgeoning immigration, the colonies joined together and gave birth to the city of Denver, named in honor of Kansas Territorial Governor, James W. Denver. On August 1, 1876, Denver became the state capital, when Colorado entered the Union.

The population of Denver is fond of professional sports, but is perhaps less partial to Olympic competitions. When the International

Olympic Committee chose Denver to host the Olympic Winter Games in 1976, the city's centennial, its residents refused to allow the municipal council to spend public funds to mop up the anticipated deficit. Denver thus became the only city in Olympic history to refuse to organize the Games after having been chosen to host them.

—៕—

Patrick didn't have a hard time adjusting to his new environment. During the season, the hockey team was his family; the players' dressing room was his home base. The daily routine was essentially the same as in Montréal. Practices in the morning, games in the evening, road trips. The only thing left was to swap the Rosemère Golf Club for the one in Castle Pines. He didn't lose out in the exchange.

When he arrived in Colorado, he could go to public areas like the mall, the grocery store or the restaurant without being approached. But his anonymity was short-lived. After the 1996 Cup, he became the superstar he had been in Montréal, and he began to attract the same attention.

Hockey lovers were behind him. The crowd at the McNichols Sports Arena was especially warm and enthusiastic. The fans went to hockey games for the show. Always behind their team, even if they occasionally voiced their displeasure with a bad play, they never weighed into the Avalanche. The supporters never mocked them. Their applause was encouraging, never derisive.

But the change was harder on the other members of the family. It meant new friends, new neighbors, new schools, and especially a new language to master. Fortunately, the Roy family and Mike Keane moved into neighboring houses in the suburb of Parker, where Jean Martineau, Jacques Cloutier and Sylvain Lefebvre were already settled. Lefebvre's four children and other kids often dropped by to play with Jana, Jonathan and Frédérick. To make their children's adaptation easier, Patrick and his wife hired an English teacher, Suzan Butcher, who gave them private English lessons at home for a few years and provided precious support with their homework. These steps allowed them to become functional fairly quickly and to get along at school and in the hockey leagues in which the two boys played.

The Columbine High School massacre, on April 20, 1999, disturbed the family's peace of mind and upset the Denver community for a long time. Eric Harris and Dylan Klebold, the two young killers, had time to murder 12 of their classmates, wounding 24 others and killing a teacher, before ending their own lives.

The slaughter unleashed an almost permanent debate in the United States about gun control. The discussions that ensued also dealt with violence on television, in films, on the Internet and in video games as well as violence promoted by certain musical genres.

Patrick was particularly shaken when he and his Avalanche teammates visited victims of the massacre in the hospital to comfort them. The players couldn't help thinking that one of their own children might have been there.

—◊◊◊—

Adam Foote, a hard-nosed defenseman, was assigned to share a room with Patrick on the road. Their cohabitation would last more than eight years, longer than many modern couples who are initially considered inseparable! At first, Foote had mixed feelings about the arrangement. Around six years younger than Patrick, he had admired the star goalie's play on television well before he himself reached the National Hockey League. And goalies had a reputation for being freaks! All in all, he felt a bit intimidated.

On their first road trip together, the day before the December 11, 1996, game with Toronto, they broke the ice. Back in the room, after the team meal, Foote felt ill at ease with Patrick, didn't know how to act or what to do with himself, so he lay down on the bed. Patrick said to him, "Hey kid, get over here; come here."

Foote was surprised, but he had a great deal of respect for the veteran, so he went over to him. Patrick leaned over the bureau on which he had placed a pad of paper and said: "Look, this is how you play a two-on-one. Give me the shot and make sure the pass doesn't get across. OK?"

A few years later, Foote revealed what had entered his mind at that moment. "Oh God!" he thought, "I made a mistake on a two-on-one in his debut, against Edmonton, and it cost a goal. This is gonna be a long year! I gotta get out of this room." He was about to leave the room when Patrick called him back:

"Where are you going, Footer?"

"Euh! . . . I'm gonna go to the mall, to do a little Christmas shopping with the guys."

"Hey! Just a minute."

Patrick handed him a few bills. "Can you grab me some underwear?"

"Yeah . . . Awright! . . . What kind do you want?"

"Just like the ones you wear, Footer, that'll be fine."

Foote could hardly believe it. He was sharing a room for the first time with Patrick Roy, whose reputation intimidated him, someone he hardly knew, and now he had to buy him underwear.

After shopping, Foote was about to come back to the hotel with two of his teammates when he realized that he had forgotten the favor Patrick had asked of him. He told them:

"Wait a minute guys. I gotta go back in there; I forgot something. Hold my bags. I'll be right back."

When he got back, his teammates asked him, "Footer, what do you have in that bag?"

"Oh! That's nothing. Don't worry about it."

But they insisted. "C'mon, Footer, what's in the bag?"

Blushing, Foote finally confessed: "Underwear . . . Just don't tell the guys, but Patty [the nickname the Anglophones called Patrick] asked me to buy him some underwear."

The three burst out laughing. "He's really weird; goalies are a race apart!"

The next day, after their victory against the Maple Leafs, Patrick's first in the Avalanche uniform, the players were changing in the dressing room when Foote sneaked a look in Patrick's direction. Patrick gave him a wink. "I couldn't figure out what that wink meant," Foote later said. "Either he liked those underwear or the way I played those two-on-one."

—⁂—

The more time passed, the more comfortable Foote felt around Patrick and the more the big defenseman felt that he wasn't so bad after all . . . for a goaltender.

An unwritten rule among hockey players has it that on the road, the roommate with the most seniority on a team controls the clicker. The only way Foote could watch his favorite TV shows was to start a pillow fight and win it, which he succeeded in doing more often than not. Victory earned him the right to control the precious remote. But then, the 1996 playoffs were getting under way, and Mike Keane had told Foote that things would be different during the series. Patrick would often be lost in thought and more distant. His mind would be even more preoccupied with upcoming games.

To be tactful and to let Patrick watch a re-run of *Murder She Wrote*, Foote was considerate enough to go downstairs to play cards with some teammates in the hotel lounge. When he got back to the room, he quietly opened the door and was stunned by the spectacle he discovered. Patrick was standing on his bed and simulating saves, crouching down in a "butterfly" on one side and then on the other, and then he stood up yelling, as he had done 20 years before in the hallway of "*Le 1330*": "And Roy makes the save, another stop by Roy, TERRIFIC! **BREATHTAKING!!!**"

Finally noticing Foote was there, he came to a dead stop, embarrassed. "Oh! Hi Footer! How's it going?"

Foote couldn't believe his eyes.

"Patty, would you mind telling me what you're doing?

"I'm getting ready for the series," Patrick replied.

—⁓—

At the beginning of the 1996–97 season, when Patrick showed up at the training camp a new backup goalie was waiting for him: Craig Billington. Pierre Lacroix had respected Stéphane Fiset's wish not to be a backup any longer and had traded him to the Los Angeles Kings in exchange for his own son, Éric, a rugged right-winger. Billington had beaten out Patrick at the Junior Team Canada selection camp in December 1984, in Belleville, Ontario. He was also chosen 28 spots before Patrick in the NHL entry draft that year by the New Jersey Devils. But the two goalies hadn't crossed paths since.

While Patrick spent the next ten years with François Allaire as his personal coach, and the two transformed the Forum into a goaltending laboratory, Billington shuttled back and forth between New Jersey and its American Hockey League farm club. After eight years in this organization, having barely gotten himself a regular spot in the NHL club, he was traded to the Ottawa Senators, where he played only two years before being traded again, this time to Boston. He spent two years with the Bruins, who used him in only 35 games.

By the summer of 1996, his career was essentially over. He found himself without a contract and in the difficult position of being obliged to peddle his wares, without much conviction, to any team that would have him. That's when Pierre Lacroix, who was searching for a backup goalie to replace Fiset, snapped him up at the waiver draft.

Billington was thrilled. Just when he was seeing himself stagnating in the International Hockey League with a minor league salary, one of the premier clubs in the National Hockey League was offering him a second chance. And he'd be working with someone he considered to be "the best goalie in the profession, the one who had revolutionized it." When Avalanche front office let him know that they were going to take care of his plane reservation for Denver, he exclaimed: "Don't worry about the flight plan; I'm starting to drive right now!"

This marked the beginning of an extremely harmonious three-year partnership between a Number 1 goalie and his backup. Both of them were devoted to the success of the team, and had complementary objectives on the personal level. Billington was at a stage in his career when he no longer aspired to Number 1 goalie status. He was perfectly content to play second fiddle, to settle for about 20 starts per season, to do his best to support Patrick and to be ready whenever his services were required.

Given everything he had read and heard about Patrick, however, Billington was nevertheless somewhat apprehensive before he saw him again. His concern quickly evaporated. "Patrick would hold himself more accountable than anybody in terms of his game and responsibility level," Billington remembers. "At times, there were some who thought he was tough on guys, but in my opinion, he wasn't at all. All he ever expected was that you'd come to the rink, give everything you've got, be passionate about it like it was the most important thing in your life. People who did that got along great with him. It was very simple and straightforward. And you didn't have to be the best guy or the best player on the team. Heck! I was a journeyman player and he respected my approach to the game, he respected the fact that I didn't have the skills or the mindset that he had, but, you know what? I never cheated the game and he would really embrace himself to those type of people. He could not support people who cheated the game and cheated the team, even in practice. That drove him nuts. And he was so right!"

Both were passionate about their profession and extremely meticulous. Ever since he was 15 years old, Billington had run a summer school for goalies with his father in Ontario. He had solid technique, but in contrast to Patrick, he had stuck with the traditional "stand-up" style and hadn't explored other ways of doing things. The result was that he had a hard time with shots along the ice that grazed the goal posts.

With his keen sense of observation and analysis, it wasn't long before he decided to borrow from Patrick's style. And Patrick opened up his "book" to Billington, particularly to help him eliminate goals he was prone to give up on low shots.

"One day, when I was working on my lateral movement to cover the low part of the net," Billington recalls, "Patrick would slide with fluidity on one knee in front of the net in his typical "butterfly" style, pushing with one leg to one side and then to the other, saying: 'See Biller, this is all you have to do to get into position.' Well, it took me at least a year of practicing every single day before my body would recognize that move; it probably took another year for my brain to pick up when to use it and it wasn't probably till my third year when I had introduced an automatic fundamental reaction into my game, before I no longer had to think about it and it just happened."

What most struck Billington about Patrick was ". . . how his passion and his analytical educated mind worked so close together in search of technical perfection, precision and efficiency. It wasn't a job to him; it was bigger than that. It was just his way of life. This was his whole life. It was all encompassing and I really respected that. I think this is why he and I got along so well. Something would happen in a game, he'd identify it, his brain and body would respond, he would try it in practice and it was done. I like to say that what took Patrick one practice to correct, took me a year.

"And he obviously had the ability," Billington continued, "to process a lot of information in his brain, very rapidly, and that allowed him to anticipate the best position to be in to stop the puck. We'd talk after a game that I had won 2–1 and he would say, 'Remember this play when the winger was coming down and you were here and he did this?'

"'Yes, what happened?'

"'Did you notice that before he shot the puck it was passed over here and the guy was on his off-wing?'

"'I remember the guy shooting the puck; I don't remember what you're talking about.'

"'Before he shot, did you notice the position of his hands on his stick? Sure enough he wasn't going to pass. He was going to fire a right-handed shot from the left wing.'

"'Patty, I didn't see any of that. What are you talking about!'"

One evening on the road, Adam Foote was nursing an injury. Exceptionally, the two goalies were assigned the same room. Billington recalls, "We often talked passionately about hockey in the locker room, at dinner or during a flight, but that night, we were up so late, talking hockey until about 4:30 in the morning. And Patrick was playing the very same night. After the game he goes: 'You know what Biller? I love talking hockey with you but we'll never room together again. It's way too exhausting!'"

—ɯ—

The two teammates encouraged each other. "The position of goaltending is such a mental psyche position," recalls Billington, "we fed off one another and it made us both play better."

Clearly, Billington made a great deal of progress during that period. His game moved to another level. The same guy whose career was just about over in the summer of 1996 raised his game so much that he stayed in the National Hockey League for seven more seasons—three in Denver and four with the Washington Capitals—as a backup goalie, one of the best at performing this thankless task. He acknowledges Patrick's contribution: "I have a tremendous appreciation for the help that Patrick brought me from a goaltending standpoint of course. But believing in me as a person, trusting my opinion and ideas, meant more to me than everything he taught me on the ice. Most people don't really know who he is."

But Patrick also benefited from Billington's advice and encouragement. In Colorado, Jacques Cloutier, a former netminder who had plied his trade for a dozen years in the National Hockey League, notably with the Nordiques, was the goalie coach. It's obvious that his role with Patrick was different from the one François Allaire had played in Montréal. Patrick was now a veteran goalie who knew what he had to do. He let Cloutier and Billington in on the bad habits he occasionally fell prey to—flopping in the "butterfly" position too early, staying too deep in his net—and he asked them to let him know if need be. So, during Billington's three years in Denver, the positive chemistry among the three was largely responsible for the goalies' superior level of performance.

On January 30, 1997, journalist Mark Kiszla of the *Denver Post* wrote:

> *Who is the best pro athlete ever to wear a Denver uniform?*
>
> *The answer is obvious.*
>
> *But it isn't John Elway.*
>
> *Pick anybody who has scored a touchdown for the Broncos, shot a jumper for the Nuggets or hit a homerun for the Rockies.*
>
> *None of them has the greatness to match Colorado Avalanche goalie Patrick Roy.*
>
> *. . . Pick any superstar of this era you like: Michael Jordan . . . Steffi Graff . . . Carl Lewis. None of them has the indomitable aura of Roy.*
>
> *. . . The most arrogant, cockiest, unbeatable SOB I've ever seen . . . has to be Roy.*

Kiszla concluded his article with the following observation:

> *To say the Duke of Denver (Elway) stands second to Roy is meant as no slap at the Bronco's quarterback. It is rather a reconfirmation of how fortunate Colorado is for the gift of St. Patrick.*
>
> *Right here and now, we are watching the greatest goalie who ever was.*

DUEL AT NAGANO 27

Before departing for Nagano, Japan, Patrick and fellow Team Canada member Éric Desjardins had recorded two TV commercials in collaboration with Esso, promoting the sale of drinking glasses decorated with the official Olympic Games logo. These rather amusing ads were aired all during the Olympics.

One of them showed Desjardins and Patrick, with their ears pressed against the wall of the adjoining dressing room, trying to listen in on the other team's coach going over game strategy with his players.

"It's the Swedish coach?" asked Patrick.

"I think he's talking about the game plan," said Desjardins.

Patrick is holding one of the Olympics glasses. He suddenly places it against the wall and places his ear to the glass and tries to listen in. Desjardins asks, anxiously:

"Well, can you hear anything? What are they saying?"

"I dunno," says Patrick, "I don't speak Swedish!"

In the other ad, Patrick gives Desjardins some food that they'll be taking on the trip.

"Salami, bread . . ."

Then, just as Patrick is about to serve Desjardins a glass of juice Desjardins stops him.

"Whoa! Whoa! Whoa! Ice?"

"Ice, Éric, you'll get all the ice you want! All the ice you want, Éric!"

The camera moves back to show the two players sitting right in the center of a big rink.

—⚂—

Patrick wasn't going to Nagano to mess around. He was going there to win. He wanted to make up for past misadventures in international hockey: his missed opportunity with Junior Team Canada in 1984, his frustrating experience in Montréal at the selection camp for the 1987 Canada Cup. And then, as he himself said, with a grin, "Adding a gold medal to my three Stanley cups wouldn't be half bad!" So far, fate had deprived him of the chance to see what he could do in international competition. In 1998, perhaps things would be different, he thought. There were a number of factors that seemed to indicate that. This time, Mark Crawford, his coach with the Avalanche, would be guiding Team Canada's destinies. Patrick felt confident. Then, for the first time in its history, the National Hockey League had scheduled an Olympic break so its players could take part. As a result, the best Canadian players, all of them from the NHL, would be there. On paper, they were a formidable team.

But there'd be stiff competition. The United States with Mike Richter, Brett Hull and John LeClair, Sweden with Mats Sundin, Nicklas Lidstrom and Peter Forsberg, the Czech Republic with Jaromir Jagr and Dominik Hasek, were powerful adversaries with every bit as good a chance to win as Canada. Like Patrick, the Buffalo Sabers' goalie Hasek could win games all by himself. That's why he was known as the "Dominator" in Buffalo. Some observers dissed his technique as "freestyle," but with this style he had won, in the previous year, his second Vézina Trophy as the best goalie in the league and the Hart trophy as the most valuable player in the regular season.

Clearly, Canada didn't have an easy task. First of all, just because players are on the ice together, no matter how good they are, doesn't mean they're a team. And Crawford had just a few days to get the chemistry right with this stellar lineup, and a few days also to convince some of them to accept less than their usual ice time. And a few days at last to get them used to playing on Olympic-size rinks, which are bigger than NHL rinks. In that respect, European teams had a slight advantage. Some of their players performed in the NHL, and all of them knew each other well, having previously played together on Olympic-size surfaces.

Furthermore, the Canadians, raised in NHL culture, would have to convince themselves that it was a unique tournament, an important competition, not a series of exhibition games.

Finally, a decision had been made to change the guard and infuse Team Canada with new blood. Though Wayne Gretzky was still part of the team, Eric Lindros, and not Gretzky, would be the captain and chief spokesman. Lindros would have a very big pair of shoes to fill. Some doubted he had the stature and maturity to galvanize the squad. But Clark, Team Canada's general manager, held the same post with the Philadelphia Flyers, Lindros's club.

—m—

After the final game on the NHL calendar before the Olympic break and an Avalanche victory against the Flyers on Saturday, February 7, Crawford informed Patrick that he would be the Number 1 goalie throughout the tournament. Martin Brodeur and Curtis Joseph would be his backups. Of course, Crawford was comfortable with

Patrick and, given his proven capacity to raise his game when the chips were on the line, no one, including Martin Brodeur himself, would contest the decision. "Patrick has always been my idol. Naturally, I'm happy for him. I'll help him as much as I can," Brodeur said sincerely.

Patrick was aware of the stakes: "It's an honor," he said, "but at the same time, it's a considerable responsibility." Then he had a few kind words for Brodeur. "I realize it's disappointing for Martin Brodeur, but our situations aren't the same. It's my last chance to play in the Olympic Games. He's only 24 years old and he'll be at his peak for the Salt Lake City Games." Two days later, on a Monday, all the Team Canada players arrived in Nagano.

With a population of 375,000, Nagano sits in the middle of the island of Honshu. The town stretches diagonally from north to south, at about the same level as Tokyo, but on the western extremity of the island. It is one of the principal cities in the Tosan district, a chain of lofty rugged mountains, over 9,850 feet high, known as the Japanese Alps.

Though Nagano was founded as far back as the 12th century, its infrastructure is ultramodern, from its hotels to its modes of transportation and its downtown buildings. Of course, the players were housed in the Olympic Village. Patrick was immediately impressed with the atmosphere and comfort. He lived in a three-room apartment. Rob Blake had one of the rooms; Adam Foote and Chris Pronger had another; Patrick and Eric Desjardins shared the third.

In the evening, he went for a stroll in the village and dropped by the Canadian pavilion to chat with other athletes like biathlete Myriam Bédard, freestyle skier Jean-Luc Brassard and short-track speed skater Marc Gagnon.

The hockey players had only four days to recover from jet lag, get acclimated to their new work environment and, above all, become a team before facing Belarus in their first game on Friday, February 13.

Three of the players attended Team Canada's first press conference: Eric Lindros, Raymond Bourque and Patrick. The media would have much preferred Wayne Gretzky, but he remained in the shadows to avoid undermining Lindros's leadership. Yet, as soon as the signal for private interviews was given, reporters flocked to Gretzky. Having participated in three Canada Cups, in one World Cup and in Rendez-Vous '87, he was undoubtedly the preeminent hockey star at the Games, the player people wanted to cheer for and, I would add, the natural leader of the team. But he was a leader Team Canada was trying to keep out of the spotlight.

—ɯ—

Most of the players had paid for family members to come and offer their support in Team Canada's march toward victory and, above all, to partake in the unique Olympic experience. In addition to his wife, Patrick invited his eldest child, Jonathan, his parents, sister and brother as well as one of his sisters-in-law.

The XVIII Winter Olympic Games had also attracted a multitude of visitors from all parts of the world and from all backgrounds. Holding the Olympic Games in the Land of the Rising Sun held a special appeal, especially for Westerners unfamiliar with this great civilization, which has introduced us to shoguns, samurai, ninjas, geishas, Buddhist temples, Zen gardens, kimonos, sushi, tempura and sake.

It was the third time that Japan had hosted the Olympic Games. In 1964, Tokyo held the Summer Games, the first significant demonstration of Japan's desire to open up to the world since the end of World War II. In 1972, it was Sapporo's turn to hold the Winter Games, the first time they took place outside of North America and

Europe. Now, Nagano was the scene of another first, with over 2,000 athletes participating.

At Tokyo's Narita International Airport, we stood in line for an hour before getting through immigration because of the hordes of travelers arriving at the same time on different flights. People waiting were consoled by fleeting glimpses of celebrities like famous supermodel Cindy Crawford, who was arriving from New York.

I boarded a chartered bus bound for Karuizawa with families of the Canadian and American players. I had left home at six in the morning on Saturday, February 14. After 26 hours in the air, with the time difference, it was 10:30 p.m. on Sunday, February 15 when the bus dropped me off at Hotel Asama.

Patrick had decided that his family would stay in Karuizawa, one of Japan's most stylish and popular summer vacation centers. In the mountains, roughly 40 miles east of Nagano, some Karuizawa establishments stay open all winter to accommodate the local ski center's clientele. Nestled in the mountains, Hotel Asama, where I shared a room with my son Stéphane, offers a panoramic view of the surrounding snowcapped mountain peaks. Through the three 20-foot-high glass walls in the spectacular dining room, we could gaze beyond the snow-covered golf course at Mount Asama, an 8,400-foot high volcano, which has erupted some 50 times in its history and whose last explosive eruption was on September 1, 2004.

The next day, a high-speed train, the Asama 519, took only 25 minutes to transport Stéphane and me all the way from Karuizawa to the heart of Nagano. At the station, we could have hopped a bus that would have driven us to the arena in no time, but with the bright February sun and the comfortable 41° Fahrenheit temperature, we preferred to go on foot.

It was a pleasant walk along the city streets lined with boutiques of all sorts. We were amused to hear the music made by the traffic lights at the intersections indicating it was safe for pedestrians to cross. There were a surprising number of bicycles parked along the sidewalks, but what most impressed us was that people left them unlocked without the least concern. That says a lot about how honest the Japanese are.

About 20 minutes later, we were standing in front of the Big Hat Arena, where the Canada–USA match would be starting in a few moments.

—⁂—

Canada had played two games on the weekend: a drab 5–0 win against Belarus and a 3–2 victory over the Swedes. Having raised eyebrows by upsetting the Americans in the opening match, Sweden was considered a major opponent. Canada dominated the second period, emerging with a 3–1 lead, but the Swedes came back in force in the third stanza, blasting 16 shots at Patrick, who had to stand on his head to keep team Canada in the game while his team managed only four shots on goal.

Hockey aficionados had been eagerly awaiting the Canada–USA duel since Team USA's triumph over Team Canada in the 1996 World Cup final. But another subject piqued Canadian fans' interest: just before the NHL Olympic break, the American Gary Suter, then a Chicago Blackhawks defenseman, had crossed-checked Canadian Paul Kariya in the face. The Anaheim Mighty Ducks left-winger was one of the foremost goal scorers in the NHL. Suter was suspended for the cheap shot but the US Olympic Committee hadn't followed suit, so he could play for the US while Kariya, the victim of a concussion as a result of the assault, was unable to represent his country. Like Team Canada, Team USA, champions of the recent World Cup, was composed of NHL players. So, the players were very familiar with each other on the ice.

It was odd to see the best professional players in the world performing in an arena with a maximum capacity of only 10,000 spectators. The atmosphere reminded me of Patrick's last round robin tournament in the Canadian Midget Hockey Championship for the Air Canada Cup in Victoria, B.C., 16 years earlier. Obviously, the stakes were different, but for parents, whatever the stakes, the anxiety and excitement are the same. Particularly for a goalie's parents, there is always the concern that a moment of inattention might cost a goal that could turn victory into defeat.

Fortunately, that wasn't the case against the Americans. The key moment in the match came in the first period when the United States had a two-man advantage for 1 minute and 40 seconds but failed to put the puck past Patrick. In all, he faced 31 shots; Richter faced 25. Patrick's performance was singled out in the Canadian Press report:

Canada remained unbeaten in Nagano by getting its revenge in a 4–1 victory over the American team that had defeated it in the World Cup, but the team may thank Patrick Roy . . . The result might have been very different if he hadn't been so solid . . .

Former Team Canada Coach Dave King, penning a column during the games for *La Presse*, a Montréal French-language paper, wrote:

Canada's victory over the USA yesterday will have an impact, and Patrick Roy is the principal architect.

He did more than keep his team in the game. He planted a seed of doubt in the Americans' minds and in the minds of all of Canada's potential opponents. Roy excels at that game. That's what he does in the NHL. Every time a team faces the Avalanche, Roy is the first player they think of.

Team USA's coach, Ron Wilson, and its star player, Pat Lafontaine, both acknowledged that Patrick's outstanding work had made the difference in the game.

The victory was important for the Canadians because it meant that they would be facing Kazakhstan, an easy prey according to the experts, in the first match of the medal round, that is, in the quarterfinal.

—⁓—

After the game, Patrick and Raymond Bourque, as well as Bourque's guests, his wife, his son and his brother, accompanied us to Karuizawa for supper and to relax with us for the rest of the evening. Patrick spent a lot of time with Bourque in Nagano. Over the years, the two had often met each other in NHL All-Star games, but in Nagano, it seemed they were becoming close friends.

The Nagano station concourse looked like a large public area in a shopping mall. On a stage, a young musician was interpreting Jimmy Smith pieces, emulating the sound of his famous Hammond B-3. People were rushing toward the platform, eager to return home after their workday. Some were carrying little bags with purchases they'd made in town. Others, with more time on their hands, gathered around the stage or leaned against the balustrade of the staircases leading to the mezzanine to listen to the one-man orchestra.

Patrick made quite a picture as he crossed the hall. Men and women kept asking him, with unfailing courtesy, to pose for a photo with them. In groups of two, three or four, they shook hands with him, bowed and left, their faces beaming.

We enjoyed a lovely family evening together at Hotel Asama. We did it another couple of times that week.

—⁓—

The much-anticipated trouncing of Kazakhstan didn't occur. The dynamic goalie Vitaly Yeremeyev kept the score down. Kazakhstan was eliminated by Canada, but lost by the respectable score of 4–1. Canada seemed to have a hard time putting the puck in the net. With the victory, Canada advanced to the semifinals against the Czech Republic, who had dashed Team USA's hopes.

The semifinal generated enormous interest in the Czech Republic, where, by 6:45 a.m. on Friday, Czech fans had already settled down in front of their TVs to watch the live action. The winner of the game would be assured of at least a silver medal with a chance for the gold, while the loser would have to battle the loser of the other semifinal for the bronze.

In goal, Patrick would be facing his great National Hockey League rival, Dominik Hasek. "Of course I expect Hasek to have a big game," he said to journalist Bertrand Raymond. "So it's doubly important for me to step up. Though we must never lose sight of the fact that it's a team sport, it's up to us, Hasek and me, to make the key saves."

The upcoming duel between the two goalies who dominated their sport was eagerly anticipated. Petr Svoboda, the Czech defenseman and Patrick's former Habs teammate, now with the Philadelphia Flyers, couldn't hide his excitement when he spoke to Réjean Tremblay after the Czechs eliminated the Americans. "It's going to be unbelievable!" he said. "Patrick Roy against Dominik Hasek, the two best goaltenders in the world. Patrick, who is very technical and is always in the right position in goal, and Dominik, who's all over the place but makes all the stops. It's unbelievable; it's incredible!"

He was right about Dominik Hasek. François Allaire was of the opinion that the Czech was always in an excellent position for the first shot, but made stopping rebounds look like a break dancing exhibition. Even so, Hasek made the saves and in a short, intense tournament like the Olympics, a good goalie at the height of his form can turn an average team into a champion.

Martin Rucinsky, another Czech who had turned up in Montréal in the trade that sent Patrick to Denver, was delighted, too. "It's the biggest victory by our country since we beat the Soviets after the Prague Spring of 1968," he said speaking of the Czech Republic's victory over the United States. Then he added, "It seems strange, Patrick Roy against Dominik Hasek at the Olympics. The best against the best!"

So far (until the Canada–Czech Republic game), Patrick had conceded a miserly four goals on 95 shots, for a save percentage of .958; Hasek had only been beaten five times on 110 shots, or an average of .954.

Patrick wanted to win; there was fire in his eyes. But the atmosphere at the Olympic Games isn't the same as the one in the Stanley Cup playoffs, for which Canadian pros prepare from the start of the season. The players on Team Canada hadn't been together long. No matter how professional they were, could they dig deep inside themselves and find the motivation and resources they needed to win a crucial game, especially since they would have to get along without Joe Sakic, who had sustained a knee ligament injury in the game against Kazakhstan?

—⁓—

The fans looking forward to a duel between two great goalies had to wait until the second period. In the first, the Canadians, seemingly unfocused, let the Czechs control the play, and as a result, there were few shots on goal. The sides were feeling each other out.

Radio-Canada TV analyst Gérard Gagnon expressed the view that Canada, the favorite and strongest team on paper, should have deployed its full arsenal from the opening face-off to take control of the game. By playing back on their heels, the Canadians helped the Czechs, who had every interest in biding their time and waiting until doubt and eventually nervousness got the better of their powerful opponent. Gagnon attributed the lack of intensity to Mark Crawford's consistent use of four lines, which prevented the team's stars, who were used to much more ice on their own clubs, from really getting into the groove. In other words, Canada wasn't following the scenario in the commercial recorded by Desjardins and Patrick. The players didn't get as much ice time as they wanted. Not enough, at any rate, to feel really involved in the game.

By contrast, the Czech Republic made full use of its stars. Jaromir Jagr, for example, the best player in the NHL—and on the Czech team, needless to say—logged a great deal of time. He played regularly on two lines, sometimes three, spearheading the play every time he was on the ice. Martin Rucinsky was also regularly employed on two lines. According to the analysts, Team Canada's coach should have responded by adapting his strategy so that his players felt more engaged.

After the intermission, on the other hand, the two teams opened up, and the goaltending duel began. In the second period, Patrick made 14 saves and Hasek made 11. No one had broken the goose egg. It was not until midway through the third period that the Czech Republic managed to put one past Patrick: the first. Defenseman Jiri Slegr skated from the blue line to the top of the face-off circle in Canada's zone and uncorked a terrific shot that Patrick didn't see coming because he was screened by the traffic in front of the net. The Czechs had taken the lead.

Just a few minutes later, near the end of the period, Hasek was beaten by a Trevor Linden shot from the slot. So the 60 minutes of regulation time expired without either team sealing the victory. The clubs were deadlocked 1–1. Patrick had made 27 saves; Hasek, 20. It wasn't normal for a powerful team like Canada, playing a weaker opponent, to be limited to 20 shots. Either the Czech Republic had been outstanding on defense, or Canada's attack lacked cohesiveness. Czech coach Ivan Hlinka ventured a response to that question by simply saying, "Canada no longer has any offense . . ."

In the 10-minute overtime period, however, Canada went on the attack, outshooting the Czech Republic 5–1. But once again, the two goalies turned everything aside.

According to Olympic rules, the teams would have to compete in a shootout to determine the victor. Five players on each side would try to beat the opposing goalie, and the team scoring the most goals would be the winner. This clearly favored the Europeans, more accustomed to this kind of exercise. In North American hockey culture, clubs had to struggle for over two months and win four games in four consecutive series against different teams, after an exhausting 82-game season, to win the ultimate honor. And sometimes, it took several periods of overtime to claim a victory. At the Olympic Games, the heads of Team Canada had already worked to convince their players of the significance of what was at stake, and now, one of the two teams would be eliminated from the race to the gold and silver medals after a simple shootout, a method yet to be adopted by the National Hockey League.

Coaches Mark Crawford of Canada and Ivan Hlinka of the Czech Republic had to give a list of their shooters to the referee and indicate the order in which they would shoot.

Hlinka was the first to submit his list. The figure in parentheses indicates the number of goals the player scored in the season preceding the Olympic Games.

1. Robert Reichel (16)
2. Martin Rucinsky (28)
3. Pavel Patera (19)
4. Jaromir Jagr (47)
5. Vladimir Ruzicka (22)

Crawford huddled with his two assistants, Andy Murray and Wayne Cashman, for a long time before settling on the following names:

1. Theoren Fleury (29)
2. Raymond Bourque (19)
3. Joe Nieuwendyk (30)
4. Eric Lindros (32)
5. Brendan Shanahan (47)

That's when Paul Kariya's absence really hurt the team. And as Joe Sakic was also sidelined with an injury, Team Canada was deprived of two 50-goal scorers.

Given the circumstances, analyst Gérard Gagnon couldn't understand, (he wasn't the only one) why Gretzky's name wasn't on the list of shooters for Team Canada. True, age had slowed him down a bit, but a player who had scored over 862 career goals in the regular season and 122 in the playoffs certainly knew what to do when he went in all alone on a goalie, especially since he had always stepped up on important occasions. He was raring to go, realizing that it was his only chance to add an Olympic medal to his impressive list of achievements.

He was shunted aside, as he had been at the press conference.

—∞—

The Czechs won the draw, and their captain, Vladimir Ruzicka, decided to let Canada go first in the shootout. More experienced in this kind of situation, the Czechs immediately lined up at the players' bench with their arms on each other's shoulders in a gesture of solidarity.

Fleury was the first to go: he went top shelf to Hasek's left; Hasek made the save. Sitting in the stands with the team management, Sakic thought he spotted a weakness in the way Hasek played the shot. It seemed the Czech goalie moved out too quickly toward the shooter, then retreated to cover the angle as the attacker moved in on goal. Sakic grabbed his cell phone to tell the coaches behind the bench that the Canadian shooters should skate in fast on Hasek, then stop right in front of him to throw him momentarily off balance. No one answered. The coaches had put down their headphones.

It was Robert Reichel's turn to go in on Patrick. The Czech made a feint and then unleashed a perfect shot, which glanced off the inside of the right post and ricocheted into the net. It was a question of millimeters, but it was all the Czechs needed for the victory.

No one else scored. The Czechs couldn't put another puck past Patrick; the Canadians couldn't beat Hasek. Lindros hit the post, too, but on the wrong side by a few millimeters, and the puck ricocheted outside the goal instead of entering it. Jagr did the same. Shanahan, Canada's last shooter, was shouldering the entire pressure of keeping the team alive as he dashed towards Hasek. The pressure made him skate too close to the Czech goalie; he no longer had a good angle to make a shot. Canada had exhausted its weapons. The players jumped on the ice to console Shanahan. Everyone, that is, except Gretzky, who sat on the bench, dejected, for a long time before joining the others.

For all intents and purposes, the tournament was over for Canada. For Patrick, too. He had wanted just one thing: to win. To him, the winner was the one who got the gold medal. The silver was for the first among the losers; the bronze, the second. Team Canada and Patrick had lost. Hasek had won the goaltending battle by a few millimeters. Sometimes, that's all that separates the winner from the loser.

In his column, Dave King wrote:

There was some doubt about their [the Czechs'] ability on defense. Some said that Hasek would have to perform miracles; they were wrong. Collectively, their defensive play was brilliant.

Patrick Roy, on the other hand, had to outdo himself every game. I hope no one holds the shootout goal against him. Of the two goalies, as brilliant as Hasek was, Roy was better. Without him, there wouldn't have been a shootout, Canada would have been out of the game a long time ago.

The Czech Republic completed its march toward victory, shutting out the Russians 1–0 in the final to claim the gold medal.

—∿—

It was something to see the forlorn expressions after the game. In the room reserved for the players and their families, Gretzky's father, Walter, walked up and down, his hands in his pockets. From time to time, he stopped, looked gloomily at his son, shrugged his shoulders and started walking again. Wayne Gretzky was shattered. "When I lost the Stanley Cup the first time, I knew there'd be another chance to win it . . ." This simple remark summed up his total disillusionment. "It's tough to swallow when you don't lose a single game but you end up going home before the final." He was referring to the fact that Canada hadn't suffered a defeat in the entire tournament, apart from the shootout loss, while the Czech Republic bowed to Russia in the preliminary round before avenging the defeat in the final. Then he concluded, "It's not often I've felt like this. It's the worst feeling in the world. This defeat is so depressing!" He had just missed the only chance he would have to be crowned an Olympic champion.

Patrick met the media after being randomly selected for the anti-doping test. He was bitterly disappointed about the defeat. "I won't make any excuses," he said. "We lost; that's it. We did everything we could, but the Czechs played very well. We came to win gold, only gold," he added. "Bronze doesn't mean the same to me; it doesn't show we've done the job."

A number of commentators, among them Bertrand Raymond, put their finger on some Team Canada weaknesses:

> *In a talent pool like the National Hockey League, there wasn't enough skill available for the shootout. Incredible! Unthinkable!*
>
> *When they have to call on Theoren Fleury, when they choose a defenseman (Raymond Bourque) to go in alone on Hasek, when everything depends on Eric Lindros, who doesn't have the best hands, and when they have to count on a player like Brendan Shanahan to take the last shot to save their honor, it's a sign that they didn't have the tools they needed for a situation in which there was no tomorrow.*

The article then discussed the selection of the players for the shootout.

> *The coaches seemed confused when it came time to choose the shooters. Yet, the list should have been prepared before the team left Canada.*
>
> *Who was responsible for the incomprehensible decision to square off against Hasek with Gretzky and Yzerman sitting on the bench when, between them, they had scored over 1,500 goals in the National Hockey League?*

The bronze medal match between Canada and Finland was a mere formality. In their heads, the Canadians wanted to win. But their hearts weren't in it. Canada was beaten 3–2 by the more opportunistic and, above all, more determined Finns.

No gold, no silver, no bronze, just a pocketful of pins. The Canadians returned from Nagano empty-handed, but for a few souvenirs from a country they found to be very hospitable.

Once again, though Patrick had put everything into it, fate had denied him the least success in international hockey. As far as he was concerned, there was absolutely no doubt that his destiny lay in the National Hockey League, where he was striving to set a few records.

FOR BETTER OR FOR WORSE

Patrick was born under the sign of Libra. But that doesn't mean that the trays of happiness and misery were always level. They had their highs and lows.

On April 24, 1997, when Patrick shut out the Chicago Blackhawks 7–0, he became the goalie with the most playoff wins. With this 89th victory, he surpassed the record previously held by Billy Smith of the New York Islanders.

From then on, he targeted the records set by the game's greatest goalies. He wanted to become the best goaltender of all time, the one with the most victories in the playoffs and in the regular season. He also aimed to pass the 1,000-game mark for the regular season. The barrier, which he would be the first goalie to crack, was, in his eyes, the fruit of the consistently excellent performance that he had strived to maintain throughout his career, game after game, from the outset.

The figure he now had in his sights was 447, the number of career wins Terry Sawchuk chalked up in the regular season. At his current pace, if he avoided injury, there was every chance he would reach the mark near the end of the 1999–2000 season or at the beginning of the next. But he still took the same approach: "I don't want to focus on winning games for the record," he said. "I want to focus on winning games for the team. The rest will take care of itself."

—⚊—

Over the years, a fierce rivalry, perhaps even a certain animosity, developed between the Detroit Red Wings and the Avalanche. In the 1996 playoffs, Claude Lemieux viciously crushed Kris Draper into the boards, causing Draper serious facial injuries. About ten months later, on March 26, 1997, on Lemieux's first visit to the Joe Louis Arena in Detroit since his assault on Draper, rugged Darren McCarthy was thirsting for revenge. At center ice, he invited Lemieux to drop the gloves. Lemieux refused. In hockey jargon, he "turtled," curling up on the ice in a fetal position and protecting his head with his gloves, while McCarty pummeled him.

Seeing his teammate in trouble, Patrick left his net and rushed to his aid. Reaching the combat zone, Detroit's Brendan Shanahan stepped in to prevent him from getting at McCarty, and the two fell to the ice. Meanwhile, Wings goalie Mike Vernon, seeing Patrick leave his net, got involved and got into a furious fight with his rival. Other skirmishes broke out later. In the end, a total of 18 major penalties were assessed during the match. Asked to explain why he got involved in a fight, Patrick said, "Hockey is a team sport, and when a teammate is in a difficult spot, you have to do what you can to help him."

The Wings recorded a 6–5 victory after dominating the shots on goal category by 47–19. And the winning goal was scored in overtime by . . . McCarty. As it was Vernon's 300th win, Patrick made an elegant gesture at the end of the encounter, by sliding the puck to him in homage.

In hindsight, Patrick believes that the game had an impact that Avalanche players took a long time to get over: "I think that game in Detroit marked a turning point in our rivalry with the Wings. As a result of those incidents, their players came together, while we had a hard time dealing with our emotions. You might say that in subsequent matches between the two clubs, we paid more attention to the side issues of the game than to the progress of the game itself. The memory of the event became a sort of distraction, a frustration, and that's, I think, what made us lose to them in the semifinals of the playoffs in 1997, even though we had finished first in the overall standings during the regular season with 107 points."

The next year, on April 1, 1998, to be exact, Patrick allowed himself to be dragged into the escalating violence when the Avalanche paid another visit to the Red Wings. With seven minutes and 11 seconds remaining in the game and Detroit leading 2–0, a fight broke out along the boards between Warren Rychel and Bob Rouse. Other players joined in and Patrick decided, rightly or wrongly, that it was time for him to do something dramatic to galvanize his teammates against their perennial rivals.

While the donnybrook was going on, he calmly removed his gloves and mask, as if he thought that the act he was about to do was a necessary evil, placed them on top of his net, skated to center ice and invited Wings goalie Chris Osgood to drop the gloves. Patrick's action surprised me. When he was younger, he got into one or two fights at school like many boys, but he was never the instigator. He wasn't the sort to look for a fight, but he didn't back down if someone stepped on his toes.

Now, Patrick thinks he exceeded his responsibilities as a leader by acting like that, especially since he had nothing personal against Osgood. But at the time, he thought he was doing the right thing and hoped that it would change the frame of mind in which his team had competed with the Red Wings since the Lemieux–McCarty incident.

Even if he acknowledges that he could have taken another approach, it helped change the Avs players' mindset and got them back on track. "That's when we realized we'd gone too far and that we hadn't reacted well after McCarty got revenge on Lemieux," says Patrick. "With the Wings we wanted to get an eye for an eye and that really wasn't the way to respond. So, we decided that, from then on, we would stick to hockey when we played them, and that's when we started to beat them. That's also why, I believe, Claude Lemieux had to go, which is what happened in the fall of 1999 when he was traded back to the Devils."

Patrick always liked to rely on his instincts; in most cases, they served him well. When they didn't, he was confident he had the resources to cope with the consequences.

I recall the astrology column in *La Presse*, which on the day Patrick was born, said that he would have a passionate nature that would lead him into numerous adventures and that he would revel in them as if he were in his natural element, but he would always land on his feet.

—◠⋘◠—

In the 1998 playoffs, the Avalanche were beaten four games to three by the Edmonton Oilers and eliminated. That defeat, combined with team Canada's problems in Nagano, cost Mark Crawford his coaching job in Denver. He was replaced by Bob Hartley on June 30, 1998.

Hartley, a Franco-Ontarian from Hawkesbury, a small Ontario town between Montréal and Ottawa, learned his trade in the American Hockey League between 1994 and 1998 with the Avalanche affiliate, the Hershey Bears, whom he guided to the Calder Cup victory in 1997. Prior to that, he had coached the QMJHL's Laval Voisins from 1991–1993. He led them to a Memorial Cup triumph in his last season with them.

In Denver, Hartley found himself behind the bench of a National Hockey league team without ever having been an assistant coach at that level. He would have to adapt. A coach can't treat NHL players, particularly his stars, like apprentices in the American Hockey League or teenagers in junior hockey. Though great players don't ask for special treatment, they do like to feel they're respected. Now, Hartley had an unfortunate habit of making derogatory remarks about the performance of players when they were on the ice within hearing distance of the men on the bench.

After the games, the players would talk to each other:

"Hey! You should hear what Hartley said about you today!"

"Oh yeah? That's nothing! Listen to what he had to say about you!"

Some of the players, disturbed by this behavior, talked about it to Patrick and asked him whether he could do something about it. They also talked about the pattern to captain Joe Sakic. Though well respected by his teammates, he was rather discreet and reserved, not the kind of guy to make waves. The players knew that with Patrick, the method would be more direct and the solution more radical. He told them he would wait for the right moment to act.

The opportunity presented itself on December 21, 1998, in Anaheim. Until then, neither the Avalanche nor Patrick had gotten off to a good start in the season. But that evening, he had an excellent match and seemed to be back on track. Though he'd been tested by a number of dangerous shots, the teams were tied 2–2 near the end of the second period. Then, two of the Mighty Ducks got two-minute penalties within one minute and 24 seconds of each other.

To give the players he wanted to use on the power play a little rest, Hartley pulled Patrick and temporarily replaced him with Craig Billington instead of calling a 30-second time-out, as he could have done. Now the rule states that the goalie who is in the game when his team takes the lead is credited with victory. With a two-man advantage, there was every chance that the Avalanche would take the lead. Milan Hejduk scored while Billington was in the net. Hartley turned to Patrick and said with a big smile:

"Good decision, eh, Pat? Good decision, eh!"

"Good decision? Listen," Patrick replied, in no mood to smile, "If I'm not the one who is credited with the victory this evening, you'd better tie your tuque on your head because I'll rattle your bones after the game like you won't believe!"

After Hejduk's goal, Patrick was sent back in and the Avalanche won 4–2. Billington, who had not made a single save, was in goal for only one minute 52 seconds. Yet, he was credited with the victory, which prevented Patrick from getting closer to his objective, despite making 27 saves against the Mighty Ducks.

In the American Hockey League, no player would have complained if the coach had made a similar decision. But in the NHL, it was a questionable move, especially since Hartley could have asked for a timeout instead of changing goalies. And Patrick used that decision as a pretext for delivering the protest he had promised teammates he would make.

He stormed into Hartley's office, and while Pierre Lacroix impassively looked on, destroyed the team's video equipment with his stick. Lacroix, who knew his protégé very well, chose not to intervene while Hartley tried to protect himself.

A number of players approved of Patrick's outburst. The team then began the month of January with an 11–game winning streak. "I really think," Patrick says today, "that the incident helped Hartley a lot because he wouldn't have lasted behind the bench very long the way he started. He began to show the players more respect, and they got back on a winning track under his leadership."

The Denver media didn't hold the incident against Patrick either. Terry Frei summed up the general feeling in the *Denver Post*:

For Colorado Avalanche goaltender Patrick Roy, the quest also is obsessive. He makes no apology for it, even when his passions boil over because a coaching maneuver and a scoring anomaly have "stolen" a victory from him. The team's video equipment could be repaired and replaced, as was the case after his infamous post-game explosion at Anaheim. The relationship with his coach, Bob Hartley, could be repaired. But the prideful competitiveness, even if it has an element of selfishness, is indispensable. And, after all, the number in Roy's sight is directly tied to team success.

By contrast, the Montréal media ripped into him and called him selfish, without really understanding the root of the problem. Patrick couldn't discuss the matter in public. To do so, he would have had to reveal the underlying reasons for his action. So he just took the criticism.

The Avalanche management decided to forget about the incident. For them, the team's future performances were more important than Patrick's affront to his coach. The following month, Lacroix offered Patrick a new agreement to replace the contract that was expiring. Patrick would earn $5 million for the 1998–99 season and $7.5 million for each of the following two seasons.

—␣␣—

Ken Dryden wrote in his book *The Game*:

I know that in any way an athlete can be measured—in strength, in speed, in height or distance jumped—he is immensely superior to one who performed twenty years ago. But measured against a memory, he has no chance. I know what I feel.

Nothing is as good as it used to be, and it never was. The "golden age of sports," the golden age of anything, is the age of everyone's childhood. For me and for the writers and commentators of my time, it was the 1950s. For those who lived in the 1950s as adults, it was the 1920s or the 1930s.

It is an interesting observation, particularly since in the 20 months or so that followed, Patrick surpassed all of my own childhood heroes, one after the other.

First, in February 1999, he reached an important milestone when he became the youngest goalie in history to record 400 victories. As luck would have it, the game took place at the Joe Louis Arena in Detroit, a hostile environment for the Avalanche. Patrick turned in a scintillating performance with 27 saves as the "Avs" downed the Wings 3–1.

Then on April 3, 1999, he passed Glenn Hall's career mark, earning his 408th victory against the Edmonton Oilers. Hall played 18 seasons (from 1952 to 1971) in the NHL, mostly with the Chicago Blackhawks, but also with the Detroit Red Wings and the St. Louis Blues. Despite being physically ill from nerves before each start, Hall accomplished the fantastic feat of playing 552 consecutive games at one point in his career.

Patrick finished the 1998–99 regular season with 412 wins. In the post-season, he recorded his hundredth playoff victory.

—ɷ—

The year before, he had sold his residence on Île Ducharme, so he spent the summer in Québec City. He drove from Denver to Québec City with a friend in a pickup truck that he had just purchased, the sort of sturdy vehicle valued by many of his teammates on the Avalanche.

In August, after making good use of his pickup during the summer, he had to go back to Denver. To keep him company, I offered to accompany him on the 2,000-mile trip across the Midwestern United States. It took us three days to reach our destination, sharing the driving. It was surprising to see how many people recognized him when we stopped to eat somewhere in the middle of nowhere—from Mississauga, Ontario, to North Platte, Nebraska, passing through Kalamazoo, Michigan.

Patrick treated me to an unforgettable week in Colorado. We played golf every day, going from one golf club to another. The courses were majestic; the landscapes were spectacular.

—m—

The Avalanche went into the 1999–2000 season in a brand-new arena, the Pepsi Center, with a seating capacity of 18,007, where the team would play before sellout audiences for years.

First, Patrick broke Tony Esposito's mark of 423 victories in a game against Vancouver on December 12, 1999. Esposito, the younger brother of the famous Phil Esposito, played 13 games for the Montréal Canadiens in 1968 before being picked up in the waiver draft by the Chicago Blackhawks, with whom he played until he retired 15 years later in 1983.

Then, Patrick moved into second place past Jacques Plante, behind Terry Sawchuk with 434 regular season victories. Counting playoff wins, Plante would have been the leader with 505, four more than Sawchuk. Anyway, Patrick beat both of Plante's marks. He won his 506th game, including the regular season and the playoffs, on March 28, 1999, against the Los Angeles Kings, and his 435th regular season victory on March 4, 2000, in Tampa Bay against the Lightning. When he accomplished that feat, Patrick couldn't help smiling. He remembered when Plante had told him he would never get to the National Hockey League.

When the 1999–2000 season ended, Patrick's victory quest stopped at 444. But the Avalanche were in for quite a surprise just before the post-season began.

—ᨑ—

On March 6, 2000, Pierre Lacroix, like Jacques Demers seven years before, rocked the hockey world by making one of the best transactions in his career as general manager. He acquired defenseman Raymond Bourque and center Dave Andreychuk in return for Brian Rolston, Martin Grenier, Samuel Pahlsson and a first-round draft choice.

Bourque was a superstar defenseman who had won the James Norris trophy, awarded to the league's best defenseman, five times. His 395 goals put him in first place among rearguards in National Hockey League history. Andreychuk, a powerful 6-foot, 4-inch, 220-pound center, had scored 551 goals so far in his career.

Clearly, Raymond Bourque was the key player in the trade. At 39 years of age, he was still one of the league's best defenseman, the kind of leader who could inspire his teammates with a simple look or gesture as well as by his determination and the quality of his play. Patrick went to Denver in late 1995 to help the Avalanche win the ultimate prize. The same now applied to Bourque, except that in his case, every player on the Avalanche would raise his game to help the veteran defenseman finally win something that had been eluding him for 21 years in the NHL: the Stanley Cup.

The trade had an immediate impact. The Avalanche, in seventh place in the Western Conference and far from certain of earning a berth in the playoffs, suffered only two defeats in the last 12 games of the regular season and finished fourth in the conference.

Patrick was delighted. Not only had his friend become a teammate, but he would also be bearing some of the leadership responsibility

(© Tim De Frisco.)

Late at night, on June 11, 1996, after a rollercoaster ride of a season full of upheavals and powerful emotions, after being run out of Montréal, denigrated by some, scorned by others, Patrick hoists the "Cup of Dignity."

(© Hans Deryk, The Canadian Press.)

At 1:06 a.m., Patrick and John Vanbiesbrouck of the Florida Panthers shake hands at the end of the 1996 Stanley Cup final. The two have waged one of the most stunning goaltending duels in NHL history, with the Avalanche winning 1-0 after a game that lasted 104 minutes and 31 seconds.

(© Paul Chiasson, The Canadian Press.)

On Tuesday, October 17, 2000, at the MCI Center in Washington, Patrick is carried around triumphantly by his two great friends, Raymond Bourque and Adam Foote, after recording his 448th regular-season victory, making him the goalie with the most wins in hockey history.

(© Nick Wass, The Canadian Press.)

After setting this historic mark, Patrick gets a hug from his father at the Avalanche bench, as his sister Alexandra and his brother Stéphane look on from the stands.

(© Tim De Frisco.)

On October 20, 2000, at the Pepsi Center in Denver, during the ceremony marking Patrick's 448th victory, the most touching moment comes when Terry Sawchuk's son, Jerry, visibly moved, raises Patrick's arm, recognizing him as the new holder of the title that his father has held since 1970.
(© David Zalubowski, The Canadian Press.)

Twice in his career, Patrick has gotten involved in fierce fights. Here we see him against Detroit's Mike Vernon. At the end of the game, in which Vernon registers the 300th victory of his career, Patrick graciously slid the "game puck" toward him.
(© Tom Pidgeon, The Canadian Press.)

On June 9, 2001, Patrick would take flight if he had wings. Mission accomplished for the Avalanche: they've won the Stanley Cup for Raymond Bourque. Patrick dubs it the "Cup of Friendship."

(© Tim De Frisco.)

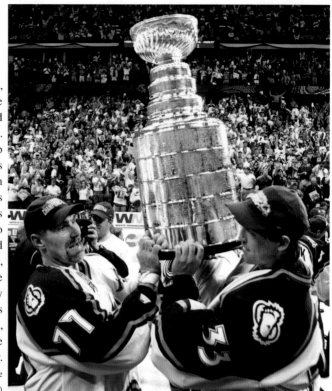

In 22 NHL seasons, Raymond Bourque had never touched the Stanley Cup. During a few Cup presentations, he's sometimes been within a few inches of it, but he has never wanted to touch it: that would be bad luck. Now, on Saturday, June 9, 2001, he finally raises it with his friend Patrick, the Conn Smythe Trophy winner.

(© Ryan Remiorz, The Canadian Press)

Gary Bettman presents Patrick with the Conn Smythe Trophy, awarded to the 2001 Playoff MVP. Patrick is the first three-time recipient of the honor. Even legendary stars like Wayne Gretzky and Mario Lemieux could not win it more than twice in their illustrious career.

(© Tim De Frisco.)

On January 20, 2003, in a 1-1 tie against the Dallas Stars, Patrick becomes the first goalie to play in a thousand regular-season games. Rogatien Vachon, his childhood hero, presents him with a silver goalie stick in a brief pre-game ceremony.
(© Tim De Frisco.)

On May 28, 2003, accompanied by Pierre Lacroix, the president of the Colorado Avalanche, Patrick serenely announces that he is retiring as an active NHL player. His retirement ends the long journey that the two men have been traveling together since 1983.
(© Tim De Frisco.)

On October 28, 2003, as his wife, his children, Pierre Lacroix and Avalanche owner Stanley Kroenke look on nostalgically, Patrick, cheered by 18,000 fans, raises the banner that represents his number 33 jersey to the rafters of the Pepsi Center.

(© Tim De Frisco.)

required to earn the Avalanche the highest honors. "He transformed the atmosphere in the dressing room when we needed it the most. He gave a lot of energy and confidence to the team," said Patrick.

Raymond Bourque's leadership carried over into the playoffs. In the first two rounds, the Avalanche beat the Phoenix Coyotes and the Detroit Red Wings, their great rivals, in five games in each series. But in the semifinals against the Dallas Stars, Colorado faced a goalie at the top of his form, Eddie Belfour, and a team every bit as strong as the Avalanche, but which enjoyed home-ice advantage. Colorado lost by a score of 3–2 in Dallas in the seventh and deciding game of a hotly contested series. Bourque would have to wait to see his dream materialize.

—⁂—

Patrick began the 2000–01 season only three victories behind Terry Sawchuk's mark. Over the phone, I told Patrick that I would like to be present when he tied the mark. Unlike most people, I considered that one as important as the one that would erase Sawchuk's record. What I most admired was the determination, the grit and the persistence that Patrick had displayed for so many years to reach the 447-victory plateau, but he would only need another win to beat the record. Asked why it was so important for him to equal and surpass the mark, Patrick replied, "Because when I started, I had one objective. It wasn't to have one very good year. It was to have a career where I would play consistently throughout. And the only way to reach that record is to have done that. That's why it's important."

I first heard of Terry Sawchuk in 1951. I was nine years old. My parents subscribed to *Life* magazine, not particularly known for its sports coverage. Nevertheless the magazine devoted an in-depth article to the spectacular goalie, who played out of a crouch. "When I'm crouching low," said Sawchuk, "I can keep better track of the puck through the players' legs on screen shots." He was 21 years old and in his first complete season in the NHL. He was considered a rising star among goaltenders. Later, he was thought to be the greatest goalie in history. He was my childhood hero among goalies. And now, Patrick was only three victories from joining him in the record book.

Sawchuk, nicknamed "Uke" because his parents were Ukrainian, played 21 seasons in the NHL from 1949 to 1970 and won the Vézina Trophy four times. He tended goal for the Detroit Red Wings, with whom he captured four Stanley Cups. He won another with the Toronto Maple Leafs in 1967. He also served brief stints with the Boston Bruins, the Los Angeles Kings and the New York Rangers, where he finished his career in 1970 with 103 shutouts in the regular season, a record still unmatched. That same year he died tragically as the result of an altercation with teammate Ron Stewart, with whom he rented a house in Long Island.

On Saturday, October 14, 2000, at the Pepsi Center in a 3–1 triumph over the Columbus Blue Jackets, Patrick joined Sawchuk in the record book. In the run-up to the event, he boned up about the legendary goalie by reading a biography on him written by David Dupuis in 1998. It was Patrick's way of paying homage to Sawchuk. Before then his only source of information about Sawchuk was his hockey card collection. "He had a difficult time off the ice," said Patrick, "but he seemed to love the game, and we have that in common."

Right after the match, I went to congratulate Patrick. We were standing side by side just before he went into the room for his press conference. Suddenly, he pulled off his game jersey and handed it to me. I was very moved by the gesture. It seemed as if every fiber of the jersey, like the lump that rose in my throat in Sherbrooke 15 years earlier, contained all the departures for the rink in the dark of the early morning, all the years when my social life consisted of going to arenas, the hopes, the disappointments, the frustrations and the anguish that were part of my life all during his career, but also the great satisfaction and excitement from the victories and accomplishments that a goalie's path can bring to a father. I was profoundly moved. By giving me the jersey, Patrick was making a gesture of acknowledgment and appreciation for all we'd been through.

During the press conference, he pointed out that he felt somewhat nostalgic about equaling Sawchuk's record. "Anytime someone gets close to a record," he said, "it brings back memories of the person who held it, and that is the beauty of it. Sawchuk has been a great athlete and competitor, he had a lot of passion for the game, and was great for goaltending because he raised that bar for a lot of us. And hopefully, I'll do the same for other goaltenders."

It would be pointless to compare Patrick with Sawchuk. They didn't behave the same away from the rink, and they played in very different eras. But when they had achieved the same number of victories, the goals-against averages were almost equal: Sawchuk's was 2.51 and Patrick's was 2.55. Given the large number of variables that enter into such an equation, it is surprising to arrive at almost identical results.

—m—

The next day, a Sunday, I accompanied Patrick and Jonathan early in the morning. Jonathan was playing in a hockey tournament in Fort Collins, about a 90-minute drive from Denver. Now it was Patrick's turn to have the same experience with his children as I had had with him and Stéphane. It made me feel a little nostalgic, too.

At the Fort Collins arena, the father of one of Jonathan's team-mates took me aside.

"Mr. Roy, I've something to tell you about your son," he began in a confidential tone. "I have an older daughter, who asked Patrick for an autograph at the beginning of the season. She told him she was honored to make his acquaintance. You know what Patrick said to her?

I waited to hear what he would say.

"He said that, on the contrary, he was the one honored to make her acquaintance because without people like her, he wouldn't be where he was today. Mr. Roy, you can be proud of your son!"

I was touched by his remarks.

—m—

The Avalanche were slated to visit the Washington Capitals the next Tuesday and the Columbus Blue Jackets the day after that. As there was every chance that Patrick would break Sawchuk's record in one of those games, Pierre Lacroix was nice enough to invite me to accompany the team on the trip.

The "Avs" covered more miles per season than any other club. For reasons of comfort and efficiency, the Avalanche management chartered two types of aircraft, a Boeing 737 and a 757, the interior of which had been adapted so that all the passengers would have first-class comfort and more space. Management personnel usually sat up front. Behind them were the guys who wanted to sleep, and way at the back, were the card players. It was an unforgettable experience for me. I was treated like an Avalanche player. I had my seat on the plane beside Patrick, between management and the sleepers. There was also a place for me on the bus. And there was a room reserved for me at the hotel.

Needless to say, ever since the previous Saturday, the sports media throughout North America had been focused on Patrick. They would be present at every game so as not to miss the event that would make him the goalie with the most career victories. When he arrived in Washington, the cameras followed him everywhere: when he got off the plane, in the bus, when he arrived at the MCI Center, in the corridor under the stands when he headed to the dressing room, during his pre-game exercises on the stationary bike, and even when he received a massage to loosen up his quadriceps and put on his uniform to get ready for the game. Patrick wanted to put the event behind him as quickly as possible so he could devote himself to one objective: winning a Stanley Cup for Raymond Bourque.

—m—

I watched practically the entire game with Pierre Lacroix from the box reserved for him high up in the arena. Everything was in place. National Hockey League Commissioner Gary Bettman and his aides had made arrangements for the ceremony that would take place if the Avalanche won. Patrick had invited his family (except for the children, who had stayed behind in Denver) and a few friends.

It was a close-fought, exciting contest. The Avalanche were on a mission for Patrick and were absolutely determined to win. They jumped off to a great start, scoring twice in the first period. But in the second, the Capitals chalked up two markers, leveling the count. Before the start of the third period, left-winger Dave Reid fired up his teammates in the dressing room. However, Peter Bondra, the Capitals right-winger, had other plans. The period had just gotten under way when he raced in on a breakaway, deked Patrick and tallied his second goal of the game, giving his team a 3–2 lead. Sakic tied the score a few minutes later. Five seconds from the end of regulation time, Jan Boulis let loose a hard drive that Patrick, who was screened, didn't see coming, but as he was in a good position and at the right spot, he made the save. "I never saw the puck," he later confessed. "It hit my pad and went out. I guess I thought the chances were on my side when that happened." The third period ended with the score tied at 3–3. The teams were going into overtime.

Pierre Lacroix couldn't stand it any more. He invited me to follow him under the stands, where we waited in a room close to the corridor that the Avalanche would take on their way to the ice. The room was bare but for a TV and a few straight-backed chairs.

The overtime began with the teams playing four to a side. But when Richard Zednik got a major penalty for cross-checking Adam Foote in the face, Bob Hartley went for the kill. He sent his big guns into the action: Joe Sakic, Peter Forsberg and Milan Hejduk up front and Raymond Bourque on defense.

A little over two minutes had gone by when Hejduk and Bourque exchanged passes in the Washington zone. Suddenly, Bourque uncorked a laser from the blue line. The puck was traveling a little off target, but Peter Forsberg managed to get his stick on it. The disk found its way behind "Caps" goaltender Olaf Kolzig at precisely 2:37 in overtime. With that, Terry Sawchuk's name slipped to second place in the number of career wins posted by a goalie. Patrick now stood at the summit of his profession.

As soon as the puck slipped into the net, Patrick leaped out of his goal—he would have flown if he could. His teammates dashed over to congratulate him, while Raymond Bourque had the presence of mind to recover the historic puck and hand it to Patrick. In the stands, their wives, jumped up and down and hugged each other, while some 13,335 spectators stood up to cheer for the hero of the moment, showing remarkable courtesy despite their team's loss. Patrick temporarily freed himself from his teammates, who went to put on navy blue caps on which was embroidered *Roy, Avalanche #33, All-Time Goaltender Wins.* Lifting his mask on top of his head, he gave a live interview for television.

During the interview, the Avalanche players and the fans, some of whom were wearing Patrick's jersey or waving signs with his name, were enjoying themselves watching a video put together by the NHL on the giant scoreboard screen. Essentially, there were excerpts from Patrick's career, including some of his most famous saves, celebrations when he was holding the Stanley Cup over his head, and even the famous wink he gave Tomas Sandstrom in 1993. The video also showed some of his most illustrious predecessors, goalies like Terry Sawchuk, Jacques Plante, Glenn Hall, Ken Dryden, Billy Smith, Lorne Worsley, Gerry Cheevers and Bernard Parent. Finally, the crowd went wild when they saw celebrities like TV hosts Alex Trebek and Denis Leary, pro wrestling personalities like Steve Austin, and legendary hockey stars like Tony Esposito and Gordie Howe offer their congratulations to Patrick.

When the goal was scored, Pierre Lacroix immediately ran out of the room where we'd been watching the game and tore down the hall leading to the ice. I followed him and ended up standing right behind the Avalanche bench beside Bob Hartley and his assistants, Bryan Trottier and Jacques Cloutier.

After the interviews and the presentation of the video, Patrick went over to his team's bench and handed his stick, mask and gloves to the equipment manager, Wayne Fleming. Patrick spotted me and came over. We shook hands and hugged. Then Patrick went back to his goal, where Gary Bettman and Tony Esposito were waiting. The commissioner handed him a pair of scissors so he could cut the net, which would be sent to the Hockey Hall of Fame in Toronto.

Patrick exchanged a few words with Esposito, and then Raymond Bourque and Adam Foote hoisted him onto their shoulders and carried him triumphantly over to the corridor leading to the team's dressing room, prompting Bourque to say, "I've seen coaches carried off, but not too many goalies. I don't know if we could have gone around the rink with him." He was alluding to the weight of his equipment, of course.

At the dressing room doorway, Patrick thanked his teammates, one after another, with a firm handshake and a big smile as they walked in. It is often said that a picture is worth a thousand words;

sometimes a few words are worth a thousand pictures. When Bob Hartley arrived, the exchange between Patrick and him was as brief as it had been with the others. But the words were warm and charged with meaning.

"Thanks, Bob," Patrick said sincerely.

"Good work, Pat," Hartley said quietly.

That was all. As time went by, the two of them had gotten to know and appreciate each other.

After a good shower, Patrick went to the media room. My family and I and some of his friends, including Fred Couples, who had made the trip to Washington so he wouldn't miss anything, could watch the conference in a place reserved for us.

During the briefing, Patrick thanked his family, all those who had supported him in his career and his teammates; he congratulated them in particular for staying focused on the game and playing extremely well despite the presence of cameras in the dressing room and a host of other unusual distractions. "To be honest, I wanted to enjoy this as much as I could but, on the other hand," he said with a grin, "I also wanted to get it over as soon as possible. I didn't want my family and friends to have to keep following me all over the country."

He was answering questions from the reporters when he got a phone call. It was the Prime Minister of Canada, Jean Chrétien, calling to congratulate him. After that, Patrick concluded the briefing by stressing that winning the Stanley Cup was still his principal objective, even though the milestone he had just passed represented the effort of an entire career: "There's a player on our team [Raymond Bourque] who, after 22 years in the National Hockey League, deserves to win a Stanley Cup, and we intend to try to get him one this year."

The players were happy to be associated with this achievement and many of them said so to the media.

"It is phenomenal what has just occurred," said Raymond Bourque. "I knew Patrick before I came here but I didn't know how he went about his business day in and day out. And what has really impressed me is how he works and how he practices. He works so hard and it's the reason why he's so good . . . How he prepares, not only on game days but on practice days as well, he'll look at videos, he'll study the game, he'll study himself and make corrections. I really admire how he goes about his business and I think that's why he's had so much success, along with the enormous amount of talent that the man has."

Craig Billington, now Kolzig's backup for the Capitals, thanked the gods of hockey for choosing Washington as the scene of this historic feat and for allowing him to witness it. "You can shed different lights on measuring goalies' performances, but basically, we get paid to win. Here, we're talking about the winningest goaltender in hockey history, which goes back more than a hundred years. He's done it year after year. In order to achieve those numbers, it had to be a consistent process and he has attained that. For me, this is his greatest accomplishment."

For Peter Forsberg, Patrick was simply the best goalie of all time. "Patrick is known as maybe a playoff goaltender," he said "but now he's got the record for most wins in the regular season too. He's unbelievable and it couldn't happen to a better person. Everybody is real happy for him."

Even celebrated ABC anchorman Peter Jennings paid tribute to him with a brief report on *World News Tonight* about his career. On the program, Patrick revealed that he often made saves without even seeing the puck: "Given the speed of the game and how fast the puck travels, it's more a matter of anticipation and positioning," he declared.

—w—

It is a bit tricky to compare goalies from different eras. Many aspects of the game have changed: strategies, techniques and equipment, as well as the speed of execution, and the power of the shots. It is worth noting, however, that while his predecessors played fewer games in a season, Patrick equaled the number of victories of Glenn Hall, Tony Esposito, Jacques Plante and Terry Sawchuk, playing respectively 131, 85, 9 and 123 games fewer than they did. Counting both the regular season and the playoffs, Plante won his 505 in 949 games; Patrick needed 929 for the feat.

After stopping off at Columbus the next day, where David Aebischer, Patrick's new backup, earned the first victory of his NHL career with a 5–2 win against the Blue Jackets, the Avalanche returned to Denver, where a remarkable party, the kind only Pierre Lacroix can throw, was awaiting the hero of the moment.

—m—

Patrick's achievement was celebrated just before a game against the Florida Panthers at the Pepsi Center on Friday, October 20. It was a truly magnificent celebration. It was extremely moving to witness the appreciation that the 18,000 fans and numerous dignitaries present showed Patrick that evening.

First, the lights were turned off so that the spectators could view the highlights of Patrick's career on the giant screen known as the Jumbotron. Then the house announcer's deep voice resounded through the entire arena: "Ladies and gentlemen, the winningest goaltender in the history of the NHL, NUMBER 33, **PATRICK ROY!!!**"

To the ovation of the crowd and the players of both teams and the sound of trumpets, Patrick emerged out of the dark from a corner of the rink, and the spotlights focused on him while he did a lap of honor before stopping by his goal. The ovation lasted several more minutes. Patrick, visibly uncomfortable about such an outpouring of love, and not quite knowing how to respond, acknowledged the applause by waving and nodding to the fans.

When the lights were turned back on, he seemed to be trying to spot his children in the crowd. When his wife, Michèle, was introduced, she went to join him. Then Jana, Frédérick and Jonathan appeared in a personalized golf cart, a gift that they and their mother were giving Patrick. He hadn't expected it. While he was chatting with distinguished guests under the stands, he'd been told casually that his children would have good seats in the stands. Pierre Lacroix had played a trick on him. The Avalanche GM knew that Patrick would be annoyed if he didn't have his children by his side. So he was elated to see them arrive on the ice. Lacroix had guessed right.

Then his parents, sister and brother came out and joined Patrick. After that, he received a flood—I better not say an avalanche—of splendid and amazing gifts.

Scott Mellanby, the Florida Panthers captain, gave Patrick a crystal vase on behalf of his team.

Guy Lafleur, representing the Montréal Canadiens, offered him a silver plate, with an inscription: "Félicitations à Patrick Roy, le gardien de but le plus victorieux de l'histoire du hockey." ("Congratulations to Patrick Roy, the goalie with the most wins in hockey history.")

Wellington Webb, the mayor of Denver, then stepped forward and asked everyone to watch the Jumbotron. There were images of city employees installing a sign along Auroria Parkway, an access road between Highway I-25 and the Pepsi Center, which would be called Patrick Roy Blvd. until the end of the season. The mayor also announced that the city was officially proclaiming the day "Patrick Roy Day."

Governor of the State of Colorado Bill Owens gave Patrick the flag that floated over the Capitol the day he won his historic victory.

The governor also made an official proclamation declaring the period of October 20 to 26 "Patrick Roy Week" throughout Colorado.

Joe Sakic, the captain of the Avalanche, unveiled a painting, an immense portrait by Samantha Wendell. A gift from his teammates, the work showed Patrick in an Avalanche uniform. But on each side, the viewer could see him in the masks of the two teams he played for in the NHL.

Then, Commissioner Gary Bettman and Terry Sawchuk's son, Jerry, appeared. "Patrick," said Bettman, "you have earned a special place in hockey history and for that, we wanted to give you a special present. This is one of your sticks dipped in silver. It has on it each building you played in and the number of wins you recorded in the NHL. And, to commemorate the fact that you are a devoted father, and very superstitious, your children's names will also be engraved on the stick.

"On behalf of all your fans, on behalf of your League and the great game of hockey, you have earned a very special place in all of our hearts. This is an amazing record at the most difficult position in all of sports. Congratulations."

The most touching moment of the ceremony came when Jerry Sawchuk, who was also quite emotional, hugged Patrick and raised his arm as the new champ.

Sawchuk hadn't known quite what to expect when he met Patrick earlier in the morning on October 20. A dyed-in-the-wool Red Wings fan, he had been in the crowd two years earlier when fans chanted, "Hit him, 'Ozzie'! Hit him!" while Patrick was exchanging blows with Osgood at the Joe Louis Arena in Detroit. But it didn't take Jerry Sawchuk long to realize that Patrick was a very different person from the one he had seen brawling at center ice. Something clicked between the two. After their meeting, Sawchuk said, "I'd be lying if I told you I wasn't a little sad to see my father's record broken.

But life moves on, and if someone has to break it, my family and I are happy Patrick is the one who did it. What a wonderful gentleman!"

After Bettman and Sawchuk spoke, Pierre Lacroix gave Patrick's wife a diamond brooch and his children gold rings.

Finally, Stan Kroenke, the owner of the team, unveiled a life-size bronze bust by sculptors Lee West and Christopher Howe, showing Patrick in the Avalanche uniform, with his mask on top of his head and "Charlotte" by his side.

Despite the tributes and display of appreciation he had received, Patrick was hungry for something else. Another victory, of course. And he got his wish when his team won by the score of 5–1 after he stopped 24 shots by the Panthers.

—⁂—

Patrick had never sought fame. But he had become famous. Now, he was a superstar, not only in Québec and Colorado, but throughout North America. At the same time, he was joining a circle of celebrities whom fame makes vulnerable because they are seen through the distorting lens of subjectivity and prejudice. The distorting lens of media people who irrevocably condemn the slightest misstep or misdemeanor just to sell newspapers or jack up the ratings. The distorting lens of talk show callers or people who write open letters to newspapers and can't wait to take it out on someone whose life seems more exciting than theirs.

In some cases, a complaint lodged for an alleged aggression might itself be a form of aggression, a way of attracting attention and sharing, if only for a moment, the spotlight with someone they envy, or of ripping off a few dollars through an out-of-court settlement that the celebrity accepts out of sheer exasperation.

Gradually, the distorting lens becomes infinitely large, attracting any number of people, including so-called psychologists or other

451

"ologists" of dubious credentials, who craftily add their theories to things they know nothing about and concoct tales that many readers or listeners eventually confuse with reality. Based on these waking dreams, judgments are formed and, sometimes, people who are considered villains may in reality be the victims.

This certainly doesn't mean that superstars are above misbehaving and that unlike everybody else they never make mistakes. It simply means that, they are more likely than anyone else to be victims of bias and to suffer the consequences. On more than one occasion, this observation would be borne out by what happened to Patrick.

On Saturday, October 21, the day after the celebrations at the Pepsi Center, we went to eat at one of Denver's finest restaurants, where we had reserved a private room. Patrick was in the company of people he loved: members of his family; old friends, like Sylvain "Ti-Pote" Doyon and his parents, Yvette and Guy, as well as Claude and Nathalie Lefebvre; newer friends like Raymond and Christiane Bourque; along with his agents, Robert and Daniel Sauvé and their spouses. After the weeks of stress, it was time to undo his tie and unwind with people close to him.

The food was exquisite and the great wines flowed freely. Around 11 p.m., I left with Barbara, Alexandra and Stéphane and asked to be dropped off at Patrick's place. When I got there, I went upstairs to sleep. As there wasn't enough room for everyone, the others stayed downtown at Hotel Monaco.

Meanwhile, the dinner carried on at the restaurant. The merrymakers were trading anecdotes and having a great time. After the wine, they moved on to liqueurs—some people downed several shooters—until nearly 2 a.m., except for people, like Patrick, who had to drive home and slowed down their alcohol consumption. Then, everyone left.

It all began on the road back. Or rather, nothing began, because, in fact, very little happened. Like any old couple, Michèle and Patrick quarreled all during the drive, with the subject veering off to Patrick's family. At the house, Patrick walked around outside for a few minutes, hoping that things would cool down and his wife would go to bed before he went back inside. That didn't happen. The argument continued; criticism flew thick and fast from both sides.

I was awakened by the sound of people shouting. According to my watch, it was 2:20 a.m. I listened, trying to find out what was going on. Michèle and Patrick were screaming at each other at the top of their lungs. Suddenly, I heard a sharp cracking sound. A few moments later, Michèle burst into my bedroom and flipped on the ceiling light. I sat up in bed.

"Mr. Roy," she said angrily, "you've won!"

"What did you say?" I said, with no idea what she was driving at.

"You've won. You can keep your son!"

"Come on, Michèle, what are you talking about? What's going on?"

"You can keep your son!" she repeated.

Then, she pointed at me and added, before leaving the room:

"Get dressed and get out of here!"

I thought I was dreaming. But the harsh ceiling light snapped me back to reality. I tried to collect my clothes . . . and my thoughts. True, Barbara and I had never had a particularly warm relationship with Michèle, but it wasn't bad either, and it had seemed to me that things were improving.

I went down to the living room. Patrick was calm, stretched out in an armchair. A police officer was already standing near him. Another officer, a woman, was interviewing Michèle in the dining room.

"What's happening?" I asked Patrick.

"She called 911. It's over," he said in a tired, almost inaudible voice.

That's when I sensed that trust had been broken. And yet, nothing had happened other than a simple quarrel in which nobody had been threatened or physically assaulted. In short, it was something of no importance for a couple who had been living together for 14 years. But, even though the receiver had been hung up without a single word being said, a call had been made to 911, and Patrick had violently pushed a door, which was not completely installed, and a hinge had given way. Fatigue and alcohol had caused the faux pas.

The law is very strict in the State of Colorado with respect to calls in which there is an appearance of a "domestic dispute." Officers are obliged to arrest the person they consider responsible for the disturbance. So, despite the protestations of both Michèle and Patrick, he ended up in a cell at a police station and wasn't released until five in the morning, after paying $750 in bail.

The case took months to resolve, until the state prosecutor withdrew the misdemeanor criminal-mischief charge. They were months that were deeply troubling for Patrick, for Michèle, for their children, and for the whole family.

THE CUP OF FRIENDSHIP

In 1998, while traveling on a high-speed train between Nagano and Karuizawa, Patrick turned to Raymond Bourque and said, "It would be fun if we could play on the same team before the end of our careers." In the spring of 2000, Pierre Lacroix's perspicacity and Boston Bruins general manager Harry Sinden's understanding turned this dream into reality.

By the fall of 2000, Patrick and Bourque had become very good friends. They often played golf and ate at restaurants together, visited each other with their wives and children, and drove to games or practices in the same car. Bourque, the epitome of quiet confidence and stability, was a good influence on Patrick. If the great defenseman had been a tree, he would have been an oak. Patrick could never have been a tree. He was solid and confident enough, but he fidgeted too much to take root. He was more like a "butterfly."

The Avs were now on a mission: to win the Stanley Cup for Raymond Bourque. They made no secret of it. Neither did Bourque, who gave every one of his teammates a cap labeled "Mission 16W" (the team needed 16 playoff wins to capture the Cup). "I had a fine career in Boston," he said, "but the ultimate prize, and that's the reason we play, is the Stanley Cup, and when we look at the team that we have here, with a good mix of veterans and talented youngsters, we have a good chance to achieve our goal. It's very exciting; you get few opportunities like this. You have to seize them when they come."

Born in the Montréal suburb of Saint-Laurent, Raymond Bourque had a brilliant start to his career with the Boston Bruins in 1979–80, winning the Calder Trophy, awarded to the NHL's Rookie of the Year, and earning a spot on the NHL's First All-Star Team, an unusual accomplishment for a player in his initial season. He spent the next 21 seasons with the Bruins and was their captain for over 14 years. During that period, he was selected to the NHL's First All-Star Team 12 times and on the second six times. In 2001, as a member of the Colorado Avalanche, he was named to the First All-Star Team for the 13th time. He had become the highest scoring defenseman in league history with the most goals, assists and overall points. He also won the James Norris Trophy as the NHL's best defenseman five times. Only Doug Harvey, Bobby Orr and Nicklas Lidstrom received the award more often.

Despite a raft of honors, attesting to an extraordinary career, he'd never been on a Stanley Cup winner, though he'd come close in 1988 and 1990 when the Bruins bowed to the Edmonton Oilers in the final.

As a consequence, the illustrious trophy became the Colorado Avs' sole objective. For them, it was "now or never." The whole organization, from the equipment manager to the president, including trainers, coaches and players, made a commitment.

It was the sort of challenge that Patrick relished.

Everyone recalled the two previous post-seasons when the Dallas Stars had beaten Colorado in the seventh and deciding game in Dallas. Experts in the town opined that Stars goalie Eddie Belfour had outplayed Patrick. Certainly, Eddie "the Eagle" sparkled in both series, but that wasn't the only reason for the victory. An even match for the Avalanche, the Stars had benefited from home-ice advantage each time. In game seven, the crowd support for the local team can make a huge difference. All the wiser from these experiences, the Avs would pull out all the stops to finish high in the season standings so they would have home-ice advantage in the post-season. They were determined that Bourque wouldn't miss out on his final opportunity to win the precious trophy.

In fact, the Avs finished a strong first with 118 points, seven better than their closest rivals, the New Jersey Devils and the Detroit Red Wings, who tied for second. It was the first and only time that Patrick ended his season with 40 wins; he suffered only 13 defeats.

—m—

In the second half of the season, the Avalanche visited Montréal on February 13, 2001. It was Patrick's first trip to the city since he had beaten Sawchuk's record, and as he had racked up 289 of his 448 victories in a Habs uniform, the Canadiens organization had decided to pay him homage before the encounter in a brief ceremony at center ice.

Since his harrowing departure from Montréal in 1995, he had played there four times, but no particular event had put the spotlight on him. This time would be different, and he was concerned about crowd reaction. He feared that fans held him solely responsible for the rupture with the Canadiens and that they hadn't forgiven him. In addition, the wounds from his marital dispute the previous fall hadn't healed. Extensive media coverage of this event, along with all sorts of interpretations, hypotheses and suppositions had hurt him and made him short-tempered. A few days before going to Montréal, he had briefly mentioned his apprehension to me on the phone. To allay his fears, I had quoted an excerpt from Milan Kundera's *The Joke*:

Everything will be forgotten and nothing will be redressed. The task of obtaining redress (by vengeance or by forgiveness) will be

457

taken over by forgetting. No one will redress the wrongs that have been done, but all wrongs will be forgotten.

Patrick had indicated that he would rather journalists avoid bringing up the subject of his domestic spat—as it was a personal matter— during his stay in Montréal. Before leaving Denver, he had granted a long telephone interview to Bertrand Raymond of the *Journal de Montréal*. When Patrick arrived at Mirabel Airport, the cameras were there to greet him. The next day, the morning of the game, Michel Villeneuve interviewed him on TQS television. Ignoring the conditions Patrick had set, Villeneuve insisted he talk about the events of the night of October 21. That's all it took to put Patrick in a very bad mood. And when he saw the title of the *Journal de Montréal* article, "When we forget, we forgive," with his nerves already raw, he exploded. Bertrand Raymond took the rap. Patrick tore into the columnist, a member of the Hockey Hall of Fame, who had always been fair to him.

And yet, Raymond had nothing to do with the heading. His article was quite complimentary: it simply referred to Patrick's relationship with the Montréal public. It was perfectly in keeping with what had been agreed upon. Nevertheless, Patrick was furious about the article's title, which, he felt, lent itself to confusion. It could be interpreted as an allusion to his troubles with his spouse. It was, in fact, possible to make that inference, but the title was taken from his own comments: "The people have put all that [his departure from Montréal] behind them and so have I," he declared. "Sometimes, the public doesn't necessarily forgive, but it forgets. And, when we forget, we always find it easier to forgive." Using these last few words ignited an already short fuse.

Patrick's apprehensions were unfounded. The crowds gave him a warm welcome. They remembered the Cup victories in 1986 and

1993 in which he played a pivotal role. Patrick was visibly moved. In a simple pre-game ceremony, his ex-teammates Patrice Brisebois, Benoît Brunet and Guy Carbonneau presented him with a painting by Michel Lapensée, depicting various stages of his career in a Canadiens uniform. Before setting up in goal for the start of the game, Patrick waved to the crowd a few times. The reconciliation had taken place.

Realizing that he had gone a bit over the top by attacking Raymond, Patrick called him up when he was in Ottawa two days later to apologize. Colorado was stopping over for a game with the Senators.

—◠◠◠—

Before the playoffs, most experts thought the Avalanche and the New Jersey Devils would be the finalists. As was his custom every March, Pierre Lacroix made moves to strengthen the team. He acquired an excellent offensive defenseman, Rob Blake, and a center, Steve Reinprecht, from the Los Angeles Kings, in exchange for right-winger Adam Deadmarsh and rearguard Aaron Miller. As in the Canadiens' heyday when they had the Big Three of Serge Savard, Guy Lapointe and Larry Robinson, the Avalanche now had their own dominant defensive trio in Raymond Bourque, Rob Blake and Adam Foote. The Avalanche, a club without weaknesses, had depth in every position. In addition to the Big Three on defense, the Avs were an offensive juggernaut with Joe Sakic, Peter Forsberg, Milan Hejduk, Alex Tanguay and Chris Drury. General Manager Lacroix had done his job. Now it was up to coach Hartley and the players to do theirs.

Right from the first playoff round, the Avalanche seemed to be on the right track. They brushed past the Vancouver Canucks in five games. It was no contest. The next opponents were the Los Angeles

Kings, who had raised eyebrows by dismissing the powerful Detroit Red Wings. But a closer look at the Kings' roster made their victory less surprising. They were solid in goal with Félix "The Cat" Potvin, on a roll after his big series against Detroit. In case Potvin faltered, Stéphane Fiset was an able backup. The rest of the team was well balanced: dangerous scorers like Luke Robitaille and Zigmund Palffy, and fine defensemen like Mathieu Schneider and Aaron Miller. Above all, in Andy Murray the Kings had a coach who knew how to get the best out of the resources at his disposal.

It did not take long for the Avs to find out. In the first match in Denver, they suffered an overtime defeat by the score of 4–3. From that game on the series became, against all expectations, a goaltending duel between Potvin and Patrick.

Criticized by the fans during the first match at the Pepsi Center, Patrick, as he had so often done after a mediocre performance, rebounded with a 2–0 shutout in the next game. In so doing, he surpassed the record of 15 playoff shutouts set by Clint Benedict, who played for the Montréal Maroons and the Ottawa Senators between 1914 and 1928. "I didn't realize before the previous playoff round that I was nearing the record," said Patrick. "I want to win the Cup above all else. I try not to put any more pressure on myself, and I avoid reading the papers."

After a 4–3 triumph in the first game in Los Angeles, Patrick produced another shutout in the following contest, this time by the score of 3–0. His solid performance helped the Avalanche take a 3–1 lead in the series, and Bob Hartley lavished praise on his goalie. "Incredible, simply incredible!" he said. "Patrick has turned in a performance that few goalies in the league can equal. Without him, we might as well have gone back to the hotel after the first period."

Even so, Patrick was cautious: "We'll have to play well," he said, "We'll have to give everything we've got to win. The Kings won't be handing us any favors."

That's for sure! With Joe Sakic shelved for three games because of a shoulder injury, Félix Potvin was unbeatable in the following two encounters, racking up two straight 1–0 shutouts. Patrick was excellent, too, making 25 saves in one game and 31 in the next, but his teammates couldn't buy a goal.

The day before the final game of the series, nothing had been decided. The league's best team during the regular season was facing elimination by a club that no one had expected to see so late in May. To make matters worse, Colorado's powerful offense had been shut out two games in a row. The Avalanche power play had managed only three meager goals since the start of this series, even with Blake or Bourque on the point, and Forsberg and Hejduk up front. There was cause for concern!

Lacroix had a lot at stake. Had he put together those deals in vain? In all, he had sacrificed nine up-and-coming players and two first-round draft picks, in addition to boosting his payroll to $56 million, in order to have a roster capable, he thought, of capturing the Cup in the short term. If he failed, the Denver media would stone him in the public square.

His honor was saved, this time, thanks to a 5–1 victory in the deciding game. The team's regular season efforts had paid off: the seventh game had taken place at the Pepsi Center. But Avalanche fans were in for bad news. After the win, Peter Forsberg complained of stomach cramps. He was taken to the hospital where the tests revealed internal injury and bleeding. He had to undergo an emergency operation to remove his spleen. The Swede would be sidelined for the rest of the series. This considerably weakened an attack that had already sputtered against the Kings.

The Western Conference final pitted the Avalanche against the St. Louis Blues, who had dispatched the Dallas Stars. In the East, the New Jersey Devils, who had disposed of the Toronto Maple Leafs, were facing the Pittsburgh Penguins.

Despite Forsberg's absence, despite the Blues' advantage in shots on goal, despite closely fought contests—three of them went into overtime—the Avalanche conquered the Blues in five games.

The Avs were nearing the objective they had set at the beginning of the season. So was Raymond Bourque: "Getting to the finals," he said in a post-game press briefing, "gives us an opportunity. I know this team is gonna be ready to go and for me that's what's left. I haven't been there in 11 years and I know the first two times that I was there (with the Bruins) we didn't even come close. So, I know what it's all about and it's not a matter of just being there. It's a matter of competing, winning hockey games, and I want to get to that point."

Colorado captain Joe Sakic had this to say: "It hasn't been easy. We lost Peter Forsberg, but Patrick Roy has led us to where we are."

In the other conference final, the Devils also eliminated their adversaries, the Pittsburgh Penguins, in five games. This was only logical. The best two teams in the regular season were going to face off in the Stanley Cup final. It is interesting to note that of the four teams that the Avalanche faced in the playoffs, three had a goalie from Québec: Dan Cloutier with Vancouver, Félix Potvin with Los Angeles and Martin Brodeur with New Jersey.

—⚏—

The Stanley Cup final would be followed more closely than it had ever been in Québec, not only because the Avalanche embodied the former Nordiques, but also because Quebecers longed to see an injustice righted. To them, the fact that Raymond Bourque had toiled away 22 seasons in the National Hockey League, made the All-Star Team 19 times and won the James Norris Trophy five times, without ever winning the Cup was an injustice. Most hockey fans in Québec would be cheering for him. And for Patrick, too, so that he could help his friend obtain reparation.

Passions were also fired at the prospect of the goaltending duel between two Quebecers. Patrick had climbed to the summit of his profession, but there were some questions as to whether Martin Brodeur, the heir apparent to the throne, was ready to supplant him. Brodeur's alternate was none other than John Vanbiesbrouck, the goalie Patrick had jousted with in the 1986 series against the Rangers and in the 1996 series against the Florida Panthers.

Just before the final got under way, Brodeur ratcheted up the pressure on his opponent by declaring, "We're going up against the best goalie in the playoffs. He has a great reputation. Competing against him will certainly be interesting. Obviously, he'll be difficult to beat. But we're in the finals and we are very enthusiastic about the idea of playing against a great team and a great goalie." But Patrick had already proven on many occasions that he wasn't paralyzed by pressure in crucial moments. He was going into the series with the league's best goals-against average (1.74); Brodeur's was 1.82.

Quebecers also remembered the famous Big Three—Robinson, Savard and Lapointe—who had ignited their enthusiasm in the 1970s. Now, the Avs stellar defensive trio of Bourque, Blake and Foote were being compared to them. Except that Larry Robinson, an authentic member of the Canadiens Big Three, was now in the other camp as the Devils head coach. Asked to comment on the comparison, Bourque was flattered. He smiled and said, "Look, I grew up in Montréal, watching those three guys play. When I think about them and their era, one word comes to mind and that's 'domination.' Those three players were dominant on the blue line, and their team won one Cup after another. It was a great era."

But the Devils were more than just a good goalie and a famous coach. They were known for their tight defensive play with rearguards like Brian Rafalski, Scott Niedermayer and Scott Stevens, and forwards like Patrick Elias, Alexander Mogilny, Petr Sykora, Scott Gomez, Jason Arnott and Bobby Holik, who made it a point of honor to help out on defense. It was a formidable lineup that would take some to be beaten.

Observers expected the opening game to be a tight checking affair with few goals. In fact, Patrick outclassed his rival, stopping 25 shots from the Devils, and the Avs notched a surprising 5–0 victory. Patrick was satisfied with his performance. It was something to see him on the ice at the end of the game waving to his little girl, Jana, with his big mitt, while in the stands she was blowing kisses to him.

Patrick was only 16 minutes and 10 seconds away from beating a 75-year-old record, another mark set by Clint Benedict in 1925–26. Benedict blanked his opponents for 229 minutes and 22 seconds straight in the final. Patrick hadn't surrendered a goal in the final since Rob Niedermayer scored against him in the first period (at 11:19) of the third game in the 1996 final between the Colorado Avalanche and the Florida Panthers.

Still, Raymond Bourque got most of the attention. A radio station in Boston (WAAF) even put up a billboard in Denver that read: "Ray, win the cup for . . . Boston!"

The defenseman was a bit annoyed by all this publicity: "I'm just here to compete and win," he said. "It would be a great story if I ended up winning (the Cup) because it's the ultimate prize, a prize that I've been chasing for a long time. But there's still a lot of work to be done. In the meantime, it's beginning to drive me crazy to see my face everywhere."

—m—

Patrick narrowly missed Benedict's record, by one minute and 41 seconds, when Bob Corkum beat him at 14:29 in the first period of the second game. Until then the Avalanche goalie had shut out his opponents for 227 minutes and 41 seconds straight in Stanley Cup final play. The Devils notched a second goal in the first period and that was enough to take the measure of the local team by a score of

2–1, robbing them of the home-ice advantage they had fought for all year. Then, the series moved to East Rutherford, New Jersey, for two consecutive games.

In game three, with only 20 seconds remaining in the second period and the score tied 1–1, Patrick moved out of his goal to his left to retrieve a loose puck-along the boards. But he didn't see Patrick Elias coming. Skating hell-bent-for-leather, Elias reached the puck at the same time. Caught out about 40 feet from his goal, Patrick was in trouble. Elias jumped on the puck and fired it at the empty cage, but fortunately for Patrick, the puck came to rest at the goal post, and Rob Blake retrieved it right away. "My heart stopped beating!" Colorado coach Bob Hartley later confessed.

It wasn't the first time that Patrick had wandered out of the net in that fashion. He was often criticized for it, but it was one of the calculated risks that he allowed himself to take. He did it first of all because he liked to do it, and it goes without saying that those adventures added a little spice to the game; it was never boring to watch Patrick play. But there was more to it than that: leaving the net helped his defensemen—they never complained about it—avoid getting creamed from behind. It was also Patrick's way of feeling more involved in the game and making an additional contribution to the team. Because of the times he got caught wandering out of his goal, critics said he had mediocre puck-handling skills. In fact, he got burned more often than other goalies because he played with fire more often than any other back-stopper in the league.

This time, he got away with it, despite what could have been perceived as a serious error on his part. He realized it. When the siren blew to end the period, he shoved his goal off its moorings, furious with himself.

In the third period, the Avalanche added two more goals, clinching the victory and regaining home-ice advantage. The teams swapped the advantage the way tennis players trade service breaks. Raymond Bourque scored the second goal—the winning goal—on a lightning bolt over Brodeur's shoulder.

In the second intermission, Bourque had predicted that he would make the difference in the game. "It's true that I said that," admitted the 40-year-old veteran, "but what did I have to lose? I just hoped it would happen! One thing for sure, it certainly was the most important goal in my whole career."

Game four was totally controlled by the Devils, who dominated play outrageously, launching 35 shots at Patrick's net, while the Avalanche managed just 12 against Brodeur. Despite everything, a dozen minutes from the end of the game, the Avalanche had a 2–1 lead. By then, Patrick had made 25 saves compared with only nine by Brodeur. The puck was fired to the Avalanche zone, went around the corner of the rink and slid along the boards toward Patrick's goal. He left his cage to get it and pass it to a teammate. He had made this play perhaps 15 times since the start of the game and thousands of times during his career. It was a routine play. But this time, just before recovering the puck, he lifted his head a little to see how the play was developing in front of him. The puck reached him on the backhand side and hopped up on his stick. He juggled with the puck and then lost control of it. It was due as much to bad luck as to a blunder. Jay Pandolfo pounced on the disk and passed it to Scott Gomez, standing alone in front of the empty net. Then, with little more than two minutes left to play, the Devils rallied again and ensured the victory by the score of 3–2. The series was now even at two games apiece.

Some commentators, journalists and analysts capitalized on Patrick's error, some going so far as to hold him responsible for the defeat. Given the Devils' domination in game four, his coach and several of his teammates came to his rescue, attempting to put things in their proper context. "The Devils would have won easily without Patrick," said Rob Blake. "He turned aside a barrage of shots from all angles. Those who want to blame him should analyze the whole game." Colorado was still in a good position despite their bad luck. They had home-ice advantage in what had become a best-of-three series.

Nothing could be taken for granted, however, since Martin Brodeur chose game five to produce his best performance of the series, while his team continued to dominate the game. The Devils surprised the Avs before their own fans, winning 4–1. A bitter blow. The Avalanche, who had seemed until then to be well in control of the situation in the final, suddenly found themselves on the edge of the abyss. There was no more room to maneuver, and the next meeting, game six, would be played before a hostile crowd at the Continental Airlines Arena in East Rutherford, home to the Devils. New Jersey needed just one more victory to thwart Raymond Bourque's career-long dream, and his teammates' ultimate objective: the Stanley Cup. Was Bourque doomed to retire as the best player never to have won the Stanley Cup? Would he forever be viewed as a loser incapable of realizing his dream? Had he just wrecked his last chance in 22 seasons to write his name on the "silver chalice"?

And what about Patrick? Would he have to bear, for the rest of his days, the blame for the failure because of his blunder in game four? Hockey observers were citing the "gaffe" as the turning point for the Devils, and even claimed that it had awakened the defending champions. The two brave warriors were facing a challenge worthy of them. They would need all the strength born of their deep friendship and a great deal of luck, to meet it. Certainly, warriors like Raymond Bourque and Patrick were not going to surrender so close to their goal.

Patrick took game six by the throat. He became an impenetrable fortress, as he had done in similar dire straits before. Not only did his virtuosity help secure a victory over the Devils playing at home, he shut them out, with 24 saves, while his teammates netted four goals against Brodeur on 18 shots. Thanks to Patrick, the series was going to a seventh and deciding game at the Pepsi Center in Denver. The hopes of Raymond Bourque were still alive. At the same time, the Doubting Thomases who had condemned him just a week earlier were now lining up behind him and singing his praises.

—m—

Just before the decisive match, Raymond Bourque said during a televised interview, "It's always been tough for me to watch that final game because at the end, you see somebody hoisting the Stanley Cup and you say, 'Man, I've played this long and I've never had the opportunity to do that!' After they hoisted the Cup, you kind of take a little walk and a lot of things come back to you. You then realize you're running out of time. So for me, it's a matter of urgency. Who knows how long we've got; there is a window of opportunity here that's open but you never know when that's gonna close. So let's get it done."

Bourque had never put his hands on the Cup. He had found himself within a few inches of it when it was being presented, but he had never wanted to touch it. There was no way he would do that; as if he wouldn't allow himself that privilege before he had earned the trophy; as if to do so could bring bad luck. Just one day before the decisive encounter, and he had never been so near or so far from his goal. All that had to be done was to defeat the Devils in one game, and the feat would be accomplished. But it was easier said than done.

Patrick understood that well. "We've given ourselves a chance to raise the Cup by winning a do-or-die game in New Jersey, but the last victory is always the most difficult to win."

According to the local media, we were about to see the biggest sports event ever to be presented in Denver. In the Pepsi Center parking lot, scalpers were offering tickets at $3,000 a pair. Over a hundred journalists were at the game to cover the action. The atmosphere was electric. During the pre-game warm-up, while a number of his teammates were skating around to loosen up their legs, Patrick could be seen meditating for a few long seconds before his team's bench, staring at a puck, before taking his turn in goal and handling some warm-up shots. After about 20 minutes, when both teams went to their dressing rooms, Bourque was the last to leave the rink.

Once the 18,007 fans were seated, and just before the players took to the ice, the lights were turned off. Color projectors swept the crowd and the ice surface, intensifying the drama. From high up in the arena, an igloo-like structure supported by cables and representing the letter "A," was lowered. The structure was placed near the door leading to the ice. One by one the Avalanche players appeared to be coming out of the igloo as they stepped onto the ice to the shouts and applause of the crowd. And as if it wasn't noisy enough already, the spectacle was accompanied by music that was so loud it would have driven a heavy metal freak crazy.

In fact, all the preparations and the suspense built up by all the analyses, hypotheses and speculation about the outcome turned out to be more exciting than the game itself. The contest took an unexpected turn early in the second period, as if determining a winner was a mere formality. Until then, while the two teams were playing close to the vest and there was no clear indication of the eventual outcome, the fans were gripped with anxiety and excitement. But when the Avalanche established a three-goal lead after only six minutes in the middle period, the Devils, predominantly known for their ability to protect a lead but obliged to play catch-up hockey, seemed less comfortable. The Avalanche victory seemed certain. Alex Tanguay had scored two goals and picked up an assist on a marker by Joe Sakic. By the end of the period, Devils center Petr Sykora had cut the margin to 3–1.

In the third stanza, the Devils struggled mightily, but Patrick was unbeatable. Alex Tanguay, with two goals and an assist, was one of the heroes of the game; Patrick was the other, having held the Devils to a single goal on 26 shots.

Bourque was on the ice for the final 90 seconds of the game because the coach wanted him to savor every remaining instant. But for the veteran defenseman, the moment was difficult and very moving. He felt pressure on his chest. He fought back the tears and struggled to contain his emotions. It got so he could hardly breathe. He had never felt like that in his whole life. With 13 seconds left in the game, he could barely make out the hazy image of the linesman who was about to do a face-off in the Avalanche zone. Bent over, exhausted, he talked to himself to keep from collapsing, "Come on," he said to himself, "pull yourself together; there are only a few seconds left!" When the siren sounded, he was the first to throw himself into Patrick's arms, followed by all his teammates who had left the bench.

Nothing resembles the collective euphoria after a Stanley Cup victory more than the collective euphoria after another Stanley Cup victory. For Patrick, it was the fourth in 15 years. But the feeling was the same. Indescribable. The players hugged and congratulated each other. Visibly moved, Bourque took time to talk to each of his comrades-in-arms. It was the high point of his career as a hockey player, the supreme reward, after such a long time.

While Pierre Lacroix was heading to his team's bench to congratulate his coaches, receiving compliments on the way from Larry Robinson, who also gave Bob Hartley a hug, and while Raymond Bourque, overwhelmed with joy, was being carried on the shoulders of teammates Adam Foote and David Reid, and while Hartley hugged Patrick in a particularly touching moment as Frédérick and Jonathan went onto the ice and congratulated their father, and after the players of both teams had exchanged the traditional handshake,

Commissioner Gary Bettman walked to center ice with the Conn Smythe Trophy.

Bettman made his announcement: "The winner of the Conn Smythe Trophy . . . for the third time . . ." —and the crowd exploded, realizing who it was—"PATRICK ROY!!!"

Earlier in the series, former commentator Dick Irvin had raised an interesting point in an interview on the CBC: "If Patrick wins it this year, it's 15 years between Stanley Cups. The only other goaltender that I can think of who did that was Terry Sawchuk, 1952 in Detroit, 1967 in Toronto. I think you've gotta take Patrick Roy and put him right up there with the Sawchuks of hockey," he added.

Now, not only had 15 years gone by since his first Cup conquest, but 15 years had also passed since his first Conn Smythe Trophy. Patrick had become the first three-time recipient of the honor awarded to the outstanding player in the playoffs. Even living legends like Wayne Gretzky and Mario Lemieux were only awarded the trophy twice in their illustrious careers. Patrick won the Stanley Cup and the Conn Smythe Trophy in three different decades: in 1986, 1993, 1996 (the Cup alone) and 2001—a mark of consistency and durability.

Patrick raised the trophy in the air for the crowd and the cameras, and he immediately put it back on the table. He was proud and happy to have won the Conn Smythe Trophy again, but it was an individual honor, and it was more important to him that his friend, Raymond Bourque, would have his name engraved on the Stanley Cup. "It is gratifying," he said, "but it gives me even greater satisfaction to see a guy like Raymond lift the Cup. There was one name missing on that great and beautiful trophy, Raymond's name."

While the hosts conducted live interviews on the ice, two NHL representatives brought the Stanley Cup and placed it on a table at center ice. Gary Bettman stepped forward, said a few words for the occasion and then called up Joe Sakic to award him the Cup.

Tradition has it that, when the captain of the victorious team receives the Stanley Cup, he begins a lap of honor around the rink before handing the trophy to his teammates. But ever since the beginning of the season, even as far back as training camp, Joe Sakic had other plans. When he took possession of the Cup, he paused to give the photographers time to take photos and then immediately handed it to Raymond Bourque. Finally touching the Cup, Bourque needed no prompting to raise it over his head, hold it there for quite a while and kiss it several times before taking a lap of honor before the rapturous fans, among whom was his whole family, including his mother and father.

Then, Bourque passed the Cup to a teammate so he too could hold it high, and this went on for minutes on end, as one player after another savored his moment of glory. Just when it seemed that the joyous scene was at an end, Bourque started all over again, grabbed the Cup again, as if he didn't want to part with it, and did another lap of the rink to the thunderous applause of the fans.

The players and coaches gathered for a group photo at center ice. As the photographer set the camera and the arena loudspeakers belted out the now famous victory anthem by Queen, I couldn't help thinking about that day in Sherbrooke 16 years earlier.

The lyrics of "We Are the Champions" filling the arena brought tears to the eyes of some of the gritty warriors crowding around Patrick and Bourque, who were holding the Stanley Cup. Then a photo was taken of Bourque standing behind the cup with his son Christopher, who exclaimed, "It's the best thing that's ever happened to us!"

Later, Bourque appeared at the post-game press conference with his wife, Christiane, and his three children, Melissa, Christopher and Ryan. "It was a tough decision for us to leave Boston last year," he said, "but it's really been worth it. We came here to win the Stanley

Cup and now it's done. I can't say enough about Harry Sinden, who's allowed me to live this experience, and everybody that I ever played with has a little piece of this. I can't thank the Boston fans enough for their support through all those years when we couldn't get it done."

Pierre Lacroix's bet had paid off. This was the second time that his team had gone all the way. Raymond Bourque finally had his Stanley Cup. No longer could anyone look at him and think, "He's a good player, but . . ." after going through a difficult season from a personal standpoint, another year of highs and lows, Patrick had his fourth Cup and third Conn Smythe Trophy. He had eclipsed the principal aspirant to his title as the league's best goalie with a goals-against average of 1.70 and a save percentage of .934 compared with Martin Brodeur's goals-against average of 2.07 and save percentage of .898.

It was the last time anyone would see Raymond Bourque on the ice, but winning the Stanley Cup with Patrick had sealed a lifelong friendship.

FULL CIRCLE 30

Patrick opened his eyes. He was alone. His bedroom curtains were closed. He had slept well enough, but he was still tired. The night before, he had played in Minnesota. The Avalanche had gone down to a 3–2 defeat in overtime. Now the Wild and the Avalanche were even with three wins each, and the deciding game in this first round of the 2003 playoffs would be contested at the Pepsi Center that evening.

He felt the team wasn't hungry enough. Not enough to win. Someone had to stand up in the dressing room and rattle the cage to wake up a few sluggards. He was the one who had to do it. He knew that. But he no longer felt like it. He no longer had the strength to fight. He wasn't hungry enough either.

During the season, he had called Raymond Bourque. He needed some advice.

"Say, Raymond, how can you tell when it's time to retire?"

"Don't worry, Pat; when the time comes, you'll know."

Suddenly, his throat tightened. His eyes misted over. In the twilight, he closed his eyelids. Tears ran down his cheeks. Highpoints of his career flashed before him.

The moment had come.

After winning the Stanley Cup with Raymond Bourque, Patrick gradually achieved all the objectives that were important to him. On December 26, 2001, he recorded a 2–0 shutout against Ed Belfour and the Dallas Stars, after making 31 saves compared with 15 by the Stars goalie. In so doing, Patrick became the first netminder in history to attain the 500 regular-season victory plateau. It was quite a Christmas gift he'd given himself.

"He's the greatest goalie in the world, greatest of all time," Rob Blake remarked after the game. "That's the significance of the 500th. It's an honor to play with him."

One day, Patrick's record of most regular-season wins will be surpassed—especially since the introduction of the shootout has eliminated draws. But no other goaltender will have the honor of being the first to win 500 games. His name will have a permanent place in the NHL record book beside that of Maurice Richard, who was the first player to score 50 goals in a season and 500 goals in a career. These two Quebecers will always have the honor of having been the first to set these illustrious marks. If for no other reason, they will always rank among the greatest to have ever played the game.

Patrick recalls an amusing anecdote about that memorable milestone. The Colorado Avalanche management gave him permission to bring Frédérick, aged 10 at the time, along on the trip—a fine treat for him as well—on which the team would be playing games on two consecutive evenings in Dallas and in Chicago. The Avalanche took off from Denver in the morning and faced off against the Stars that evening. The Avalanche hopped a flight to Chicago immediately after the match. Frédérick was looking forward to sharing a room with Adam Foote—who liked to tease him—and his dad to help him win the pillow fight.

When they arrived in Chicago in the middle of the night, Patrick and Frédérick checked into the hotel, rushed up to the room and hid in the closet so they could scare Foote when he came in. Time passed. Foote didn't show up. All of a sudden, Patrick's cell rang:

"Patrick, it's 'Footer.'"

"Footer? Where are you?" asked Patrick.

"Me? I'm in the room. What about you, where are you?"

"No way, you can't be in the room; I'm the one in the room. What's going on?"

"I tell you I'm in the room," Foote insisted, "I'm hiding in the closet, waiting for you!"

As Frédérick was on the trip, the travel organizer had taken the initiative, unbeknownst to Foote and Patrick, of booking them in separate rooms. So, they had both wasted their time hiding in a closet to spring a surprise on their teammate.

—⁓—

A little earlier that season, on November 6 to be exact, Patrick and the Avalanche had played the Canadiens in Montréal. For the occasion, host Michel Beaudry had asked me to work as an analyst in TV between periods, and especially to comment on the work of the goaltenders. I had plenty to talk about, since the two goalies, José Théodore and Patrick, were named the first and second stars of a game that ended in a 1–1 draw.

Right after overtime, I was asked to interview my son by the boards before he went to the dressing room. As I had already consulted the NHL schedule for the rest of the season and I knew that the Avalanche wouldn't be returning to Montréal the following season, I had a scoop that no one, not even Patrick, had considered.

After a few routine questions and answers, I asked "the killer question" just as the interview was about to end:

"Was this your last game in Montréal?"

"Uh, I don't know ..." Patrick hesitated; he hadn't thought about it. "It's hard to say."

"According to the schedule, you won't be coming back to Montréal next season," I informed him.

"Is that so? Well, if the Avalanche aren't coming back to Montréal next year, this was my last game here!"

—m—

Early in 2002, Hockey Canada invited Patrick to join the team representing the country at the Olympic Games in Salt Lake City, Utah. But Patrick had never had much success on the international hockey scene. When he played for his country in Nagano, and gave everything he had, it turned out to be an experience that didn't leave him with fond memories. He came back from Japan firmly convinced that international hockey competition was not part of his future.

Besides, Patrick was involved in an increasing number of activities outside of professional hockey, such as his investment in the Junior Québec Remparts, in addition to his children's education and development. As a matter of fact, for the second year in a row, his son, Jonathan, would be tending goal for the Littleton team in the Québec International Pee-Wee Hockey Tournament. Patrick didn't want to miss a moment of that experience. He was keeping a close eye on the progress Jonathan and Frédérick were making in hockey in Denver; it had become a part of his life. This was the last time he could see Jonathan play in the Québec tournament, a major event he had taken part in as a child. He fully intended to avail himself of the unique opportunity provided by the NHL Olympic Break.

He called up Team Canada Executive Director Wayne Gretzky to say that he was declining the invitation. The conversation was very cordial, and Gretzky readily understood Patrick's reasoning. It wasn't an easy decision; Patrick had mulled it over for a long time. Yet, it was met with misunderstanding and resentment by many Canadian fans. If he had feigned an injury and claimed that he needed to use the Olympic break to heal it, he wouldn't have been criticized. But it wasn't in his nature to prevaricate.

Of course, if Canada had been short of goalies, he would have agreed to represent his country again. But there was Martin Brodeur, who valued Olympic competition highly and had graciously accepted his role as backup in Nagano, where he didn't play a single game. Denis Brodeur, Martin's father, had returned from Cortina d'Ampezzo, Italy, with a bronze medal as the goalie for the Canadian hockey team in 1956; now, he fervently hoped that his son would participate in the Winter Games. Patrick knew that Martin Brodeur was ready and more than willing.

And Hockey Canada could call on other goaltenders: Curtis Joseph, Sean Burke, José Théodore, Roberto Luongo, and others. It's not as if Canada was suffering from a dearth of talented candidates.

People who couldn't accept his decision would have immediately understood if they had been in Québec City and had seen Patrick's eyes sparkle when he ran a peewee practice with the kids from Denver. He had rented one of the two rinks in the Sainte-Foy arena (the one where it had all begun for him 20 years earlier), to prepare the team for the tournament. He seemed to have rediscovered the true meaning of hockey, the love of the game. He was having the time of his life. It was as if he was still a peewee.

—⁂—

In 2001–02, Patrick had what he considers to be his best season, with a goals-against average of 1.94 and a save-percentage of .925. He won the Jennings Trophy as the goaltender who allowed the fewest number of goals in the league. That year, his work was the principal reason that the Avalanche finished first in the division, despite the absence of Peter Forsberg and the departure of Raymond Bourque, Dave Reid and John Klemm. Adam Foote, Milan Hejduk and Alex Tanguay were also sidelined for long stretches of the season with injuries.

Named on the First All-Star Team for the fourth time, Patrick thought he had a good chance to win the Hart and Vézina trophies. Unfortunately for him, both the journalists who voted for the recipient of the Hart Trophy, awarded to the player deemed the most valuable to his team, and the general managers who chose the season's top goalie, decided on José Théodore of the Montréal Canadiens by a narrow margin. Although Théodore had a less sparkling goals-against average (2.11) than Patrick, he'd had an excellent season and it was thanks to his goaltending exploits that the Habs had earned a berth in the playoffs.

Nonetheless, Patrick was very disappointed not to win the trophies—particularly the Hart, which would have been his first—after having the best season of his career and helping his team finish first in its division.

The playoffs were also disappointing for the Colorado Avalanche. The club reached the semifinals, but the road was long and difficult. The Avs defeated the Los Angeles Kings and San Jose Sharks in the first two rounds, but were pushed to the seven-game limit each time.

Patrick probably experienced the most embarrassing moment of his career at the Pepsi Center in game six of the semifinal series with the Detroit Red Wings. After making an incredible glove save—with a little bit of luck—on a point-blank shot from the slot by Brendan Shanahan, he raised "Charlotte" high in the air to show opposing players and the referee, in particular, that he had caught the puck, the way an outfielder does after making a spectacular catch against the fence. But both the referee and Shanahan spotted something that had escaped Patrick's notice: "Charlotte"'s grasp of the puck loosened—perhaps it was victim of time, too—and the puck fell, without Patrick noticing it, right at his feet. Shanahan kept on skating and just tucked the puck into the net. Detroit won 2–0, and the series was level.

The Colorado Avalanche suffered a humiliating 7–0 trouncing in the deciding game of the semifinals in Detroit, and then saw the Red Wings capture the Stanley Cup, easily sweeping aside the Carolina Hurricanes by four games to one in the final.

The unfortunate end to the series probably cost Bob Hartley his job. He was replaced in December of the following season by his assistant, Tony Granato, who had played for the New York Rangers, Los Angeles Kings and San Jose Sharks in his 13-year NHL career.

—⁓—

During the summer, Patrick seriously considered retirement. But because he'd just had an outstanding season, he decided to stay on for another year to see if it would be as good, and to find out how far he could go. He was convinced that it would be his last campaign, but he kept the door ajar in case something happened to change his mind.

The 2002–03 campaign was the second year of the three-year contract he had signed after his most recent Cup victory. The agreement guaranteed him $8.5 million a season in American dollars, then amounting to about $12 million Canadian.

He was conscious, however, that he could no longer do certain little things as well as he could in the past. He was surprised when he first discovered this. His vast experience and, particularly, his excellent technique compensated for the decline in his physical capacities. "I wasn't the quickest," he recalls, "or the strongest or the fittest; my "butterfly" posture wasn't necessarily the best, but what I did have, more than anyone else, was the ability to anticipate the play, to be in the right place before the puck got there. I broke down the game, the strategy and the tactics of my opponents in minute detail."

He also felt that he was coping less well with criticism when things weren't going the way he wanted. His mood kept changing. "I was 37 years old and I was expected to play like a 25-year-old goalie," he recalls. "I found it frustrating."

It should be pointed out that goaltending is the most demanding job in competitive sports. One day, I was leafing through a magazine on a plane when I came across an article listing the three most stressful jobs in professional team sports. The author mentioned baseball relief pitchers, who go in late in the game with runners on base when the team's victory depends on their ability to retire the next hitter; football place-kickers, who can also make the difference between victory and defeat with a single 30-, 40- or 50-yard kick; and goalies, whose slightest mistake can prove fatal to their team.

It is true that relief pitchers and place-kickers have to perform before thousands of tense and anxious fans, who immediately express their disapproval if they fail, but the article ignored the fact that pitchers and kickers feel the pressure for only the brief time that they are in the game, while goalies are subjected to the same pressure all during the game, nearly a hundred times a year, including exhibition games and the playoffs.

As a consequence, the goalie undergoes constant stress, day after day, year after year. In the long run, the tension wears him down, and that's what Patrick felt now. Mental fatigue had gotten the better of him. He had lost his enthusiasm and fire. Throughout his career, the will to win had never left him for an instant; the desire to do everything it took to prevail had never deserted him. For the first time in his life, he no longer felt like taking shots that left bruises on his arms and shoulders. He no longer felt like facing hundreds of 95-mile-an-hour shots in practice. Showing up for at the arena took more and more effort. Now he had to warm up for a good 15 minutes to feel right. He no longer felt like suffering. That's when he spoke to Raymond Bourque.

On January 20, 2003, in a 1–1 draw against the Dallas Stars, Patrick became the first goaltender to play 1,000 games in the regular season. For the occasion, Jim Gregory, Vice President in Charge of Hockey Operations for the NHL, presented him with a crystal sculpture to mark the achievement in a brief pre-game ceremony. Then the Avalanche management had Rogatien Vachon, his childhood hero, give him a silver-coated goalie stick.

After the contest, Dallas Stars goaltender Marty Turco raised his mask to praise Patrick. "I don't know if I can really comprehend a thousand games; it is mind boggling," said Turco—he had started 97 matches up to then. "He didn't just play 1,000 mediocre games; he's played 1,000 of the best hockey games any goaltender's ever played," he added, showing his admiration.

His new coach, Tony Granato, recalled the 1993 final, in which he had played with the Los Angeles Kings against Patrick. "We talked all day about how do we beat this guy? What do we have to do as shooters?" he said. "I think that's the advantage he has. Psychologically, you try to adjust your shots and try to do something that maybe you're not capable of, or something you're not comfortable with."

Patrick was particularly proud of the new mark. At the beginning of his career with the Canadiens, an appendix to his first contract, dated July 1984, provided for a $5,000 bonus if he played at least 40 games. "At first," he said, "my only goal was to earn a job in the league. Then, it was to survive, then to produce consistently excellent performances and to apply myself, with intensity and perseverance, in practices and games." The 1000th game was an eloquent testimony to his personal success.

He won 35 games and suffered only 15 defeats in that final season. He played his last game of the regular season on April 6, 2003:

a 5–2 victory over the St. Louis Blues. It was his 1,029th game and his 551st victory.

In the beginning of the first playoff round in 2003, the Avalanche took a 3–1 lead against the Minnesota Wild. Patrick notched his 151st playoff win, a record that will not soon be broken. But the team lost the next two games by the identical scores of 3–2, so the series was now even at three wins apiece.

—⁂—

On Tuesday, April 22, 2003, after his usual afternoon nap, Patrick was driving along Santa Fe Boulevard on his way to the Pepsi Center. Now he was certain of his decision. This would be his last season. Despite that, it was the game that was uppermost in his mind. What do you have to do to win it? He didn't find the answer. The Avalanche lost again by the score of 3–2 in overtime. The Wild had been hungrier and more determined.

While the players were shaking hands at center ice, I looked at Cliff Ronning as he was receiving congratulations from Patrick. I could still see him, with his long blonde hair, standing on the deck of the ferry from Victoria to Vancouver, 21 years before. He and his Burnaby team had just ended Patrick's career in the midget division by eliminating the Sainte-Foy Gouverneurs in the Air Canada Cup final. Now, he and the Wild had just put an end to Patrick's career in the National Hockey League by eliminating the Avalanche.

After the game, Patrick slowly removed his goalie equipment and took a shower as usual. But before leaving the Pepsi Center, he gathered all his personal belongings. He even removed the plaque with his name on it from his locker door. He removed everything. It was over.

In the days that followed, Pierre Lacroix invited Patrick to his home in Las Vegas. Lacroix wanted to find out what Patrick intended to do.

"So you made your decision, eh?"

"Yes," Patrick simply said.

"Could you give yourself a few days to think it over, at least until the end of May before making the decision final?"

Patrick agreed.

A month later, nothing had changed. The press conference was set for May 28, 2003, the day after the opening game of the Stanley Cup final, in which two goaltenders in Patrick's lineage were meeting: Martin Brodeur of the New Jersey Devils and Jean-Sébastien Giguère of the Anaheim Mighty Ducks.

—ᴍ—

"Pierre, members of the media, and all the hockey fans who have supported me and followed my career, I'm here today to officially announce that I have made my decision to retire as an active NHL player."

It was with those words that Patrick, accompanied by his wife, Michèle, Pierre Lacroix and his agent Robert Sauvé, started the press conference. Jana, Jonathan and Frédérick were sitting in the first row of the room overflowing with journalists. The conference was held in Denver and transmitted by satellite to a number of countries in the world. It was broadcast in Montréal, where journalists were invited to gather in a room at the Marriott Château Champlain Hotel. A giant screen had been installed so that people could see the event live, and technical provisions had been made so the media could ask Patrick questions directly from Montréal.

"I'm leaving with the feeling that I've done everything I could to be the best in my profession. My passion and respect for the game have guided me over my career. I played for two of the best organizations in all of professional sports: one that possesses a great history, the other that has established a winning tradition in a very short time. To my wife and children, you've always been an inspiration to me all those years. To my parents and all of those who have guided me in my career, I thank you."

Patrick was serene when he made these remarks. No tears. No sobs. He was satisfied with the road he had traveled. He'd given all he had for 18 years in the National Hockey League. He had given his all. He had gone as far as he could go. He couldn't have done more. Athletes are often overcome by emotion in these circumstances. Not Patrick. For him, the moment meant a release from the constant pressure he'd borne from the beginning of his career, for nearly 30 years. His journey had ended, and in his mind he was already beyond the press briefing, as if it was a thing of the past.

The decision to retire was his, and his alone. His general manager, Pierre Lacroix, would have preferred him to carry on, but he respected Patrick's wishes, as he had always done when he was the goalie's agent.

Lacroix was the one who cried. The two men had traveled a long way together. They had lived through some great moments since 1983.

"Maybe Pierre experienced those moments more intensely than I did," Patrick explained. "In the heat of the action, you're not always aware of what's going on around you."

No one pushed Patrick into retirement—unless it was the warrior within him that said he no longer had the tools to be the best. According to some experts, he could have carried on for another few years and still been among the four or five top goalies in the league. Patrick didn't want to be one of the four or five best. He wanted to be *the* best.

It was no longer possible.

He was calmly turning the page and going back to live in Québec City, the city closest to his heart. He was taking on a new and exciting challenge: managing the Québec Remparts, of which he was a part owner. It wasn't a matter of money. By accepting the million dollars that the Avalanche owed him in case he retired before the end of his contract, Patrick was walking away from $7.5 million—over $10 million in Canadian currency at the time—to head up a junior team.

"Money has never affected my attitude," he confided to Bertrand Raymond. "I never tried to give more on the ice because I was in the last year of my contract. I didn't give a damn about that. My contract was not the thing that brought me to the arena. Staying in hockey just to pocket my salary isn't the way I am. Rake in the money and pretend, no thanks!"

A number of television stations did a special program on the occasion of Patrick's retirement, including Radio-Canada's news network (RDI), which devoted over two and a half hours of airtime to him. Of course, the press conference was broadcast in its entirety in addition to a montage of the highlights of his career. There were comments by journalists and hockey analysts as well as by personalities who knew Patrick well.

Once again, in those discussions, people confused combativeness with arrogance; self-confidence, determination and hardheadedness with presumptuousness and conceit; pride with ostentation. True, the dividing line between these virtues and flaws is sometimes very thin; it often comes down to the amount of respect one person has for another in a relationship. Patrick sometimes resorted to intimidating behavior in an effort to weaken his opponents mentally and to give his teammates a competitive edge, but he always respected his adversaries. People who said that he was arrogant, conceited, haughty and egotistical did not understand that combativeness, determination, hardheadedness, self-confidence and pride were the principal ingredients of his formula for success. He often beat his opponents with bravado.

These character traits were the source of the lightest, most amusing moment at the press conference. When everyone seemed tenser than Patrick, a journalist asked him:

"What player did you fear the most on breakaways?

"I've always had a lot of respect for the players," Patrick said, "but I also had a lot of confidence in my ability to stop them. There wasn't anyone."

The rejoinder made everyone in the room break up. Then, tossing a mischievous look at Joe Sakic and Mike Keane, Patrick continued with a little grin:

"You see, some things don't change."

Among the celebrities who spoke during the TV program were artists such as author, songwriter and singer Daniel Boucher: "He's one of the best; it's quite simple," he said. "He's one of the best and is also one of those with the hardest head. That's just the way it is. He's a guy who always knew what he wanted, like Guy Lafleur, like Félix Leclerc. He is another great Quebecer."

The final word was left to Richard Garneau, René Lecavalier's worthy successor on Radio-Canada's *La Soirée du hockey*: "During my career, I've seen many athletes who had the will to win or what we call a kind of 'killer instinct.' Maurice Richard had the killer instinct, Rocky Marciano had the killer instinct in boxing. But I've rarely seen one like Patrick Roy. In his case, it's obvious, he had only one direction that he has followed and he's never gotten away from it. That's why, in my opinion, Patrick has been the greatest goalie in history."

—⁂—

Four months later, on October 28, 2003, the Colorado Avalanche retired Patrick's jersey in a brief but grand and touching ceremony before fervent fans. Once again, team owner Stanley Kroenke and Pierre Lacroix gave Patrick and his family gifts, including an immense superbly executed painting depicting a typical Colorado landscape.

But the most touching moment came when Patrick received a standing ovation from the 18,007 partisans at the Pepsi Center. Their

487

outpouring of love seemed to last forever and sent shivers up and down my spine. In his navy blue suit, standing on the red carpet that had been rolled onto the ice, Patrick, moved by this demonstration of affection, acknowledged the crowd by nodding and waving.

Then he started to speak, but he was interrupted by the fans who applauded and shouted every time he thanked them for their support and the warm welcome they had given him during his eight years in Denver.

He briefly recalled the 30 years that had passed since the first time he donned a pair of skates, his arrival in Denver with his family who couldn't speak English, his fears about not being able to meet Colorado hockey fans' lofty expectations. He made sure to thank his friend and teammate Adam Foote, his roommate on the road for eight seasons, who also helped him out greatly with his English.

When he said a few words in French, the audience listened with respect in silence. Back to English, he concluded, "Playing for the Avalanche, wearing this uniform these past eight years, and working behind a group of players that was never satisfied with anything else but victory was a great honor. Thank you all from the bottom of my heart."

Then with the help of his wife and three children, Patrick unveiled the banner, which was in the colors of his jersey and emblazoned with his name and number. The banner joined that of Raymond Bourque, whose jersey had been retired the year before. So the two players and friends would be together forever.

As Patrick's jersey was being raised high up in the Pepsi Center, the hockey world saluted the goalie who was, in the opinion of many, the greatest in history, the one who had revolutionized the goaltending art and given it its legitimacy.

And, on November 2008, during a very touching ceremony, the red, blue and white jersey with the number 33 joined those of

488

Morenz, Vézina, Richard, Plante, Béliveau, Dryden and other immortals of the Montreal Canadiens Hockey Club in the rafters of the Bell Centre.

That evening, the warrior returned from exile.

EPILOGUE

Patrick returned to Québec City to serve as Vice President of Hockey Operations and General Manager of the Québec Remparts of the QMJHL. To keep in touch with the game on the ice and to get a feel of what it was like behind the bench, he coached the Beaubourg Seigneurs, his son Frédérick's bantam team. He loved working with the youngsters and giving them the benefit of his knowledge and expertise.

Patrick took up with old friends again, including Claude Lefebvre, whom he invited to join him as assistant coach of the Beaubourg team. Lefebvre valued his friendship with Patrick. The depth of their relationship had helped Lefebvre overcome life's trials and tribulations. "I wish everyone had a friendship like ours," Lefebvre told Albert Ladouceur in an interview for the *Journal de Québec* newspaper. "It's precious. We could have lost touch along the way. We played on different teams in junior hockey. And while Patrick knew glory in Montréal, I played in Europe for eight seasons." Lefebvre finished the interview by remarking that Patrick was still the same unaffected person he had known years before. "He still has a bit of the teenager inside him," he said. "That's why he gets so much fun out of hockey."

After spending two years on the Colisée's "second floor," looking after the management side of the Remparts' operations, Patrick yearned to get closer to ice level, and his passion for competition resurfaced. Confident that his experience behind the Beaubourg bench had prepared him for the task, he took over from his coach on September 29, 2005, after the team had gotten off to a bad start. Throwing himself into his new role with his accustomed ardor, passion and determination in his first season behind their bench, he propelled the Remparts to the summit, capturing the Memorial Cup, emblematic of Canadian junior hockey supremacy. Québec City had not won the Cup since 1971 when Guy Lafleur was in the lineup.

During the Memorial Cup tournament, held in Moncton, New Brunswick, Patrick drew on his vast experience in championship competition to coach his troops to victory. Throughout the event, his declarations distracted opponents, and focused attention on him, allowing his players to work in peace.

The warrior galvanized his players and showed them what they had to do to win even against a stronger team. Patrick got under Moncton Wildcats coach Ted Nolan's skin and got into his players' heads. Patrick was also the tournament's best salesman, attracting unprecedented nation-wide attention. Every day, the public couldn't wait to discover what surprise the Remparts' coach had in store.

When it was all over, the Warrior retreated. He made sure his players were in the limelight. He praised them in interviews. At the banquet in their honor, he stayed in the background. He wanted victory. Nothing else.

—⁄⁄⁄—

Patrick never liked talking about himself. Nor did he like other people talking about him. All he ever wished to do was play hockey and win games. He considers himself privileged that he could do what he loved for a living and win at it. I think he still doesn't quite understand why so much attention is lavished on him and why what he has to say is given so much importance. In fact, other people think he is much more important than he thinks he is. He's not stuck in the past. He keeps moving ahead at 100 miles an hour.

That's why Serge Savard, Pierre Lacroix and even the Canadiens' president, Pierre Boivin, had to step in to convince him to attend the ceremony for his induction into the Hockey Hall of Fame in Toronto. He was reluctant to do so because he didn't want to miss a game as the Remparts' coach. Patrick can be stubborn when events force him to stray from the path he's traced for himself.

But induction into the Hockey Hall of Fame isn't just another event. It's the ultimate recognition of consistently outstanding performance throughout an entire career. In addition, the inductee will be forever enshrined with his peers.

On that Monday, November 13, 2006, three other hockey personalities entered the Hockey Hall of Fame: Harley Hotchkiss, co-owner of the Calgary Flames; Dick Duff, who played for the Toronto Maple Leafs and the Montréal Canadiens in the 1960s; and Herb Brooks, honored posthumously, who coached a group of college students representing the United States at the 1980 Lake Placid Winter Olympics to the miraculous victory over the Soviet Union and went on to defeat Finland for the gold medal.

Three days of celebrations were organized around the ceremony: first there was a game between the Leafs and the Canadiens on Saturday evening; this was followed by the Hockey Hall of Fame Legends Classic the next day, a game pitting former NHL stars against each other. The induction ceremony, which took place on Monday evening, was preceded by several activities and meetings during the day. At each of these events, the new "legends" were presented to the audience and were given various keepsakes: the plaque that would immortalize their exploits in the Hall of Fame, a blazer, a ring, etc.

Patrick didn't realize the scope of the induction celebrations until he was there. "Now I can appreciate the significance of the Hall of Fame induction," he said. "When I saw how proud Larry Robinson, Peter Stastny, Michel Goulet, Billy Smith and Brian Trottier were to be enshrined, it opened my eyes." He became more relaxed and started enjoying some aspects of the celebrations. As he said later on: "I really had a good time in the evenings when we got together as friends, with Pierre Lacroix, Raymond Bourque, Jacques Tanguay, my father and others, in a little lounge near the hotel lobby, where we could spend hours reminiscing."

The journalists had gotten wind that Patrick would be delivering three quarters of his acceptance speech in French. This was a bold and unusual step in a milieu where English was the working language, and especially in the heart of English Canada—Toronto, home to the famous Hockey Hall of Fame. Asked how he had come to the decision, Patrick answered: "I'm not into politics; it's just natural for me to deliver my speech this way. People are well aware that I'm a French-speaking Quebecer and that I'm proud of it. It's normal for me to express myself in my language. That's all there is to it."

Barely two hours before the commencement of the ceremony, he called me in my room. He was concerned about his speech, but not because it was mostly in French:

"Hey, p'pa! I just reread my speech, and it doesn't work; it's way too long!"

"Wait, I'll come right over."

I went up to his room and asked him to read it slowly and calmly. The organizers had suggested his speech last about five minutes; it was more than six minutes long. But I was moved by the way he read his speech; it came from the heart. It would have been a shame to cut any of the words.

To reassure him, I reminded him that the ceremony was intended to celebrate his extraordinary career, that he fully deserved it, that the moment belonged to him and that he could take all the time he wanted.

He agreed with me, but it wasn't until he realized that the inductees preceding him at the podium were speaking well over five minutes that he felt fully confident. And he delivered his induction speech with great poise before a vast audience, his three children, his family and the television cameras.

Mesdames et Messieurs,
Chers amis du hockey,
Bonsoir,

Je voudrais tout d'abord remercier les membres du comité de sélection de me faire un si grand hommage.

Je profite aussi de l'occasion pour féliciter mes confrères, Dick Duff, Herb Brooks et Harley Hotchkiss, qui sont intronisés ce soir.

Alors qu'il n'y a pas si longtemps, je chaussais les patins pour jouer mon premier match de hockey dans la Ligue nationale de hockey, je réalise, ce soir, tout le chemin parcouru.

Un chemin rempli de défis, d'efforts et de persévérance, mais aussi de profondes amitiés, de camaraderie, de solidarité et d'entraide.

Un parcours surtout teinté d'une passion et d'une soif de victoire qui m'animent encore aujourd'hui.

Mon passage dans la Ligue nationale au sein du Canadien de Montréal et de l'Avalanche du Colorado est rempli de souvenirs et d'émotions.

My first memory goes back to when I was about eight years old, when my parents brought me to the arena for the first time. It was then that I started believing in my dream: becoming a professional goaltender in the National Hockey League.

C'est à ce moment que j'ai décidé de m'y consacrer entièrement, en m'inspirant de modèles comme Daniel Bouchard et Rogatien Vachon, et en y mettant tout mon coeur, toute ma rigueur et toute ma passion.

J'ai rêvé de cette ligue réservée à l'élite.

J'ai rêvé de faire partie des étoiles et des gagnants.

J'ai rêvé de pouvoir y jouer avec les plus grands.

J'ai rêvé de voir mon talent, ma fougue et ma soif de vaincre faire vibrer les partisans.

Today, when I look back, I feel very lucky to have been a part of the National Hockey League and to have played in the best possible conditions on teams such as the Canadiens and the Avalanche.

I sure do remember the pain, the sacrifices, the discipline and the efforts.

But I also remember the partnerships, the friendships and, mostly, this awesome feeling of being part of a team.

Je me rappelle ce que notre soif de gagner nous permet de réaliser.

La sensation de se retrouver au sein d'un groupe de gars qui s'est donné comme mission de gagner la Coupe Stanley.

Hockey taught me discipline.

It also taught me to believe in my dreams, to go for it and to never give up.

Tonight, I feel very lucky to have been supported by many people who have believed in me, and I would like to take a few moments to thank them.

N'eût été ma mère et mon père qui ont cru en moi et qui m'ont donné tout le support nécessaire pour donner vie à mes ambitions;

n'eût été mes enfants, Jana, Jonathan et Frédérick ainsi que leur mère qui m'ont donné toute la liberté nécessaire pour mener à bien ma destinée;

n'eût été mes agents, Robert Sauvé, Pierre Lacroix et leurs précieux conseils tout au long de ma carrière avec le Canadien de Montréal, puis avec l'Avalanche du Colorado;

n'eût été tous mes coéquipiers, leur soutien et leur confiance;

n'eût été mes adversaires qui m'ont amené à me surpasser;

n'eût été mes entraîneurs qui m'ont appris la persévérance, la constance, et qui ont su cultiver et mettre à profit mon désir de gagner;

n'eût été les nombreux et fidèles amateurs qui appuient et qui adorent le hockey;

n'eût été le hockey lui-même, le sport le plus excitant au monde;

jamais je n'aurais pu connaître un cheminement aussi valorisant, un destin aussi exaltant qui est l'objet de tant d'hommages en cette soirée qui restera mémorable pour moi.

Thanks to Adam Foote, my friend, my roommate during eight years and probably *my best English teacher!*

Merci à Raymond Bourque qui m'a inspiré et qui nous a tous poussés à nous dépasser pour remporter la Coupe Stanley en 2001.

Merci à Mike Keane et à Pierre Turgeon avec qui j'ai développé de grandes amitiés.

Je suis également fier, et je voudrais le souligner, de la présence ici ce soir, de ma sœur Alexandra et de mon frère Stéphane.

On a souvent dit que j'étais un excessif et que j'avais la tête bien dure!

Aujourd'hui, avec le recul, je pense plutôt que j'étais, et que je serai toujours, un passionné, un «guerrier» avide de nouveaux défis.

Et puis, pour devenir champion, ne faut-il pas à un certain moment sortir du rang?

On a aussi dit que j'étais un précurseur du style « papillon ». En réalité, ce style existait déjà, mais c'est avec la vision et le travail inlassable de François Allaire que j'ai pu en perfectionner la technique.

Aujourd'hui, je suis particulièrement fier de voir la relève s'en inspirer, et de laisser derrière un legs pour les futures générations.

À tous ces jeunes qui rêvent, en ce moment même, de faire un jour partie de la Ligue nationale de hockey, je veux profiter de l'occasion pour vous inviter à croire en vous, à persévérer, à faire fi de la pression et à vous surpasser.

Nobody will become a champion without efforts.

Nobody will become a winner without discipline, faith and passion.

Chaque jour, dans mon rôle d'entraîneur, je vois des jeunes qui ont, tout comme moi, le feu sacré et un profond respect pour le hockey.

Ce soir, je voudrais que vous ne reteniez qu'un seul mot, celui qui a guidé mon parcours et qui m'a fait chausser les patins chaque matin:

PERSÉVÉRANCE

Il n'en tient qu'à vous de tirer le meilleur profit de la passion qui vous habite et de la transformer en une expérience inoubliable teintée de réussite, de défis, d'amitiés et de leçons de vie!

Finally, I would like to congratulate my fellow inductees and award recipients, Dick Duff, Herb Brooks and Harley Hotchkiss. Thank you very much and long live hockey!

PATRICK ROY
IN THE NATIONAL
HOCKEY LEAGUE

TROPHIES AND HONORS

Stanley Cup (4):
 1986, 1993, 1996, 2001
Conn Smythe Trophy (3):
 1986, 1993, 2001
Vézina Trophy (3):
 1988–1989, 1989–1990, 1991–1992
William M. Jennings Trophy (5):
 1986–1987, 1987–1988, 1988–1989, 1991–1992, 2001–2002
Trico Goaltending Award (3):
 1988–1989, 1989–1990
NHL All-Rookie Team:
 1985–1986
First All-Star Team (4):
 1988–1989, 1989–1990, 1991–1992, 2001–2002
Second All-Star Team (2):
 1987–1988, 1990–1991
All-Star Game Appearances (11):
 1988, 1990, 1991, 1992, 1993, 1994, 1997, 1998, 2001, 2002, 2003,

REGULAR SEASON

SEASON	TEAM	GP	W	L	T	SA	GA	GAA	SV%	SO
1984–1985	Canadiens	1	1	0	0	2	0	0.00	1.000	0
1985–1986	Canadiens	47	23	18	3	1,185	148	3.35	.875	1
1986–1987	Canadiens	46	22	16	6	1,210	131	2.93	.892	1
1987–1988	Canadiens	45	23	12	9	1,248	125	2.90	.900	3
1988–1989	Canadiens	48	33	5	6	1,228	113	2.47	.908	4
1989–1990	Canadiens	54	31	16	5	1,524	134	2.53	.912	3
1990–1991	Canadiens	48	25	15	6	1,362	128	2.71	.906	1
1991–1992	Canadiens	67	36	22	8	1,806	155	2.36	.914	5
1992–1993	Canadiens	62	31	25	5	1,814	192	3.20	.894	2
1993–1994	Canadiens	68	35	17	11	1,956	161	2.50	.918	7
1994–1995	Canadiens	43	17	20	6	1,357	127	2.97	.906	1
1995–1996	Canadiens	22	12	9	1	667	62	2.95	.907	1
TOTALS	Canadiens	551	289	175	66	15,359	1,476	2.68	.904	29
1995–1996	Avalanche	39	22	15	1	1,130	103	2.68	.909	1
1996–1997	Avalanche	62	38	15	7	1,861	143	2.32	.923	7
1997–1998	Avalanche	65	31	19	13	1,825	153	2.39	.916	4
1998–1999	Avalanche	61	32	19	8	1,673	139	2.29	.917	5
1999–2000	Avalanche	63	32	21	8	1,640	141	2.28	.914	2
2000–2001	Avalanche	62	40	13	7	1,513	132	2.21	.913	4
2001–2002	Avalanche	63	32	23	8	1,629	122	1.94	.925	9
2002–2003	Avalanche	63	35	15	13	1,723	137	2.18	.920	5
TOTALS	Avalanche	478	262	140	65	12,994	1,070	2.27	.917	37
CANADIENS/ AVALANCHE TOTALS		1,029	551	315	131	28,353	2,546	2.54	.910	66

PLAYOFFS

SEASON	TEAM	GP	W	L	SA	GA	GAA	SV%	SO
1985–1986	Canadiens	20	15	5	506	39	1.92	.923	1
1986–1987	Canadiens	6	4	2	173	22	4.00	.873	0
1987–1988	Canadiens	8	3	4	218	24	3.35	.890	0
1988–1989	Canadiens	19	13	6	528	42	2.09	.920	2
1989–1990	Canadiens	11	5	6	292	26	2.43	.911	1
1990–1991	Canadiens	13	7	5	394	40	3.06	.898	0
1991–1992	Canadiens	11	4	7	312	30	2.62	.904	1
1992–1993	Canadiens	20	16	4	647	46	2.13	.929	0
1993–1994	Canadiens	6	3	3	228	16	2.57	.930	0
1994–1995	Canadiens	–	–	–	–	–	–	–	–
TOTALS	Canadiens	114	70	42	3,298	285	2.46	.914	5
1995–1996	Avalanche	22	16	6	649	51	2.10	.921	3
1996–1997	Avalanche	17	10	7	559	38	2.21	.932	3
1997–1998	Avalanche	7	3	4	191	18	2.52	.906	0
1998–1999	Avalanche	19	11	8	650	52	2.66	.920	1
1999–2000	Avalanche	17	11	6	431	31	1.79	.928	3
2000–2001	Avalanche	23	16	7	622	41	1.70	.934	4
2001–2002	Avalanche	21	11	10	572	52	2.51	.909	3
2002–2003	Avalanche	7	3	4	177	16	2.27	.910	1
TOTALS	Avalanche	133	81	52	3,851	299	2.18	.922	18
CANADIENS/ AVALANCHE TOTALS		247	151	94	7,149	584	2.30	.918	23

COMBINED REGULAR SEASON AND PLAYOFFS

1984 to 2003	GP	W	L	T	SA	GA	GAA	SV%	SO
	1,276	702	409	131	35,502	3,130	2.49	.912	89

GP: Games Played

W: Wins

L: Losses

T: Ties

SA: Shots Against

GA: Goals Against

GAA: Goals-Against Average

SV%: Save Percentage (percentage of saves per shots against)

SO: Shut Outs

INDEX

511

P

513